The Zohar

by
Rav Shimon bar Yochai
From The Book of Avraham

with
The Sulam Commentary

by
Rav Yehuda Ashlag

The First Ever Unabridged
English Translation with Commentary

Published by
The Kabbalah Centre International Inc.
Dean Rav S. P. Berg Shlita

Edited and Compiled by
Rabbi Michael Berg

Published by
The Kabbalah Centre International Inc.

155 E. 48th St., New York, NY 10017
1062 S. Robertson Blvd., Los Angeles, CA 90035

Director Rav Berg

First Printing 2001
Revised Edition 2008

Printed in USA

ISBN: 1-57189-189-7

May spreading the Light of the Zohar elevate the soul
of my beloved father Bruce

יצחק משה בן ארנולד

for all the blessings he gave me.

For all the love that he brings me, for which
I am forever indebted, may the Light I reveal from all my actions
in my life, reflect back to his soul.

For my dear son, may he live forever. I thank the Creator for
bringing him into my life. My son is the one who opened
the doors for my study, understanding and giving me the deepest
appreciation for the present.

And my daughter, my angel, for the light that you shine
on the world.

With love and gratitude, Gwyneth

APPLYING THE POWER OF THE ZOHAR

The Zohar is a book of great mystical power and wisdom. It is Universally recognized as the definitive work on the Kabbalah – and it is also so Much more.

The Zohar is a wellspring of spiritual energy, a fountainhead of metaphysical power that not only reveals and explains, but literally brings blessing, protection, and well-being into the lives of all those who read or peruse its sacred texts. All that is required is worthy desire, the certainty of a trusting heart, and an open and receptive mind. Unlike other books, including the great spiritual texts of other traditions, The Zohar is written in a kind of code, through which metaphors, parables, and cryptic language at first conceal but ultimately reveal the forces of creation.

As electrical current is concealed in wire and cable before disclosing itself as an illuminated light bulb, the spiritual Light of the Creator is wrapped in allegory and symbolism throughout the Aramaic text of the Zohar. And while many books contain information and knowledge, the Zohar both expresses and embodies spiritual Light. The very letters on its pages have the power to bring spiritual wisdom and positive energy into every area of our lives.

As we visually scan the Aramaic texts and study the accompanying insights that appear in English, spiritual power is summoned from above – and worlds tremble as Light is sent forth in response.

It's primary purpose is not only to help us acquire wisdom, but to draw Light from the Upper Worlds and to bring sanctification into our lives. Indeed, the book itself is the most powerful of all tools for cleansing the soul and connecting to the Light of the Creator. As you open these pages, therefore, do not make understanding in the conventional sense your primary goal.

Although you may not have a knowledge of Aramaic, look first at the Aramaic text before reading the English. Do not be discouraged by difficulties with comprehension. Instead, open your heart to the spiritual transformation the Zohar is offering you.

Ultimately, the Zohar is an instrument for refining the individual soul – for removing darkness from the earth – and for bringing well being and blessing to our fellow man.

Its purpose is not only to make us intellectually wise, but to make us spiritually pure.

Torah

Also known as the Five Books of Moses, the Torah is considered to be the physical body of learning, whereas the Zohar is the internal soul. The literal stories of the Torah conceal countless hidden secrets.` The Zohar is the Light that illuminates all of the Torah's sublime mysteries.

Beresheet	Genesis
Shemot	Exodus
Vayikra	Leviticus
Bemidbar	Numbers
Devarim	Deuteronomy

Prophets

Amos	Amos
Chagai	Haggai
Chavakuk	Habakkuk
Hoshea	Hosea
Malachi	Malachi
Melachim	Kings
Michah	Micah
Nachum	Nahum
Ovadyah	Obadiah
Shmuel	Samuel
Shoftim	Judges
Tzefanyah	Zephaniah
Yechezkel	Ezekiel
Yehoshua	Joshua
Yeshayah	Isaiah
Yirmeyah	Jeremiah
Yoel	Joel
Yonah	Jonah
Zecharyah	Zechariah

Writings

Daniel	Daniel
Divrei Hayamim	Chronicles
Eicha	Lamentations
Ester	Esther
Ezra	Ezra
Nechemiah	Nehemiah
Iyov	Job
Kohelet	Ecclesiastes
Mishlei	Proverbs
Rut	Ruth

Sir Hashirim	Songs of Songs
Tehilim	Psalms

The Ten Sfirot – Emanations

To conceal the blinding *Light* of the Upper World, and thus create a tiny point into which our universe would be born, ten *curtains* were fabricated. These ten *curtains* are called Ten Sfirot. Each successive Sfirah further reduces the emanation of *Light*, gradually dimming its brilliance to a level almost devoid of *Light* – our physical world known as *Malchut*. The only remnant of Light remaining in this darkened universe is a *pilot light* which sustains our existence. This Light is the life force of a human being and the force that gives birth to stars, sustains suns and sets everything from swirling galaxies to busy ant hills in motion. Moreover, the Ten Sfirot act like a prism, refracting the Light into many *colors* giving rise to the diversity of life and matter in our world.

The Ten Sfirot are as follows:

Keter	Crown
Chochmah	Wisdom
Binah	Understanding
Da'at	Knowledge
Zeir Anpin	Small Face,
	(includes the next six Sfirot):
Chesed	Mercy (Chassadim - plural)
Gvurah	Judgment (Gvurot - Plural)
Tiferet	Splendor
Netzach	Victory (Eternity)
Hod	Glory
Yesod	Foundation
Malchut	Kingdom

The Partzufim - Spiritual forms

One complete structure of the Ten Sfirot creates a *Partzuf* or Spiritual Form. Together, these forces are the building blocks of all reality. As water and sand combine to create cement, the Ten Sfirot combine to produce a Spiritual Form *[Partzuf]*. Each of the Spiritual Forms below are therefore composed of one set of Ten Sfirot.

These Spiritual Forms are called:

Atik	Ancient
Atik Yomin	Ancient of Days
Atika Kadisha	Holy Ancient
Atik of Atikin	Anceint of Ancients
Aba	Father
Arich Anpin	Long Face
Ima	Mother
Nukva	Female
Tevunah	Intelligence
Yisrael Saba	Israel Grandfather
Zachar	Male

These names are not meant to be understood literally. Each represents a unique spiritual force and building block, producing a substructure and foundation for all the worlds make up reality.

The Five Worlds

All of the above Spiritual Forms *[Partzufim]* create one spiritual world. There are Five Worlds in total that compose all reality, therefore, five sets of the above Spiritual Forms are required.

Our physical world corresponds to the world of: Asiyah – Action

Adam Kadmon	Primordial Man
Atzilut	Emanation
Briyah	Creation
Yetzirah	Formation
Asiyah	Action

The Five Levels of the soul

Nefesh	First, Lowest level of Soul
Ruach	Second level of Soul
Neshamah	Third level of Soul
Chayah	Fourth level of Soul
Yechidah	Highest, fifth level of Soul

Names of God

As a single ray of white sunlight contains the seven colors of the spectrum, the one Light of the Creator embodies many diverse spiritual forces. These different forces are called *Names of God.* Each Name denotes a specific attribute and spiritual power. The Hebrew letters that compose these Names are the interface by which these varied Forces act upon our physical world. The most common Name of God is the Tetragrammaton (the four letters, *Yud Hei Vav Hei* יהוה.) Because of the enormous power that the Tetragrammaton transmits, we do not utter it aloud. When speaking of the Tetragrammaton, we use the term *Hashem* which means, *The Name.*

Adonai, El, Elohim, Hashem, Shadai, Eheyeh, Tzevaot, Yud Hei Vav Hei

People

Er	The son of Noach
Rabbi Elazar	The son of Rabbi Shimon bar Yochai
Rabbi Shimon bar Yochai	Author of the Zohar
Shem, Cham, Yefet	Noach's children
Shet	Seth
Ya'akov	Jacob
Yishai	Jesse (King David's father)
Yitzchak	Isaac
Yosef	Joseph
Yitro	Jethro
Yehuda	Judah

Angels

Angels are distinct energy components, part of a vast communication network running through the upper worlds. Each unique Angel is responsible for transmitting various forces of influence into our physical universe.

Adriel, Ahinael, Dumah (name of Angel in charge of the dead), Gabriel, Kadshiel, Kedumiel, Metatron, Michael, Rachmiel,

Raphael, Tahariel, Uriel

Nations

Nations actually represent the inner attributes and character traits of our individual self. The nation of Amalek refers to the doubt and uncertainty that dwells within us when we face hardship and obstacles. Moab represents the dual nature of man. Nefilim refers to the sparks of Light that we have defiled through our impure actions, and to the negative forces that lurk within the human soul as a result of our own wrongful deeds.

Amalek, Moab, Nefilim

General

Aba	Father
	Refers to the male principle and positive force in our universe. Correlates to the proton in an atom.
Arvit	The Evening prayer
Chayot	Animals
Chupah	Canopy (wedding ceremony)
Et	The
Avadon	Hell
Gehenom	Hell
Sheol	Hell
	The place a soul goes for purification upon leaving this world.
Ima	Mother
	The female principle and minus force in our universe. Correlates to the electron in an atom.
Kiddush	Blessing over the wine
Klipah	Shell (negativity)
Klipot	Shells (Plural)
Kriat Sh'ma	The Reading of the Sh'ma
Mashiach	Messiah
Minchah	The Afternoon prayer
Mishnah	Study
Mochin	Brain, Spiritual levels of Light
Moed	A designated time or holiday
Negev	The south of Israel
Nukva	Female

Partzuf	Face
Shacharit	The Morning prayer
Shamayim	Heavens (sky)
Shechinah	The Divine presence, *The female aspect of the Creator*
Tefilin	Phylacteries
The Dinur river	The river of fire
Tzadik	Righteous person
Zion	Another name for Jerusalem
Yisrael	The land of Israel *The nation of Israel or an individual Israelite*
Zohar	Splendor

The Hebrew vowels

Chirik **א**, Cholam **וא א**, Kamatz **א**, Patach **א**, Segol **א**, Sh'va **א**, Shuruk **וא א**, Tzere **א**.

The Twelve Tribes

Asher, Dan, Ephraim, Gad, Issachar, Judah, Levi, Menasheh, Naphtali, Reuben, Shimon, Zebulun

Jewish Holidays

Rosh Hashanah	The Jewish New Year
Yom Kippur	Day of Atonement
Sukkot	Holiday of the Booths
Shmini Atzeret	The day of Convocation
Simchat Torah	Holiday on which we dance with the Torah
Pesach	Passover
Shavout	Holiday of the Weeks

כרך יז

פרשת במדבר, נשא (האידרא רבא),
בהעלותך

Vol. XVII

**Bemidbar, Naso (including the Idra Raba),
Beha'alot'cha**

A Prayer from The Ari

To be recited before the study of the Zohar

Ruler of the universe, and Master of all masters, The Father of mercy and forgiveness, we thank You, our God and the God of our fathers, by bowing down and kneeling, that You brought us closer to Your Torah and Your holy work, and You enable us to take part in the secrets of Your holy Torah. How worthy are we that You grant us with such big favor, that is the reason we plead before You, that You will forgive and acquit all our sins, and that they should not bring separation between You and us.

And may it be your will before You, our God and the God of our fathers, that You will awaken and prepare our hearts to love and revere You, and may You listen to our utterances, and open our closed heart to the hidden studies of Your Torah, and may our study be pleasant before Your Place of Honor, as the aroma of sweet incense, and may You emanate to us Light from the source of our soul to all of our being. And, may the sparks of your holy servants, through which you revealed Your wisdom to the world, shine.

May their merit and the merit of their fathers, and the merit of their Torah, and holiness, support us so we shall not stumble through our study. And by their merit enlighten our eyes in our learning as it stated by King David, The Sweet Singer of Israel: "Open my eyes, so that I will see wonders from Your Torah" (Tehilim 119:18). Because from His mouth God gives wisdom and understanding.

"May the utterances of my mouth and the thoughts of my heart find favor before You, God, my Strength and my Redeemer" (Tehilim 19:15).

BEMIDBAR

Names of the articles

1. The counting and the reckoning

A Synopsis

Rabbi Aba speaks about the creation of man, saying that God made him in the image of the higher and the lower ones as the combination of them all. Man was composed of both male and female, and the female side was composed of both Chesed and Judgment. After they sinned they became concerned with only worldly matters and they no longer knew wisdom. Neither of Adam's sons, Abel, from the upper aspects, nor Cain, from the lower aspects, inherited the earth because neither of them left any offspring. The world was founded from Seth, but it was not complete until Abraham came; once Isaac and Jacob came everything was included in the Central Column and the world stood firm. Even with this it still required the twelve tribes and seventy persons that came from Jacob, and it required Israel to receive the Torah and erect the Tabernacle. Then God wished to count all his legions of people, the children of Yisrael, in order to link them to their roots above. After Yisrael left the land of Egypt they achieved both the Torah and the Tabernacle, and then they were perfectly complete. Rabbi Yitzchak says that when one speaks of his own blessings he must also bless God and acknowledge those blessings. He says that blessings from above do not rest on anything that has been counted, but the counting of the children of Yisrael was an exception. We hear that God will bless the women, who were not counted among the census, the priests and the Levites, and the children under the age of twenty. Rabbi Shimon explains to Rabbi Yehuda what the source of the blessings is, and says that when God's illumination is awakened everything is in love, in perfection, and in peace.

א. וַיְדַבֵּר יְיָ׳ אֶל מֹשֶׁה בְּמִדְבַּר סִינַי בְּאֹהֶל מוֹעֵד וְגוֹ׳, ר׳ אַבָּא פָּתַח, וַיִּבְרָא אֱלֹהִים אֶת הָאָדָם בְּצַלְמוֹ וְגוֹ׳, הַאי קְרָא אִתְּמַר. ת״ח, בְּשַׁעֲתָא דְּבָרָא קוּדְשָׁא בְּרִיךְ הוּא לְאָדָם עָבֵד לֵיהּ בְּדִיּוּקְנָא דְּעִלָּאֵי וְתַתָּאֵי, וַהֲוָה כָּלִיל מִכֹּלָּא, וַהֲוָה נְהוֹרֵיהּ נָהִיר, מִסַיְיפֵי עָלְמָא עַד סַיְיפֵי עָלְמָא. וַהֲווֹ דַּחֲלִין קָמֵיהּ כֹּלָּא.

1. "And Hashem spoke to Moses in the wilderness of Sinai, in the Tent of Meeting..." (Bemidbar 1:1). Rabbi Aba opened the discussion with, "So Elohim created man in His own image..." (Beresheet 1:27). We have learned

-3-

this verse. Come and behold: at the time the Holy One, blessed be He, created the man, He made him in the image of the upper beings and lower beings, and he was the combination of all. His light illuminated from one end of the world to the other end of the world, and everyone feared him.

2. וְאע״ג דְּהָא אוּקְמוּהָ, אִית לְאִסְתַּכְּלָא בֵּיה בְּהַאי קְרָא, וַיִּבְרָא אֱלֹהִים אֶת הָאָדָם בְּצַלְמוֹ בְּצֶלֶם אֱלֹהִים בָּרָא אוֹתוֹ, כֵּיוָן דְּאָמַר בְּצַלְמוֹ, מַאי בְּצֶלֶם אֱלֹהִים בָּרָא אוֹתוֹ. אֶלָּא וַדַּאי תְּרֵין דַּרְגִּין דִּכְלִילָן דְּכַר וְנוּקְבָּא, חַד לִדְכַר, וְחַד לְנוּקְבָּא.

2. And though it was settled, we must look into this verse: "So Elohim created man in His own image, in the image of Elohim He created him." Since it already said, "His image," why REPEAT AGAIN, "in the image of Elohim He created him"? HE ANSWERS: There were two levels IN THE MAN, SINCE he was composed of male and female. THEREFORE, there is one for the male, THAT IS, "SO ELOHIM CREATED..." and one for the female, THAT IS, "IN THE IMAGE..."

3. וּבְגִין כַּךְ דּוּ פַּרְצוּפִין הֲווֹ וַדַּאי, וְסֵיפָא דִּקְרָא אוֹכַח, דִּכְתִּיב זָכָר וּנְקֵבָה בָּרָא אוֹתָם. וְכָלִיל הֲוָה מִתְּרֵין סִטְרִין ואע״ג דְּנוּקְבָּא אֲחִידַת בְּסִטְרוֹי. הָא הִיא נָמֵי כְּלִילָא מִתְּרֵין סִטְרִין, לְמֶהֱוֵי שְׁלִים בְּכֹלָּא.

3. And as a result of this, there were assuredly two faces, MALE AND FEMALE, and the end of the verse proves it, since it is written, "male and female He created them" (Ibid.). And he was composed of both aspects. Although the female was attached to his side, she ON HER OWN was also composed of two sides, WHICH ARE CHESED AND JUDGMENT, to be complete in all.

4. וַהֲוָה מִסְתַּכַּל בְּחָכְמְתָא, לְעֵילָּא וְתַתָּא. כֵּיוָן דְּסָרַח, אִתְמַעֲטוּ פַּרְצוּפִין, וְחָכְמְתָא אִסְתַּלְקַת מִנֵּיה, וְלָא הֲוָה מִסְתַּכַּל אֶלָּא בְּמִלֵּי דְגוּפֵיה. לְבָתַר אוֹלִיד בְּנִין מֵעֵלָּאֵי וְתַתָּאֵי, וְלָא אִתְיַישְּׁבוּ דָּא וְדָא בְּעָלְמָא, עַד דְּאוֹלִיד בַּר, וּמִנֵּיה אַשְׁתִּיל עָלְמָא, דְּאִקְרֵי שֵׁת, וְהָא אוּקְמוּהָ.

-4-

4. And he used to observe with wisdom up and down. Because he sinned, these faces diminished, the wisdom disappeared from him, and he was only concerned with his own bodily matters. And afterwards he begot sons from above and below – THAT IS, ABEL WAS FROM THE UPPER ASPECTS AND CAIN FROM THE LOWER – and neither of them inhabited the earth, SINCE NONE OF THEM LEFT ANY DESCENDANTS IN THE WORLD. Then he fathered a son, NAMELY SETH, and from him the world was planted. This has been explained.

5. וְעכ"ד, עָלְמָא תַּתָּאָה לָא אִשְׁתְּלִים, וְלָא הֲוָה שְׁלִים, וְלָא אִשְׁתְּכַח בְּקִיּוּמֵיהּ, עַד דְּאָתָא אַבְרָהָם, וְאִתְקַיַּים עָלְמָא. אֲבָל לָא אִשְׁתְּלִים, עַד דְּאַבְרָהָם אִשְׁתְּכַח בֵּיהּ בְּעָלְמָא וְאָחִיד בֵּיהּ בִּימִינָא, כְּמַאן דְּאָחִיד בִּימִינֵיהּ, לְמַאן דְּנָפִיל. אָתָא יִצְחָק, וְאָחִיד בִּידֵיהּ דְּעָלְמָא בִּשְׂמָאלָא, וְאִתְקַיַּים יַתִּיר. כֵּיוָן דְּאָתָא יַעֲקֹב, אָחִיד בְּאֶמְצָעִיתָא בְּגוּפָא, וְאִתְכְּלִיל בִּתְרֵין סִטְרִין, אִתְקַיַּים עָלְמָא וְלָא הֲוָה מִתְמוֹטֵט.

5. In spite of all this, the world below was not finished and complete and was not sustained on its own until Abraham came along. The world was sustained but not completed until Abraham was present in the world and held on TO THE WORLD with his right hand, THAT IS CHESED, as one who holds and assists the right hand of someone who fell. Isaac came along and held the world's hand with the left hand, THAT IS GVURAH, and THE WORLD was sustained even more. When Jacob came along, he held on to the center, with the body, THAT IS THE CENTRAL COLUMN, and became included in both sides, THE RIGHT AND THE LEFT. And the world stood firm and did not collapse.

6. וְעִם כָּל דָּא לָא אִשְׁתִּיל בְּשָׁרְשׁוֹי, עַד דְּאוֹלִיד תְּרֵיסָר שִׁבְטִין, וְשִׁבְעִין נַפְשָׁאן, וְאִשְׁתִּיל עָלְמָא. וְעכ"ד לָא אִשְׁתְּלִים, עַד דְּקַבִּילוּ יִשְׂרָאֵל אוֹרַיְיתָא בְּטוּרָא דְּסִינַי, וְאִתְּקַם מַשְׁכְּנָא. כְּדֵין אִתְקַיְימוּ עָלְמִין וְאִשְׁתְּלִימוּ, וְאִתְבַּסְמוּ עִלָּאִין וְתַתָּאִין.

6. And with all this, THE WORLD was not properly planted with its roots until JACOB begot twelve tribes and seventy persons, and the world was planted. Even so, it was not completed until the time Yisrael received the Torah and the Tabernacle was erected. At that time, the worlds could exist and were completed, and the higher and lower beings were scented.

7. כֵּיוָן דְּאוֹרַיְיתָא וּמַשְׁכְּנָא אִתּוֹקָמוּ, בָּעָא קוּדְשָׁא בְּרִיךְ הוּא לְמִפְקַד חֵילוֹי דְּאוֹרַיְיתָא, כַּמָּה חַיָּילִין אִינּוּן דְּאוֹרַיְיתָא, כַּמָּה חַיָּילִין אִינּוּן דְּמַשְׁכְּנָא. ת״ח, כָּל מִלָּה דְּבָעֵי לְאִתְיַישְׁבָא בְּדוּכְתֵּיה, לָא מִתְיַישְׁבָא עַד דְּאִדְכַּר בְּפוּמָא, וְאִתְמְנֵי עָלָה. אוֹף הָכָא, בָּעָא קוּדְשָׁא בְּרִיךְ הוּא לְמִפְקַד חַיָּילִין דְּאוֹרַיְיתָא, וְחַיָּילִין דְּמַשְׁכְּנָא, וְכֻלְּהוּ הֲווֹ כְּחַד וְלָא מִתְפָּרְשֵׁי דָּא מִן דָּא, כֹּלָּא כְּגַוְונָא דִּלְעֵילָּא, דְּהָא אוֹרַיְיתָא וּמַשְׁכְּנָא לָא מִתְפָּרְשֵׁי דָּא מִן דָּא, וְאָזְלִין כַּחֲדָא.

7. Since the Torah and the Tabernacle were erected, NAMELY, ZEIR ANPIN AND MALCHUT, the Holy One, blessed be He, wanted to count the troops of the Torah. How many legions are there in the Torah, IN ZEIR ANPIN? How many hosts are in the Tabernacle, WHICH IS MALCHUT? (THIS MEANS THAT HE WANTED TO COUNT YISRAEL, WHO ARE THE LEGIONS OF ZEIR ANPIN AND MALCHUT.) Come and behold: every item that needs to be settled in its place, THAT IS, TO LINK PROPERLY THE BRANCH BELOW TO ITS ROOT ON TOP, does not settle until it is uttered by mouth and is counted. Here, also, the Holy One, blessed be He, wanted to count the soldiers of the Torah and the soldiers of the Tabernacle, IN ORDER TO TIE YISRAEL TO THEIR ROOTS ABOVE, WHICH ARE ZEIR ANPIN AND MALCHUT, CALLED 'TORAH' AND 'TABERNACLE'. And they are all united and are inseparable from each other. Everything is in a likeness of above, since THEIR ROOTS, the Torah and Tabernacle, are JOINED AND inseparable from each other, and are in unison.

8. וּבְגִין כָּךְ, חַיָּילֵיהוֹן עָאלִין בְּחוּשְׁבְּנָא לְאִשְׁתְּמוֹדְעָא גַּבַּיְיהוּ, בַּר אִינּוּן אַחֲרָנִין דְּלֵית לוֹן חוּשְׁבְּנָא. וּבְגִין כָּךְ כְּתִיב, וַיְדַבֵּר יְיָ׳ אֶל מֹשֶׁה בְּמִדְבַּר סִינַי בְּאֹהֶל מוֹעֵד. אִי בְּאֹהֶל מוֹעֵד, אֲמַאי בְּמִדְבַּר סִינַי. אֶלָּא חַד לְאוֹרַיְיתָא וְחַד לְמַשְׁכְּנָא.

8. Therefore, YISRAEL, WHO ARE the legions OF ZEIR ANPIN AND

MALCHUT, are counted so that they are known, in addition to the others who have no number, NAMELY THE WOMEN AND THOSE YOUNGER THAN TWENTY YEARS. Therefore, it is written: "And Hashem spoke to Moses in the wilderness of Sinai, in the Tent of Meeting." If it is in the Tent of Meeting why IS IT REQUIRED TO MENTION that it was in the wilderness of Sinai, SINCE IT IS KNOWN THAT THE TENT OF MEETING WAS IN NO OTHER PLACE EXCEPT IN THE WILDERNESS OF SINAI? HE REPLIES: Once is for the Torah, NAMELY ZEIR ANPIN, and once is for the Tabernacle, THAT IS, MALCHUT.

9. וְהַאי וְהַאי, בְּאֶחָד לַחֹדֶשׁ הַשֵּׁנִי בַּשָּׁנָה הַשֵּׁנִית, וְכֹלָּא חַד, וְהַאי אִקְרֵי חֹדֶשׁ זִיו רֶמֶז לְהַהוּא יַרְחָא וְשַׁתָּא דְּנָהִיר לְסִיהֲרָא, דְּהָא כְּדֵין עָלְמִין כֻּלְּהוּ אִשְׁתְּכָחוּ בִּשְׁלִימוּ. לְצֵאתָם מֵאֶרֶץ מִצְרַיִם, לְאִשְׁתְּמוֹדְעָא דְּהָא כַּד נָפְקוּ יִשְׂרָאֵל מִמִּצְרַיִם, בַּחֹדֶשׁ הָרִאשׁוֹן הֲוָה.

9. And both TORAH AND TABERNACLE were, "on the first day of the second month, in the second year" (Ibid.). THAT IS THE SECRET OF GVURAH AND THE ILLUMINATION OF CHOCHMAH OF THE LEFT, SINCE THE MONTH OF NISSAN IS THE RIGHT COLUMN AND CHESED AND IYAR IS THE LEFT COLUMN AND GVURAH. And all is one – THAT IS, THE RIGHT AND THE LEFT WERE JOINED IN HARMONY AS ONE. This month is also called "the month Ziv (lit. 'brightness')" (I Melachim 6:1), alluding to the month and year that is luminous to the moon, THAT IS, MALCHUT, SINCE THE MAIN PERFECTION OF MALCHUT IS FROM THE LEFT COLUMN – THE SECRET OF THE SECOND MONTH AND SECOND YEAR. At that time, all the worlds are whole, LIKE MALCHUT THAT IS THEIR ROOT. "...after they were come out of the land of Egypt..." (Ibid.). THE SCRIPTURE informs us here that when Yisrael left Egypt, it was the first month, THAT IS TO SAY, THEY WENT OUT FROM THE ASPECT OF THE FIRST MONTH, WHICH IS CHESED AND THE RIGHT COLUMN. AND THEN THEY WERE PERFECTED ALSO FROM THE ASPECT OF THE SECOND MONTH, WHICH IS GVURAH AND THE LEFT COLUMN.

10. רִבִּי יִצְחָק פָּתַח, יְיָ' זְכָרָנוּ יְבָרֵךְ יְבָרֵךְ אֶת בֵּית וְגוֹ'. יְיָ' זְכָרָנוּ יְבָרֵךְ, אִלֵּין גּוּבְרִין. דַּהֲווֹ עָאלִין בְּחוּשְׁבָּנָא בְּמַדְבְּרָא, וְקוּדְשָׁא בְּרִיךְ הוּא מְבָרֵךְ לוֹן, וְאוֹסִיף עֲלַיְיהוּ בְּכָל זִמְנָא.

10. Rabbi Yitzchak began the discussion with: "Hashem has been mindful of us; He will bless us; He will bless the house..." (Tehilim 115:12). "Hashem has been mindful of us; He will bless us," refers to the men who were included in the count of the desert, whom the Holy One, blessed be He, blesses and to whom He adds more each time.

11. ת״ח, הַאי מַאן דְּאָמַר שְׁבָחָא דְחַבְרֵיה, דִּבְנוֹי, אוֹ דְמָמוֹנֵיה, בָּעֵי לְבָרְכָא לֵיה, וּלְאוֹדָאָה עֲלֵיה בִּרְכָאן. מְנָלָן. מִמֹּשֶׁה. דִּכְתִּיב וְהִנְּכֶם הַיּוֹם כְּכֹכְבֵי הַשָּׁמַיִם לָרוֹב, לְבָתַר מַה כְּתִיב, יְיָ' אֱלֹהֵי אֲבוֹתֵיכֶם יוֹסֵף עֲלֵיכֶם כָּכֶם אֶלֶף פְּעָמִים וְגוֹ'. תְּרֵין בִּרְכָאן הֲווֹ, חַד יְיָ' אֱלֹהֵי אֲבוֹתֵיכֶם וְגוֹ'. הָא חַד. לְבָתַר וִיבָרֵךְ אֶתְכֶם כַּאֲשֶׁר דִּבֶּר לָכֶם. לְאוֹדָאָה עֲלַיְיהוּ, בִּרְכָאן עַל בִּרְכָאן.

11. Come and behold: he who speaks in praise of his friend, of his children, or of his money or wealth, must also bless Him and acknowledge those blessings. From where do we learn this? From Moses, since it is written, "behold, you are this day like the stars of heaven for multitude." And afterwards, what does he say? "Hashem, the Elohim of your fathers, makes you a thousand times many more than you are..." (Devarim 1:10-11). There are two blessings here. One is the "Hashem, the Elohim of your fathers..." That is one, and the one following that is, "and bless you, as He has promised you"; (Ibid.). He promised to acknowledge them and add blessings, benedictions upon those benedictions!

12. וְאִי אִיהוּ מָנֵי שְׁבָחָא דְחַבְרֵיה, וְלָא אוֹדֵי עֲלֵיה בִּרְכָאן. הוּא נִתְפַּס בְּקַדְמֵיתָא מִלְעֵילָא. וְאִי אִיהוּ מְבָרֵךְ לֵיה, הוּא מִתְבָּרֵךְ מִלְעֵילָא. וּבִרְכְתָא בָּעֵי לְבָרְכָא לָה בְּעֵינָא טָבָא, וְלָא בְּעֵינָא בִּישָׁא. וּבְכֹלָּא בָּעֵי קוּדְשָׁא בְּרִיךְ הוּא רְחִימוּתָא דְלִבָּא. וּמַה מַאן דִּמְבָרֵךְ לְחַבְרֵיה, בָּעֵי קוּדְשָׁא בְּרִיךְ הוּא דִיבָרֵךְ לֵיה בְּעֵינָא טָבָא, בְּלִבָּא טָבָא. מַאן דִּמְבָרֵךְ לְקוּדְשָׁא בְּרִיךְ הוּא, עאכ״ו, דְּבָעֵי עֵינָא טָבָא, וְלִבָּא טָבָא, וּרְחִימוּתָא דְלִבָּא. בג״כ וְאָהַבְתָּ אֵת יְיָ' אֱלֹהֶיךָ בְּכָל לְבָבְךָ וְגוֹ'.

12. And if he counts the praises of his friend but does not acknowledge these benedictions, he will be punished because of this, first from above,

THAT IS, HE WILL BE HARMED BECAUSE OF IT. And if he blesses him, he will be blessed HIMSELF from above. And he should bless him with a good eye and not with an evil eye. And in all things, the Holy One, blessed be He, wishes to have the blessings given with a good heart WHEN HE BLESSES. And since when one blesses his friend, the Holy One, blessed be He, wishes one to bless with a good eye and a good heart, when one gives grace to the Holy One, blessed be He, most certainly it must be in good eye, and with a good and loving heart. Therefore, IT IS WRITTEN: "And you shall love Hashem your Elohim with all your heart" (Devarim 6:5).

13. ת״ח, הָא אוּקְמוּהָ לֵית בִּרְכָתָא דִלְעֵילָא שַׁרְיָא, עַל מִלָה דְּאִתְמְנֵי. וְאִי תֵּימָא, יִשְׂרָאֵל אֵיךְ אִתְמְנוּן. אֶלָא כּוּפְרָא נָטְלֵי מִנַּיְיהוּ, וְהָא אוּקְמוּהָ, וְחוּשְׁבָּנָא לָא הֲוֵי עַד דְּיִתְכְּנִישׁ כָּל הַהוּא כּוּפְרָא, וְסָלִיק לְחוּשְׁבָּנָא, וּבְקַדְמֵיתָא מְבָרְכָן לְהוּ לְיִשְׂרָאֵל, וּלְבָתַר מְנָאן הַהוּא כּוּפְרָא, וּלְבָתַר מְהַדְרִין וּמְבָרְכִין לוֹן לְיִשְׂרָאֵל. אִשְׁתְּכָחוּ דְּיִשְׂרָאֵל מִתְבָּרְכִין בְּקַדְמֵיתָא וּבְסוֹפָא, וְלָא סָלִיק בְּהוּ מוֹתָנָא.

13. Come and behold: it has been established that the blessing of above does not rest on something that has been counted. You may question: how could they have counted Yisrael? It is because they took ransom from them and it was settled, and the count did not take place until all the ransom was gathered and counted. At first they would bless Yisrael and then they would count the ransom, and they would repeat and bless Yisrael again. So the result is that we find that Yisrael were blessed in the beginning and at the end, and there was no death amongst them.

14. מוֹתָנָא אֲמַאי סָלִיק בְּמִנְיָינָא. אֶלָא בְּגִין דְּבִרְכָתָא לָא שַׁרְיָא בְּמִנְיָינָא, כֵּיוָן דְּאִסְתַּלַּק בִּרְכָתָא, סִטְרָא אַחֲרָא שָׁארֵי עֲלוֹי, וְיָכִיל לְאַתְזְקָא. בְּגִין דָּא בְּמִנְיָינָא נַטְלִין כּוּפְרָא וּפִדְיוֹנָא, לְסַלְּקָא עֲלֵיהּ מִנַּיְיהוּ.

14. HE ASKS: Why does death result from counting? AND HE ANSWERS: It is because the blessing does not dwell when you count, and when the blessing departs, the Other Side rests upon it and one could be damaged. Therefore, they used to substitute a monetary ransom for the count, and

thereby remove the threat OF DEATH.

15. יְבָרֵךְ אֶת בֵּית יִשְׂרָאֵל, אִלֵּין נָשִׁין, דְּלָא סַלְקִין בְּמִנְיָינָא. יְבָרֵךְ אֶת בֵּית אַהֲרֹן, דְּאִינוּן מְבָרְכִין לְעַמָּא, בְּעֵינָא טָבָא וּבְלִבָּא טָבָא, וּבִרְחִימוּתָא דְּלִבָּא. אֶת בֵּית אַהֲרֹן, הָכִי נָמֵי נָשִׁין, דְּאִתְבָּרְכָן בְּבִרְכָתָא.

15. "He will bless the house of Yisrael..." (Tehilim 115:12). These are the women, WHO ARE CALLED 'HOUSE', which were not included in the count, BECAUSE WOMEN WERE NOT COUNTED IN THE DESERT. "He will bless the house of Aaron" (Ibid.), because they ARE THE PRIESTS AND THEY bless the people with a benevolent eye, a good heart, and heartfelt love. "...the house of Aaron..." WHY DOES IT MENTION THE HOUSE? IT ALLUDES also to the women who are blessed by the blessing OF AARON.

16. יְבָרֵךְ יִרְאֵי יְיָ' אִלֵּין אִינוּן לֵיוָאֵי, וְכֻלְּהוּ מִתְבָּרְכִין, בְּגִין דְּדַחֲלִין לֵיהּ לְקוּדְשָׁא בְּרִיךְ הוּא. הַקְּטַנִים עִם הַגְּדוֹלִים, אע"ג דְּלָא עָאלִין בְּמִנְיָינָא.

16. "He will bless those who fear Hashem" (Ibid. 13). These are the Levites, all of whom are blessed because they fear Hashem. It is written, "both small and great" (Ibid.), because although THE YOUNG were not included in the count, SINCE THEY WERE COUNTING THE POPULATION ONLY FROM TWENTY YEARS AND OLDER, STILL THEY SHOULD BE BLESSED TOGETHER WITH THE OLDER ONES.

17. ת"ח לָא אִשְׁתְּכַח מִנְיָינָא בְּהוּ בְּיִשְׂרָאֵל דְּאִתְבָּרְכָן בֵּיהּ, כְּהַאי מִנְיָינָא. דְּהַאי מִנְיָינָא לְאִתְבָּרְכָא הֲוָה, וּלְאַשְׁלְמָא שְׁלִימוּתָא דְּעָלְמִין הֲוָה, וּבַאֲתַר דְּבִרְכָּאן נָפְקִין אִתְמְנוּן, דִּכְתִיב בְּאֶחָד לַחֹדֶשׁ הַשֵּׁנִי, דְּאִיהוּ זִיוָא דְּבִרְכָּאן דְּעָלְמָא, דְּמִנֵּיהּ נָפִיק זִיוָא לְעָלְמָא. וְעַל דָּא אִקְרֵי חֹדֶשׁ זִי"ו, דְּזִיוָא דְּכֹלָּא נָפִיק מִנֵּיהּ, וְעַל דָּא כְּתִיב, יְבָרֶכְךָ יְיָ' מִצִּיּוֹן, וְכֹלָּא חַד מִלָּה וּכְתִיב כִּי שָׁם צִוָּה יְיָ' אֶת הַבְּרָכָה וְגו'.

17. Come and behold: we do not find another counting among Yisrael by which they received blessings from it as in this count, IN WHICH THEY USED THE HALF-SHEKEL FOR THE COUNTING, because this counting was purposely meant for a blessing, and it was meant to perfect the completeness of the worlds. At the place whence blessings emanate, they were counted, as it is written, "on the first day of the second month" (Bemidbar 1:1), that is Ziv, of the world's blessings, out of which emanates and radiates brightness (Heb. *ziv*) to the world. Hence this SECOND month, WHICH IS THE LEFT COLUMN, is called BY THE NAME OF 'Ziv' because the brightness of everything radiates from it. And therefore it is written, "May Hashem...bless you out of Zion" (Tehilim 134:3), THAT IS THE SECRET OF MALCHUT. And it all pertains to the same thing, BECAUSE MALCHUT WAS BUILT FROM THE SECOND MONTH, WHICH IS THE SECRET OF THE LEFT COLUMN. It is also written, "for there Hashem has commanded the blessing, even life for evermore" (Tehilim 133:3).

18. רְבִּי יְהוּדָה הֲוָה שְׁכִיחַ קַמֵּיהּ דר"ש, א"ל יִשְׂרָאֵל מֵאָן אֲתָר אִתְבְּרְכָן. א"ל, וַוי לְעָלְמָא, דְּלָא מַשְׁגִּיחִין וְלָא מִסְתַּכְּלִין בְּנֵי נָשָׁא, בִּיקָרָא דְמַלְכָּא עִלָּאָה. תָּא חֲזֵי, בְּשַׁעֲתָא דְּאִשְׁתְּכָחוּ יִשְׂרָאֵל זַכָּאִין קַמֵּי קוּדְשָׁא בְּרִיךְ הוּא, וַהֲווֹ עָלְמִין שְׁכִיחִין בְּחַד אִילָנָא עִלָּאָה קַדִּישָׁא, דִּמְזוֹנָא דְּכֹלָּא בֵּיהּ, הֲוָה מִתְבְּרֵךְ מֵאֲתָר דְּכָל בִּרְכָאן כְּנִישִׁין בֵּיהּ. וּבֵיהּ אִתְנְטַע וְאִשְׁתִּילוּ שָׁרְשׁוֹי.

18. Rabbi Yehuda was present before Rabbi Shimon. He said to him: From where do Yisrael draw their blessings? He answered him: Woe to the world that does not pay attention, and to men who do not observe the glory of the most high King. Come and behold: at a time when Yisrael are worthy before the Holy One, blessed be He, the worlds were in one uppermost and holy tree, THAT IS, ZEIR ANPIN, where all the sustenance is. And it received blessings from the place where all the blessings were gathered, THAT IS BINAH, where, it was planted and rooted. SINCE MOCHIN OF ZEIR ANPIN WERE PLANTED IN BINAH IN THE SECRET OF THE 'THREE THAT EMANATE FROM ONE, ONE EXISTS IN THREE'.

19. וְיִשְׂרָאֵל לְתַתָּא, הֲווֹ מִתְבְּרְכָן מֵאֲתָר דְּכָל אִינּוּן בִּרְכָאן נָפְקִין בֵּיהּ, וְלָא מִתְעַכְּבֵי לְמֵיפַק, הה"ד יְבָרֶכְךָ יְיָ' מִצִּיּוֹן, וּכְתִיב כְּטַל חֶרְמוֹן

-11-

שֶׁיּוֹרֵד עַל הַרְרֵי צִיּוֹן כִּי שָׁם צִוָּה יְיָ' אֶת הַבְּרָכָה חַיִּים עַד הָעוֹלָם. וְדָא אִיהוּ נְהִירוּ דְעַלְמָא. דִּכְתִיב מִצִּיּוֹן מִכְּלַל יוֹפִי אֱלֹהִים הוֹפִיעַ. הוֹפִיעַ: נָהִיר. כד"א הוֹפִיעַ מֵהַר פָּארָן. וְכַד יְנָהֵר, יְנָהֵר לְכֻלְּהוּ עָלְמִין.

19. And Yisrael below were blessed from the place out of which all blessings emanate and are not prevented from leaving, THAT IS MALCHUT, as is written: "may Hashem...bless you out of Zion," and: "like the dew of Hermon descending upon the mountains of Zion" (Tehilim 133:3); THAT IS, MALCHUT. AND IT IS FURTHER WRITTEN: "because it is there that Hashem commanded the blessing, life forever" (Ibid.). And that is the light of the universe. It is written: "Out of Zion, the perfection of beauty, Elohim has shone forth" (Ibid. 50:2); "has shone forth," MEANS illuminates, as in, "He shone forth from Mount Paran" (Devarim 33:2). And when He lights up, He illuminates all the worlds.

20. וְכַד הַאי נְהִירוּ אִתְּעַר, כֹּלָא הוּא בְּחַבְרוּתָא, כֹּלָא הוּא בִּרְחִימוּתָא, כֹּלָא הוּא בִּשְׁלִימוּ, כְּדֵין הוּא שְׁלָמָא דְכֹלָא, שְׁלָמָא דְעֵילָא וְתַתָּא, הה"ד יְהִי שָׁלוֹם בְּחֵילֵךְ שַׁלְוָה בְּאַרְמְנוֹתָיִךְ.

20. And when this light, MEANING THE BLESSING AND LIFE MENTIONED ABOVE, awakens, all is joined, THAT IS, IN THE SECRET OF UNION. Everything is with love, all is with perfection, and then it is all peaceful – peace above and peace below. That is the meaning of, "Peace be within your walls, and prosperity within your palaces" (Tehilim 122:7).

2. "Rejoice with Jerusalem"

A Synopsis

Rabbi Elazar begins by saying that God and all His hosts pay attention to whoever speaks the words of the Torah because the Torah is so loved by Him. Whoever performs one precept of the Torah causes it to awaken above; this makes peace above and below. Rabbi Elazar says that people are to rejoice only when they are in the Holy Land but not when they do not live there. Rabbi Aba adds that one may rejoice only when Jerusalem is in a state of happiness, but never when Yisrael is in exile. We learn of why Hashem should be served with gladness and yet also with fear and trembling.

21. אִישׁ עַל דִּגְלוֹ בְאוֹתוֹת לְבֵית אֲבוֹתָם יַחֲנוּ בְּנֵי יִשְׂרָאֵל וְגוֹ'. רִבִּי אֶלְעָזָר פָּתַח, שִׂמְחוּ אֶת יְרוּשָׁלַם וְגִילוּ בָה כָּל אוֹהֲבֶיהָ וְגוֹ'. כַּמָּה חֲבִיבָא אוֹרַיְיתָא קַמֵּי קוּדְשָׁא בְּרִיךְ הוּא, דְּהָא בְּכָל אֲתָר דְּמִלֵּי דְאוֹרַיְיתָא אִשְׁתְּמָעוּ, קוּדְשָׁא בְּרִיךְ הוּא וְכָל חַיָּילִין דִּילֵיה כֻּלְּהוּ צַיְיתִין לְמִלּוּלֵיה. וְקוּדְשָׁא בְּרִיךְ הוּא אָתֵי לְדַיְירָא עִמֵּיה, הה"ד בְּכָל הַמָּקוֹם אֲשֶׁר אַזְכִּיר אֶת שְׁמִי וְגוֹ'. וְלֹא עוֹד, אֶלָּא דְשַׂנְאוֹי נַפְלִין קַמֵּיה, וְהָא אוֹקְמוּהָ.

21. "Every man of the children of Yisrael shall pitch by his own standard, with the ensign of their father's house" (Bemidbar 2:2). Rabbi Elazar began the discussion with, "Rejoice with Jerusalem and be glad with her, all you that love her..." (Yeshayah 66:10). How beloved the Torah is before the Holy One, blessed be He, for wherever the words of the Torah are heard, the Holy One, blessed be He, and all His hosts pay attention to His words. And the Holy One, blessed be He, comes to live with him. That is the meaning of, "in all places where I cause My Name to be pronounced..." (Shemot 20:21). And in addition to this, his enemies fall before him. This has already been explained.

22. ת"ח, פִּקּוּדֵי אוֹרַיְיתָא עִלָּאִין אִינּוּן לְעֵילָּא. אָתֵי בַּר נָשׁ וְעָבֵיד פִּקּוּדָא חֲדָא, הַהוּא פִּקּוּדָא קַיְּימָא קַמֵּי קוּדְשָׁא בְּרִיךְ הוּא, וּמִתְעַטְּרָא קַמֵּיה, וְאָמַר פְּלַנְיָיא עֲבַד לִי, וּמִן פְּלַנְיָיא אֲנָא, בְּגִין דְּאִיהוּ אִתְּעַר

לֵיהּ לְעֵילָּא. כְּגַוְונָא דְּאִיהוּ אִתְּעַר לֵיהּ לְתַתָּא, ה"נ אִתְּעַר לְעֵילָּא,
וְעָבֵיד שְׁלָמָא לְעֵילָּא וְתַתָּא, כְּמָה דְּאַתְּ אָמֵר, אוֹ יַחֲזֵק בְּמָעוּזִּי יַעֲשֶׂה
שָׁלוֹם לִי שָׁלוֹם יַעֲשֶׂה לִי. יַעֲשֶׂה שָׁלוֹם לִי, לְעֵילָּא. שָׁלוֹם יַעֲשֶׂה לִי,
לְתַתָּא. זַכָּאָה חוּלָקֵיהּ דְּהַהוּא בַּר נָשׁ, דְּעָבֵיד פִּקּוּדֵי אוֹרַיְיתָא.

22. Come and behold: the commandments of the Torah are supernal above. A man comes and performs one precept. That precept stands up before the Holy One, blessed be He, and decorates itself and says, 'this person has made me and I am from him.' For he awakens it above. As he arouses it below, it awakens above and makes peace above and below, THAT IS, HE BRINGS ABOUT A BOND BETWEEN ZEIR ANPIN AND MALCHUT, WHICH ARE REFERRED TO AS 'ABOVE' AND 'BELOW', as it was said, "Or let him take hold of My strength, that he may make peace with Me; and he shall make peace with Me" (Yeshayah 27:5). "That he may make peace with Me," that is, above IN ZEIR ANPIN; "and he shall make peace with Me," that is below, IN MALCHUT. Happy is the lot of that man who performs the precepts of the Torah.

23. שִׂמְחוּ אֶת יְרוּשָׁלַם וְגוֹ', בְּגִין דְּחֶדְוָה לָא אִשְׁתְּכַח, אֶלָּא בְּזִמְנָא
דְיִשְׂרָאֵל קַיְימֵי בְּאַרְעָא קַדִּישָׁא. דְּתַמָּן אִתְחַבְּרַת אִתְּתָא בְּבַעְלָהּ,
וּכְדֵין הוּא חֶדְוָותָא דְּכֹלָּא, חֶדְוָותָא דְּעֵילָּא וְתַתָּא. בְּזִמְנָא דְיִשְׂרָאֵל לָא
אִשְׁתְּכָחוּ בְּאַרְעָא קַדִּישָׁא, אָסִיר לֵיהּ לְב"נ לְמֶחְדֵי, וּלְאַחֲזָאָה חֵידוּ.
דִּכְתִיב, שִׂמְחוּ אֶת יְרוּשָׁלַם וְגִילוּ בָהּ וְגוֹ', וְגִילוּ בָהּ דַּיְיקָא.

23. "Rejoice with Jerusalem..." That is because festivity is prevalent only when Yisrael reside in the Holy Land. It is there that the woman conjugates with her husband, THAT IS, ZEIR ANPIN AND MALCHUT. Then it is time for everyone to rejoice, above and below. During the time when Yisrael are not living in the Holy Land, a man is not permitted to rejoice and show joy, as is written: "Rejoice with Jerusalem, and be glad with her." This is meant precisely, THAT IS, WHEN YISRAEL ARE IN IT.

24. רִבִּי אַבָּא חָמָא חַד ב"נ, דַּהֲוָה חַדֵי בְּבֵי טְרוֹנְיָיא דְּבָבֶל, בָּטַשׁ בֵּיהּ,
אָמַר שִׂמְחוּ אֶת יְרוּשָׁלַם כְּתִיב, בְּזִמְנָא דִירוּשְׁלֵם בְּחֶדְוָה, בָּעֵי בַּר נָשׁ

לְמֶחֱדֵי. ר' אֶלְעָזָר לְטַעֲמֵיהּ, דְּאָמַר שִׂמְחוּ אֶת יְרוּשָׁלַם, הַיְינוּ דִכְתִּיב עִבְדוּ אֶת יְיָ' בְּשִׂמְחָה.

24. Rabbi Aba observed one man who was rejoicing in the house of a tyrant in Babylon. He kicked and scolded him and said: It is written, "Rejoice with Jerusalem." During a time when Jerusalem is in happiness, a person is required to rejoice, AND NOT DURING THE TIME OF THE EXILE. Rabbi Elazar follows this reasoning in saying, "Rejoice with Jerusalem," namely as is written, "serve Hashem with gladness" (Tehilim 100:2) – WHICH MEANS THAT JERUSALEM IS THE SHECHINAH, AND IT IS OBLIGATORY TO SERVE HER AND MAKE HER HAPPY.

25. כָּתוּב אֶחָד אוֹמֵר, עִבְדוּ אֶת יְיָ' בְּשִׂמְחָה, וְכָתוּב אֶחָד אוֹמֵר, עִבְדוּ אֶת יְיָ' בְּיִרְאָה וְגִילוּ בִּרְעָדָה. מַה בֵּין הַאי לְהַאי. אֶלָּא, כָּאן בְּזִמְנָא דְיִשְׂרָאֵל שָׁרָאן בְּאַרְעָא קַדִישָׁא. כָּאן בְּזִמְנָא דְיִשְׂרָאֵל שָׁרָאן בְּאַרְעָא אָחֳרָא. עִבְדוּ אֶת יְיָ' בְּיִרְאָה, דָּא כ״י, בְּזִמְנָא דְאִיהִי בְּגָלוּתָא בֵּינֵי עַמְמַיָא.

25. One verse says, "Serve Hashem with gladness" (Tehilim 100:2), and one says, "Serve Hashem with fear, and rejoice with trembling" (Tehilim 2:11). What is the difference between them? HE ANSWERS: One speaks of the time when Yisrael live in the Holy Land, THAT IS, WHEN THEY SERVE HASHEM HAPPILY, and one speaks of a time when Yisrael live in other lands – THEN IT IS NECESSARY TO SERVE HASHEM IN FEAR AND REJOICE WHILE TREMBLING. "Serve Hashem with fear." This refers to the Congregation of Yisrael, NAMELY MALCHUT at a time when she is in exile among the nations.

26. אָמַר ר' יְהוּדָה, וְהָא כְּתִיב כִּי בְשִׂמְחָה תֵצֵאוּ, וְדָא הִיא כ״י, כֵּיוָן דְּאָמַר תֵצֵאוּ, מִן גָּלוּתָא הוּא, וְאִקְרֵי שִׂמְחָה. א״ל, וַדַּאי הָכִי הוּא, דְּכָל זִמְנָא דְאִיהִי בְּגָלוּתָא וּשְׁכִיבַת לְעַפְרָא, לָא אִקְרֵי שִׂמְחָה, עַד דְקוּדְשָׁא בְּרִיךְ הוּא יֵיתֵי לְגַבָּהּ, וְיוֹקִים לָהּ מֵעַפְרָא, וְיֵימָא הִתְנַעֲרִי מֵעָפָר וְגוֹ'. קוּמִי אוֹרִי וְגוֹ'. כְּדֵין חֶדְוָותָא אִקְרֵי.

חֶדְוָותָא דְּכֹלָּא, וּכְדֵין בְּשִׂמְחָה תֵצֵאוּ וַדַּאי. כְּדֵין כַּמָּה חַיָּילִין יִפְּקוּן
לְקָבְלָא דְּמַטְרוֹנִיתָא, לְחֶדְוָותָא דְּהִלּוּלָא דְּמַלְכָּא, כד"א הֶהָרִים
וְהַגְּבָעוֹת יִפְצְחוּ וְגוֹ', וּכְתִיב כִּי הֹלֵךְ לִפְנֵיכֶם יְיָ' וּמְאַסִּפְכֶם וְגוֹ'.

26. Rabbi Yehuda said the scripture says, "For you shall go out with joy" (Yeshayah 55:12), referring to the Congregation of Yisrael. And since it says, "you shall go out," IT MEANS from exile, and it is called 'a rejoicing'; THUS, EVEN WHILE STILL RESIDING IN THE EXILE, WE CALL IT 'A REJOICING'. He replied to him: Certainly, that is the way it is. During all the time she is in exile and lies in the dust, you can not call it 'happiness' until the Holy One, blessed be He, comes and raises her from the dust, and says to her, "Shake yourself from the dust" (Yeshayah 52:2); "Arise, shine..." (Yeshayah 60:1). And then they will join together. At that point it is called 'rejoicing'. That will be happiness for everyone and then certainly, "you shall go out with joy." Then, many legions will go out to greet and receive the Matron to the joyous festivity of the King, as it is written: "the mountains and the hills shall break forth" (Yeshayah 55:12); and further, "for Hashem will go before you; and the Elohim of Yisrael will be your rearguard" (Yeshayah 52:12).

3. The standards

A Synopsis

Rabbi Yehuda talks about the four camps of Yisrael and the twelve tribes and twelve boundaries. He brings into his discussion the four faces in the four corners of the universe, all of which are integrated in man. He tells of the movement of the two standards of Judah and Reuben that traveled with the Tent of Meeting and the two standards of Ephraim and Dan that followed. Rabbi Yehuda correlates the various Sfirot and the four Archangels and the letters in the Holy Name with these standards and events. He talks about the direction of circling the altar, the direction of sunrise, and the importance of the direction of the bed for creating a male child.

27. אִישׁ עַל דִּגְלוֹ בְאוֹתוֹת. אִלֵּין אַרְבַּע מַשְׁרְיָין דִּכְנֶסֶת יִשְׂרָאֵל, דְּאִינּוּן תְּרֵיסַר שְׁבָטִין, תְּרֵיסַר תְּחוּמִין, סְחוֹר סְחוֹר לָהּ. כֹּלָּא כְּגַוְונָא דִלְעֵילָּא, כְּתִיב שֶׁשָּׁם עָלוּ שְׁבָטִים שִׁבְטֵי יָהּ וְגוֹ'. שֶׁשָּׁם עָלוּ שְׁבָטִים, אִלֵּין י"ב שְׁבָטִין, י"ב תְּחוּמִין דִּלְתַתָּא.

27. "Every man...shall pitch by his own standard, with the ensigns" (Bemidbar 2:2). These are the four camps of the Congregation of Yisrael – THAT IS THE SECRET OF CHESED, GVURAH, TIFERET AND MALCHUT – AND THEY ARE MICHAEL, GABRIEL, URIEL, RAPHAEL, who represent the twelve tribes and twelve boundaries all encircled around her, BECAUSE CHESED, GVURAH, TIFERET AND MALCHUT EACH HAVE THREE COLUMNS FOR A TOTAL OF TWELVE. Everything reflects the above, THE TWELVE BOUNDARIES OF ZEIR ANPIN. The Scripture says, "there the tribes used to go up, the tribes of Yah..." (Tehilim 122:4). The words, "there the tribes used to go up," refer to the twelve tribes, which are the twelve boundaries below OF MALCHUT, WHO WENT UP TO THE TWELVE BOUNDARIES OF ZEIR ANPIN.

28. שִׁבְטֵי יָהּ, הָא אוּקְמוּהָ בְּגִין דְּיָ"הּ עֵדוּת לְיִשְׂרָאֵל וַדַּאי. וּבְגִין דָּא, הָראוּבֵנִי, הַשִּׁמְעוֹנִי, יָ"הּ בְּכָל חַד וְחַד. אֲבָל וַדַּאי הָכִי הוּא, דְּהָא אִילָנָא עִלָּאָה קַדִּישָׁא, בְּהוּ אַחְתָּם בְּחוֹתָמוֹי. וְאוּקְמוּהָ דִּכְתִיב, וּדְמוּת פְּנֵיהֶם פְּנֵי אָדָם וּפְנֵי אַרְיֵה אֶל הַיָּמִין וְגוֹ'. דִּיּוּקְנָא דְּאָדָם אִתְכְּלִיל

בְּכֻלְּהוּ, וְאַפִּין הֲווֹ לְד׳ סִטְרִין דְּעָלְמָא, וּמִתְפָּרְשָׁן בְּדִיּוּקְנֵיהוֹן, וְכֻלְּהוֹן כְּלִילָן בֵּיה בְּאָדָם.

28. "...the tribes of Yah..." It has been explained that this is because *Yud-Hei*, THE SECRET OF CHOCHMAH AND BINAH, is assuredly "an appointed practice (also: 'a testimony') for Yisrael." And therefore IT IS WRITTEN, "the Reubenite (with Hei as prefix and Yud as suffix)" (Bemidbar 26:7); "the Shimonite" (Ibid. 14). This is because each individual contains *Yud-Hei, HEI* IN THE BEGINNING AND *YUD* AT THE END. But assuredly it is so, because the uppermost holy Tree, THAT IS THE NAME OF YUD HEI VAV HEI, has stamped them with its seal. And this has been explained according to the scripture: "As for the likeness of their faces, the four had the face of a man, the face of a lion on the right..." (Yechezkel 1:10), IN WHICH the image of a man, WHICH IS MALCHUT, is included in all. And there were four faces to the four directions of the world. They are distinguished in their appearances, NAMELY A LION, AN OX, AND AN EAGLE, and all are integrated in man, THE SECRET OF MALCHUT. THE LION, OX, AND EAGLE ARE CHESED, GVURAH AND TIFERET, AND THE FACE OF MAN IS MALCHUT, WHICH DRAWS FROM ALL, AND ALL ARE INCLUDED IN IT.

29. מִיכָאֵל מִימִינָא, גַּבְרִיאֵל מִשְּׂמָאלָא, אוּרִיאֵל לְקַדְמַיְיהוּ, רְפָאֵל לַאֲחוֹרַיְיהוּ, שְׁכִינְתָּא עֲלַיְיהוּ. תְּרֵין מִכָּאן, וּתְרֵין מִכָּאן, וְהִיא בְּאֶמְצָעִיתָא. כְּגַוְונָא דָא בְּאַרְעָא דִלְתַתָּא, תְּרֵי מִכָּאן, וּתְרֵי מִכָּאן, וְי"ה בֵּינַיְיהוּ.

29. Michael is to the right, WHICH IS SOUTH. Gabriel is to the left, WHICH IS TO THE NORTH. Uriel is to the front, WHICH IS EAST. Raphael is to the back, WHICH IS WEST. And the Shechinah is on top of them. Two are on this side, FROM SOUTH AND NORTH, and two are on that side, FROM EAST AND WEST, and she, MALCHUT, is in the center. Likewise, it is on the earth below AT THE STANDARDS. Two are on this side, THE STANDARD OF JUDAH'S CAMP AND THE STANDARD OF REUBEN'S CAMP, and two are on that side, WHICH INCLUDES THE STANDARD OF EPHRAIM'S CAMP AND THE STANDARD OF DAN'S CAMP. And *Yud-Hei* is in the center, WHICH IS THE SECREAT OF THE TWO TABLETS OF TESTIMONIAL IN THE ARK THAT

TRAVELED IN THEIR MIDST. AND THE CHANGE OF ORDER THAT WE FIND HERE AT THE STANDARDS, IS THAT EAST MOVES FIRST, NAMELY, TIFERET, WILL BE EXPLAINED FURTHER.

30. כֵּיוָן דְּנַטְלִין תְּרֵין דְּגָלִים, מַה כְּתִיב. וְנָסַע אֹהֶל מוֹעֵד מַחֲנֵה הַלְוִיִּם וְגוֹ'. וּלְבָתַר, אִינּוּן תְּרֵין אַחֲרָנִין ד' מַשְׁרְיָין אִינּוּן לְד' סִטְרֵי עָלְמָא, וְאִשְׁתְּכָחוּ תְּרֵיסַר. אוֹף הָכִי לְתַתָּא כְּגַוְונָא דִּלְעֵילָּא.

30. Since the two standards traveled, THAT OF JUDAH AND REUBEN, what does the scripture say? "Then the Tent of Meeting shall set forward with the camp of the Levites..." (Bemidbar 2:17). And following them were the other two STANDARDS OF EPHRAIM AND DAN, which compose the four camps in the four directions of the world – EAST, SOUTH, WEST AND NORTH, for a total of twelve. This is BECAUSE EACH STANDARD COMPRISES THREE TRIBES, SINCE below it is the same as above, IN MALCHUT.

31. וְנָסַע בָּרִאשׁוֹנָה דֶּגֶל מַחֲנֵה יְהוּדָה, לָקֳבֵיל מַשְׁרְיָיא דְּאוּרִיאֵל. וּמַחֲנֵה דִּרְאוּבֵן לָקֳבֵיל מַשְׁרְיָיא דְּמִיכָאֵל. דָּא לַדָּרוֹם, וְדָא לְמִזְרָח. מִזְבֵּחַ ה"נ דְּרוֹמִית מִזְרָחִית. וּמַחֲנֵה דָּן לַצָּפוֹן. מַחֲנֵה אֶפְרַיִם יָמָּה. מַחֲנֵה דָּן לָקֳבֵיל מַשְׁרְיָיא דְּגַבְרִיאֵל. מַחֲנֵה אֶפְרַיִם לְמַעֲרָב, לָקֳבֵיל מַשְׁרְיָיא דִּרְפָאֵל מִזְבֵּחַ ה"נ צְפוֹנִית מַעֲרָבִית. כֹּלָּא אָחִיד דָּא בְּדָא, עַד דְּסַלְּקָא כֹּלָּא וְאִתְאֲחָד בִּשְׁמָא קַדִּישָׁא, דְּאִיהוּ שֵׁירוּתָא דְּכֹלָּא. עֵלָּאָה דְּכֹלָּא קַדִּישָׁא דְּכֹלָּא. כֹּלָּא אִתְכְּלִיל בֵּיהּ.

31. The standard of the Judah camp traveled first, the representative of the camp of Uriel. And AFTERWARDS, THE STANDARD OF the Reuben camp followed, representing the camp of Michael. That is, REUBEN to the south, WHICH IS CHESED, and that OF JUDAH to the East, WHICH IS TIFERET. AND THE SPRINKLING ON the altar ALSO BEGAN in the south-east CORNER, WHICH SIGNIFIES CHESED AND TIFERET. And the camp of Dan was to the north, and the camp of Ephraim was westward. The camp of Dan, TO THE NORTH, is representative of the camp of Gabriel, and the camp of Ephraim, to the west, is representative of the camp of Raphael. AND THE SPRINKLING ON the altar was also north-west, WHICH IS THE SECRET OF GVURAH AND MALCHUT. Everything is connected with the other until all ascends and unites with the Holy Name, YUD HEI VAV HEI, which is the beginning of everything, NAMELY THE *Yud* OF YUD HEI VAV HEI, WHICH IS CHOCHMAH. It is supreme over all, THE FIRST *HEI*, BINAH. Overall holiness is *VAV*, TIFERET. Everything is comprised in it, THE LAST *HEI*, WHICH IS MALCHUT.

32. י' מִזְרָח הוּא שֵׁירוּתָא דִּנְהוֹרָא, אָזִיל וְשָׁאט וְאַפִּיק לְדָרוֹם. וְדָרוֹם נָפִיק וְתַלְיָיא בְּשֵׁירוּתָא דְּמִזְרָח. ה' דָּרוֹם. מִנֵּיהּ נָפִיק דָּרוֹם בְּעָלְמָא. וְעָיֵיל י' בְּשֵׁירוּתָא דְּמִזְרָח, וְאַפִּיק לֵיהּ.

32. The *Yud* OF YUD HEI VAV HEI OF ZEIR ANPIN is east, and that is the beginning of light. It travels and wanders and produces the south, THAT IS CHESED. And the south goes out, suspended from beginning of the east, THAT IS THE *YUD* OF YUD HEI VAV HEI, CHOCHMAH. *Hei* OF YUD HEI VAV HEI OF ZEIR ANPIN is south, MEANING THAT from it the south goes forth to the world, SINCE *HEI* IS BINAH AND FROM BINAH THE CHESED IS DRAWN, THAT IS, SOUTH. But the *Yud*, REPRESENTING CHOCHMAH, enters at the beginning of the east and takes out CHESED, WHICH EVOLVES FROM BINAH TO ZEIR ANPIN.

33. וּמִן ה' תַּלְיָיא דָּרוֹם וְצָפוֹן, וְהַהוּא דְּבֵינַיְיהוּ, י' מִזְרָח יָ"ה דָּרוֹם וְצָפוֹן תַּלְיָין בֵּיהּ. ו' בְּאֶמְצָעִיתָא. וְדָא הוּא בֵּן דְּכַר. בְּגִ"כ אִיהוּ בֵּין צָפוֹן לְדָרוֹם. וע"ד תָּנֵינָן, מַאן דְּיָהִיב מִטָּתוֹ בֵּין צָפוֹן לְדָרוֹם, הָוְיָין לֵיהּ בָּנִים זְכָרִים. דְּהַאי בֵּן דְּכַר אִיהוּ בֵּין צָפוֹן לְדָרוֹם. ה' עִלָּאָה בָּהּ תַּלְיָא צָפוֹן וְדָרוֹם, וּבֵן דְּכַר בֵּינַיְיהוּ, בְּרָזָא דְיו"ה. ה' בַּתְרָאָה מַעֲרָב.

33. From *Hei* come south and north and that which is in between, WHICH IS THE CENTRAL COLUMN THAT UNITES THEM, from *Yud* east, and from *Yud-Hei*-south and north depend on them – SOUTH FROM *YUD*, AND NORTH FROM *HEI*, *Vav* in the center, WHICH UNITES THEM. And that is a male child, NAMELY, TIFERET THAT IS A SON OF *YUD-HEI*. And for this reason, it is between north and south, therefore, we are taught that whoever places his bed between the north and the south shall have male children, because this male child, WHO IS TIFERET, is situated between north and south. FOR from the supreme *Hei*, BINAH, came out north and south, WHICH ARE THE

TWO COLUMNS IN IT. The male child, NAMELY TIFERET, is between them, UNITING THEM in the mystery of *Yud-Vav-Hei*. YUD IS THE RIGHT COLUMN ON THE SOUTH. *VAV* IS THE CENTRAL COLUMN ON WHOSE RIGHT IS SOUTH AND ON WHOSE LEFT IS NORTH. *HEI* IS THE LEFT COLUMN ON THE NORTH. The last *Hei* OF YUD HEI VAV HEI is west, NAMELY MALCHUT.

34. וע"ד דָּרוֹם אָחִיד מִזְרָח, דְּאִיהוּ שֵׁירוּתָא דְּשִׁמְשָׁא וְתַלְיָיא בֵּיהּ. וע"ד תְּנֵינָן, מִסְטְרָא דְּאַבָּא אָחִיד וְתַלְיָיא חֶסֶד עִלָּאָה. מִסְטְרָא דְּאִימָא תַּלְיָיא גְּבוּרָה. כְּגַוְונָא דָּא אָחִיד כֹּלָּא דָּא בְּדָא.

34. Consequently, the south holds to the east, where the sun rises, and depends on it. Therefore, we are taught that the aspect of Aba - THAT IS THE *YUD*, bonds and depends on the supreme Chesed. And on the side of Ima, THAT IS THE *Hei*, Gvurah depends. Likewise, everything holds to each other.

35. זַוְויָין דְּמַדְבְּחָא ה"נ אִסְתַּחֲרָן, וּבָא לוֹ לְקֶרֶן דְּרוֹמִית מִזְרָחִית. דְּדָרוֹם תּוּקְפֵּיה בְּמִזְרָח, דְּאִיהוּ שֵׁירוּתָא דְּשִׁמְשָׁא, וְתוּקְפָּא דְּשִׁמְשָׁא לָא שַׁרְיָיא אֶלָּא בְּשֵׁירוּתָא. מִזְרָחִית צְפוֹנִית. כֵּיוָן דְּדָרוֹם נָטִיל תּוּקְפֵּיה דְּמִזְרָח, הוּא אַנְהִיר לְצָפוֹן וְצָפוֹן אִתְכְּלִיל בְּדָרוֹם, דְּהָא שְׂמָאלָא אִתְכְּלִיל בִּימִינָא.

35. The corners of the altar were also circled in that manner. It comes to the south-east corner, because the south is strengthened in the east, THE CENTRAL COLUMN, which is the sunrise, and the strength of the sun only stays at the start. IT THEN APPROACHES the north-east CORNER. Since after the south, NAMELY CHESED, received the strength of the east – THAT IS, AFTER THE CENTRAL COLUMN UNITED SOUTH AND NORTH – THE EAST illuminated to the north, and the north was included in the south because the left is combined in the right THROUGH THE CENTRAL COLUMN.

36. צְפוֹנִית מַעֲרָבִית, דְּהָא מַעֲרָב דְּאִיהִי בָּהּ בַּתְרָאָה, נָטְלָא מִצָּפוֹן. וע"ד צָפוֹן אָזִיל לְמַעֲרָב. מַעֲרָבִית דְּרוֹמִית, הִיא אַזְלָא לְאִתְחַבְּרָא בְּדָרוֹם, כְּמָה דְּדָרוֹם תַּלְיָיא בְּמִזְרָח, וְתוּקְפֵּיה אָזִיל בְּשֵׁירוּתָא. ה"נ

מַעֲרָב, אַזְלָא לְאִתְאַחֲדָא בִּדְרוֹם, הה"ד וִימִינוֹ תְּחַבְּקֵנִי. יְמִינָא דָּא
הוּא דָרוֹם. בְּג"כ יַנְקָא מִתְּרֵין סְטְרִין, מִצָּפוֹן וּמִדָּרוֹם. הה"ד שְׂמֹאלוֹ
תַּחַת לְרֹאשִׁי וִימִינוֹ תְּחַבְּקֵנִי. שְׂמֹאלוֹ דָּא הוּא צָפוֹן, וִימִינוֹ דָּא הוּא
דָרוֹם.

36. IT THEN COMES TO the north-west CORNER, since the west that is in the last *Hei*, NAMELY MALCHUT, receives from the north. And therefore the north moves west, SINCE MALCHUT IS BUILT FROM THE LEFT COLUMN. IT THEN FOLLOWS TO the south-west CORNER, BECAUSE MALCHUT moves to join in the south, NAMELY, TO DRESS UP CHOCHMAH WITH CHASSADIM, since the south is dependent on the east, THE CENTRAL COLUMN. And THEREFORE, its strengthening, WHICH IS THE EAST, moves first; the west moves to grasp the south, AND THE SOUTH, WHICH IS ITS STRENGTHENING, MOVES FIRST. That is the meaning of the words: "and his right hand embraces me" (Shir Hashirim 2:6); right meaning south. Therefore, it nourishes from two sides, from the north and south, FROM LEFT AND RIGHT. That is the meaning of, "His left hand is under my head, and his right hand embraces me;" left is north and right is south.

37. וְרָזָא דָּא אוֹלִיפְנָא, קוּדְשָׁא בְּרִיךְ הוּא יָהִיב מִטָּתֵיהּ, בֵּין צָפוֹן
לְדָרוֹם. וַאֲחִידַת לְהַאי בֵּן וַדַּאי. וע"ד אִית לְהוּ לִבְנֵי נָשָׁא לְמֵיהַב
מִטָּתַיְיהוּ בֵּין צָפוֹן לְדָרוֹם. וְהָכִי אוֹלִיף לִי אַבָּא. דִּיהֲבִין לְהוּ בְּנִין
דִּכְרִין. דְּהָא אִיהוּ אִתְכְּוָון כְּלַפֵּי מְהֵימְנוּתָא שְׁלֵימָא עִלָּאָה,
בִּשְׁלֵימוּתָא דְּכֹלָּא. לְגַבֵּי קוּדְשָׁא בְּרִיךְ הוּא דְּאִיהוּ בֵּין צָפוֹן לְדָרוֹם,
וּלְגַבֵּי כְּנֶסֶת יִשְׂרָאֵל דְּאִיהִי בֵּין צָפוֹן לְדָרוֹם. וַדַּאי יֶהֱוֹון לֵיהּ בְּנִין
דִּכְרִין.

37. And this mystery I learned: that the Holy One, blessed be He, places His bed from north and south, SINCE HIS BED IS THE MYSTERY OF MALCHUT, and it is certainly attached to the son, THAT IS ZEIR ANPIN, WHO IS THERE, FROM SOUTH AND NORTH. And therefore people should place their bed between north and south; THE RIGHT OF THE BED SHOULD BE TO THE SOUTH AND THE LEFT OF THE BED TO THE NORTH, JUST AS ZEIR ANPIN STANDS BETWEEN SOUTH AND NORTH. And so my father taught me, that one is given male children because he concentrated on the complete, whole supernal Faith, NAMELY the Holy One, blessed be He, Who is situated between north and south, and the Congregation of Yisrael, NAMELY MALCHUT ALSO CALLED 'BED', situated between north and south. Most certainly he shall have male children.

38. וּבְכֹלָּא בָּעֵי לְאַחֲזָאָה עוֹבָדָא כְּגַוְונָא דִּלְעֵילָא, וּכְמָה דְּאַחֲזֵי עוֹבָדָא לְתַתָּא, ה"נ אִתְּעַר לְעֵילָא, וְאוּקְמוּהָ. שָׁמַע ר' פִּנְחָס, וּנְשָׁקֵיהּ לְר' אֶלְעָזָר, וּבָכָה וְחַיִּיךְ אָמַר, זַכָּאָה חוּלָקִי בְּהַאי עָלְמָא וּבְעָלְמָא דְּאָתֵי.

38. And in all things, we must show a deed, WHICH SHOULD BE in the likeness of the higher. As one manifests a deed below, likewise it awakens on him above. This has been explained. Rabbi Pinchas heard this explanation and kissed Rabbi Elazar and cried and smiled. He said: Blessed is my lot in this world and the World to Come.

4. "Hashem is my light and my salvation"

A Synopsis

Rabbi Pinchas tells us that as soon as God has shone on a person and as soon as the person has gazed on the supreme Light, he no longer has fear of anyone above or below. We hear an explanation of the scripture that says, "Let your father and your mother be glad and let her who bore you rejoice."

39. פָּתַח וְאָמַר, יְיָ' אוֹרִי וְיִשְׁעִי מִמִּי אִירָא וְגוֹ'. יְיָ' אוֹרִי וְיִשְׁעִי, כֵּיוָן דְּבַר נָשׁ אִסְתָּכַּל בִּנְהוֹרָא דִּלְעֵילָא, וְקוּדְשָׁא בְּרִיךְ הוּא אַנְהִיר עֲלֵיהּ, לָא דָּחִיל מֵעִלָּאִין וְתַתָּאִין. כד"א. וְעָלַיִךְ יִזְרַח יְיָ' וּכְבוֹדוֹ עָלַיִךְ יֵרָאֶה. יְיָ' מָעוֹז חַיַּי, כֵּיוָן דְּקוּדְשָׁא בְּרִיךְ הוּא אָחִיד בֵּיהּ בְּבַר נָשׁ, לָא מִסְתָּפֵי בְּהַהוּא עָלְמָא מִכָּל מָארֵיהוֹן דְּדִינִין. אוּף אֲנָא כְּהַאי גַּוְונָא, כֵּיוָן דְּאֲחִידְנָא בְּאָבוּךְ וּבָךְ לָא אֶסְתַּפֵּינָא בְּהַאי עָלְמָא וּבְעָלְמָא אַחֲרָא.

39. RABBI PINCHAS opened the discussion and said: "Hashem is my light and my salvation; whom shall I fear?" (Tehilim 27:1) "Hashem is my light and my salvation," MEANING, as soon as a man has gazed on the supreme light, and the Holy One, blessed be He, has shone on him, he no longer has fear from anyone above or below, as it says, "but Hashem shall arise upon you, and His glory shall be seen upon you" (Yeshayah 60:2). "Hashem is the stronghold of my life" (Tehilim 27:1); THAT IS, once the Holy One, blessed be He, gives support to man, he has no fear in that world from any prosecutor. And so am I. As soon as I cling to your father and you, I have no fear in this world or the other world.

40. וְעָלָךְ כְּתִיב, יִשְׂמַח אָבִיךְ וְגוֹ'. כֵּיוָן דְּכְתִיב יִשְׂמַח אָבִיךְ וְאִמֶּךָ, מַאי וְתָגֵל יוֹלַדְתֶּךָ, דְּהָא בְּאִמֶּךְ סַגְיָא. אֶלָּא יִשְׂמַח אָבִיךָ: דָּא קוּדְשָׁא בְּרִיךְ הוּא. וְאִמֶּךְ: דָּא כְּנֶסֶת יִשְׂרָאֵל. וְתָגֵל יוֹלַדְתֶּךָ: יוֹלַדְתֶּךְ דִּלְתַתָּא. ר' שִׁמְעוֹן אָבוּךְ אָן חֶדְוָותָא דִּילֵיהּ. אֶלָּא קְרָא הוּא בִּלְחוֹדוֹי דִּכְתִיב גִּיל יָגִיל אֲבִי צַדִּיק: דָּא קוּדְשָׁא בְּרִיךְ הוּא. וְיוֹלֵד חָכָם יִשְׂמַח בּוֹ: דָּא אָבִיךְ דִּלְתַתָּא. דָּבָר אַחֵר, גִּיל יָגִיל אֲבִי צַדִּיק: דָּא אָבִיךְ דִּלְתַתָּא. וְיוֹלֵד חָכָם יִשְׂמַח בּוֹ, כְּתִיב בְּתוֹסֶפֶת וָא"ו, דָּא קוּדְשָׁא בְּרִיךְ הוּא הוּא לְעֵילָא.

40. Of you it is written: "Let your father and your mother be glad" (Mishlei 23:25). HE ASKS: Since it is written, "Let your father and your mother be glad," what is the meaning of, "and let her who bore you rejoice" (Ibid.)? It would seem sufficient with the mention of the mother. AND HE ANSWERS: ONLY, "your father," means the Holy One, blessed be He, "and your mother" is the Congregation of Yisrael, WHICH IS MALCHUT. The words, "and let her who bore you rejoice," MEANS she who bore you below, THAT IS, YOUR MOTHER IN THIS WORLD. AND IF SO, Rabbi Shimon, your father, where is his joy – SINCE HE IS NOT EVEN ALLUDED TO IN THIS? AND HE REPLIES: It is because he has a verse of his own, as it is written, "The father of the righteous shall greatly rejoice" (Ibid. 24), which refers to the Holy One, blessed be He. "...and he who begets a wise child shall have joy of him..." (Ibid.) is your father below, NAMELY RABBI SHIMON. An alternate explanation: "The father of the righteous shall greatly rejoice," is the father below. "...and (Heb. *ve, Vav*) he who begets a wise child shall have joy of him," is written with an extra *Vav*. SINCE IT WOULD HAVE SUFFICED TO WRITE, "HE WHO BEGETS..." it refers to the Holy One, blessed be He, above, WHO IS CALLED '*VAV*'.

5. "Into Your hand I commit my spirit"

A Synopsis

Rabbi Elazar explains that at night the Tree of Death rules in the world and therefore one must deposit his soul with God to keep it safe. During sleep everyone gets a taste of death, until morning comes and the Tree of Life awakens again. Rabbi Yehuda wonders why even gentiles can rise in the middle of the night even though the Tree of Death still reigns. Rabbi Elazar explains that even the idolatrous nations are joined to their aspect of the Defiled Spirit of the left, as everything that is above is likewise down below. He talks about the time when Bila'am could not curse Yisrael because there was no judgment hanging over them. Rabbi Elazar uses the analogy of a snake with the movements of its head and its tail to explain what is driving and controlling events below and above. The section closes with an explanation of "peculiar possession" which is deemed to be God's possession of the three Patriarchs and the priests, Levites and Yisrael.

41. אָמַר ר' אֶלְעָזָר, כְּתִיב בְּיָדְךָ אַפְקִיד רוּחִי פָּדִיתָה אוֹתִי יְיָ' אֵל אֱמֶת. הַאי קְרָא אִית לֵיה לְאִסְתַּכְּלָא בֵּיה, חֲמִיתּוּן מַאן דְּאַפְקִיד בִּידָא דְּמַלְכָּא מִידִי. אֶלָּא, וַדַּאי זַכָּאָה הוּא בַּר נָשׁ, דְּאָזִיל בְּאוֹרְחוֹי דְּמַלְכָּא קַדִּישָׁא, וְלָא חָטֵי קַמֵּיה תָּא חֲזֵי, כֵּיוָן דְּעָאל לֵילְיָא, אִילָנָא דְּמוֹתָא שַׁלִּיט בְּעָלְמָא, וְאִילָנָא דְּחַיֵּי אִסְתַּלָּק לְעֵילָא לְעֵילָא. וְכֵיוָן דְּאִילָנָא דְּמוֹתָא שַׁלִּיט בְּעָלְמָא בִּלְחוֹדוֹי, כָּל בְּנֵי עָלְמָא טַעֲמִין טַעֲמָא דְּמוֹתָא. מ"ט. בְּגִין דְּהַהוּא אִילָנָא גָּרִים.

41. Rabbi Elazar said: It is written, "Into Your hand I commit my spirit: You have redeemed me, Hashem, El of Truth" (Tehilim 31:5). This verse must be examined. Have you ever seen someone who would deposit something in the hands of the King, WHO IS THE HOLY ONE, BLESSED BE HE? AND HE REPLIES: Therefore most certainly, happy is the man that follows the ways of the Holy King and does not sin before Him. Come and behold: as soon as night falls, the Tree of Death rules in the world and the Tree of Life disappears high above. Then the Tree of Death is the sole ruler in the universe, and all inhabitants of the world taste of death – SINCE SLEEP IS A ONE-SIXTIETH PORTION OF DEATH. What is the reason? Because this tree causes this; MALCHUT THAT REIGNS ALONE, WITHOUT

ZEIR ANPIN, GIVES RISE TO THIS, SINCE, MALCHUT IS CALLED 'NIGHT'.

42. וּבַר נָשׁ בָּעֵי לְאַקְדְּמָא וּלְמִפְקַד בִּידֵיהּ נַפְשֵׁיהּ בְּפִקְדוֹנָא. כְּפִקְדוֹנָא דְּבַר נָשׁ, דְּיָהִיב פִּקְדוֹנָא לְאַחֲרָא, דְּאַף עַ"ג דְּאִיהוּ אִתְחַיָּיב לְגַבֵּיהּ יַתִּיר מֵהַהוּא פִּקְדוֹנָא, לָאו כְּדַאי לְאִתְאַחֲדָא בֵּיהּ, הוֹאִיל וּפִקְדוֹנָא אִתְמְסַר לְגַבֵּיהּ, וְאִי יְסָרֵב בֵּיהּ, וַדַּאי נִבְדּוֹק אֲבַתְרֵיהּ, דְּלָאו מִזַּרְעָא קַדִּישָׁא הוּא, וְלָאו מִבְּנֵי מְהֵימְנוּתָא.

42. And a person should take precautions and entrust his soul in His hand for deposit. This is as a man provides another man with a deposit, THAT IS, A PLEDGE. Even if he owes more than the value of the security, it is not worthy for him to be involved IN A CONFLICT with him, since he gave a deposit. However, if he refuses TO GIVE HIM A DEPOSIT, we should certainly examine him, because he is not from the holy seed or from the faithful.

43. כַּךְ הַהוּא אִילָנָא, בְּנֵי נָשָׁא אַקְדִּימוּ וְיָהֲבִין לֵיהּ פִּקְדוֹנָא דְּנַפְשַׁיְיהוּ, וְכָל נִשְׁמָתִין דִּבְנֵי עָלְמָא נָטִיל. וְכֻלְּהוּ טַעֲמִין טַעֲמָא דְּמוֹתָא, בְּגִין דְּהַאי אִילָנָא דְּמוֹתָא הוּא. וּבְגִין דְּכָל אִינּוּן נַפְשָׁתָא, אע"ג דְּכֻלְּהוּ אִתְחַיָּיבוּ לְגַבֵּיהּ, וְלָאו כְּדַאי הוּא לְאָתָבָא פִּקְדוֹנָא לְגַבֵּיהּ דְּבַר נָשׁ, אֶלָּא כֵּיוָן דְּכֻלְּהוּ אִתְמְסָרֵי לֵיהּ בְּפִקְדוֹנָא, אָתִיב כָּל פִּקְדוֹנִין לְמָארֵיהוֹן.

43. Likewise is this tree, WHICH IS MALCHUT, to which people give their soul as a deposit. It receives all the souls of the inhabitants of the world. And everyone tastes of death because this is the Tree of Death. DURING THE TIME THAT MALCHUT IS SEPARATED FROM ZEIR ANPIN, WHICH IS THE TREE OF LIFE, IT IS A TREE OF DEATH. In spite of the fact that these souls are all guilty before it and it is not appropriate to return the deposit to man, nonetheless, since they were presented to it as a pledge deposit, it returns all these deposits to their owners.

44. ת"ח, לָאו כְּדַאי הוּא הַאי אִילָנָא דְּמוֹתָא לְאָתָבָא פִּקְדוֹנָא לְגַבֵּיהּ דְּבַר נָשׁ. אֶלָּא בְּשַׁעֲתָא דְּאִילָנָא דְּחַיֵּי אִתְּעַר בְּעָלְמָא. וְאֵימָתַי אִתְּעַר

הַהוּא אִילָנָא דְּחַיֵּי. בְּשַׁעֲתָא דְּסָלִיק צַפְרָא. וּכְדֵין, כֵּיוָן דְּהַאי אִתְּעַר בְּעָלְמָא, כָּל בְּנֵי עָלְמָא חַיִּין, וְשָׁבִיק וְאַהְדָר הַהוּא אִילָנָא דְּמוֹתָא כָּל פִּקְדּוֹנִין דְּאִתְפְּקָדוּ לְגַבֵּיה, וְאָזִיל לֵיה. מַ"ט חַיִּין. בְּגִין דְּהַהוּא אִילָנָא דְּחַיֵּי גָּרִים.

44. Come and behold: this Tree of Death is not obligated to return the man the deposit IN THE MORNING, only when the Tree of Life awakens in the world. And when does that Tree of Life awaken? When the morning comes. Then, SINCE THIS TREE OF LIFE awakens in the universe and all people COME OUT alive, that Tree of Death leaves and returns all the deposits provided to it and goes away. What is the reason that they live? It is because of that Tree of Life, THAT IS, ZEIR ANPIN THAT REIGNS DURING THE DAY.

45. וְאִי תֵּימָא, הָא בְּנֵי נָשָׁא סַגִּיאִין אִינוּן דְּמִתְעָרִין בְּלֵילְיָא, בְּעוֹד דְּאִילָנָא דְּמוֹתָא שַׁלִּיט. אֶלָּא, וַדַּאי הַהוּא אִילָנָא דְּחַיֵּי קָא עָבֵיד. מַ"ט. בְּגִין דִּכְתִּיב לִרְאוֹת הֲיֵשׁ מַשְׂכִּיל דּוֹרֵשׁ אֶת אֱלֹהִים. וְלָא יְהֵא לֵיה פִּתְחוֹן פֶּה לְבַר נָשׁ, דְּיֵימָא, אִלְמָלֵי שְׁלִיטָנָא בְּנַפְשַׁאי בְּלֵילְיָא אִשְׁתַּדַּלְנָא בְּאוֹרַיְיתָא. אָ"ר יְהוּדָה, הַאי בְּיִשְׂרָאֵל וַדַּאי וְהָכִי הוּא. אֲבָל בְּאוּ"ה דַּחֲמֵינָא כְּהַאי גַּוְונָא, מַ"ט. אָ"ל וַדַּאי שַׁפִּיר הוּא דְּקָא אַמְרַת.

45. And you may ask why, if this is so, we see many people getting up at night from their sleep, AND THEIR LIFE IS RETURNED TO THEM, while the Tree of Death still reigns. AND HE REPLIES: Most certainly the Tree of Life does this. What is the reason? Because it is written: "to see if there were any that understood, and sought Elohim" (Tehilim 14:2), so there will be no excuse for the person to say that if he had been in control of his soul at night, he would have RISEN AND studied the Torah. Rabbi Yehuda said: That is certainly CORRECT for Yisrael, and so it is. However, for the nations of the world, we also see likewise, THAT THEY WAKE UP FROM THEIR SLEEP AT NIGHT. What is the reason? He told him: Most certainly, what you said is true.

46. פָּתַח וְאָמַר, מָה אָקוֹב לֹא קַבֹּה אֵל וּמָה אֶזְעֹם לֹא זָעַם יְיָ'. ת"ח,

כְּגַוְונָא דְּאִית לְעֵילָא, אִית לְתַתָּא. לְעֵילָא אִית יְמִינָא וְאִית שְׂמָאלָא.
לְתַתָּא יִשְׂרָאֵל וְעַמִּין. יִשְׂרָאֵל אִתְאַחֲדָן לִימִינָא, בִּקְדוּשָׁא דְּמַלְכָּא
קַדִּישָׁא. עַמִּין עכו״ם לִשְׂמָאלָא, לְסִטְרָא דְּרוּחַ מְסָאֲבָא. וְכֻלְּהוּ לְתַתָּא
מִכֻּלְּהוּ דַּרְגִּין דִּשְׂמָאלָא. וְכֻלְּהוּ דַּרְגִּין אֲחִידָן דָּא בְּדָא, עַד דְּתַלְיָין מִן
רֵישָׁא. וּכְגַוְונָא דְּרֵישָׁא נָטִיל, בְּהַהוּא גַוְונָא נָטִיל זַנְבָּא, דְּאִיהִי תַתָּאָה.
מ״ט. בְּגִין דְּאָחִיד בֵּיהּ. וּבְגִין כָּךְ, עַמִּין עכו״ם, בְּהַהוּא סְטַר מְסָאֲבָא
דִּלְהוֹן, הָכִי אִתְדַּבְּרוּ.

46. He opened the discussion and said: "How shall I curse whom El has not cursed? Or how shall I denounce whom Hashem has not denounced?" (Bemidbar 23:8) Come and behold: that which is there above, likewise is down below. Above IN MALCHUT, there is right and there is left. ALSO, down below are Yisrael and the other nations. Yisrael hold on to the right, to the holiness of the Holy King. The idolatrous nations hang on to the left, NAMELY ONLY on the side of the Defiled Spirit, which is the lowest level of the left. And all the levels are attached to each other FROM BELOW until they hang from the top, THAT IS, EROM THE LEFT SIDE OF MALCHUT ABOVE. And in the same manner the head moves ABOVE, the tail also moves below, which is THE LOWEST LEVEL, WHICH IS THE DEFILED SPIRIT. The reason is that it is attached to it, SINCE THEY ARE INTERLINKED FROM BELOW UPWARDS, LIKE A CHAIN, the idolatrous nations are guided after the MANNER, WHICH IS THEIR aspect of the Defiled Spirit.

47. בִּלְעָם הוּא אִשְׁתַּמַּשׁ בְּכֻלְּהוּ דַּרְגִּין תַּתָּאִין. וְהוּא הֲוָה חָמֵי בְּהַאי
תַתָּאָה דְּאִיהוּ זַנְבָּא, דְּלָא יָכִיל לְאִתְדַּבְּרָא אֶלָּא בְּרֵישָׁא. בְּגִין כָּךְ
אָמַר, מָה אֶקּוֹב לֹא קַבֹּה אֵל, דְּהַהוּא רֵישָׁא עִלָּאָה, לָא אִשְׁתְּכַח
בְּדִינָא בְּאִינּוּן יוֹמִין.

47. Bilaam employed all the lowest levels THAT DESCEND FROM THE LEFT ASPECT OF MALCHUT. He used to gaze at the lowest LEVEL, the tail, AND HE FIGURED OUT WHAT WAS ABOVE, SINCE THE LOWEST is controlled solely by the head. He therefore declared, "How shall I curse whom El has not cursed?" SINCE HE COULD SEE THE LOWER, AND KNEW that the supreme head, WHICH IS THE LEFT OF MALCHUT, is not in a state of

Judgment during that period.

48. ואע״ג דְּהַאי אֵל אוּקִימְנָא, הַאי מַלְכוּתָא קַדִּישָׁא נָטִיל שְׁמָא כְּגַוְונָא דִּלְעֵילָא, וְהַאי טַב וְחֶסֶד דְּהַאי עָלְמָא וּבְגִין כַּךְ אִקְרֵי אֵל, אֶלָּא דְּאִיהוּ זוֹעֵם בְּכָל יוֹם, דְּאִשְׁתְּכַח בֵּיהּ דִּינָא.

48. And even though we explained the name El TO BE SUPERNAL CHESED, holy Malchut receives this name in the likeness of above and becomes goodness, and Chesed in this world. Therefore, it is called BY THE NAME 'El'. However, it displays anger every day, ACCORDING TO THE MEANING OF, "EL WHO HAS INDIGNATION EVERY DAY" (TEHILIM 7:11), because there is Judgment in it. BUT IN THAT PERIOD THERE WAS NO JUDGMENT IN IT. THEREFORE, BILAAM SAID, "HOW SHALL I CURSE WHOM EL HAS NOT CURSED?"

49. ותָ״ח, אֵל שַׁדַּי הָא אוּקִימְנָא דְּבֵיהּ סְפוּקָא דְּעָלְמָא וְאִיהוּ אָמַר לְעוֹלָם דַּי, דְּהָא הַאי אֵל הוּא דְּאִזְדַּוֵּוג בַּהֲדֵיהּ, וּבְגִין כַּךְ אִקְרֵי אֵל שַׁדַּי, אֵל דְּשַׁדַּי. וְעַל דָּא מַה אֵקּוֹב לֹא קַבֹּה אֵל. בְּגִין כַּךְ, כְּגַוְונָא דְּאִתְּעַר רֵישָׁא, ה״נ אִתְּעַר תַּתָּאָה.

49. Come and behold: we explained about El Shadai, that satiates the world and said to the world, 'Enough (Heb. *dai*)' – THAT HE, YESOD, PROVIDES ENOUGH BOUNTY TO MALCHUT THAT IS CALLED 'WORLD'. This El, WHO IS MALCHUT, conjugates with him, and therefore it is called 'El-Shadai', SINCE EL, WHICH IS MALCHUT, UNITES WITH SHADAI, WHICH IS YESOD. And therefore, HE DECLARED, "How shall I curse whom El has not cursed?" REFERRING TO MALCHUT, WHICH IS CALLED 'EL'. HE KNEW THAT as the head awakens, WHICH IS MALCHUT, so the lower also awakens, WHICH IS THE TAIL – NAMELY THE SPIRIT OF DEFILEMENT. AND BILAAM OBSERVED THE TAIL AND KNEW WHAT WAS IN THE HEAD.

50. בָּכָה רִבִּי אֶלְעָזָר, פָּתַח וְאָמַר קוֹלָהּ כַּנָּחָשׁ יֵלֵךְ וְגוֹ'. הַשְׁתָּא דְיִשְׂרָאֵל בְּגָלוּתָא, אִיהִי וַדַּאי אַזְלָא כְּנָחָשׁ. חִוְיָא כַּד אִיהוּ כָּפִיף רֵישָׁא לְעַפְרָא, סָלִיק זַנְבָא, שַׁלִּיט וּמָחֵי לְכָל אִינוּן דְּאִשְׁתְּכָחוּ קַמֵּיהּ. אוֹף

הָכִי הַשְׁתָּא בְּגָלוּתָא, כְּהַאי גַּוְונָא, רֵישָׁא כָּפִיף לְעַפְרָא, וְזַנְבָּא שַׁלִּיט. מַאן עָבֵיד לְזַנְבָּא דְּיִסְתְּלִיק לְעֵילָא וְשַׁלִּיט וּמָחֵי, רֵישָׁא דְּאִתְכַּפְיָא לְתַתָּא. וְעִם כָּל דָּא, מַאן מַדְבַּר לֵיהּ לְזַנְבָּא, וּמַאן נָטִיל לֵיהּ לְמַטַּלְנוֹי. הַאי רֵישָׁא. אע״ג דְּאִיהוּ כָּפִיף לְעַפְרָא, הוּא מַדְבַּר לְמַטַּלְנוֹי, בְּגִין דָּא קוֹלָהּ כַּנָּחָשׁ יֵלֵךְ.

50. Rabbi Elazar wept. He opened the discussion and said: "Her sound is like that of a snake on the move..." (Yirmeyah 46:22). Now that Yisrael are in exile, most certainly MALCHUT goes on like a snake – BECAUSE THE WAY of a snake is that when it bows its head to the dust, it raises its tail. THE TAIL controls and hits those who are in its way. And now it is also that way; WHEN YISRAEL ARE in exile, MALCHUT BEHAVES LIKEWISE. In the same manner as OF THE SNAKE, the head is in the ground and the tail, NAMELY THE LOWEST LEVEL MENTIONED ABOVE, rules. Who caused the tail to rise above to guide and hit? That is the head, which is bowed downwards. Who drives the tail, and who propels the tail on its journeys? It is the same head. Although it is lowered to the dust, it still leads the movements OF THE TAIL. Therefore, SAYS THE SCRIPTURE, "Her sound is like that of a snake on the move..."

51. וְהַשְׁתָּא שְׁאַר עַמִּין דְּאִינּוּן אֲחִידָן בְּזַנְבָּא, סַלְקִין לְעֵילָא, וְשַׁלְטִין וּמָחְיָין, וְרֵישָׁא כָּפִיף לְעַפְרָא, כד״א נָפְלָה לֹא תוֹסִיף קוּם וְגוֹ'. וְעִם כָּל דָּא, הַאי רֵישָׁא מַדְבַּר לְזַנְבָּא וְנָטִיר לֵיהּ, כד״א שָׂמוּנִי נוֹטֵרָה אֶת הַכְּרָמִים, אִלֵּין עַמִּין עעכו״ם, דְּאִינּוּן זַנְבָּא. אָתָא רַבִּי יְהוּדָה וְנָשִׁיק יְדוֹי, אָמַר אִלְמָלֵי לָא שָׁאִילְנָא מִלָּה בְּעָלְמָא, אֶלָּא דְּשָׁאִילְנָא דָּא וְרַוַוחְנָא לֵיהּ, דַּי לִי. דְּהַשְׁתָּא יְדַעְנָא עַמִּין עכו״ם, וְשׁוּלְטָנוּתָא דִּלְהוֹן הֵיךְ מִתְדַּבַּר. זַכָּאָה חוּלָקֵיהוֹן דְּיִשְׂרָאֵל, דַּעֲלַיְיהוּ כְּתִיב, כִּי יַעֲקֹב בָּחַר לוֹ יָהּ וְגוֹ'.

51. And now the other nations that hold to the tail OF MALCHUT, rise above and dictate and harm, and the head is bowed to the dust, as it was said, "is fallen; she shall no more rise" (Amos 5:2). Still, the head guides the tail and preserves it, as it says, "they made me the keeper of the vineyards" (Shir Hashirim 1:6). Which refers to the idolatrous nations, who are in the tail.

Rabbi Yehuda then came close and kissed his hands and said: If I had not asked anything in this world except this question, and I gained this answer, it would have been sufficient. For now I understand THE ASPECT OF the idolatrous nations, and how their dictatorship is led. Praiseworthy is the lot of Yisrael, for about them it is written: "For Hashem has chosen Jacob to Himself, Yisrael for His peculiar possession" (Tehilim 135:4).

52. א״ל רְבִּי אֶלְעָזָר, מַהוּ לִסְגוּלָתוֹ. א״ל, תְּלַת אֲבָהָן אִלֵּין אִקְרוּן סְגוּלָה, בֵּין לְעֵילָּא בֵּין לְתַתָּא, כְּגַוְונָא דָא כֹּהֲנִים לְוִיִּם וְיִשְׂרְאֵלִים, וְכֹלָּא חַד. וְאִלֵּין סְגוּלָתוֹ שֶׁל קוּדְשָׁא בְּרִיךְ הוּא לְעֵילָּא, וּסְגוּלָתוֹ לְתַתָּא, וְדָא הוּא דִכְתִיב וִהְיִיתֶם לִי סְגוּלָה מִכָּל הָעַמִּים.

52. Rabbi Elazar asked him: What is the definition of, "peculiar possession," WHEN THE SCRIPTURE SAYS, "YISRAEL FOR HIS PECULIAR POSSESSION"? He said to him: The three patriarchs are alluded to, and they are called 'possession', both above, WHERE THEY ARE REFERRED TO AS CHESED, GVURAH AND TIFERET, and below, NAMELY ABRAHAM, ISAAC AND JACOB. And likewise are the priests, Levites and Yisrael, THAT ALSO CORRESPOND TO CHESED, GVURAH AND TIFERET, and everything is the same. And they are the possession of the Holy One, blessed be He, above, and the possession of the Holy One, blessed be He, below. And that is what is written: "then you shall be My own treasure (also: 'possession') from among all peoples" (Shemot 19:5). THAT IS, BECAUSE THEY HAVE PRIESTS, LEVITES AND YISRAEL, WHO ARE CALLED 'POSSESSION'.

6. "His litter, that of Solomon," between north and south

A Synopsis

The rabbis return to their discussion of the standards of the tribes that traveled with the Tent of Meeting. We hear that holy Yisrael will not bless the universe except through the Shechinah. The question arises how Israel could have seen the Shechinah when his eyes were dim with age, and the answer is that he perceived Her fragrance. We learn that the Shechinah is in the west, and are told of the importance of direction in the union of the Shechinah with the body. We read of the ten Hallelujah's in the five psalms and how a person accepts the yoke of the heavenly kingdom in the morning when he recites praises to God. The summary of this section is that if one wishes to create a unification, to put the lights in order, one must take upon himself the yoke of the Holy Kingdom in order to elevate himself through the hallowed connection of the south, Chesed. One must encircle the four corners of the universe, Chesed Gvurah Tiferet and Malchut, until he joins them together into one knot. And in the south he should arrange a place and dwell there.

53. וְנָסַע אֹהֶל מוֹעֵד מַחֲנֵה הַלְוִיִּם וְגוֹ'. לְבָתַר מַה כְּתִיב, וְנָסַע דֶּגֶל מַחֲנֵה אֶפְרַיִם לְצִבְאֹתָם יָמָּה. הַיְינוּ שְׁכִינָה שַׁרְוָיָה בְּמַעֲרָב, וְאוּקְמוּהָ. כְּתִיב וַיְבָרְכֵם בַּיּוֹם הַהוּא לֵאמֹר בְּךָ יְבָרֵךְ יִשְׂרָאֵל לֵאמֹר וְגוֹ'. וַיָּשֶׂם אֶת אֶפְרַיִם וְגוֹ'. בְּךָ יְבָרֵךְ יִשְׂרָאֵל, יִשְׂרָאֵל סָבָא. מַאי קמ"ל.

53. "Then the Tent of Meeting shall set forward with the camp of the Levites..." (Bemidbar 2:17). After this, it is written, "On the west side shall be the standard of the camp of Ephraim by their hosts" (Ibid. 18). That refers to the Shechinah that rests on the west, as it was explained THAT EPHRAIM TRAVELED ON THE WEST, THE SECRET OF MALCHUT, AND THEREFORE HE TRAVELED AFTER THE STANDARD OF REUBEN, WHO IS ON THE SOUTH, WHICH IS CHESED, AND SO ON. It is written: "And he blessed them that day, saying, 'By you shall Yisrael bless, saying...' and he set Ephraim..." (Beresheet 48:20). HE ASKS: "By you shall Yisrael bless," referring to Yisrael-Saba. HE QUESTIONS: What does this teach us?

54. אֶלָּא בְּךָ יִתְבָּרֵךְ יִשְׂרָאֵל לָא כְּתִיב, אוֹ בְּךָ יְבוֹרַךְ יִשְׂרָאֵל, מַהוּ יְבָרֵךְ יִשְׂרָאֵל. אֶלָּא, יִשְׂרָאֵל קַדִּישָׁא לָא יְבָרֵךְ לְעָלְמָא, אֶלָּא בְּךָ, דְּאַנְתְּ

בְּמַעֲרָב. וּכְתִיב אֲנִי אֵל שַׁדַּי פְּרֵה וּרְבֵה. אוֹלִיפְנָא דְּחָכְמָא עֲמֵיהּ
שְׁכִינְתָּא, וּכְדֵין אָמַר בְּךָ יְבָרֵךְ יִשְׂרָאֵל לֵאמֹר. בְּךָ יְבָרֵךְ לְעָלְמָא.

54. AND HE REPLIES: 'By you shall Yisrael be blessed', is not what is actually written, nor is, 'By you will Yisrael be blessed'. What then is the meaning of, "By you shall Yisrael bless," WHICH REFERS TO OTHERS GETTING BLESSED? THE EXPLANATION is that holy Yisrael, MEANING ZEIR ANPIN, will not bless the world, except through you, EPHRAIM, who resides in the west, MEANING THE SHECHINAH. And it is written: "I am El Shadai: be fruitful and multiply" (Beresheet 35:11). WE THEREFORE SEE THAT THE BLESSING RESTS WITH THE SHECHINAH THAT IS CALLED 'EL SHADAI'. We learn that he saw the Shechinah with him, and then he declared, "By you shall Yisrael bless, saying," MEANING by THE SHECHINAH shall he bless the world.

55. וְהָאֵיךְ חָמָא, וְהָכְתִיב וְעֵינֵי יִשְׂרָאֵל כָּבְדוּ מִזוֹקֶן וְגוֹ'. אֶלָּא שֶׂכֵּל
אֶת יָדָיו כְּתִיב. מַאי שֶׂכֵּל. אֶלָּא יְמִינָא הֲוָה זָקִיף, וְסָטֵי לֵיהּ שְׁכִינְתָּא
כְּלַפֵּי אֶפְרַיִם, וְאָרַח רֵיחָא דִּשְׁכִינְתָּא עַל רֵישֵׁיהּ, כְּדֵין אָמַר בְּךָ יְבָרֵךְ
יִשְׂרָאֵל. וְחָמָא דְּאִיהוּ לְמַעֲרָב.

55. HE QUESTIONS: How could he see THE SHECHINAH, since it is also written: "Now the eyes of Israel were dim from old age..." (Beresheet 48:10), WHICH ALSO ALLUDES TO THE SPIRITUAL EYES. AND HE REPLIES: However, it is written, "changing his hands" (Ibid. 14). Why the crossing? AND HE ANSWERS: The right hand was raised CORRESPONDING TO EPHRAIM, and the Shechinah turned in the direction of Ephraim, and ISRAEL had smelled the fragrance of the Shechinah over his head. He then said, "By you shall Yisrael bless," and saw Her in the west – MEANING THAT HE DID NOT SEE WITH HIS EYES, BUT PERCEIVED IT BY THE SENSE OF SMELL, WHICH MEANS FROM BELOW UPWARD.

56. וַדַּאי שְׁכִינְתָּא בְּמַעֲרָב, וְהָא אוֹקִימְנָא בְּגִין דִּלְהֱוֵי בֵּין צָפוֹן
לְדָרוֹם, וּלְאִתְחַבְּרָא בְּגוּפָא, וּלְמֶהֱוֵי בְּזִוּוּגָא חַד. וְצָפוֹן מְקַבְּלָא לָהּ
תְּחוֹת רֵישָׁא, וְדָרוֹם מְחַבְּקָא לָהּ, הה"ד שְׂמֹאלוֹ תַּחַת לְרֹאשִׁי וִימִינוֹ
תְּחַבְּקֵנִי. וְהָא אוֹקִימְנָא וַדַּאי, מִטָּתוֹ שֶׁלִשְׁלֹמֹה בֵּין צָפוֹן לְדָרוֹם,

וּלְאִתְחַבְּרָא בְּגוּפָא, וּכְדֵין כְּלָלָא חַד לְאִתְבָּרְכָא עָלְמָא. תְּנָן, כָּל הָאוֹמֵר תְּהִלָּה לְדָוִד ג׳׳פ בְּכָל יוֹמָא, מוּבְטַח לוֹ שֶׁהוּא בֶּן העוה׳׳ב, וְהָא אוֹקִימְנָא בְּגִין לְזַוְּוגָא לָהּ לְהַאי תְּהִלָּה, וּלְאִשְׁתַּכְּחָא בְּכָל יוֹמָא בֵּין צָפוֹן לְדָרוֹם.

56. Certainly, the Shechinah is in the west, and we explained that this is in order that she should be between the north and south, BECAUSE THE WEST IS SITUATED BETWEEN NORTH AND SOUTH. And so She will unite with the body, THE SECRET OF ZEIR ANPIN, CALLED 'BODY' – WHICH MEANS THE SEVEN LOWER SFIROT – and be WITH IT in one union. And the north, WHICH IS THE LEFT COLUMN OF ZEIR ANPIN, receives Her under its head, and the south, WHICH IS THE RIGHT OF ZEIR ANPIN, embraces Her. That is what is written, "His left hand is under my head" (Shir Hashirim 2:6), SINCE FROM THE LEFT, THE SECRET OF THE ILLUMINATION OF CHOCHMAH, SHE RECEIVES THE FIRST THREE SFIROT, ALSO CALLED 'HEAD'. "...and His right hand embraces me..." (Ibid.) AND FROM THE RIGHT, THE SECRET OF CHASSADIM, SHE RECEIVES THE ILLUMINATION OF THE SEVEN LOWER SFIROT, THAT ARE REFERRED TO AS 'BODY'. And we explained, certainly Solomon's bed, WHICH IS THE MYSTICAL REFERENCE TO MALCHUT, CALLED 'BED', is situated between north and south, THAT ARE CHESED AND GVURAH, in order that it should adhere to the body THAT IS TIFERET. Then they are one wholeness by which the universe is blessed. We learned that whoever recites "A praise of David" (Tehilim 145) three times daily is assured to be worthy of the World to Come. And we concluded THAT ITS MEANING IS that he unites this praise, WHICH REFERS TO MALCHUT, to be WITH ZEIR ANPIN, every day between the north and south.

57. אָתֵי בַּר נָשׁ בְּצַפְרָא, מְקַבֵּל עָלֵיהּ עוֹל מַלְכוּת שָׁמַיִם בְּאִינּוּן תּוּשְׁבְּחָן דְּקָאמַר תְּהִלָּה לְדָוִד, וְכֻלְּהוּ הַלְלוּיָה דְּאִינּוּן סִדּוּרָא דַּעֲשָׂרָה תּוּשְׁבְּחָן, דַּעֲשָׂרָה כִּתְרִין קַדִּישִׁין דִּשְׁמָא קַדִּישָׁא. וּבְגִין כָּךְ עֲשָׂרָה אִינּוּן הַלְלוּיָה. לְבָתַר סִיֵּים בַּעֲשָׂרָה תּוּשְׁבְּחָן, דְּאִינּוּן הַלְלוּיָה הַלְלוּ אֵל בְּקָדְשׁוֹ וְגוֹ׳. הַלְלוּהוּ וְגוֹ׳. מַאן אִינּוּן עֲשָׂרָה הַלְלוּיָה, וְהָא חֲמִשָּׁה אִינּוּן. אֶלָּא שָׁרֵי שְׁבָחָא בְּהַלְלוּיָה, וְסִיֵּים בְּהַלְלוּיָה.

-35-

57. A person comes in the morning and accepts upon himself the yoke of the heavenly kingdom with these praises that he recites, referring to, "A praise of David," and the rest of the Haleluyah's which are the order of the ten praises of the ten holy Sfirot of the Holy Name. Therefore, there are ten Haleluyah's, concluding with ten praises, that are, "Haleluyah, Praise El in His Sanctuary: praise Him..." (Tehilim 150:1). HE QUERIES: Where do we find ten Haleluyah's? There are only five, SINCE THERE ARE ONLY FIVE PSALMS THAT BEGIN WITH HALELUYAH. AND HE RESPONDS: It is because each psalm begins with Haleluyah and concludes with Haleluyah, FOR A TOTAL OF TEN.

58. לְבָתַר עִלְוֵיָא דְּסִדּוּר שְׁבָחָא, בְּאָז יָשִׁיר מֹשֶׁה, דְּאִית בֵּיהּ כֹּלָּא. וּבְדָא מְקַבֵּל עָלֵיהּ עוֹל מַלְכוּתָא קַדִּישָׁא. לְבָתַר אַשְׁרֵי לֵהּ בְּחֶסֶד, בְּסִיּוּמָא דִּצְלוֹתָא, לְאִתְקַדְּשָׁא בֵּיהּ. לְבָתַר בִּצְלוֹתָא דְּמִנְחָה דִּגְבוּרָה תַּלְיָיא, וְדִינָא שָׁרֵי. אִשְׁתְּכַח בְּכָל יוֹמָא דָא מִטָּה דְּאִתְיְהִיבַת בֵּין צָפוֹן לְדָרוֹם. לְאִתְחַבְּרָא בְּזִוּוּגָא דָא בְּגוּפָא כַּדְקָא יָאוֹת. וּמַאן דִּמְסַדֵּר וּמְחַבֵּר לָהּ בְּכָל יוֹמָא כְּהַאי גַּוְונָא, וַדַּאי הוּא בֶּן העוה"ב.

58. Afterwards he established the sequence of praise of the Song of the Sea (Shemot 15) that includes everything. And with this he accepts upon himself the yoke of the holy Kingdom. He then causes Chesed to rest it in the conclusion of the prayers, which makes it hallowed, SINCE THE MORNING PRAYER CORRESPONDS TO ABRAHAM, WHO IS CHESED AND THE RIGHT COLUMN. Afterwards, in the afternoon prayer, Gvurah is impending and Judgment is prevalent, WHICH CORRESPONDS TO ISAAC, WHO IS GVURAH AND THE LEFT COLUMN. We find that this bed, WHICH REFERS TO MALCHUT, is placed daily between north and south, BETWEEN THE MORNING PRAYER, THE SECRET OF THE SOUTH, AND THE AFTERNOON PRAYER, THE SECRET OF THE NORTH, so that it will properly join in unity with the body, WHICH IS ZEIR ANPIN, THE CENTRAL COLUMN. And whoever daily arranges and joins MALCHUT in this manner is most assuredly worthy of the World to Come. THIS MEANS THAT ABOUT THIS IT WAS SAID THAT WHOEVER DAILY RECITES, "A PRAISE OF DAVID," is assured to be of the World to Come.

59. בְּגִין כַּךְ הַאי דֶּגֶל מַחֲנֵה אֶפְרַיִם יָמָּה, וְאִיהוּ בֵּין צָפוֹן לְדָרוֹם.

דָּרוֹם רְאוּבֵן מִן סִטְרָא חַד, דִּכְתִּיב דֶּגֶל מַחֲנֵה רְאוּבֵן תֵּימָנָה. צָפוֹן דָּן מִסִּטְרָא אַחֲרָא, דִּכְתִּיב דֶּגֶל מַחֲנֵה דָן צָפוֹנָה. אֶפְרַיִם, בֵּין דָּא לְדָא. אִשְׁתְּכַח מַעֲרָב דְּאִיהוּ אֶפְרַיִם, בֵּין צָפוֹן לְדָרוֹם, כֹּלָּא כְּגַוְונָא דִלְעֵילָא.

59. Consequently, the standard of Ephraim is to the west, which is between north and south. South is Reuben. He is from one side, as it is written: "On the south side shall be the standard of the camp of Reuben" (Bemidbar 2:10). Dan was from the opposite side to the north, as is written: "The standard of the camp of Dan shall be on the north side" (Ibid. 25). Ephraim was situated between this one and that one, SINCE REUBEN, WHO IS SOUTH, IS BEFORE DAN, WHO IS NORTH, BEHIND HIM. Therefore, the west, which is Ephraim, is situated between north and south, all reflecting MALCHUT above.

60. רָזָא לְיַתְבֵי דְרוֹמָא אֲחוּנָא. וְהָכִי שָׁדַר לוֹן אֲחוּנָא, מְסַדְּרֵי בּוּצִינִין בְּרָזִין קְטִירִין, דְּבָעֵיתוּ לְיַחֲדָא יִחוּדָא בְּטוּפְסְרָא דִּקְטִירָא עִלָּאָה, קַבִּילוּ עֲלַיְיכוּ עוֹל מַלְכוּתָא קַדִּישָׁא בְּכָל יוֹמָא בְּקַדְמֵיתָא, וּבְדָא תַּעֲלוּן בְּקִשּׁוּרָא קַדִּישָׁא דְּדָרוֹם, וְאַסְחֲרוּ סִטְרֵי עָלְמָא, עַד דְּמִתְקַשְּׁרָן בְּקְטוּרָא חֲדָא, וּבְדָרוֹם תְּקִיעוּ דּוּכְתָּא, וְתַמָּן תִּשְׁרוּן.

60. This secret is of our brothers, the southern inhabitants. And so our brothers' message was to us, those who put the lights in order, in the mystical connections, MEANING THE UNIFICATIONS. You who wish to create a unification in the sequence of the supreme connection. Firstly, undertake upon yourselves daily the yoke of the holy Kingdom, and by doing so, you will elevate yourselves WITH HER through the hallowed connection of the south, MEANING CHESED. And encircle the FOUR directions of the world, CHESED, GVURAH, TIFERET AND MALCHUT, until you join them together into one knot. And in the south you should arrange a place and dwell there, SIMILAR TO THE ENCIRCLING OF THE ALTAR, AS EXPLAINED BEFORE.

7. The sign of unification

A Synopsis
Rabbi Shimon repeats to his son the importance and the mystical meaning of the direction for encircling the altar. Only when this is properly done can a person create the perfect unification.

61. ר' אֶלְעָזָר שָׁאִיל לר"ש אֲבוֹי, א"ל, סִימָנָא לְזִוּוּגָא דְּיִחוּדָא מְנַיִן. א"ל בְּרִי, אע"ג דְּאוֹקִימְנָא מִלִין לְכָל סְטַר וּסְטַר, וְאִתְבַּדְּרוּ הָכָא מִלָה וְהָכָא מִלָה סִימָנָא דָא נְקוֹט בִּידָךְ, וְהָכִי הוּא, כְּעֵין סָחֲרָא דְּמַדְבְּחָא, דִּתְנָן, וּבָא לוֹ לְקֶרֶן דְּרוֹמִית מִזְרָחִית, מִזְרָחִית צְפוֹנִית, צְפוֹנִית מַעֲרָבִית, מַעֲרָבִית דְּרוֹמִי. א"ל וְהָא לָא יָכִיל עַד דְּמְקַבֵּל עֲלֵיה ב"נ עוֹל מַלְכוּתָא קַדִּישָׁא בְּקַדְמֵיתָא, וְיָהִיב עֲלֵיה עוֹל דָּא, וְאַתְּ אֲמַרְתְּ דְּיֵיתֵי לְדָרוֹם בְּקַדְמֵיתָא.

61. Rabbi Elazar asked his father Rabbi Shimon: Where do we find this sign of unification, SO THAT WE DO NOT ERR? He told him: My son, although we explained this in many facets and THESE WORDS were scattered here and there, keep this sign in your hand. This is similar to the encircling of the altar, which we have previously learned. One should approach the south-east corner, north-east, north-west, and south-west, AS WE DESCRIBED BEFORE. So he asked him: It is inconceivable TO DO ANYTHING until a person accepts upon himself the yoke of the Holy Kingdom first and carries that yoke, yet you said he should first come to the south, WHICH IS CHESED.

62. א"ל, כֹּלָּא הָא אֲמֵינָא לָךְ, דְּהָא וּבָא לוֹ לְקֶרֶן, אֲמֵינָא בְּקַדְמֵיתָא, וְהָא יְדַעְתָּא רָזָא דְּקֶרֶן, וְדָא הוּא עוֹל מַלְכוּתָא קַדִּישָׁא. לְבָתַר דְּרוֹמִית מִזְרָחִית, דְּתַמָּן הוּא אִילָנָא דְחַיֵּי. וְדָא לְאִזְדַּוְּוגָא לֵיה בְּמִזְרָח דְּאִיהוּ אַבָּא עִלָּאָה. דְּהָא בֵּן מִסְּטְרָא דְּאַבָּא קָא אָתֵי. וּבְגִין כַּךְ, מִדָּרוֹם לְמִזְרָח, דְּתוּקְפָּא דְּדָרוֹם בְּמִזְרָח הוּא, וּבָעֵי לְאִתְקַשְּׁרָא כַּחֲדָא, דָּרוֹם בְּמִזְרָח.

62. He told him: I have already told you everything. I said first that one

-38-

approaches the corner. And you know the hidden meaning of corner – THAT IS, MALCHUT, which is the yoke of holy Malchut. Following that is south-east; ONE SHOULD CONNECT THE SOUTH, CHESED, TO THE EAST, WHICH IS TIFERET, THE CENTRAL COLUMN, because there, IN THE EAST, is the Tree of Life, WHICH IS TIFERET. This is in order to bring together THE SOUTH with the east, who is supernal Aba, MEANING CHOCHMAH, ALSO CALLED 'SUPERNAL ABA AND IMA', because the son, WHICH IS TIFERET, comes from the father's side – BECAUSE THE ROOT OF TIFERET IS IN THE CONCEALED DA'AT OF SUPERNAL ABA AND IMA. Hence, ONE UNITES from south to the east, for the fortitude of the south is in the east, NAMELY IN THE CONCEALED DA'AT OF SUPERNAL ABA AND IMA, WHICH IS THE BEGINNING OF THE EAST. And therefore it is imperative that south and east should be bound together.

63. וּמִזְרָח דְּאִתְקְשַׁר בְּצָפוֹן, בְּגִין דְּהַאי אַשְׁלִים וּמַלֵּי נַחֲלִין וּמַבּוּעִין, וע״ד מִזְרָחִית צְפוֹנִית, אִלֵּין אַבָּא וְאִמָּא דְּלָא מִתְפָּרְשָׁן לְעָלְמִין, וְהָא אוֹקִימְנָא. וּמַה דְּאִתְּמַר צְפוֹנִית, דְּאִיהוּ טְמִירָא עִלָּאָה, וּמִסְטַר דִּילָהּ נָפִיק צָפוֹן, וְדִינִין מִסְּטְרָא דִּילָהּ מִתְעָרִין, אע״ג דְּהִיא רַחֲמֵי וְחֵידוּ. וְהָא אוֹקִימְנָא. וְכַד אִיהִי נָפְקַת, צָפוֹן נָפְקַת בֵּיהּ, דְּאִיהוּ אִתְכְּלִיל וְאִתְקְשַׁר בְּדָרוֹם.

63. And east connects to the north, WHICH IS IN IMA, REFERRING TO BINAH, ALSO CALLED 'YISRAEL-SABA AND TEVUNAH', FROM WHICH THE NORTH IS DRAWN FORTH – THAT IS, THE LEFT COLUMN, since it, MEANING BINAH, completes and fills the rivers and springs OF THE EAST, WHICH IS THE REVEALED DA'AT AND TIFERET. And therefore, IT IS IMPERATIVE TO UNITE north-east, MEANING TO CONNECT THE EAST WITH BINAH. However, these EAST AND NORTH are Aba and Ima that never separate, BECAUSE EAST IS DA'AT OF SUPERNAL ABA, THAT IS, THE SECRET OF SUPERNAL ABA AND IMA. DA'AT OF SUPERNAL ABA CLEAVES TO DA'AT OF SUPERNAL IMA, AND THE LEFT COLUMN THAT IS REVEALED IN HER THAT IS CALLED 'NORTH', as we already explained. And the reason she, THE SUPERNAL IMA, is called northern (Heb. *tzefonit*), is because it is the supernal hidden one (Heb. *tzefunah*), and from her end the north emanates, WHICH IS THE LEFT COLUMN. THIS IS BECAUSE FROM ABA'S END, THE NORTH IS HIDDEN AND CONCEALED. The Judgments arise from her side, although she is merciful and happy. And we already

explained it. When she, IMA, emerges, the north emanates from her; IT IS
FROM HER THAT THE NORTH REVEALS ITSELF, because he, ABA, was
included in and connected to the south, AND THE NORTH IS HIDDEN IN IT.

64. לְבָתַר צְפוֹנִית מַעֲרָבִית, דְּהָא מִסְטְרָא דְאַבָּא נָפִיק בֵּן, וּמִסְטְרָא
דְאִמָּא נְפִיקַת בַּת. וּבְגִין כַּךְ צְפוֹנִית מַעֲרָבִית, וְדָא הוּא קֶרֶן
קַדְמֵיתָא, דְּהַשְׁתָּא אִתְקְשַׁר בַּצְפוֹן סְתָם. לְבָתַר בָּעֵי לְקַשְׁרָא לָהּ
בַּדָרוֹם, דְּתַמָּן הוּא קִשּׁוּרָא דְכֹלָּא, וְגוּפָא בֵּיה אִשְׁתְּכַח, וע"ד מַעֲרָבִית
דְּרוֹמִית.

64. Following that, HE WILL COME TO THE north-western CORNER. From
Aba's side the son emerges, WHICH IS TIFERET, EAST. And from Ima's
side, WHICH IS NORTH, the daughter emerges, WHICH IS MALCHUT, WEST.
And because of that it is north-western; FROM NORTH WHICH IS IMA, TO
WEST, WHICH IS MALCHUT. And that is the first corner, SINCE CORNER IS
THE MEANING OF MALCHUT THAT ONE MUST ACCEPT UPON HIMSELF
FIRST OF ALL. And now it is simply referred to as north, MEANING IN IMA
AND LEFT COLUMN. Then one must connect it to the south, WHICH IS
CHESED AND THE RIGHT COLUMN, where everything is connected, where
the body, THAT IS, ZEIR ANPIN, is situated. SINCE ZEIR ANPIN EMANATES
FROM ABA, AS MENTIONED ABOVE, HE IS THEREFORE CONTAINED
COMPLETELY IN THE SOUTH, LIKE ABA, AND THE NORTH IS CONCEALED
IN HIM. It is therefore south-western.

65. אִשְׁתְּכַח הַאי קֶרֶן ג' זִמְנִין, חַד לְקַבְּלָא לֵיה בַּר נָשׁ בְּקַדְמֵיתָא,
וּלְבָתַר הָכִי לְקַשְׁרָא לָהּ בִּתְרֵי דְרוֹעֵי, לְאִתְחַבְּרָא בְּגוּפָא, וּלְמֶהֱוֵי כֹלָּא
חַד. וְדָא הוּא סְדוּרָא דְיִחוּדָא שְׁלִים. וְכָל סְטַר וּסְטַר בְּהַהוּא קִשּׁוּרָא
דְאִתְחֲזֵי לֵיה, וְלָא יַחֲלִיף סִטְרָא בְּסִטְרָא אַחֲרָא דְלָא אִתְחֲזֵי לֵיה, בְּגִין
דְּלָא יִתְעֲנַשׁ. מַאן דְּעָבֵיד יִחוּדָא דָא כַּדְקָא חֲזֵי כְּמָה דְּאַמֵינָא, זַכָּאָה
חוּלָקֵיה בְּהַאי עָלְמָא וּבְעָלְמָא דְּאָתֵי, דְּהָא יָדַע לְסַדְרָא שְׁבָחָא
דְּמָארֵיה, וְיִחוּדָא דְמָארֵיה, וְלָא עוֹד אֶלָּא דְקוּדְשָׁא בְּרִיךְ הוּא מִשְׁתְּבַח
בֵּיה. עֲלֵיה כְּתִיב וַיֹּאמֶר לִי עַבְדִּי אָתָּה יִשְׂרָאֵל אֲשֶׁר בְּךָ אֶתְפָּאָר.

65. And we find this corner, WHICH ALLUDES TO MALCHUT, three times.

One is that a person must first accept upon himself. And the following is to connect MALCHUT with both arms, THAT ARE SOUTH AND NORTH, RIGHT AND LEFT, so as to join in the body, WHICH IS TIFERET, THE CENTRAL COLUMN, so that all should be united in one. And that is the order of the perfect unification, TO UNITE every aspect with the appropriate bond. And one must not substitute one side with another side that is not appropriate for it, so as not to be punished. Whoever operates this unification properly as I described, happy is his share in this world and the World to Come, since he knows how to prepare the sequence of praise for his Master and the unification of his Master. And furthermore, the Holy One, blessed be He, takes praise in him. About him the verse is written, "and said to me, 'You are My servant, Yisrael, in whom I will be glorified'" (Yeshayah 49:3).

8. The meditation of prayer

A Synopsis

Rabbi Shimon reiterates much of the information in previous sections to do with the consignment of the soul at night and the requirement to give praise to God in the morning. He speaks about entering the synagogue and donning the Tefilin and the Tzitzit and giving offerings and saying the prescribed prayers in the proper order. But he adds that although the prayers depend on speech, everything is primarily dependent first upon action. He says that a person must not say a prayer until he first observes the act of conforming to the prayer. If his physical act of cleansing himself or donning the Tefilin, for example, is flawed, the prayer will also be flawed and so will the person become flawed below and above. If he does make his prayers correctly then the upper and lower grades are blessed through him. At the end of the prayers he should imagine himself as if he were dying since he gave his soul as a pledge. Rabbi Shimon says that there are some sins that do not get atoned for until a person dies. He tells us about the importance of doing the ceremony of prayer with a full attention of the heart and how one must not approach God with any false intention.

66. רַ׳ שִׁמְעוֹן פָּתַח לְדָוִד אֵלֶיךָ יְיָ׳ נַפְשִׁי אֶשָּׂא אֱלֹהַי בְּךָ בָטַחְתִּי וְגוֹ׳, מַאי קָא חָמָא דָוִד לְסַדְרָא הַאי שְׁבָחָא הָכִי. וְכֻלְּהוּ שְׁבָחֵי דְאִינּוּן בְּאַלְפָא בֵּיתָא כֻּלְּהוּ שְׁלֵמִין, וְהַאי חַסְרָא דְלָא אִית בֵּיהּ ו׳. וַאֲמַאי סְדוּרָא דָא לְמִנְפַּל עַל אַנְפִּין.

66. Rabbi Shimon began the discussion with, "Of David. 'To You, Hashem, do I lift up my soul. O my Elohim, I trust in You...'" (Tehilim 25:1-2). AND HE ASKS: Why did David see fit to prepare this praise so, since all praises that are in alphabetical order are complete, while this one is missing the *Vav*? And why is this arranged for the prostration upon the face?

67. אֶלָּא רָזָא עִלָּאָה הוּא, גָּנִיז בֵּין חַבְרַיָּיא. בְּשַׁעֲתָא דְלֵילְיָא עָאל, אִילָנָא תַּתָּאָה דְתַלְיָיא בֵּיהּ מוֹתָא פָּרִישׁ עַנְפוֹי וּמְכַסְיָא לְכֹלָּא. וע״ד אִתְחֲשָׁךְ. וְכָל בְּנֵי עָלְמָא טַעֲמִין טַעֲמָא דְמוֹתָא, וְאַקְדִּים בַּר נָשׁ וְיָהִיב לֵיהּ פִּקְדוֹנָא דְנַפְשֵׁיהּ, וְאַפְקְדֵיהּ בִּידֵיהּ בְּפִקְדוֹנָא. וּבְגִין דְנָטִיל לוֹן בְּפִקְדוֹנָא, תָּב פִּקְדוֹנָא לְמָארֵיהּ בְּשַׁעֲתָא דְּאָתֵי צַפְרָא. כַּד אָתֵי צַפְרָא

וְתָב לְגַבֵּיה פְּקִדוֹנֵיה, בָּעֵי לְבָרְכָא לֵיה לְקוּדְשָׁא בְּרִיךְ הוּא, דְּאִיהוּ מְהֵימָנָא עִלָּאָה.

67. HE ANSWERS: It is because it is a supreme mystery concealed among the friends. During the time night falls, the lower tree on which death depends, WHICH IS MALCHUT FROM THE JUDGMENT ASPECT, spreads its branches and covers everything. Therefore, it becomes dark, and all the inhabitants of the world a taste of death. And man hastens to give the deposit of his soul, and deposit it as a pledge in its hand FOR THE NIGHT TIME, SO IT WOULD BE RETURNED AT DAY BREAK. And since IT took the soul as a deposit, the deposit returns to its owner when morning comes. When morning arrives and the pledge is returned to him, he is required to bless the Holy One, blessed be He, who is the highest trustee.

68. לְבָתַר דְּקָם, עָאל לְבֵי כְּנִישְׁתָּא, מְעַטַּר בְּטוֹטָפֵי. אִתְכַּסֵּי בִּכְסוּי דְּצִיצִית. עָאל וּמְדַכֵּי גַּרְמֵיה בְּקוּרְבְּנִין בְּקַדְמֵיתָא. לְבָתַר קַבִּיל עֲלֵיה עוֹל מַלְכוּתָא בְּסִדּוּרָא דְּשַׁבְחֵי דְּדָוִד, דְּאִינוּן סִדּוּרָא דְּעוֹל מַלְכוּתָא. וּבְסִדּוּרָא דְּשַׁבְחָא דָּא, אַשְׁרָא עֲלֵיה הַהוּא עוֹל. לְבָתַר סִדּוּרָא דִּצְלוֹתָא דִּמְיוּשָׁב, וּצְלוֹתָא דִּמְעוֹמָד, לְקַשְּׁרָא לוֹן כַּחֲדָא.

68. After waking FROM HIS SLEEP, he enters the synagogue, decorates himself with his Tefilin, covers himself with Tzitzit, enters, and cleanses himself, first with the offerings. After that, he accepts upon himself the yoke of Malchut in the order of David's praises, which are the arranging of the yoke of the Kingdom. And in this order of praises he steeps himself in that yoke. Following that is the order of prayer while seated, WHICH IS PARALLEL TO MALCHUT, and the order of prayer while standing, WHICH IS PARALLEL TO ZEIR ANPIN, to connect them, ZEIR ANPIN AND MALCHUT, together.

69. ת"ח רָזָא דְּמִלָּה אע"ג דִּצְלוֹתָא תַּלְיָיא בְּמִלּוּלָא וְדִבּוּרָא דְּפוּמָא, כֹּלָּא תַּלְיָיא בְּעִקָּרָא דְּעוֹבָדָא בְּקַדְמֵיתָא, וּלְבָתַר בְּדִבּוּרָא וּבְמִלּוּלָא דְּפוּמָא. מַאן עוֹבָדָא, אֶלָּא הַהוּא עוֹבָדָא דְּעָבֵיד בַּר נָשׁ בְּקַדְמֵיתָא, כְּגַוְונָא דִּצְלוֹתָא הוּא, וְלָא יְצַלֵּי בַּר נָשׁ צְלוֹתָא, עַד דְּיִתְחֲזֵי עוֹבָדָא

בְּקַדְמֵיתָא כְּגַוְונָא דִּצְלוֹתָא.

69. Come and behold the mystery of it. Although the prayer depends on speech and the utterance of the mouth, everything is mostly and first dependent upon action, and afterwards upon speech and uttering with the mouth. And what is the deed? It is only the action that a person performs first that resembles prayer. And a person must not say a prayer until he first displays an act of that resembles prayer.

70. עוֹבָדָא דְּקַדְמֵיתָא בְּשַׁעֲתָא דְּבַר נָשׁ קָאִים, בָּעֵי לְדַכְּאָה גַּרְמֵיהּ בְּקַדְמֵיתָא. וּלְבָתַר יְקַבֵּל עֲלֵיהּ הַאי עוֹל, לְפָרְשָׁא עַל רֵישֵׁיהּ פְּרִישׁוּ דְּמִצְוָה. לְבָתַר יִתְקְשַׁר קִשּׁוּרָא דְּיִחוּדָא דְּאִינוּן תְּפִלִּין, תְּפִלָּה שֶׁל רֹאשׁ, וְשֶׁל יַד. וּלְאַתְקְנָא לוֹן בְּקִשּׁוּרָא חֲדָא בִּשְׂמָאלָא, וְעַל לִבָּא, כְּמָה דְּאוֹקִימְנָא שְׂמָאלוֹ תַּחַת לְרֹאשִׁי וְגוֹ'. וּכְתִיב שִׂימֵנִי כַחוֹתָם עַל לִבֶּךָ כַּחוֹתָם עַל זְרוֹעֶךָ. וְהָא אוֹקִימְנָא. וְדָא הוּא עוֹבָדָא בְּקַדְמֵיתָא.

70. The first activity is when a person gets up FROM HIS SLEEP. He must cleanse himself first, MEANING RELIEVE HIMSELF. Following that, he must accept the yoke upon himself, to cover his head with the passages of the commandments. Afterwards, he shall tie the knot of unification – these are the Tefilin, one on the head and ONE TEFILIN on the hand – and fix them into a knot on the left hand and on the heart, as we explained concerning, "His left hand is under my head" (Shir Hashirim 2:6), and: "Set Me as a seal upon your heart, as a seal upon your arm" (Shir Hashirim 8:6), A REFERENCE TO THE HAND TEFILIN, WHICH IS THE SECRET OF MALCHUT, THAT IS PUT ON THE ARM AGAINST THE HEART. And we already explained that this is the action THAT ONE MUST PERFORM at first.

71. לְבָתַר בְּשַׁעֲתָא דב"נ עָאל לְבֵי כְנִישְׁתָּא, יְדַכֵּי גַּרְמֵיהּ בְּקַדְמֵיתָא, בְּקָרְבָּנִין, בְּמִלּוּלָא דְּפוּמָא. לְבָתַר יְקַבֵּל עֲלֵיהּ הַאי עוֹל מַלְכוּת, לְפָרְשָׁא עַל רֵישֵׁיהּ בְּשִׁבְחֵי דְּדָוִד מַלְכָּא. כְּגַוְונָא דְּעוֹבָדָא דְּפָרִישׁ עַל רֵישֵׁיהּ פְּרִישׁוּ דְּמִצְוָה. וּלְבָתַר צְלוֹתָא דִּמְיוּשָׁב, לָקֳבֵל תְּפִלָּה שֶׁל יַד. לְבָתַר צְלוֹתָא דִּמְעוּמָּד, דְּהִיא לָקֳבֵל תְּפִלָּה דְּרֵישָׁא. וְדָא כְּגַוְונָא דְּדָא. עוֹבָדָא כְּגַוְונָא דְּדִבּוּרָא. וַדַּאי בְּעוֹבָדָא וּמִלּוּלָא תַּלְיָיא צְלוֹתָא.

71. Following this, when a person enters the synagogue, he should first purify himself with offerings, by means of speech – THAT IS, BY RECITING THE PASSAGES OF THE OFFERINGS. Then, one should accept the yoke of Malchut to spread over his head with the praises of King David, with the same action as of one who spreads on his head the passages of the commandments, WHICH CORRESPONDS TO THE ACTION OF WEARING THE TZITZIT. Following this is the seated prayer, which corresponds to THE TYING ON OF the hand Tefilin, DENOTING MALCHUT. Then is the standing prayer, WHICH IS THE SECRET OF ZEIR ANPIN, which parallels THE DONNING OF the head Tefilin. And one corresponds to the other; the deed MUST CONFORM to speech, since certainly prayer depends on both speech and the deed.

72. וְאִי פָּגִים עוֹבָדָא, מִלּוּלָא לָא אַשְׁכַּח אֲתָר דְּשַׁרְיָא בֵּיהּ, וְלָאו אִיהוּ צְלוֹתָא, וְאִתְפְּגִים הַהוּא בַּר נָשׁ לְעֵילָּא וְתַתָּא. דְּבָעֵינָן לְאַחֲזָאָה עוֹבָדָא, וּלְמַלְּלָא מִלּוּלָא עֲלֵיהּ, וְדָא הוּא צְלוֹתָא שְׁלִים. וַוי לֵיהּ לְבַר נָשׁ דְּפָגִים צְלוֹתֵיהּ, פּוּלְחָנָא דְּמָארֵיהּ. עֲלֵיהּ כְּתִיב, כִּי תָבוֹאוּ לֵרָאוֹת פָּנַי וְגו'. גַּם כִּי תַרְבּוּ תְפִלָּה אֵינֶנִּי שׁוֹמֵעַ, דְּהָא בְּעוֹבָדָא וּבְמִלּוּלָא תַּלְיָא מִלְּתָא.

72. If his deed is flawed, SPEECH does not find a place upon which to dwell, and this is not considered a prayer. And that person becomes flawed above and below, since it is necessary to demonstrate a deed and say the proper speech about it, and then it is considered a perfect prayer. Woe unto the person who flaws his prayer, the service of his Master! About him it is written: "When you come to appear before Me...even when you make many prayers, I will not hear" (Yeshayah 1:12-15), because this depends upon both deed and speech.

73. ת"ח, כֵּיוָן דְּבַר נָשׁ עָבֵיד צְלוֹתָא כְּגַוְונָא דָא, בְּעוֹבָדָא וּבְמִלּוּלָא, וְקָשִׁיר קִשּׁוּרָא דְּיִיחוּדָא, אִשְׁתְּכַח דְּעַל יְדֵיהּ מִתְבָּרְכָן עֶלָּאִין וְתַתָּאִין. כְּדֵין בָּעֵי לֵיהּ לְבַר נָשׁ לְאַחֲזָאָה גַּרְמֵיהּ, בָּתַר דְּסַיֵּים צְלוֹתָא דַּעֲמִידָה, כְּאִלּוּ אִתְפְּטַר מִן עָלְמָא, דְּהָא אִתְפְּרַשׁ מִן אִילָנָא דְּחַיֵּי, וְכָנִישׁ רַגְלוֹי לְגַבֵּי הַהוּא אִילָנָא דְּמוֹתָא, דְּאַהֲדַר לֵיהּ פִּקְדוֹנֵיהּ. כד"א וַיֶּאֱסוֹף רַגְלָיו

אֶל הַמִּטָּה. דְּהָא אוֹדֵי חֲטָאוֹי, וְצַלֵּי עֲלַיְיהוּ. הַשְׁתָּא בָּעֵי לְאִתְכַּנְשָׁא
לְגַבֵּי הַהוּא אִילָנָא דְּמוֹתָא, וּלְמִנְפַּל, וְלֵימָא לְגַבֵּיה יְיָ' נַפְשִׁי
אֶשָּׂא. בְּקַדְמֵיתָא, יָהִיבְנָא לָךְ בְּפִקְדּוֹנָא, הַשְׁתָּא דְּקַשִׁירְנָא יִחוּדָא,
וְעֲבֵידְנָא עוֹבָדָא וּמִלּוּלָא כַּדְקָא יָאוֹת, וְאוֹדֵינָא עַל חֲטָאַי, הָא נַפְשִׁי
מָסִירְנָא לָךְ וַדַּאי.

73. Come and behold: if a person makes his prayer in this manner, with deeds and speech consistent, and ties the knot of unification, the result is that upper and lower beings are blessed through him. Then, after he concludes his Amidah prayer, the person must exhibit himself as if he departed from this world. This is because he took leave from the Tree of Life, THAT IS, ZEIR ANPIN, THE SECRET OF AMIDAH PRAYER, and gathered his feet to that Tree of Death, that returned his pledge, GIVING HIM BACK HIS SOUL IN THE MORNING, as it says, "he gathered up his feet into the bed" (Beresheet 49:33). Since he has already confessed his sins and prayed for forgiveness, now he must necessarily be gathered to that Tree of Death and fall ON HIS FACE, and say to Him, "To You, O Hashem, do I lift up my soul" (Tehilim 25:1). In the beginning WHEN I WENT TO SLEEP, I gave You MY SOUL in pledge. Now that I have tied the unification, fulfilled my deed and speech properly, and confessed my sins, certainly I entrust You with my soul – MEANING THAT HE ACCEPTS UPON HIMSELF TO SACRIFICE HIS LIFE (SOUL).

74. וְיֶחֱזֵי בַּר נָשׁ גַּרְמֵיהּ כְּאִילּוּ פָּטִיר מִן עָלְמָא, דְּנַפְשֵׁיהּ מָסִיר לְהַאי
אֲתָר דְּמוֹתָא, בְּגִין כָּךְ לָא אִית בֵּיהּ וָא"ו, דְּוָא"ו אִילָנָא דְּחַיֵּי הוּא,
וְהַאי אִילָנָא דְּמוֹתָא הוּא. וְהָא קַמְּ"ל, דְּרָזָא דְּמִלָּה, דְּאִית חוֹבִין דְּלָא
מִתְכַּפְּרָן, עַד דְּאִתְפְּטַר בַּר נָשׁ מֵעָלְמָא, הה"ד אִם יְכוּפַּר הֶעָוֹן הַזֶּה
לָכֶם עַד תְּמוּתוּן, וְהַאי יָהִיב גַּרְמֵיהּ וַדַּאי לְמוֹתָא, וּמָסִיר נַפְשֵׁיהּ לְהַאי
אֲתָר. לָאו בְּפִקְדּוֹנָא כְּמָה בְּלֵילְיָא, אֶלָּא כְּמַאן דְּאִתְפְּטַר מִן עָלְמָא
וַדַּאי.

74. And a person should imagine himself as if he departed from this world, since he gave his soul to that place of death. That is the reason there is no *Vav* IN THE ALPHABETICAL ORDER OF THE PRAYER BEGINNING WITH THE

VERSE, "TO YOU, O HASHEM, DO I LIFT UP MY SOUL." For *Vav* is the Tree of Life, MEANING ZEIR ANPIN, WHICH IS THE SECRET OF *VAV* OF YUD HEI VAV HEI. And the one, THAT HE ENTRUSTED WITH HIS SOUL, is the Tree of Death, MEANING MALCHUT. And that teaches us that the mystery of it is that there are sins that are not atoned for until a person departs from this world. That is what is written: "surely this iniquity shall not be forgiven you till you die" (Yeshayah 22:14). AND THEREFORE, this person most certainly gives himself to death and sacrifices his soul to this place, TO MALCHUT, not for a pledge as that at night, but rather as one departs the world, most certainly.

75. וְתִקּוּנָא דָא בָּעֵי בְּכַוְּונָא דְּלִבָּא וּכְדֵין קוּדְשָׁא בְּרִיךְ הוּא מְרַחֵם עֲלוֹי, וּמְכַפֵּר לֵיה לְחוֹבֵיה. זַכָּאָה הוּא בַּר נָשׁ דְּיָדַע לְמִפְתֵּי לֵיה, וּלְמִפְלַח לְמָארֵיה, בִּרְעוּתָא וּבְכַוְּונָא דְּלִבָּא. וַוי לֵיה לְמַאן דְּאָתֵי לְמִפְתֵּי לְמָארֵיה, בְּלִבָּא רְחִיקָא, וְלָא בִּרְעוּתָא. כד"א וַיְפַתּוּהוּ בְּפִיהֶם וּבִלְשׁוֹנָם יְכַזְבוּ לוֹ וְלִבָּם לֹא נָכוֹן עִמּוֹ. הוּא אוֹמֵר אֵלֶיךָ יְיָ' נַפְשִׁי אֶשָּׂא, וְלָאו כָּל מִלּוֹי אֶלָּא בְּלִבָּא רְחִיקָא, הָא גָּרַם עֲלֵיה לְאִסְתַּלְּקָא מֵעָלְמָא, עַד לָא מָטוּן יוֹמוֹי, בְּזִמְנָא דְּהָא אִילָנָא אִתְּעַר בְּעָלְמָא לְמֶעְבַּד דִּינָא.

75. And this correction must be with the meditation of the heart, and then the Holy One, blessed be He, has mercy on him and forgives his sins. Happy is the person who knows to entice and serve his Master willingly and with his heart's devotion. Woe unto him who comes to tempt his Creator with a distant heart, unwillingly. It says, "Nevertheless they did flatter Him with their mouths, and they lied to Him with their tongues. For their heart was not steadfast with Him" (Tehilim 78:36-37). He says, "to You, O Hashem, do I lift up my soul," yet all his talk is with a distant heart. And this causes him to depart from the world before his time, during a period when this tree is awakened in this world to exact punishment.

76. וְעַל דָּא בָּעֵי בַּר נָשׁ לְאַדְבְּקָא נַפְשֵׁיה וּרְעוּתֵיה בְּמָארֵיה, וְלָא יֵיתֵי לְגַבֵּיה בִּרְעוּתָא כְּדִיבָא, בְּגִין דִּכְתִיב דּוֹבֵר שְׁקָרִים לֹא יִכּוֹן לְנֶגֶד עֵינָי. מַאי לֹא יִכּוֹן. אֶלָּא בְּשַׁעֲתָא דְּהוּא אַתְקִין גַּרְמֵיה לְהַאי, וְלִבֵּיה רְחִיקָא

מְקוּדְשָׁא בְּרִיךְ הוּא, קָלָא נָפִיק וְאָמַר, לֹא יִכּוֹן לְנֶגֶד עֵינָי. הַאי בָּעֵי לְאַתְקְנָא גַּרְמֵיהּ, לֹא יִכּוֹן, לָא בָּעֵינָא דְיִתְתַּקַּן. כ״ש אִי אָתֵי לְיַחֲדָא שְׁמָא קַדִּישָׁא, וְלָא מְיַחֵד לֵיהּ כַּדְקָא יָאוֹת.

76. And therefore, a person must devote his soul and will to his Master, and not approach Him with a false intention, because, "he that tells lies shall not remain in My sight" (Tehilim 101:7). What is the meaning of "remain"? AND HE REPLIES: It is when one readies himself for that, FOR THE DEVOTION OF HIS SOUL, WHEN HE FALLS ON HIS FACE, and his heart is far from the Holy One, blessed be He. A voice calls out, "'he...shall not remain in My sight." This person wants to make amends for himself, but "he shall not remain," I do not wish to have him corrected'. Most certainly, this is so if he comes to unify the Holy Name, but does not bring about unison properly.

77. זַכָּאָה חוּלָקֵהוֹן דְּצַדִּיקַיָּא בְּעָלְמָא דֵין וּבְעָלְמָא דְּאָתֵי, עֲלַיְיהוּ כְּתִיב וּבָאוּ וְרָאוּ אֶת כְּבוֹדִי וְגוֹ'. וּכְתִיב, אַךְ צַדִּיקִים יוֹדוּ לִשְׁמֶךָ וְגוֹ'. אָתָא ר׳ אֶלְעָזָר וְנָשִׁיק יְדוֹי. אָמַר, אִלְמָלֵא לָא אֲתֵינָא לְעָלְמָא אֶלָּא לְמִשְׁמַע מִלִּין אִלֵּין דַּיַּי. אָמַר ר׳ יְהוּדָה, זַכָּאָה חוּלְקָנָא, וְזַכָּאָה חוּלָקֵהוֹן דְּיִשְׂרָאֵל, דְּאִינּוּן מִתְדַּבְּקִין בְּקוּדְשָׁא בְּרִיךְ הוּא, דִּכְתִיב וְאַתֶּם הַדְּבֵקִים וְגוֹ'. וְעַמֵּךְ כֻּלָּם צַדִּיקִים וְגוֹ'.

77. Praiseworthy is the portion of the righteous in this world and the World to Come. About them it is written, "and they shall come, and see My Glory..." (Yeshayah 66:18), and: "surely the righteous shall give thanks to Your Name..." (Tehilim 140:14). Rabbi Elazar approached and kissed his hands. He told him: If I had come to this world only to listen to these words, it would have been enough. Rabbi Yehuda said: Happy is our lot and happy is the lot of Yisrael, who cling to the Holy One, blessed be He, as it says, "But you that did cleave..." (Devarim 4:4), and, "Your people also shall be all righteous" (Yeshayah 60:21). Blessed be Hashem for evermore. Amen, and Amen. May Hashem reign for evermore. Amen, and Amen.

NASO
THE IDRA RABA

Names of the articles

Continuation of Naso

1. At midnight

A Synopsis

Rabbi Aba speaks about the time of day and how judgment and joy and praise are aroused at different times of the day and night. He says that during sleep the soul rises above and is examined about its daily activities that are then recorded in the book.

וַיְדַבֵּר יְיָ' אֶל מֹשֶׁה לֵּאמֹר, נָשֹׂא אֶת רֹאשׁ בְּנֵי גֵרְשׁוֹן וְגוֹ'. ר' אַבָּא .1
פָּתַח, אַשְׁרֵי אָדָם לֹא יַחְשֹׁב יְיָ' לוֹ עָוֹן וְאֵין בְּרוּחוֹ רְמִיָּה. הַאי קְרָא,
לָאו רֵישֵׁיהּ סֵיפֵיהּ, וְלָאו סֵיפֵיהּ רֵישֵׁיהּ. וְאִית לְאִסְתַּכְּלָא בֵּיהּ, וְהָא
אוּקְמוּהָ.

1. "And Hashem spoke to Moses, saying, 'Take also the sum of the sons of Gershon'" (Bemidbar 4:21-22). Rabbi Aba opened the discussion saying, "Blessed is the man to whom Hashem imputes no iniquity, and in whose spirit there is no guile" (Tehilim 32:2). The beginning and the end of this verse do not agree, BECAUSE THE BEGINNING SAYS, "IMPUTES NO INIQUITY," SEEMINGLY THAT HE HAS SIN BUT IT IS NOT ASCRIBED TO HIM. BUT AT THE END IT SAYS, "AND IN WHOSE SPIRIT THERE IS NO GUILE." We should look into it, and it has already been established.

ת"ח, בְּשַׁעֲתָא דִּצְלוֹתָא דְּמִנְחָה דִּינָא שַׁרְיָא בְּעָלְמָא, וְיִצְחָק תִּקֵּן .2
צְלוֹתָא דְּמִנְחָה, וּגְבוּרָה עִלָּאָה שַׁלְטָא בְּעָלְמָא, עַד דְּאָתֵי וְעָאל
לֵילְיָא, בְּגִין לְקַבְּלָא לֵיהּ לְלֵילְיָא, וּמִזְמְנָא דְּשָׁארֵי צְלוֹתָא דְּמִנְחָה,
אִתְפְּרַשׁ שְׂמָאלָא לְקַבְּלָא וְאִתְּעַר לֵילְיָא.

2. Come and see, Minchah (the afternoon prayers), Judgment dwells in the world and Isaac, WHO IS SUPERNAL GVURAH AND THE LEFT COLUMN OF ZEIR ANPIN, instituted Minchah. FOR THEN THE UNION WAS COMPLETED IN THE SECRET OF: "HIS LEFT HAND IS UNDER MY HEAD" (SHIR HASHIRIM 2:6). THEREFORE, supernal Gvurah rules the world until the onset of night, because Gvurah receives the night, MEANING THAT NIGHT IS MALCHUT DRAWN FROM GVURAH, WHICH IS MINCHAH. When the time of Minchah begins, the left separates to receive MALCHUT and the night is aroused, WHICH IS MALCHUT.

3. בָּתַר דְּאִתְּעַר כָּל אִינּוּן נְטוּרֵי פִּתְחִין דִּלְבַר, כֻּלְּהוּ מִתְעָרִין בְּעָלְמָא וְאִתְפָּשְׁטוּ. וְכָל בְּנֵי עָלְמָא טַעֲמִין טַעֲמָא דְּמוֹתָא.

3. After THE NIGHT is aroused, all the guards of the external gates are aroused in the world and spread out, and all the inhabitants of the world taste death.

4. וְהָא אִתְּמַר. בְּפַלְגוּת לֵילְיָא מַמָּשׁ, אִתְּעַר שְׂמָאלָא כְּמִלְקַדְמִין, וְוַרְדָּא קַדִּישָׁא סַלְקָא רֵיחִין, וְהִיא מְשַׁבַּחַת וַאֲרִימַת קָלָא, וּכְדֵין סַלְקָא וְשַׁרְיָא רֵישָׁא לְעֵילָּא בִּשְׂמָאלָא, וּשְׂמָאלָא מְקַבֵּל לָהּ.

4. It has been said that at exactly midnight, the left is aroused as before, AS DURING MINCHAH. The holy lily, WHICH IS MALCHUT, exudes fragrances, WHICH IS THE SECRET OF THE ILLUMINATION OF CHOCHMAH OF THE LEFT, and raises a voice in praise. Then her head rises and dwells above in the left, IN THE SECRET OF: "HIS LEFT HAND IS UNDER MY HEAD," and the left receives her.

5. כְּדֵין כָּרוֹזָא קָארֵי בְּעָלְמָא, דְּהָא עִידָן הוּא לְאִתְּעָרָא לְשַׁבְּחָא לֵיהּ לְמַלְכָּא. וּכְדֵין תּוּשְׁבְּחָן מִתְעָרִין, וְאִתְבַּסְּמוּתָא דְּכֹלָּא אִשְׁתְּכַח. זַכָּאָה חוּלָקֵיהּ מַאן דְּאִתְּעַר לְזַוּוּגָא זַוּוּגָא דָּא. כַּד אָתֵי צַפְרָא, וִימִינָא אִתְּעַר וּמְחַבְּקָא לָהּ, כְּדֵין זַוּוּגָא דְּכֹלָּא אִשְׁתְּכַח כַּחֲדָא.

5. This is then proclaimed in the world: The time has come to rise from sleep and praise the King. Praises then awaken and everything is fragrant. Praised is the lot of the one who awakens to effect this bond. When morning approaches and the right, WHICH IS CHESED, awakens and hugs her, there is universal union BETWEEN CHOCHMAH AND CHASSADIM. THIS IS NOT THE CASE AT NIGHT WHEN THERE ARE NO CHASSADIM.

6. ת"ח, בְּשַׁעֲתָא דִּבְנֵי נָשָׁא דְּמִיכִין, וְטַעֲמִין טַעֲמָא דְּמוֹתָא, וְנִשְׁמָתָא סַלְקָא לְעֵילָּא, קַיְּימָא בְּאֲתָר דְּקַיְּימָא, וְאִתְבְּחִינַת עַל עוֹבָדָהָא דְּעַבְדַת כָּל יוֹמָא, וְכַתְבִין לְהוּ עַל פִּתְקָא. מ"ט. בְּגִין דְּנִשְׁמָתָא סַלְקָא לְעֵילָּא, וְאִסְהֲדַת עַל עוֹבְדוֹי דב"נ, וְעַל כָּל מִלָּה וּמִלָּה דְּנָפִיק מִפּוּמֵיהּ.

6. Come and see, During the time when people sleep and taste of death, the soul rises up and gets to stand in a certain place, where it is examined about its daily activities which are recorded in the book. What is the reason for this? Because the soul rises up and testifies about all the person's activities and every single word that came out from his lips.

7. וְכַד הַהִיא מִלָּה דְּאַפִּיק ב״נ מִפּוּמֵיהּ אִיהִי כַּדְקָא יָאוּת, מִלָּה קַדִּישָׁא דְאוֹרַיְיתָא וּצְלוֹתָא. הַהִיא מִלָּה סַלְּקָא, וּבָקַע רְקִיעִין, וְקַיְימָא בְּאֲתָר דְּקַיְימָא, עַד דְּעָאל לֵילְיָא, וְנִשְׁמָתָא סַלְּקָא וְאָחִיד לְהַהִיא מִלָּה, וְעָאִיל לָהּ קַמֵּי מַלְכָּא.

7. When that word that exits from the mouth of a person is worthy, a holy word of Torah study and prayer, that word then rises and cleaves the firmaments. It stands there until nightfall, when the soul rises and grasps that word and brings it before the King.

8. וְכַד הַהִיא מִלָּה לָאו אִיהִי כַּדְקָא יָאוּת, וְאִיהִי מִלָּה מִמִּילִין בִּישִׁין, מִלִּישָׁנָא בִּישָׁא, הַהִיא מִלָּה סַלְּקָא לַאֲתָר דְּסַלְּקָא, וּכְדֵין אִתְרְשִׁים הַהִיא מִלָּה, וְהַהוּא חוֹבָה עֲלֵיהּ דב״נ, הה״ד מִשּׁוֹכֶבֶת חֵיקֶךָ שְׁמוֹר פִּתְחֵי פִּיךָ. וּבג״כ אַשְׁרֵי אָדָם לֹא יַחְשׁוֹב יְיָ׳ לוֹ עָוֹן. אֵימָתַי. כְּשֶׁאֵין בְּרוּחוֹ רְמִיָּה.

8. When the word is improper, one of evil words or of evil speech, that word rises wherever it rises to be recorded as a sin of that person. This is the meaning of: "Keep the doors of your mouth from her that lies in your bosom" (Michah 7:5), MEANING FROM THE SOUL THAT GIVES TESTIMONY ABOUT HIS DEEDS. Therefore, IT IS WRITTEN: "Blessed is the man to whom Hashem imputes no iniquity"; NAMELY, WHEN THE SOUL DOES NOT BEAR TESTIMONY AGAINST HIM, SO THAT A CERTAIN SIN WILL BE RECORDED. When is that? When "in whose spirit there is no guile" – THAT IS, WHEN HE DOES NOT SIN.

2. "And in the night his song shall be with me"

A Synopsis

We learn about the role of the Levites and the role of the priest in the Temple, and are told that the priest is the angel Michael and the Levite is the angel Gabriel, who must make the music. Information is given about how the songs and chants should be done with the lungs and the windpipe. We learn about the heart and the mouth, two thrones, and the meaning of the Shofar and the implements of speech. Lastly we are told that the Torah is more important to God than all the offerings and burnt offerings.

רעיא מהימנא

9. מִבֶּן שְׁלֹשִׁים שָׁנָה וָמַעְלָה וְעַד בֶּן חֲמִשִּׁים שָׁנָה כָּל הַבָּא לַעֲבוֹד עֲבוֹדַת עֲבוֹדָה וַעֲבוֹדַת מַשָּׂא בְּאֹהֶל מוֹעֵד. פְּקוּדָא דָא לְהֱיוֹת הַלְוִיִּם מְשׁוֹרְרִים בַּמִּקְדָּשׁ. וְאע״ג דְּאוֹקִימְנָא לְעֵילָא, הָכָא צָרִיךְ לְחַדֵּשׁ מִלִּין, דְּהָא כֹּהֵן אִיהוּ מַקְרִיב קָרְבְּנָא, וְאִיהוּ מִיכָאֵל. לֵוִי אִיהוּ גַּבְרִיאֵל. אִיהוּ צָרִיךְ לְנַגְּנָא.

Ra'aya Meheimna (the Faithful Shepherd)

9. "From thirty years old and upward to fifty years old, everyone that came to do the service of the ministry, and the service of carrying in the Tent of Meeting" (Bemidbar 4:47). This commandment IS THAT the Levites should sing in the Temple. Although this was already explained before, we need to add something new, for it is the priest who sacrifices the offering and he is THE ANGEL Michael, WHO IS CHESED, CHESED BEING THE PRIEST. The Levite is Gabriel, WHO IS GVURAH, AND GVURAH IS CALLED LEVITE. And he should play music.

10. וְרָזָא דְמִלָּה, יוֹמָם יְצַוֶּה יְיָ' חַסְדּוֹ, דָּא חֶסֶד כַּהֲנָא רַבָּא דְּמִיכָאֵל אִיהוּ כֹּהֵן הֶדְיוֹט לְגַבֵּי מָארֵיהּ, וְעִם כָּל דָּא דְּהֶדְיוֹט אִיהוּ אֵצֶל מָארֵיהּ. מֶלֶךְ דְּחַיּוֹת הַקֹּדֶשׁ אִיהוּ. וּבִרְכַּת הֶדְיוֹט אַל תְּהִי קַלָּה בְּעֵינֶיךָ, וְהַאי אִיהוּ יוֹמָם יְצַוֶּה יְיָ' חַסְדּוֹ.

10. The secret of: "Yet Hashem will command His steadfast love (Heb. *Chesed*) in the daytime" (Tehilim 42:9). That is Chesed OF ZEIR ANPIN, which is the High Priest, because Michael is a common priest in relation to his Master, CHESED OF ZEIR ANPIN. Nevertheless, EVEN THOUGH he is a common priest in relation to his Master, he is a king over the holy living creatures THAT ARE IN YETZIRAH, AND IT WAS SAID OF HIM: Let not the blessing of a common priest be light in your eyes. That is what is meant by: "Yet Hashem will command his Chesed in the daytime."

11. וּבַלַּיְלָה שִׁירֹה עִמִּי, דָּא גְּבוּרָה. שִׁירָה: בְּכוֹר שׁוֹרוֹ הָדָר לוֹ. וּפְנֵי שׁוֹר מֵהַשְּׂמֹאל, וְגַבְרִיאֵל שְׁלוּחֵיהּ, וְצָרִיךְ לְשׁוֹרֵר וּלְנַגֵּן בְּחֶדְוָה בְּחַמְרָא דְאוֹרַיְיתָא, לְאִתְעַסְּקָא בְּאוֹרַיְיתָא, יְקַיֵּים קוּמִי רֹנִּי בַּלַּיְלָה לְרֹאשׁ אַשְׁמוּרֹת.

11. "And in the night his song shall be with me" (Ibid.), which is Gvurah OF ZEIR ANPIN, since *Shirah* (lit. 'song') is similar to "The firstling of his herd (Heb. *shoro*), grandeur is his" (Devarim 33:17) and "the face of an ox (Heb. *shor*) on the left side" (Yechezkel 1:10). SHIRAH AND SHOR ARE IDENTICAL. Gabriel is the messenger OF GVURAH. It is incumbent upon him to sing and play music happily with the wine of Torah, study the Torah and fulfill: "Arise, cry out in the night: in the beginning of the watches" (Eichah 2:19).

12. וְיֵימָא בְּאַשְׁמוּרוֹת, כַּמָּה סְלִיחוֹת וְתַחֲנוּנִים וּבַקָּשׁוֹת, בְּכָל מִינֵי רְנָה בִּגְרוֹנֵיהּ, דְּאִיהוּ כִּנּוֹר לְאַפָּקָא בֵּיהּ קָלָא, בְּשִׁית כַּנְפֵי רֵיאָה עִם וַורְדָּא. בְּשִׁית עִזְקָאן דְּקָנֶה. וְדָא ו'. וְיִפּוֹק לֵיהּ מַלְבָּא, דְּתַמָּן בִּינָה. כַּמָּה דְּאוּקְמוּהָ מָארֵי מַתְנִיתִין, הַלֵּב מֵבִין. יִפּוֹק בֶּן מִבִּינָה, מִבֶּן יָה, דְּאִיהוּ ו', דְּאִיהוּ אֶפְרוֹחַ בְּשִׁית גַּדְפִּין. וְיִסַּלֵּק לֵיהּ בְּשִׁית עִזְקָאן דְּקָנֶה, דְּאִינּוּן שֵׁשׁ מַעֲלוֹת לַכִּסֵּא.

12. He should say at dawn several penitential prayers (*Slichot*), supplications and petitions with all kinds of joyful chants in his throat, which is like a fiddle to produce the voice with the six parts of his lungs – THAT IS, FIVE LOBES OF THE LUNGS, with the rose lobe, WHICH IS A SMALL VENOUS LOBE THAT IS ATTACHED TO THE LUNG, and in the six rings of the windpipe, that is ALLUDING TO the Vav THAT CORRESPONDS TO ZEIR ANPIN, that comes out from the heart, where Binah is situated. As the authors of the Mishnah have explained, the heart has understanding. A son, THAT IS ZEIR ANPIN, comes out from Binah, the son (Heb. *ben*) of Yud Hei. THE LETTERS OF BINAH ARE BEN YUD HEI, that is Vav which alludes to a newborn chick with six wings, NAMELY ZEIR ANPIN THAT HAS SIX SFIROT – CHESED, GVURAH, TIFERET, NETZACH, HOD AND YESOD. He shall raise them by the six rings of the windpipe, which are the six rungs of the throne, BECAUSE CHESED, GVURAH, TIFERET, NETZACH, HOD AND YESOD OF ZEIR ANPIN ARE SIX STEPS TO BINAH THAT IS REFERRED TO AS THE THRONE TO CHOCHMAH.

13. וב' כָּרְסְיָין אִינּוּן כִּסֵּא כָבוֹד מָרוֹם מֵרֵאשׁוֹן, וְאִינּוּן לִבָּא וּפוּמָא. לֵ"ב, וַיֹּאמֶר כִּי יָד עַל כֵּס יָה מִלְחָמָה לַיְיָ' בַּעֲמָלֵק, כָּבֵד, סָמָאֵ"ל, פּוּמָא דְכַסֵּ"ה, כְּ"ס ה', הה"ד תִּקְעוּ בַחֹדֶשׁ שׁוֹפָר וְגוֹ'.

13. There are two thrones, AS IT IS WRITTEN: "A glorious throne exalted from the beginning" (Yirmeyah 17:12), MEANING THAT IT IS HIGHER THAN THE FIRST THRONE, INDICATING THAT THERE ARE TWO THRONES. They are the heart, WHICH IS BINAH AND the mouth, WHICH IS MALCHUT. The heart, AS WRITTEN: "Because Yah has sworn by his throne" (Shemot 17:16), IS BINAH, WHICH IS A THRONE FOR YUD-HEI, CHOCHMAH. AND THE HEART IS THE SECRET OF: "That Hashem will have war with Amalek" (Ibid.), WHICH IS THE SECRET OF the liver, THAT IS, Samael. The mouth is THE SECRET OF the seat (Heb. *kiseh*), that is, the throne (Heb. *kes*) of Hei. This is what is meant by: "Blow a Shofar at the new moon, at the full moon (lit. 'covering') (Heb. *keseh*)" (Tehilim 81:4), WHICH IS THE MOUTH, MEANING MALCHUT THAT IS THE THRONE OF THE LAST HEI OF YUD HEI VAV HEI. IT CONTAINS THE FIVE RESTORATIONS OF THE MOUTH, AS EXPLAINED BEFORE.

14. מַאי שׁוֹפָר. קָנֶה, ו', קוֹל דְּסָלִיק מִן הַקָּנֶה, לְגַבֵּי פוּמָא, דְּתַמָּן ה'. בָּה' מִינֵי תִּקּוּנִין דְּדִבּוּרָא, דְּאִינּוּן שִׂפְוָון וְשִׁינַּיִם וְחֵיךָ. שִׂפְוָון תְּרֵין. שִׁינַּיִם וְטוֹחֲנוֹת תְּרֵין מִינִין. וְחֵיךָ, הָא חָמֵשׁ. דְּטַחֲנִין כְּנַהֵר דְּאִיהוּ קוֹל, כְּגַוְונָא דְּטַחֲנִין רֵיחַיָּיא. לְאַפָּקָא קוֹל וְדִבּוּר, דְּנָפִיק מִבִּינָה דְּלִבָּא בְּמַחֲשָׁבָה.

-58-

14. HE EXPLAINS: What is the meaning of Shofar, WHEN IT SAYS: "BLOW A SHOFAR AT THE NEW MOON"? The windpipe alludes to the Vav, WHICH IS THE MYSTERY OF ZEIR ANPIN THAT IS REFERRED TO BY THE VAV. IT IS ALSO CALLED VOICE. It is the voice that ascends from the windpipe to the mouth, WHICH IS MALCHUT, where the Hei is. THAT IS THE MEANING OF THE WORDS: "AT THE FULL MOON (HEB. *KESEH*) ON OUR FEAST DAY" (IBID.), WITH THE THRONE (HEB. *KES*) OF HEI, MEANING the five articulation points of speech: the lips, the teeth and the palate. There are two lips, TEETH INCLUDING regular teeth and molars, which makes them two kinds of teeth and a palate, so we have a total of five. THESE ARE THE FIVE ARTICULATION POINTS OF SPEECH. When they mill like a riverbed, they make noise like the milling of grindstones to produce sound and speech that emanates from Binah WHICH IS the heart, and with thought, WHICH IS THE SECRET OF CHOCHMAH.

15. דְּאִיהוּ שְׁמָא מְפֹרָשׁ בְּעֶשֶׂר מִינֵי תִּלִּים. וּבְשׁוֹפָר, אֵין פּוֹחֲתִין מֵעֲשָׂרָה שׁוֹפָרוֹת. וְאוֹרַיְיתָא, קָלָא דִּילָהּ, דִּיבּוּר דִּילָהּ, בִּינָה דִּילָהּ, דְּאוּקְמוּהָ אֵיזֶהוּ חָכָם הַמֵּבִין דָּבָר מִתּוֹךְ דָּבָר. מַחֲשָׁבָה דִּילֵיהּ. חָשִׁיב קַמֵּי קוּדְשָׁא בְּרִיךְ הוּא, מִכָּל קָרְבְּנִין וְעִלָּוָון, הה"ד זֹאת הַתּוֹרָה לְעוֹלָה וְלַמִּנְחָה.

ע"כ רעיא מהימנא

15. That is the Name pronounced in full in ten various praises, WHICH PARALLEL THE TEN SFIROT. HERE TOO, THOUGHT IS CHOCHMAH, THE HEART IS BINAH AND THE WINDPIPE IS THE SECRET OF ZEIR ANPIN, IN WHICH ARE CHESED, GVURAH, TIFERET, NETZACH, HOD AND YESOD – THE SIX RINGS OF THE WINDPIPE. THE MOUTH IS MALCHUT AND WITH THE ROOT, WHICH IS KETER, THEY AMOUNT TO TEN SFIROT. THEREFORE, when blowing the Shofar, we never blow less than ten times, WHICH CORRESPONDS TO THE TEN SFIROT. As for the Torah, the voice is hers and the speech is hers, and hers is Binah, as we have explained: 'A wise man understands one thing from another.' Hers is the faculty of thought, WHICH IS CHOCHMAH. THERE ARE TEN SFIROT, BECAUSE VOICE IS ZEIR ANPIN – IN WHICH ARE CHESED, GVURAH, TIFERET, NETZACH, HOD AND YESOD. SPEECH IS MALCHUT, AND WITH BINAH

AND HER CHOCHMAH WITH THE ROOT, KETER, THEY AMOUNT TO TEN SFIROT. THEREFORE, THE TORAH is more important to the Holy One, blessed be He, than all the offerings and burnt offerings. This is what is meant by: "This is the Torah of the burnt offering, of the meal offering" (Vayikra 7:37).

End of Ra'aya Meheimna (the Faithful Shepherd)

3. "To do trespass against Hashem"

A Synopsis

We are told about Heber the Kenite who went into the desert to find God, separating himself from his people; whenever a person follows the ways of the Torah he draws the spirit of the most Holy upon himself, but when he diverts his ways from the Torah he draws upon himself a spirit from the unclean side. Whoever clings to God and does the commands of the Torah upholds the world above and the world below, but whoever transgresses those commands makes a flaw above and below.

16. אִישׁ אוֹ אִשָּׁה כִּי יַעֲשׂוּ מִכָּל חַטֹּאת הָאָדָם וְגוֹ'. ת"ח, כְּתִיב וְחֶבֶר הַקֵּינִי נִפְרָד מִקַּיִן מִבְּנֵי חוֹבָב חֹתֵן מֹשֶׁה וְגוֹ', וְחֶבֶר הַקֵּינִי מִבְּנֵי בְנוֹי דְּיִתְרוֹ הֲוָה, כד"א וַיֹּאמֶר שָׁאוּל אֶל הַקֵּינִי וְגוֹ'. אֲמַאי אִקְרֵי קֵינִי. וְהָא אוּקְמוּהָ. וּכְתִיב אֶת הַקֵּינִי וְאֶת הַקְּנִזִּי. וְאִתְּמַר דְּעָבַד קֵנָא בְּמַדְבְּרָא, כְּעוֹפָא דָא, בְּגִין לְמֶעְלֵי בְּאוֹרַיְיתָא, וְאִתְפְּרַשׁ מִן מָתָא, נִפְרַד מִקַּיִן, אִתְפְּרַשׁ מֵהַהוּא עַמָּא דַּהֲוָה בְּקַדְמֵיתָא, וְאִתְדַּבָּק בֵּיהּ בְּקוּדְשָׁא בְּרִיךְ הוּא, נִפְרַד מִקַּיִן.

16. "When a man or a woman shall commit any sin that men commit..." (Bemidbar 5:6). Come and see that it is written: "Now Heber the Kenite, who was of the children of Hobab the father-in-law of Moses" (Shoftim 4:11). Heber the Kenite was from the great-grandchildren of Jethro, as it says, "And Saul said to the Kenite..." (I Shmuel 15:6). We have already explained why he was called Kenite. Another verse says, "The Kenite and the Kenizzites" (Beresheet 15:19). We learned that he made a nest (Heb. *ken*) in the desert like a bird to study the Torah. He left the city, took leave of Cain and split away from that nation, MEANING FROM THE MIDIANITES to whom he originally belonged. Then he adhered to the Holy One, blessed be He, AND THEREFORE, he separated from Cain.

17. זַכָּאָה ב"נ דְּזָכֵי בְּאוֹרַיְיתָא, לְמֵיזַל לְאִתְדַּבְּקָא בְּאוֹרְחוֹי. דְּכַד בַּר נָשׁ אָזִיל בְּאוֹרְחוֹי דְּאוֹרַיְיתָא, מָשִׁיךְ עָלֵיהּ רוּחָא קַדִּישָׁא עִלָּאָה. כד"א, עַד יֵעָרֶה עָלֵינוּ רוּחַ מִמָּרוֹם. וְכַד בַּר נָשׁ סָטֵי אוֹרְחוֹי, מָשִׁיךְ

עֲלֵיהּ רוּחָא אַחֲרָא מִסִּטְרָא אַחֲרָא, דְּהוּא סִטְרָא דִּמְסָאֲבָא וְסִטְרָא דִּמְסָאֲבָא אִתְּעַר מִסִּטְרָא דְּנוּקְבָּא דִּתְהוֹמָא רַבָּא, דְּתַמָּן מָדוֹרִין דְּרוּחִין בִּישִׁין, דְּנַזְקֵי לִבְנֵי נָשָׁא, דְּאִקְרוּן נַזְקֵי עָלְמָא. דְּהָא מִסִּטְרָא דְּקַיִן קַדְמָאָה אִשְׁתְּכָחוּ.

17. Happy is the person who merits the Torah, to follow and adhere to his ways. When a person follows the ways of the Torah, he draws upon himself a holy supernal spirit, as it says: "Until a spirit be poured upon us from on high" (Yeshayah 32:15). When a person diverts his ways FROM THE TORAH he draws upon himself a spirit from the Other Side, which is the unclean side. That defiled side awakens from the side of the hole of the great abyss, wherein lie the wicked spirits that harm people and are called the world's destroyers that originate in Cain.

18. וְיִתְרוֹ בְּקַדְמֵיתָא כּוּמָרָא לַע"ז הֲוָה, וּלְהַהוּא סְטָר הֲוָה פָּלַח, וּמָשַׁךְ עֲלֵיהּ רוּחָא מֵהַהוּא אֲתָר. וְע"ד אִקְרֵי קֵינִי לְבָתַר נִפְרָד מִקַּיִן, וְאִתְדַּבַּק בֵּיהּ בְּקוּדְשָׁא בְּרִיךְ הוּא, דְּכָל מַאן דְּאִתְדַּבַּק בֵּיהּ בְּקוּדְשָׁא בְּרִיךְ הוּא, וְעָבֵיד פְּקוּדֵי אוֹרַיְיתָא, כִּבְיָכוֹל, הוּא קַיֵּים עָלְמִין, עָלְמָא דִּלְעֵילָּא וְעָלְמָא דִּלְתַתָּא. וְהָא אוּקְמוּהָ, וַעֲשִׂיתֶם אוֹתָם כְּתִיב.

18. Jethro was originally a priest to idols and he served that side. He drew upon himself a spirit of that side. Therefore he was also called the Kenite later, since he separated from Cain and adhered to the Holy One, blessed be He. Whoever bonds to the Holy One, blessed be He, and performs the commandments of the Torah, it is as if he upholds the worlds, the world above and the world below. This was already explained, as is written: "And do them" (Vayikra 26:3).

19. וְכָל מַאן דְּעָבַר עַל פְּקוּדֵי אוֹרַיְיתָא, כִּבְיָכוֹל פָּגִים לְעֵילָּא, פָּגִים לְתַתָּא, פָּגִים לְגַרְמֵיהּ, פָּגִים לְכָל עָלְמִין. מָתַל לְאִינּוּן מַפְרֵישֵׁי יָמִין דְּשָׁאטֵי בְּאַרְבָּא, קָם חַד שַׁטְיָיא בֵּינַיְיהוּ, בָּעָא לְנַקְבָּא וְכוּ'.

19. Anyone who transgresses the commandments of the Torah, he, as it were, makes a flaw above and impairs below, becomes flawed and impairs all worlds. This is similar to the seafarers on a ship, when a fool among them stands up and wishes to punch a hole IN THE BOAT. HIS NEIGHBOR ASKS HIM: WHY ARE YOU DRILLING AND HE ANSWERS: WHY ARE YOU CONCERNED, I AM DRILLING ONLY UNDER MY OWN SPOT. HE REPLIES: BECAUSE WE'LL BOTH DROWN IN THE BOAT TOGETHER.

20. וע״ד אִישׁ אוֹ אִשָּׁה כִּי יַעֲשׂוּ וְגוֹ׳, הָאָדָם וְגוֹ׳. וְהֵמָּה כְּאָדָם עָבְרוּ בְרִית. אָדָם עָבַר עַל פִּקוּדָא חַד דְּאוֹרַיְיתָא, גָּרִים לֵיהּ לְגַרְמֵיהּ מִיתָה, וְגָרַם לְכָל עָלְמָא, פָּגִים לְעֵילָא, פָּגִים לְתַתָּא, וְהַהוּא חוֹבָא תַּלְיָיא, עַד דִּיקַיֵּים קוּדְשָׁא בְּרִיךְ הוּא עָלְמָא כְּמִלְּקַדְמִין, וְיִתְעֲבַר הַהוּא פְּגִימוּ מֵעָלְמָא, הה״ד בִּלַּע הַמָּוֶת לָנֶצַח וּמָחָה יְיָ׳ אֱלֹהִים דִּמְעָה מֵעַל כָּל פָּנִים וְגוֹ׳. ובג״כ כִּי יַעֲשׂוּ מִכָּל חַטֹּאת הָאָדָם. הָאָדָם אָדָם קַדְמָאָה.

20. Therefore, "when a man or a woman shall commit...that men (Heb. *adam*)..." is REFERRING TO ADAM, AS IT IS WRITTEN: "But they like Adam have transgressed the covenant" (Hoshea 6:7). Adam transgressed one command in the Torah, and he caused death to himself and he caused to the whole world a blemish above and a blemish below. That sin is still impending until the Holy One, blessed be He, will restore the world to its original state, when that flaw will disappear from the world. It is written: "He will destroy death for ever; and Hashem Elohim will wipe away tears from all faces..." (Yeshayah 25:8). Therefore, IT IS WRITTEN HERE: "Shall commit any sin that Adam commit," with "Adam" REFERRING TO the first man.

21. לִמְעוֹל מַעַל בַּיְיָ׳, דְּמַאן דְּיִפּוֹק מֵרַחֲמֵי, וְיַנְקָא מִן דִּינָא, הוּא גָּרִים פְּגִימוּ וְכוּ׳, ועַ״ד, רַחֲמָנָא לִישֵׁזְבָן מֵחַיָּיבֵי דְּהַאי עָלְמָא, וּמִן פְּגִימוּ דִּלְהוֹן, כַּמָה זַכָּאִין מִסְתַּלְּקֵי בְּגִינַיְיהוּ, בַּר כָּל מַה דְּגַרְמֵי לְעֵילָא וְתַתָּא.

21. "To do trespass against Hashem" (Bemidbar 5:6), because whoever abandons Mercy and draws on Judgment causes a flaw. Therefore, the Merciful One should redeem us from the wicked of this world and from their damage, as many righteous pass away because of them, on top of what they caused to happen above and below.

4. Repentance

A Synopsis

Rabbi Yehuda wonders why if someone's sins actually harmed the whole universe, his repentance should help. Rabbi Yitzchak replies that when someone makes repentance it restores whatever he damaged above; repentance restores everything, including the man himself and the whole universe. We hear that although God has steeped the world in Judgment, He wishes the children of Yisrael to repent in order to better their position in this world and in the World to Come. We are told that Jonah's repentance saved a great many people in the world.

22. רִבִּי יִצְחָק וְר' יְהוּדָה הֲווֹ אָזְלֵי מֵאוּשָׁא לְלוּד, אָמַר רִבִּי יְהוּדָה נֵימָא מִילִין דְּאוֹרַיְיתָא וְנֵזִיל. פָּתַח רִבִּי יְהוּדָה וְאָמַר, כִּי יִפְתַּח אִישׁ בּוֹר אוֹ כִּי יִכְרֶה אִישׁ בּוֹר וְגוֹ'. מַה כְּתִיב בַּתְרֵיהּ, בַּעַל הַבּוֹר יְשַׁלֵּם וְגוֹ'. וּמַה עַל דָּא כָּךְ, מַאן דְּגָרִים לְאַבְאָשָׁא עָלְמָא בְּחוֹבוֹי עאכ"ו. אֶלָּא תַּוַוהְנָא דאע"ג דְּאַבְאִישׁ עָלְמָא, אֲמַאי אִית לֵיהּ תְּשׁוּבָה, כְּמָה דִּכְתִיב אִישׁ אוֹ אִשָּׁה כִּי יַעֲשׂוּ וְגוֹ' וְהִתְוַדּוּ אֶת חַטָּאתָם וְהֵשִׁיב.

22. Rabbi Yitzchak and Rabbi Yehuda were traveling from Usha to Lod. Rabbi Yehuda said, Let's discuss some Torah as we go. Rabbi Yehuda opened the discussion with the verse: "If a man shall open a pit, or if a man shall dig a pit..." (Shemot 21:33). The following verse says: "The owner of the pit shall make it good..." (Ibid. 34). Therefore whoever harms the world with his sins should most certainly make it good. However, I wonder. Since he caused harm to the universe, why does repentance help as it says, "When a man or a woman shall commit any sin...then they shall confess their sins...and he shall make restitution" (Bemidbar 5:6-7).

23. אֶלָּא וַדַּאי דָּא מְהַנְיָא לְהוּ, בְּגִין דְּעָבֵיד תְּשׁוּבָה, כִּבְיָכוֹל הוּא עָבֵיד לֵיהּ מַמָּשׁ. דְּהָא מַה דְּפָגִים לְעֵילָּא, אַתְקִין לֵיהּ, וּבַמֶה בִּתְשׁוּבָה. דִּכְתִיב אִישׁ אוֹ אִשָּׁה כִּי יַעֲשׂוּ וְגוֹ', וְהִתְוַדּוּ אֶת חַטָּאתָם וְהֵשִׁיב, וּתְשׁוּבָה אַתְקִין כֹּלָּא, אַתְקִין לְעֵילָּא, אַתְקִין לְתַתָּא, אַתְקִין לְגַרְמֵיהּ, אַתְקִין לְכָל עָלְמָא.

23. HE REPLIES: Assuredly it helps them because when he repents, it is as if he causes it in reality, SINCE REPENTANCE (LIT. 'RETURN') RETURNS THE HEI TO THE VAV. He restored whatever he damaged above. How? By repentance, as it is written: "When a man or a woman shall commit any sin...then they shall confess their sins...and he shall make restitution (return)." Repentance restores everything. It repairs above and it repairs below, restoring himself and restoring the whole universe.

24. פָּתַח ר' יִצְחָק אַבַּתְרֵיהּ וְאָמַר, בַּצַּר לְךָ וּמְצָאוּךָ כָּל הַדְּבָרִים הָאֵלֶּה וְגוֹ'. בַּצַּר לְךָ, מִכָּאן דִּתְשׁוּבָה מֵעַלְיָא מִכֹּלָּא, עַד לָא יִשְׁרֵי דִּינָא בְּעָלְמָא. דִּבָתַר דְּשָׁרֵי דִּינָא תַּקִּיף חֵילֵיהּ מַאן יַעֲבַר לֵיהּ מֵעָלְמָא וִיסַלֵּק לֵיהּ. דְּהָא כֵּיוָן דְּשָׁארֵי דִּינָא, לָא אִסְתְּלִיק עַד דְּיִשְׁתַּלִּים. בָּתַר דְּאִשְׁתְּלִים, וְעָבַד תְּשׁוּבָה, אַתְקִין עָלְמִין כֻּלְּהוּ. מַשְׁמַע, דִּכְתִיב וּמְצָאוּךָ כָּל הַדְּבָרִים הָאֵלֶּה בְּאַחֲרִית הַיָּמִים, וּכְתִיב וְשַׁבְתָּ עַד יְיָ' אֱלֹהֶיךָ וְגוֹ'. כִּי אֵל רַחוּם יְיָ' אֱלֹהֶיךָ וְגוֹ'.

24. Rabbi Yitzchak opened next the discussion saying, "When you are in distress, and all these things are come upon you..." (Devarim 4:30). "When you are in distress": From here, we see that best of all is repentance before Judgment steeps the world, because once Judgment has settled, its power increases. Who will be able to remove it or make it go away? Once the Judgment begins, it does not disappear until it is fulfilled. Following the completion OF THE JUDGMENT and repenting, he restores the worlds. That is deduced from the scripture: "And all these things are come upon you, in the latter days...if you turn to Hashem your Elohim...for Hashem your Elohim is a merciful El" (Ibid. 30-31).

25. בְּאַחֲרִית הַיָּמִים, מַאי אִיכָּא הָכָא. אֶלָּא לְאַכְלָלָא כְּנֶסֶת יִשְׂרָאֵל, דְּאִיהִי בְּגָלוּתָא, וְאִשְׁתְּכָחַת בְּעָאקוּ דִּלְהוֹן, וְלָא שַׁבְקַת לוֹן לְעָלְמִין. וּבְגִין כַּךְ קוּדְשָׁא בְּרִיךְ הוּא אע"ג דְּאַשְׁרֵי דִּינָא בְּעָלְמָא, בָּעֵי דְּיָהַדְרוּן יִשְׂרָאֵל בִּתְשׁוּבָה, לְאוֹטָבָא לְהוּ בְּהַאי עָלְמָא, וּבְעָלְמָא דְּאָתֵי, וְלֵית לָךְ מַאן דְּקָאֵים קַמֵּי תְּשׁוּבָה.

25. HE INQUIRES: "In the latter days"? What is the connection of this verse to here? HE REPLIES: It is in order to include the Congregation of Yisrael, WHICH IS REFERRED TO AS THE LATTER DAYS, that is in exile, being with them in their distress and never leaving them. Although the Holy One, blessed be He, has steeped the world in Judgment, He wishes that Yisrael will repent to better their position in this world and in the World to Come. There is nothing that can withstand repentance.

26. ת״ח, אֲפִילוּ כְּנֶסֶת יִשְׂרָאֵל, תְּשׁוּבָה אִקְרֵי. וְאִי תֵּימָא תְּשׁוּבָה עִלָּאָה מִכָּל אֲתָר לָא שְׁכִיחַ, אֶלָּא דָּא אִקְרֵי תְּשׁוּבָה, כַּד אֲהַדָּר רַחֲמֵי לְקַבְּלָהָא, וְהִיא תָּבַת עַל כָּל אִינוּן אוֹכְלוֹסִין וְיָנְקָא לוֹן. וּתְשׁוּבָה מֵעַלְיָא, כַּד אִתְמְסַר נַפְשָׁא לְגַבָּהּ, וְנָטִיל לָהּ בְּזִמְנָא דְּאִיהִי בִּתְשׁוּבָה, כְּדֵין כֹּלָּא אִתְתָּקַן לְעֵילָּא וְתַתָּא, וְאִתְתָּקַן הוּא, וְכָל עָלְמָא.

26. Come and see that even the Congregation of Yisrael, WHICH IS MALCHUT, is called repentance. You might say the uppermost repentance, WHICH IS BINAH, is not found everywhere. But MALCHUT is called repentance when mercy THAT IS ZEIR ANPIN returned before her, and she returned again to nourish all her multitudes. The best way to repent is when the sinner risks his life for it. It is received during a time that he is in repentance. Then everything is restored above and below, and he and the worlds are restored.

27. חַיָּיבָא חַד בְּעָלְמָא, קִלְקוּלָא דְּכַמָּה אַחֲרָנִין בְּגִינֵיהּ. וַוי לְחַיָּיבָא, וַוי לִשְׁבִיבֵיהּ. ת״ח, יוֹנָה, בְּגִין דְּלָא בָּעָא לְמֵהַךְ בִּשְׁלִיחוּתָא דְּמָארֵיהּ, כַּמָּה בְּנֵי נָשָׁא הֲווֹ אִתְאָבִידוּ בְּגִינֵיהּ בְּיַמָּא, עַד דְּכֻלְּהוּ אָהַדְרוּ עֲלוֹי, וְדָאִינוּ לֵיהּ בְּדִינָא בְּיַמָּא, וּכְדֵין אִשְׁתְּזִיבוּ כֻּלְּהוּ, וְקוּדְשָׁא בְּרִיךְ הוּא חָס עֲלֵיהּ לְבָתַר, וְשֵׁזִיב כַּמָּה אוֹכְלוֹסִין בְּעָלְמָא. אֵימָתַי. כַּד אֲהַדָּר לְמָארֵיהּ מִגּוֹ עָקְתֵּיהּ. הֲדָא הוּא דִכְתִיב, קָרָאתִי מִצָּרָה לִי אֶל יְיָ' וַיַּעֲנֵנִי. וּכְתִיב, מִן הַמֵּצַר קָרָאתִי יָהּ עָנָנִי בַּמֶּרְחָב יָהּ וְגוֹ'.

27. How many others are hurt because of one wicked person in the world. Woe to the wicked and woe to his neighbor. Look at Jonah. Because he had no wish to go on his Master's mission, how many people could have perished at sea because of him, until they all gathered about him to judge

and convict him, TO THROW HIM into the sea. Then all were saved and the Holy One, blessed be He, had mercy upon him. Afterwards, he saved a great many in the world; THAT IS, THE PEOPLE OF NINEVEH. When WAS THIS? When he repented before his Master, in his distress. This is what is meant by: "I cried to Hashem out of my distress, and he heard me" (Yonah 2:3), and: "Out of my distress I called upon Yah: Yah answered me with liberation..." (Tehilim 118:5).

A Synopsis

We hear what the letters in the Holy Name have to do with repentance, that is Binah. This repentance is called life, and the "issues of life" are the souls of Yisrael. We are told of the importance of breath, and the words that issued from the mouth of God. The question arises where the breath that exists in the heathen nations comes from if the Shechinah does not dwell on them, and the answer is that not all faces are equal even among the children of Yisrael. We are told about another soul that hovers over a man's head that moves all his limbs to follow the precepts. There follows an elaboration of the sense of the Nefesh, Ruach, Neshamah, Chayah and Yechidah of Ruach that are drawn to a deserving person. We are told that there is a good kind of breath and a breath that is wicked. The countenance of the animal that resides in a person is apparent in the likeness that dwells on his face; upon every face is someone in charge over him. This is also true for the six days of creation, as there is no day that has no good in it, but not every person is able to enter into that goodness due to their unworthiness. There are various types of repentance, and all of them are good but they are not all equal. The most important thing is to study the Torah with awe and love for God; awe and love reside in the brain and the heart. We are told how the holy grades are able to discern anyone who has become impaired through his misdeeds, and how they distance themselves from him. And yet complete repentance causes God to return to him.

רעיא מהימנא

28. פְּקוּדָא דָא, הִיא מִצְוַת תְּשׁוּבָה. וְדָא אִיהִי בִּינָה. וּבַעֲוֹונוֹתֵינוּ מִדְחָרַב בֵּי מַקְדְּשָׁא, לָא אִשְׁתְּאַר לָנוּ אֶלָּא וִדּוּי דְּבָרִים לְבַד, וְדָא מַלְכוּת. וּמַאי בִּינָה. בֶּן יָ"ה. וְהַאי בֵּן, ו' אִיהוּ וַדַּאי. וְכָל מַאן דְּחָזַר בְּתִיוּבְתָּא, כְּאִילוּ חָזַר אָת ה' לְאָת ו', דְּאִיהוּ בֶּן יָ"ה, וְאִשְׁתְּלִים בֵּיה יְדֹנ"ד. וְדָא אִיהוּ תְּשׁוּבָה, תָּשׁוּב ה' וַדַּאי לְגַבֵּי ו'.

Ra'aya Meheimna (the Faithful Shepherd)

28. This commandment is that of repentance, and that is Binah. Because of our sins when the Temple was destroyed, nothing was left for us, only verbal confession alone, which is Malchut THAT IS REFERRED TO AS A

VERBAL CONFESSION. What is Binah? IT CONSISTS OF THE LETTERS Ben (Eng. 'son') Yud-Hei, and that son is surely Vav, WHICH ALLUDES TO ZEIR ANPIN WHO IS CALLED SON THAT IS ATTACHED TO HER AND RECEIVES THE MOCHIN OF YUD-HEI FROM HER. For everyone who repents, it is as if he returned the letter Hei, WHICH IS MALCHUT, to the letter Vav, WHICH IS ZEIR ANPIN, which is the son of Yud Hei. Thus, through him Yud Hei Vav Hei is completed, BECAUSE THE SON IS THE SECRET OF VAV AND TOGETHER WITH YUD-HEI IT FORMS YUD-HEI-VAV, AND WITH MALCHUT, THAT IS THE HEI THAT RETURNED TO HIM, THE WHOLE NAME WAS MADE COMPLETE. That is repentance (Heb. *teshuvah*) for sure, WHICH CONSISTS OF THE LETTERS *tashuv* (Eng. 'return') Hei to the Vav.

29. דְּאָת ה' וַדַּאי אִיהוּ וִדּוּי דְּבָרִים, וְרָזָא דְּמִלָּה, קְחוּ עִמָּכֶם דְּבָרִים וְשׁוּבוּ אֶל יְיָ' אָמְרוּ אֵלָיו וְגוֹ' וּנְשַׁלְּמָה פָּרִים שְׂפָתֵינוּ. דְּוַדַּאי כַּד ב"נ אִיהוּ חוֹטָא, גָּרִים לְאִתְרַחֲקָא ה' מֵאָת ו'. דְּאִסְתְּלַק בֵּן יָ"ה, דָּא יה"ו, מֵאָת ה'. וּבְגִ"ד אִתְחֲרַב בֵּי מַקְדְּשָׁא, וְאִתְרַחֲקוּ יִשְׂרָאֵל מִתַּמָּן, וְאִתְגְּלוּ בֵּינֵי עַמְמַיָּא. וּבְגִ"ד, כָּל מַאן דְּעָבֵיד תְּשׁוּבָה, גָּרִים לְאַחְזְרָא ה' לְאָת ו', וּפוּרְקָנָא בְּדָא תַּלְיָיא. וּבְגִ"ד הַכֹּל תָּלוּי בִּתְשׁוּבָה. דְּכָךְ אָמְרוּ קַדְמָאֵי, כָּל הַקִּצִּים כָּלוּ, וְאֵין הַדָּבָר תָּלוּי אֶלָּא בִּתְשׁוּבָה, דְּאִיהוּ שְׁלִימוּ דִּשְׁמֵיהּ.

29. The letter Hei definitely is verbal confession and the secret meaning of: "Take with you words, and turn to Hashem: say to him...so we will offer the words of our lips instead of calves" (Hoshea 14:3). When a person sins, he certainly causes the Hei to distance itself from the Vav, since the son of Yud -Hei, MEANING THE VAV THAT CONTAINS Yud-Hei-Vav, removes himself from the Hei. Because of this, the Temple was destroyed and Yisrael were driven away from there and dispersed among the nations. Because of this, whoever repents affects the return of the Hei to the letter Vav, and redemption depends upon it. Consequently, everything depends on repentance. That is what the ancient sages said. The intimated term for the coming of Messiah has passed – worse has come to worst – and it is contingent upon repentance only, which is the completion of his Name, WHICH IS THE SECRET MEANING OF HEI THAT COMPLETES HIS NAME WHEN ADDED TO YUD-HEI-VAV.

30. וע״ד וָאֶעֱשֶׂה לְמַעַן שְׁמִי. וְעוֹד לְמַעֲנִי לְמַעֲנִי אֶעֱשֶׂה. וְאִם לָאו חַזְרִין, אֲנָא אֲעַמִּיד לוֹן מַלְכָּא, שֶׁקַּשִׁין גְּזֵרוֹתָיו מִשֶּׁל פַּרְעֹה, וְיַחְזְרוּן עַל כָּרְחַיְיהוּ. הה״ד וְשַׁבְתָּ עַד יְיָ׳ אֱלֹהֶיךָ, עַד יְדֹנָ״ד וַדַּאי.

30. Therefore, "I acted for my name's sake" (Yechezkel 20:14), NAMELY TO COMPLETE THE NAME YUD HEI VAV HEI and also "for my own sake, for my own sake, will I do" (Yeshayah 48:11). If they do not return, then I will set upon them a king whose decrees are harsher than those of Pharaoh. Then they will repent in spite of themselves. This is what is meant by: "If you turn to Hashem your Elohim" (Devarim 4:30), to Yud Hei Vav Hei certainly, NAMELY TO COMPLETE THE NAME YUD HEI VAV HEI.

31. וּתְשׁוּבָה דָּא אִתְקְרִיאַת חַיִּים, כִּי מִמֶּנּוּ תּוֹצְאוֹת חַיִּים, דְּאִינּוּן נִשְׁמָתִין דְּיִשְׂרָאֵל. וְאִיהוּ הֶבֶל דְּנָפַק וְעָאל בְּפוּמָא דב״נ, בְּלָא עָמָל וּבְלָא יְגִיעָה. ה׳ דִּבְהִבָּרְאָם. וְעָלָהּ אִתְּמַר, כִּי עַל כָּל מוֹצָא פִּי יְיָ׳ יִחְיֶה הָאָדָם. וְהִיא עַל רֵישֵׁיהּ דב״נ. עָלָהּ אִתְּמַר, וּתְמוּנַת יְיָ׳ יַבִּיט. אַךְ בְּצֶלֶם יִתְהַלֶּךְ אִישׁ.

31. This repentance, WHICH IS MALCHUT AND THE HEI OF YUD HEI VAV HEI, is called life, AS IS WRITTEN: "For out of it are the issues of life" (Mishlei 4:23). These are the souls of Yisrael, THE ISSUES OF MALCHUT, REFERRED TO AS LIFE, and MALCHUT is the breath that a person exhales and inhales through the mouth without toil or effort. IT IS THE SECRET OF Hei of "When they were created (Heb. *BeHibar'am*)" (Beresheet 2:4), SINCE THE LETTER HEI IS VOCALIZED THROUGH THE MOUTH MORE EASILY THAN THE REST OF THE LETTERS. About this, it is written: "But by every word that proceeds out of the mouth of Hashem does man live" (Devarim 8:3), SINCE MALCHUT IS REFERRED TO AS "WORD THAT PROCEEDS OUT OF THE MOUTH OF HASHEM," which is above the head of the man, THAT IS, 'AND OVER MY HEAD THE SHECHINAH OF EL'. About it, it says: "And the likeness of Hashem does he behold" (Bemidbar 12:8), BECAUSE MALCHUT IS REFERRED TO AS THE LIKENESS OF HASHEM, AND ALSO: "Surely every man walks in a vain show (image)" (Tehilim 39:7).

32. וּבְגִין דְּאִיהִי עַל רֵישֵׁיהּ דב״נ, אָסִיר לֵיהּ לב״נ לְמֵיזַל ד׳ אַמּוֹת

בְּגִלּוּי דְּרֵישָׁא, דְּאִם הִיא אִסְתַּלָּקַת מֵעַל רֵישֵׁיהּ דב״ּנ, מִיַּד אִסְתַּלָּקוּ חַיִּים מִנֵּיהּ.

32. Because it is over a person's head, a man is prohibited to walk four cubits with his head uncovered. If she departs from over his head, his life is immediately gone.

33. וְאִי תֵּימָא דְּכַךְ שַׁרְיָא עַל אוּמִין דְּעָלְמָא, אע״ג דְּלָא אִתְבְּרֵי בְּהוֹן שְׁמַיָּא וְאַרְעָא וְכָל תּוֹלְדִין דִּבְהוֹן. לָא שַׁרְיָא וַדַּאי, דְּמֹשֶׁה בָּעָא מְקוּדְשָׁא בְּרִיךְ הוּא, דְּלָא תִּשְׁרֵי שְׁכִינָה עַל אוּמִין דְּעָלְמָא, וְיָהִיב לֵיהּ. הֶבְלָא דְּקַיְּימָא עַל אוּמִין דְּעָלְמָא מֵאָן נָפְקָא. אוֹ עַל חַיָּיבַיָּא דְּאִינּוּן עֵרֶב רַב מְעוּרְבִין עִם יִשְׂרָאֵל. אֶלָּא וַדַּאי לֵית כָּל אַפַּיָּיא שָׁוִין, אֲפִילוּ יִשְׂרָאֵל לָאו אִינּוּן שַׁוְיָן, כָּל שֶׁכֵּן אַחֲרָנִין.

33. You might say that this is also the way MALCHUT dwells on the nations of the world, even though the heavens and earth and all their hosts were not created through them, SINCE *BeHibar'am* IS COMPOSED OF THE LETTERS OF 'WITH ABRAHAM', THROUGH WHOM THE HEAVENS AND EARTH AND ALL THAT SPRANG FORTH FROM THEM WERE CREATED, AND THE OFFSPRING OF ABRAHAM, BUT NOT THE NATIONS OF THE WORLD. HE RESPONDS: She definitely does not dwell ON THEM, since Moses asked the Holy One, blessed be He, that the Shechinah shall not dwell on the nations of the world and it was granted to him. BUT IF SO, where does the breath present for the nations of the world come from? WHAT IS THE SOURCE OF THE ONE FOUND over the wicked, which are the mixed multitudes mingled among Yisrael? HE REPLIES: It therefore must be that not everyone is equal. Even among Yisrael, everyone is not equal and this is certainly true for others, AS WILL BE EXPLAINED.

34. אֶלָּא וַדַּאי עַל הַאי דִּיּוּקְנָא דְּאָת ה׳ אוּקְמוּהָ, מַתָּנָה טוֹבָה יֵשׁ לִי בְּבֵית גְּנָזַי וְשַׁבָּת שְׁמָה. וְכַד הַאי שַׁרְיָא עַל יִשְׂרָאֵל, לֵית לוֹן יְגִיעָה וְלָא שִׁעְבּוּד. וּבָה נֶפֶשׁ עֲמֵלָה וִיגִיעָה שָׁבַת וַיִּנָּפַשׁ.

34. We definitely expounded on the form of the letter Hei: I have a beautiful gift in My storehouse by the name Shabbat, BECAUSE SHABBAT IS MALCHUT WHEN SHE ASCENDS TO BINAH. When MALCHUT, THE SECRET MEANING OF SHABBAT, dwells on Yisrael, they do not toil and are not under enslavement. In it, the working, tired soul "rested, and was refreshed" (Shemot 31:17).

35. דְּנֶפֶשׁ אַחֲרָא אִית עַל רֵישֵׁיהּ דב"נ, דְּאִתְקְרִיאַת עֶבֶד. וְאִיהוּ דִּיּוּקְנָא עַל ב"נ. וְאִיהִי עֶבֶד דְּמַלְכָּא, דִּמְנַעְנָעָא כָּל אֵבְרִין דב"נ, לְמֵיזָל בְּאָרְחִין טָבִין, וּלְקַיְּימָא בְּהוֹן רמ"ח פִּקּוּדִין, לְשַׁרְיָא עֲלַיְיהוּ ה' דִּבְהִבָּרְאָם, דְּכַךְ סָלִיק הִבָּרְאָם לרמ"ח.

35. There is another soul above a man's head, WHICH IS NOT OF MALCHUT, that is called a servant, SINCE IT DRAWS FROM METATRON THAT IS REFERRED TO AS SERVANT. It is the form above man's head. It is the King's servant that moves all the limbs of a person to follow the good ways and observe with them the 248 precepts, so that the Hei of BeHibar'am, WHICH IS THE SECRET MEANING OF MALCHUT, shall dwell on them, since the numerical value of BeHibar'am is 248.

36. וּדְיוּקְנָא אַחֲרָא עַל רֵישֵׁיהּ, דְּאִתְקְרִיאַת יִרְאָה, וְדָא י'. וַעֲלַיְיהוּ אִתְּמַר, וַיִּבְרָא אֱלֹהִים אֶת הָאָדָם בְּצַלְמוֹ בְּצֶלֶם אֱלֹהִים. תְּרֵין דִּיּוּקְנִין טָבִין, דְּאִינּוּן דְּכַר וְנוּקְבָא. דְּכַר מִסִּטְרָא דְּאָת י'. נוּקְבָּא מִסִּטְרָא דְּאָת ה'.

36. AFTER EXPLAINING THE ASPECT OF THE HUMAN NEFESH, HE ELABORATES ON THE ASPECTS OF NEFESH, RUACH, NESHAMAH, CHAYAH AND YECHIDAH OF THE RUACH THAT IS DRAWN TO A DESERVING PERSON FROM THE ASPECT OF THE FOUR LETTERS OF YUD HEI VAV HEI OF ZEIR ANPIN, THAT REST OVER HIS HEAD. HE SAYS: There is another form on his head called awe, and that is the Yud OF YUD HEI VAV HEI, THE SECRET MEANING OF KETER AND CHOCHMAH, WHICH ARE THE LIGHTS OF YECHIDAH AND CHAYAH OF RUACH. SINCE IT IS THE HIDDEN MEANING OF KETER, IT IS THE ASPECT OF AWE, SINCE AWE COMES FROM KETER. About them, it is written: "So Elohim created man in his own image, in the image of Elohim" (Beresheet 1:27), NAMELY "IMAGE"

TWICE, which are two goodly images, male and female. The male is from the side of the letter Yud OF YUD HEI VAV HEI, THE HIDDEN MEANING OF YECHIDAH AND CHAYAH, and the female from the side of the letter Hei OF YUD HEI VAV HEI, THE HIDDEN MEANING OF NESHAMAH.

37. וּתְרֵין אַתְוָון אִתְּעֲרִין לֵיהּ לב״נ לְתוֹרָה וְלַמִּצְוָה. י׳ יִרְאָה, וְדָא אִיהִי עַל רֵישֵׁיהּ דב״נ, וּמִנָּהּ יֵיעוּל דְּחִילוּ לְלִבָּא דב״נ, לְמִדְחַל מִקוּדְשָׁא בְּרִיךְ הוּא, וּלְנַטְרָא גַּרְמֵיהּ דְּלָא יַעֲבַר עַל פִּקּוּדִין דְּלָא תַעֲשֶׂה. ה׳ אַהֲבָה עַל רֵישֵׁיהּ דב״נ, וּמִנֵּיהּ עָאל רְחִימוּ דְּקוּדְשָׁא בְּרִיךְ הוּא, עַל רמ״ח אֵבָרִין דִּילֵיהּ, לְקַיְּימָא בְּהוֹן פִּקּוּדִין דַּעֲשֵׂה. ו׳ אִיהִי עַל רֵישֵׁיהּ דב״נ, וּמִנֵּיהּ יֵיעוּל עַל פּוּמָא דב״נ מִלּוּלִין לְאוֹלָפָא בְּאוֹרַיְיתָא.

37. The two letters – YUD-HEI – awaken man to the Torah and the precepts. VAV IS THE HIDDEN MEANING OF THE TORAH AND HEI OF THE PRECEPTS. Yud is awe, which is over man's head, whence awe goes into man's heart to fear the Holy One, blessed be He, and guard himself not to transgress the negative commandments. Hei is the love over a person's head and, from it, the love of the Holy One, blessed be He, is imbued on his 248 body parts with which he performs the 248 positive commandments. Vav OF YUD HEI VAV HEI, FROM WHICH ASPECT DWELLS THE ILLUMINATION OF RUACH OF RUACH ON MAN, rests over man's head and through it words enter his mouth with which to learn Torah. THAT IS MALCHUT, WHICH IS THE SECRET OF THE NEFESH OF RUACH CALLED 'WORDS,' THE SECRET OF HEI. THUS THE YUD HEI VAV HEI IS MADE COMPLETE.

38. וּבְהַאי קְחוּ עִמָּכֶם דְּבָרִים וְשׁוּבוּ אֶל יְיָ׳. וּבְהַאי דִּיהֵא בְּכוֹן הַיִּרְאָה וְהָאַהֲבָה וְהַתּוֹרָה יִתְחֲזַר יְדֹו״ד בִּינָה דְּאִיהוּ תְּשׁוּבָה, ו׳ תָּשׁוּב לְגַבֵּי ה׳, דְּאִיהוּ עוֹבָדָא דִּבְרֵאשִׁית. וְאִיהִי ל״ב אֱלֹהִים. וְיִשְׁתַּלִּים יְדֹו״ד וּבָהּ יְהֵא לְכוֹן נַיְיחָא מִכֹּלָּא, וּבָהּ שָׁבַת וַיִּנָּפַשׁ.

38. Of THE WORDS THAT ARE DRAWN INTO HIS MOUTH TO STUDY TORAH, IT SAYS, "Take with you words, and turn to Hashem" (Hoshea 14:3), BECAUSE THE WORDS COMPLETE THE YUD-HEI-VAV WITH THE LAST HEI CALLED WORDS. By this, you will have the awe and love and Torah,

WHICH IS THE SECRET OF YUD HEI VAV HEI, BECAUSE AWE AND LOVE
ARE THE SECRET OF YUD-HEI, THE TORAH IS THE SECRET OF VAV AND
WORDS OF MOUTH ARE THE SECRET OF HEI. Yud Hei Vav Hei, THAT IS
ZEIR ANPIN, will return to be Binah, which is Repentance, WHICH MEANS
the Vav – WHICH REFERS TO ZEIR ANPIN – will return to the FIRST Hei,
which is the act of Creation and the 32 times Elohim IS MENTIONED IN THE
ACT OF CREATION, NAMELY BINAH, and thus Yud Hei Vav Hei will be
complete. WITH MALCHUT RISING TO BINAH, you will have rest from
everything and in it, one "rested, and was refreshed." THAT IS TO SAY,
WHEN MALCHUT ASCENDS TO BINAH, SHE IS CALLED SHABBAT AND
PERTAINS TO THE SECRET OF REST AND REFRESHMENT. AS LONG AS
SHE DOES NOT ASCEND TO BINAH, MALCHUT IS NOT CONSIDERED
SHABBAT.

39. וּבָהּ יִתְכְּלִיל יד״ו, ובג״ד וַיְכֻלּוּ: שְׁלִימוּ דְּכֹלָּא. בָּהּ, אִתְבְּרֵי כָּל
עָלְמָא, וְעָלָהּ קַיְימִין שְׁמַיָא וְאַרְעָא וְיַמָּא וְכָל בִּרְיָין דְּאִתְבְּרוּן, דִּכְתִּיב
אֵלֶּה תוֹלְדוֹת הַשָּׁמַיִם וְהָאָרֶץ בְּהִבָּרְאָם, בְּה׳ בְּרָאָם. וְאִם הִיא
אִתְרַחֲקַת מֵעָלְמָא אֲפִילוּ רִגְעָא, כֹּלָּא אִתְחָרֵב וְאִתְבַּטֵּל, וְלָא הֲוֵי
קִיּוּמָא בְּעָלְמָא.

39. In MALCHUT, WHICH IS THE LAST HEI THAT ASCENDED TO BINAH,
the Yud-Hei-Vav will be concluded, AND THE NAME WILL BE COMPLETE.
"THUS THE HEAVENS AND THE EARTH were finished" (Beresheet 2:1),
WHICH WAS ON SHABBAT, which is total perfection. The whole world was
created through her, and on her stand firmly the heavens, the earth, the seas
and all creatures that were created, since it is written: "These are the
generations of the heavens and of the earth when they were created (Heb.
BeHibar'am)." THIS CONSISTS OF THE SAME LETTERS OF: 'With Hei they
were created (Heb. *be Hei bra'am*)', WHICH IS MALCHUT. If she would
have departed from the world even for a moment, everything would have
collapsed and dissolved, and the world could not have been preserved.

40. הַאי ה׳ לָא תֵּיזִיל מִגּוּפָא, וּבָהּ קַיְימָא וְכַד הִיא תֵּיזִיל מִינֵּיהּ, הוּא
סַם הַמָּוֶת תֵּיתֵי וְתִשְׁרֵי עֲלֵיהּ, דְּתִתְקְרֵי טוּמְאָה, נְבֵלָה, פְּסוּלָה, מַלְאַךְ
הַמָּוֶת, חֹשֶׁךְ, אֲפֵלָה, וְשַׁרְיָא עַל גּוּפָא דב״נ. וּבְהַהוּא זִמְנָא אִתְקְרֵי ב״נ

-74-

מֵת. וְרָזָא דְמִלָּה, כִּי לֹא אֶחְפּוֹץ בְּמוֹת הַמֵּת נְאֻם יְיָ׳ אֱלֹהִים וְהָשִׁיבוּ וְחָיוּ.

40. This Hei will not leave the body OF A MAN and therein it stays. When it does leave him, the poison of death will come and rest on him, which is called defilement, a carcass, unfit, the Angel of Death, darkness and obscurity; and it dwells on the corpse of men. At that point, the man is called dead. The secret of it is: "'For I have no pleasure in the death of him that dies', says Hashem Elohim: therefore turn, and live" (Yechezkel 18:32). IT SHOULD HAVE SAID, 'THE DEATH OF HIM THAT LIVES.' THIS IS BECAUSE THE WICKED IS ALREADY DEAD, SO IT SAYS, "THE DEATH OF HIM THAT DIES."

41. כָּל פִּקוּדִין דַּעֲשֵׂה, דַּהֲווֹ עֲתִידִין לְשַׁרְיָא בְּרַמָ״ח אֵבָרִין דִּילֵיהּ, כֻּלְּהוּ מִתְאַבְּלִין עֲלֵיהּ. וְרָזָא דְמִלָּה, דְּרָכָיו רָאִיתִי וְאֶרְפָּאֵהוּ וְגוֹ׳. וְלַאֲבֵלָיו. מַאי וְלַאֲבֵלָיו. אִלֵּין רמ״ח אֵבָרִין, דְּקָא מִתְאַבְּלִין עֲלֵיהּ, דְּאִינּוּן דִּיּוּקְנָא עִלָּאָה דְּשַׁרְיָא עַל רֵישֵׁיהּ, דְּבָהּ שַׁרְיָא הֲוָיֶ״ה. דִּכְמָה דְּאִית דִּיּוּקְנָא טָבָא עַל צַדִּיק, וּמַנְהִיג לֵיהּ לְכָל עוֹבָדִין טָבִין, לְזַכָּאָה לֵיהּ לְעָלְמָא דְּאָתֵי. כָּךְ אִית דִּיּוּקְנָא בִּישָׁא, עַל רֵישָׁא דְּחַיָּיבַיָּא, לְאַנְהָגָא לוֹן בְּעוֹבָדִין בִּישִׁין, דְּיַרְתּוּן גֵּיהִנָּם. וּבְג״ד אִית הֶבֶל וְאִית הֶבֶל, אִית הֶבֶל טַב, דְּאִתְּמַר בֵּיהּ, כִּי עַל כָּל מוֹצָא פִי יְיָ׳ יִחְיֶה הָאָדָם. וְאִית הֶבֶל בִּישׁ, דְּאִתְּמַר בֵּיהּ גַּם זֶה הֶבֶל וּרְעוּת רוּחַ.

41. All the positive commandments that were to imbue his 248 organs grieve for him. The hidden meaning is that "I have seen his ways and I will heal him...and on his mourners" (Yeshayah 57:18). What are "his mourners"? These are the 248 limbs that grieve for him. That is the uppermost likeness resting on his head, where Yud Hei Vav Hei rests. As there is a good likeness over the righteous, which leads him to do good deeds and merit the World to Come, so is there a bad likeness over the heads of the wicked that leads them to act wrongly and deserve Gehenom. Therefore, there are different kinds of breath. There is the good kind of breath, about which is written: "But by every word that proceeds out of the mouth of Hashem does man live" (Devarim 8:3) and there is breath that is wicked, about which is written: "This also is vanity (breath) and a striving after wind" (Kohelet 2:26).

42. וְת"ח בְּעוֹבָדִין דב"נ אִשְׁתְּמוֹדַע פַּרְצוּפָא, דְּאִיהִי עֲלֵיהּ, וּפַרְצוּפָא דְאַנְפּוֹי. הה"ד, הַכָּרַת פְּנֵיהֶם עָנְתָה בָּם. בְּדִיּוּקְנָא, אִשְׁתְּמוֹדַע פַּרְצוּפָא דְּחַיָּה דְּשַׁרְיָא עֲלֵיהּ, אִם הוּא אַרְיֵה, אוֹ שׁוֹר אוֹ נֶשֶׁר, אוֹ אָדָם. מֵהַמֶּרְכָּבָה דְקוּדְשָׁא בְּרִיךְ הוּא וּשְׁכִינְתֵּיהּ. אוֹ מֵהַמֶּרְכָּבָה דְּמַלְאָךְ שַׂר הַפָּנִים. אוֹ מֵהַמֶּרְכָּבָה בִּישָׁא דְּסָמָאֵל. אוֹ מֵהַמֶּרְכָּבָה דְּאַרְבַּע יְסוֹדִין דְּעָלְמָא. וְלֵית בְּהוֹן לָא הַיֵּצֶר טוֹב, וְלָא הַיֵּצֶר הָרַע, אֶלָּא כִּבְעִירִין דְּעָלְמָא. וּבג"ד כַּמָּה הֲבָלִים אִית בִּבְנֵי נָשָׁא, כָּל חַד לְמִינֵיהּ. וְרָזָא דְמִלָּה, תּוֹצֵא הָאָרֶץ נֶפֶשׁ חַיָּה לְמִינָהּ. וּבג"ד, בְּמִדָּה שֶׁאָדָם מוֹדֵד בָּהּ מוֹדְדִין לוֹ. וּבְכָל פַּרְצוּפָא אִית מְמָנָא עֲלֵיהּ.

42. Come and see that through people's actions, the spiritual form (lit. 'countenance) is recognized that hovers over them, and so is the appearance. This is what is meant by, "The show of their countenance witnesses against them" (Yeshayah 3:9). In the likeness THAT DWELLS OVER ONE is apparent the face of the living creature that resides over him, whether it is a lion, an ox, an eagle or a man, OR FROM the Chariot of the Holy One, blessed be He and his Shechinah, from the Chariot of the angel, the chief prince, from the wicked Chariot of Samael or from the Chariot of the four elements of the universe, which contain neither the Good Inclination nor the Evil Inclination but are like common beasts. Therefore, there are many types of breath in people, each one according to his own kind, the secret meaning of, "Let the earth bring forth living creatures after their kind" (Beresheet 1:24). It follows that a person is treated the same way he treats others. And upon every spiritual form is an angel in charge over it.

43. ת"ח, לְשִׁית יוֹמֵי בְּרֵאשִׁית, לְכָל חַד אִית לֵיהּ פַּרְצוּפֵיהּ, דְּהַהוּא דַרְגָּא דְּאַנְהִיג לֵיהּ, וְלָא תִּשְׁכַּח יוֹם דְּלֵית בֵּיהּ טוֹב. וְאע"ג דְּבְיוֹמָא תִּנְיָינָא לָא אִית בֵּיהּ טוֹב, בְּיוֹמָא תְּלִיתָאָה תִּשְׁכַּח לֵיהּ. וּבג"ד אִתְּמַר בֵּיהּ תְּרֵי זִמְנֵי טוֹב.

43. Come and see: each of the six days of Creation has its own form of the grade that guides it. You will not find a day that has no good in it. THAT IS, IT SAYS OF THEM: "AND ELOHIM SAW THAT IT WAS GOOD" (BERESHEET 1:10). Although "that it is good" was not mentioned on the second day,

you will find it on the third day. Therefore, "good" is mentioned twice in it.

44. וְכָל יוֹמָא אִית לֵיהּ גָּדֵר מִלְּבַר, דְּלָא יֵיעוּל כָּל ב"נ לְהַהוּא טוֹב. כְּגוֹן חֹשֶׁךְ דְּכַסֵּי לִנְהוֹרָא. דְּתִשְׁכַּח בְּיוֹמָא קַדְמָאָה אוֹר, וְתִשְׁכַּח בֵּיהּ חֹשֶׁךְ. בְּכָל יוֹמָא תִּשְׁכַּח נְטִירָא. וְאִינּוּן נְטִירִין אִינּוּן, כְּגוֹן קוֹצִים לַכֶּרֶם. וְאִית נְטִירִין אַחֲרָנִין, כְּגוֹן נְחָשִׁים וְעַקְרַבִּים וּשְׂרָפִים, וְנַטְרִין הַהוּא טוֹב, דְּלָא יֵיעוּל תַּמָּן דְּלָאו אִיהוּ רָאוּי לְמֵיעַל. וְאִי לָאו, כָּל חַיָּיבַיָּא הֲווֹ עָאלִין בְּרָזִין דְּאוֹרַיְיתָא.

44. Every day has its exterior barrier, so that not everyone would be able to enter into the goodness in it, MEANING there is darkness that veils the light, as you will find light in the first day, and also find darkness in it. AND SO, in every day there are barriers that guard like thorns THAT GUARD the vineyard, SO THAT STRANGERS WILL NOT ENTER IT. There are other types of guardians, like snakes, scorpions and poisonous serpents that protect the good, so that unworthy people will be unable to enter. If there were no barriers, all the wicked would have the ability to access the secrets of the Torah.

45. וּבג"ד מַאן דְּאִיהוּ חַיָּיבָא, וְיֵיעוּל לְמִנְדַּע רָזִין דְּאוֹרַיְיתָא, כַּמָּה מַלְאֲכֵי חַבָּלָה דְּאִתְקְרִיאוּ חֹשֶׁךְ וַאֲפֵלָה, נְחָשִׁים וְעַקְרַבִּים חֵיוַת בָּרָא אִתְקְרִיאוּ, וּמְבַלְבְּלִין מַחֲשַׁבְתֵּיהּ, דְּלָא יֵיעוּל לַאֲתַר דְּלָאו דִילֵיהּ.

45. Therefore, many angels of destruction that are called darkness and obscurity, and snakes and scorpions that are called wild animals, confuse the mind of whoever is wicked and has access to the secrets of the Torah to prevent his entry where he does not belong.

46. אֲבָל מַאן דְּאִיהוּ טוֹב, כָּל אִלֵּין נְטִירִין אִינּוּן לְמֶמְרֵיהּ, וְקָטֵיגוֹר נַעֲשָׂה סַנֵיגוֹר, וְיֵיעַלּוּן לֵיהּ לְטוֹב הַגָּנוּז, וְיֵימְרוּן לֵיהּ מָרָנָא, הָא בַּר נָשׁ טוֹב וְצַדִּיק יְרֵא שָׁמַיִם, בָּעֵי לְאַעֲלָא קַדְמָךְ, אֲמַר לָנוּ, פִּתְחוּ לִי שַׁעֲרֵי צֶדֶק אָבֹא בָם אוֹדֶה יָהּ. הַהוּא טוֹב הַגָּנוּז יֵימָא לוֹן, פִּתְחוּ לֵיהּ בְּהַאי תַּרְעָא דְּאִתְקְרֵי אַהֲבָה, אוֹ בְּהַאי תַּרְעָא דְּאִיהִי תְּשׁוּבָה. כָּל צַדִּיק

וְיֵעוֹל כְּפוּם דַּרְגָּא דִילֵיה, וְרָזָא דְמִלָּה פִּתְחוּ שְׁעָרִים וְיָבֹא גוֹי צַדִּיק וְגוֹ'.

46. However, all these guardians are at the assistance of whoever is good, and the prosecutor becomes a defendant. They bring him to the concealed goodness and they will say TO THE CONCEALED GOODNESS: Our Master, here is a good person, virtuous, heaven fearing, who wishes to enter before You. And he tells us, "Open to me the gates of the righteous. I will go in to them, and I will praise Yah" (Tehilim 118:19). THEN, that concealed goodness will reply to them to open for him the gate of love or the gate of repentance. Every righteous person shall enter according to his degree, the meaning of it being: "Open the gates, that the righteous nation...may enter" (Yeshayah 26:2).

47. כְּעַן צָרִיךְ לְאָהַדְרָא עַל פֶּתַח הַתְּשׁוּבָה. וְכִי מִכַּמָּה מִינִין אִיהוּ תְּשׁוּבָה דְעַבְדִין בְּנֵי נָשָׁא, כֻּלְּהוּ טָבִין, אֲבָל לָאו כָּל אַפַּיָּיא שָׁוִין. אִית בַּ"נ דְּאִיהוּ רָשָׁע גָּמוּר כָּל יָמָיו, וְאִיהוּ עוֹבֵר עַל כַּמָּה פְּקוּדִין דְּלָא תַּעֲשֶׂה, וּמִתְחָרֵט וּמוֹדֶה עֲלַיְיהוּ, וּלְבָתַר כֵּן לָא עָבֵד לָא טַב וְלָא בִיש. לְדָא וַדַּאי יִמְחוֹל לֵיה קוּדְשָׁא בְּרִיךְ הוּא, אֲבָל לָא דְיִזְכֶּה לִתְשׁוּבָה עִלָּאָה. אִית בַּ"נ לְבָתַר דְּיֵיתוּב מֵחַטָּאוֹי, וּמִתְכַּפֵּר לֵיה, אִיהוּ אָזִיל בְּדֶרֶךְ מִצְוָה, וּמִתְעַסֵּק בְּכָל כֹּחוֹ בִּדְחִילוּ וּרְחִימוּ דְקוּדְשָׁא בְּרִיךְ הוּא. דָּא זָכֵי לִתְשׁוּבָה תַּתָּאָה, דְּאִתְקְרֵי ה'. וְדָא אִיהוּ תְּשׁוּבָה תַּתָּאָה.

47. Now we must return to the gate of repentance. The repentance that people do consists of various types. All are good but all are not equal. There is a person who is completely wicked all his life and transgressed many negative commandments, but he regrets and confesses them. He then does neither good nor bad. Surely, the Holy One, blessed be He, will forgive him, but he will not merit the highest repentance. There is also a person who has repented and has his sins wiped clean. He pursues the way of the precepts and performs them with all his might, with awe and love for the Holy One, blessed be He. That person will acquire the lower repentance, called Hei, WHICH IS MALCHUT, which is a lower degree of repentance.

48. וְאִית בַּ"נ דְּמִתְחָרֵט מֵחוֹבוֹי, וְיַעֲבִיד תְּשׁוּבָה, וְיִתְעַסַּק

-78-

בְּאוֹרַיְיתָא בִּדְחִילוּ וּרְחִימוּ דְקוּדְשָׁא בְּרִיךְ הוּא, וְלָא ע"מ לְקַבֵּל פְּרָס. דָּא זָכֵי לְאָת ו', וְאִיהוּ בֵּן יָ"ה, וְעַל שְׁמֵיהּ אִתְקְרֵי בִּינָה, וְדָא גָּרִים דְּתָשׁוּב ו' לְגַבֵּי ה'. וּמִלַּת תְּשׁוּבָה כָּךְ הִיא, תָּשׁוּב ו' לְה'.

48. Then there is a person that studies the Torah with awe and love for the Holy One, blessed be He, after regretting his sins and repenting but not for any reward. That person acquires the letter Vav OF YUD HEI VAV HEI, WHICH IS ZEIR ANPIN and is the son of Yud-Hei. Binah is named after him. That causes the return of Vav, WHICH IS ZEIR ANPIN, to Hei, WHICH IS MALCHUT. The word *teshuvah* (lit. 'repentance') CONSISTS OF THE LETTERS: Vav shall return (Heb. *tashuv*) to Hei.

49. וּלְעוֹלָם לָא שַׁרְיָא ה' בְּבַר נָשׁ, וְלָא ו', בְּלָא דְּחִילוּ וּבְלָא רְחִימוּ, דְּאִינּוּן יָ"ה, יִרְאָה וְאַהֲבָה קָרֵינָן לֵיהּ וַדַּאי. וּמִתַּמָּן אִתְיְיהִיבוּ הַתּוֹרָה וְהַמִּצְוָה דְּאִינּוּן בֵּן וּבַת. וּבְגִין דְּיִשְׂרָאֵל מְקַיְימִין הַתּוֹרָה וְהַמִּצְוָה, אִתְקְרִיאוּ בָּנִים לְקוּדְשָׁא בְּרִיךְ הוּא, הה"ד בָּנִים אַתֶּם לַיְיָ' אֱלֹהֵיכֶם.

49. Neither Hei nor Vav ever dwell on a person without awe and love, which are Yud-Hei, which we surely call awe and love. From there, the Torah and the precepts were given, which are the son and daughter – NAMELY VAV AND HEI, ZEIR ANPIN AND MALCHUT. Since Yisrael observe the Torah and its commandments, they are called the children of the Holy One, blessed be He, as it is written: "You are the children of Hashem your Elohim" (Devarim 14:1).

50. הַנִּסְתָּרוֹת: יִרְאָה וְאַהֲבָה, דְּאִינּוּן בְּמוֹחָא וְלִבָּא. בַּחֲלָלָא דְגוּפָא. וּבְרֵישָׁא. וְהַנִּגְלוֹת: הַתּוֹרָה וְהַמִּצְוָה, דְּאִינּוּן בְּגוּפָא וּבְרֵישָׁא לְבַר. וְרָזָא דְּמִלָּה הָכִי הוּא וַדַּאי, דְּאִי ב"נ דָּחִיל לְקוּדְשָׁא בְּרִיךְ הוּא, אוֹ רָחִים לֵיהּ, דָּא לָא יָדַע ב"נ אַחֲרָא, בְּגִין דְּאִיהוּ מִלָּה דְּלָא אִתְגַּלְיָא אֶלָּא בֵּינוֹ לְבֵין קוֹנוֹ.

50. "The secret things BELONG TO HASHEM OUR ELOHIM" (Devarim 29:28). These are awe and love, which reside inside the brain and heart. They are present in the cavities of the body and in THE INTERIOR OF the head, THE SECRET OF YUD-HEI. "But those things which are revealed BELONG TO US AND TO OUR CHILDREN" (Ibid.). These are the Torah and the precepts, which are on the exterior of the body and head, THE SECRET OF VAV-HEI. The basis of this is that if a person is in awe of the Holy One, blessed be He, or loves him, no one else knows, for it is unknown except to himself and his Master.

51. אֲבָל ב"נ דְּמִתְעֲסַק בְּאוֹרַיְיתָא, וְאָזִיל בְּפִקּוּדִין דַּעֲשֵׂה, דָּא אִתְגַּלְיָא לְכָל ב"נ, בְּגִין דְקוּדְשָׁא בְּרִיךְ הוּא עָבֵד לֵיהּ פּוּמָא בְּאִתְגַּלְיָא, לְאִתְעַסְּקָא בְּאוֹרַיְיתָא, וְעַיְינִין לְאִסְתַּכְּלָא בָּהּ, וְאוּדְנִין לְמִשְׁמַע בָּהּ. וְעָבֵד קוּדְשָׁא בְּרִיךְ הוּא בב"נ, יְדִין וְרַגְלִין וְגוּפָא, לְמֶעְבַּד בְּהוֹן פִּקּוּדִין דַּעֲשֵׂה.

51. However, if a person studies the Torah and pursues positive commandments, it is known to everyone. For the Holy One, blessed be He, made him a visible mouth with which to study the Torah, eyes with which to behold the Torah and ears with which to listen to it. The Holy One, blessed be He, also made hands, legs and a body for man with which to perform positive commandments.

52. א"כ חוֹטָמָא לְמַאי נָפְקָא מִנֵּיהּ. וַיִּפַּח בְּאַפָּיו נִשְׁמַת חַיִּים, דָּא אִיהִי דִּיּוּקְנָא דְּעַל ב"נ, דְּאִתְּמַר בֵּיהּ וַיַּחֲלוֹם וְהִנֵּה סֻלָּם. סֻלָּם וַדַּאי אִיהִי נִשְׁמַת חַיִּים, כֻּרְסְיָיא לְשֵׁם יְדֹו"ד דְּאִיהוּ הַיִּרְאָה וְהָאַהֲבָה הַתּוֹרָה וְהַמִצְוָה וּבָהּ שַׁרְיָא, וְהַאי כֻּרְסְיָיא, מִנָּהּ גְּזוּרוֹת כָּל נִשְׁמָתִין דְּיִשְׂרָאֵל, וְאִיהִי דִּיּוּקְנָא עַל רֵישָׁא דב"נ.

52. HE ASKS: If so, what is the purpose of the person's nose? WHY DID THE HOLY ONE, BLESSED BE HE, MAKE IT? HE RESPONDS: "And breathed into his nostrils the breath of life" (Beresheet 2:7). This is the form over the person, of which is said: "And he dreamed, and behold a ladder" (Ibid. 28:12). A ladder is assuredly the breath of life, WHICH IS MALCHUT, the throne to the Name – Yud Hei Vav Hei – which is awe, love, Torah and the precepts, SINCE AWE AND LOVE ARE YUD-HEI AND TORAH AND THE PRECEPTS ARE VAV-HEI. In it, IN THE BREATH (SOUL) OF LIFE, dwells THE NAME OF YUD HEI VAV HEI and that is the throne, THE LADDER,

from which all the souls of Yisrael are hewn. That is the form over the person's head.

53. וְהִנֵּה מַלְאֲכֵי אֱלֹהִים עוֹלִים וְיוֹרְדִים בּוֹ. אִלֵּין הַבְלִים דְּסַלְקִין וְנָפְקִין בְּגוּפָא, בְּהַאי סֻלָּם. אִיהוּ חַד, שְׁבִיעָאָה דְּכֻלָּא. וְאִיהוּ מֻצָּב אַרְצָה, תְּרֵין. וְרֹאשׁוֹ מַגִּיעַ הַשָּׁמַיְמָה, תְּלַת. וְהִנֵּה מַלְאֲכֵי אֱלֹהִים עוֹלִים, תְּרֵי. וְיוֹרְדִים תְּרֵי. אִינּוּן לָקֳבֵל ד' רוּחוֹת וְהַשָּׁמַיִם וְהָאָרֶץ. וְרָזָא, דְּמִלָּה הֲבֵל הֲבָלִים אָמַר קֹהֶלֶת הֲבֵל הֲבָלִים הַכֹּל הָבֶל. אִינּוּן שִׁבְעָה, לָקֳבֵל כּוּרְסְיָיא, דְּאִיהוּ הַסֻּלָּם, וְהַשָּׁמַיִם וְהָאָרֶץ, וְד' יְסוֹדִין דְּעָלְמָא, וְאִינּוּן שִׁבְעָה. לָקֳבֵל שִׁבְעָה יוֹמֵי בְּרֵאשִׁית. אִית כָּל בִּרְיָין דִּשְׁמַיָא, וְיַמָּא, וְאַרְעָא. כְּגוֹן חַיּוֹת עוֹפוֹת בְּהֵמוֹת דָּגִים, וְכַמָּה תוֹלָדִין דְּתַלְיָין מִינֵיהּ.

53. "And behold the angels of Elohim ascending and descending on it" (Ibid.). This refers to the breaths that go up and leave the body through this ladder. That LADDER is one, the seventh among them. That which is "set up on the earth" (Ibid.) IS ANOTHER ONE, MAKING two. "And the top of it reached to heaven" (Ibid.) IS ANOTHER ONE, SO TOGETHER THERE ARE three. "And behold the angels of Elohim ascending": THESE ARE ANOTHER two, SO THEY AMOUNT TO FIVE; "and descending" are two MORE, FOR A TOTAL OF SEVEN. They correspond to the four directions OF THE UNIVERSE, the heavens and earth, WHICH ILLUMINATE THAT LADDER, being the secret meaning of: "'Vanity of vanities,' says Kohelet, 'vanity of vanities; all is vanity'" (Kohelet 1:2). These are the seven breaths (or: 'vanities') corresponding to the throne, SINCE "VANITY OF VANITIES" ARE THREE. WITH THE SECOND "VANITY OF VANITIES," IT IS SIX AND WITH THE LAST "VANITY," IT IS SEVEN ALTOGETHER. They are the ladder, the heavens AND THE SEA, the earth and the four elements of the universe, totaling seven, congruent with the seven days of Creation – WHICH ARE CHESED, GVURAH, TIFERET, NETZACH, HOD, YESOD AND MALCHUT – AND CORRESPONDING TO THEM are all the creatures of the sky, sea and land; that is, the animals, birds, beasts, fish and many other offspring coming from them.

54. וּבְגִין דְּכֹלָּא אִתְבְּרֵי בְּהַאי צוּלְמָא, דְּעַל כָּל יִשְׂרָאֵל דְּאִיהִי צַדִּיק,

אִתְּמַר בְּהוֹן וּמוֹרַאֲכֶם וְחִתְּכֶם יִהְיֶה עַל כָּל חַיַּת הָאָרֶץ וְעַל כָּל עוֹף
הַשָּׁמַיִם וְגוֹ'. וְדָא מְמַלֵּל עַל בְּנֵי נָשָׁא, דְּאִינּוּן מְתִילִין לְחֵיוָן בָּרָא,
וּלְבְעִירָן, וּלְעוֹפִין, וּלְנוּנֵי יַמָּא. דְּאִית בַּר נָשׁ דְּמַזָּלֵיהּ שׁוֹר, וּמַזָּלֵיהּ
אַרְיֵה, וּמַזָּלֵיהּ נֶשֶׁר, וּמַזָּלֵיהּ אָדָם.

54. Since everything was created in the image that is on all Yisrael, which is the Righteous, BEING YESOD, it says about them: "And the fear of you and the dread of you shall be upon every beast of the earth, and upon every bird of the air..." (Beresheet 9:2). This SCRIPTURE talks about people who are compared to wild animals, to beasts, birds and fish of the sea. There are people whose astrological sign is the ox, SOME whose sign is the lion, SOME whose sign is the eagle AND SOME whose sign is a man.

55. וְכָל אִלֵּין, לָמָּה מִתְפַּחֲדִין מֵהַאי דִּיּוּקְנָא דְּאִינּוּן מִתַּמָּן אִתְבְּרִיאוּ.
אֶלָּא מִשּׁוּם דְּשֵׁם יְדֹוָ"ד שַׁרְיָא עֲלֵיהּ. רָזָא דְּמִלָּה, וְרָאוּ כָּל עַמֵּי הָאָרֶץ
וְגוֹ'. וְכָל מַאן דְּפָגִים עוֹבָדוֹי, אִתְפְּגִים דִּיּוּקְנֵיהּ, וְשֵׁם יְיָ' לָא שַׁרְיָא
בַּאֲתָר פָּגִים, וּבְהַהוּא פְּגִימוּ שַׁרְיָא חֹשֶׁךְ, בְּגִין פְּגִימוּ דְּסִיהֲרָא דְּשַׁרְיָא
בֵּיהּ חֲשׁוֹכָא. וְהַאי ב"נ כְּמָה דְּאִיהוּ פָּגִים דִּיּוּקְנֵיהּ, כַּךְ אִתְפְּגִים אִיהוּ
לְתַתָּא, אוֹ אִתְעֲבֵיד אִלֵּם, אוֹ חֵרֵשׁ, אוֹ סוּמָא, אוֹ חִגֵּר. בְּגִין דִּיְהֵא
רָשִׁים לְעֵילָּא וְתַתָּא.

55. Why are they all afraid of this likeness OVER MAN, seeing that they were also created from it? It is only because the name of Yud Hei Vav Hei dwells on him. That is the secret meaning of: "And all people of the earth shall see THAT YOU ARE CALLED BY THE NAME OF HASHEM; AND THEY SHALL BE AFRAID OF YOU" (Devarim 28:10). Whoever impairs his deeds, his form is impaired, and the name of Yud Hei Vav Hei does not reside in an impaired place. In that blemish, darkness prevails because at the time of impairment of the moon, WHICH IS MALCHUT, darkness prevails. As this person has damaged his form, so is he damaged below, and he either becomes mute, deaf, blind or lame, so that he is marked above and below.

56. וְהַהוּא חֹשֶׁךְ שַׁרְיָא בְּפַגִּימוּ דִּילֵיהּ, וּמִיַּד אִשְׁתְּמוֹדְעָאן בֵּיהּ דַּרְגִּין
קַדִּישִׁין, דְּאִינּוּן חֵילוֹי דְּקוּדְשָׁא בְּרִיךְ הוּא, וּמִתְרַחֲקִין מִנֵּיהּ, דִּכְבָר

יַדְעִין דִּבְהַהוּא פְּגִימוּ לָא שַׁרְיָא מַלְכָּא. וּבג״ד חֵילוֹי דְּמַלְכָּא מִתְרַחֲקִין
מִנֵּיהּ, דְּחַיָּילִין דְּמַלְכָּא לָא שַׁרְיָין, וְלָא מִתְקָרְבָן, אֶלָּא בְּאֲתָר דְּמַלְכָּא
שַׁרְיָא, דְּכַךְ אִינּוּן מִתְנַהֲגִין אֲבַתְרֵיהּ, כְּאֶבְרִין בָּתַר גּוּפָא.

56. That darkness prevails on his blemish and the holy grades discern him instantly. They are the hosts of the Holy One, blessed be He, who distance themselves from him since they already know that the King does not reside in that blemish. Therefore, the King's legions distance themselves from him, since the armies of the King reside and are near only where the King dwells. They follow him like limbs follow the body.

57. וּבְהַהוּא אֲתָר דְּשַׁרְיָ הַהוּא חֹשֶׁךְ, כַּמָּה מַלְאֲכֵי חַבָּלָה, דְּאִתְקְרִיאוּ
נְחָשִׁים וְעַקְרַבִּים, מִתְקָרְבִין לֵיהּ, וְיַהֲבִין לֵיהּ כַּמָּה נְשִׁיכִין, וְאִלֵּין אִינּוּן
יְסוּרִין. וְאִי אִית לֵיהּ מָמוֹנָא דְּעוֹבָדִין טָבִין דְּעָבֵיד, אִתְמַעֲטוּן מִנֵּיהּ.
וְאֵיךְ אִתְמַעֲטוּן מִנֵּיהּ, אֶלָּא כָּל זְכוּת דְּנָחִית לֵיהּ מִלְעֵילָא, יָהִיב לֵיהּ
לְאִלֵּין מַלְאֲכֵי חַבָּלָה, וּבַטְלִין מִנֵּיהּ יְסוּרִין. וְאִי לֵיהּ לֵיהּ זְכוּ, וְלָא
חוֹבָא לְעֵילָא, אֶלָּא כֹּלָּא לְתַתָּא, בְּכָל זְכוּ דְּעָבֵיד נָחִית לֵיהּ מָמוֹנִין,
וְאוּמִין דְּעָלְמָא מִתְקָרְבִין לֵיהּ, לָקֳבֵל מַלְאֲכֵי חַבָּלָה, וְיָהִיב לוֹן מָמוֹנָא,
וְאִשְׁתְּזִיב מִנַּיְיהוּ.

57. In the place where darkness prevails, various angels of destruction called snakes and scorpions come near him and bite him many times, and these are sufferings. If he has money, THAT IS, PROPERTY of his good deeds that he has done, MEANING IF HIS PROPERTY CONSISTS OF GOOD DEEDS, they diminish. How do they diminish? Every merit, MEANING EVERY ILLUMINATION that descends on him from above AS A REWARD FOR HIS GOOD DEEDS is given to the angels of destruction. In lieu of that, they suspend the sufferings from him. If he has neither merit nor debts above, because all HIS PROPERTY is below and with every merit he accumulates MATERIAL money, THEN the nations of the world approach him instead of the angels of destruction, and he gives them his money to save himself.

58. וּבג״ד הֲווֹ יִשְׂרָאֵל מַקְרְבִין לַעֲזָאזֵל, לְגַבֵּי הַהוּא חֹשֶׁךְ. וְשִׁבְעִים

פָרִים, לָקֳבֵל שִׁבְעִים אֻמִּין, לְקַיְּימָא קְרָא, אִם רָעֵב שֹׂנַאֲךָ הַאֲכִילֵהוּ
לֶחֶם וְאִם צָמֵא הַשְׁקֵהוּ מָיִם. וּמִיַּד דְּהַדְרִין בְּתִיוּבְתָּא, אִתְעַבַּר הַהוּא
חֹשֶׁךְ מֵהַהוּא פְּגִימוּ, וְיִשְׁתְּלִים. וְרָזָא דְמִלָּה, גַּם יְיָ' הֶעֱבִיר חַטָּאתְךָ לֹא
תָמוּת. וּמִיַּד אִתְהַדַּר בֵּיהּ שְׁמָא דַיְיָ', וְיִתְרְפֵי בֵּיהּ, מֵאִנּוּן נְשִׁיכִין
דְּיִסּוּרִין, הֲדָא הוּא דִּכְתִיב וְשָׁב וְרָפָא לוֹ. וּמְנַיִן דְּאִתְהַדַּר קוּדְשָׁא בְּרִיךְ
הוּא מִיַּד דְּהָדַר בְּתִיוּבְתָּא וְאִשְׁתְּלִים הַהוּא פְּגִימוּ. הֲדָא הוּא דִּכְתִיב
שׁוּבוּ אֵלַי וְאָשׁוּבָה אֲלֵיכֶם.

58. This is the reason that Yisrael used to sacrifice to Azazel, to that same darkness. And the seventy oxen that correspond to the seventy nations, WHICH THEY SACRIFICED DURING SUKKOT (HOLIDAY OF THE BOOTHS), fulfill the words: "If your enemy be hungry, give him bread to eat; and if he be thirsty, give him water to drink" (Mishlei 25:21). Once they repent, that darkness is removed from that blemish and they attain perfection. That is the meaning of: "Hashem also has commuted your sin; you shall not die" (II Shmuel 12:13). The name of Yud Hei Vav Hei immediately returns to him and heals him from the bites of affliction, as is written: "And return, and be healed" (Yeshayah 6:10). How do we know that the Holy One, blessed be He, returns immediately after he repents and the blemish is perfected? It is written: "Return to me, and I will return to you" (Malachi 3:7).

59. וְדָא אִיהוּ בִּתְשׁוּבָה גְמוּרָה, דְּגָרִים לְאַהֲדָרָא בִּינָה דְּאִיהוּ יד"ו,
לְגַבֵּי ה' דְּאִיהִי מַלְכוּת. דְּאַזְלָא מְנַדְּדָא מִן קִנָּהּ, דְּאִיהִי הַהִיא
דִּיּוּקְנָא, דְּמִתְקַטְּרִין בָּהּ כָּל פִּקוּדִין. וּבָהּ מִתְקַטְּרִין עֶשֶׂר סְפִירָן. כַּד ב"נ
עָבֵד פִּקוּדָא חֲדָא וְלָא יַתִּיר, וְעָבֵיד לָהּ בִּדְחִילוּ וּרְחִימוּ דְקוּדְשָׁא בְּרִיךְ
הוּא. בְּגִינָהּ שַׁרְיָין עֲלֵיהּ י' סְפִירָן. וְכָל מַאן דְּקַיֵּים פִּקוּדָא חַד כַּדְקָא
יָאוּת, כְּאִלּוּ מְקַיֵּים רמ"ח פִּקוּדִין דַּעֲשֵׂה, דְּלֵית פִּקוּדָא לָאו אִיהוּ
כְּלִילָא מִכֻּלְּהוּ רמ"ח.

ע"כ רעיא מהימנא

59. All this happens with complete repentance, which effects the return of Binah, that is Yud-Hei-Vav, to Hei, which is Malchut that left her nest and

is the same form ON THE HEAD OF A PERSON, to which all the precepts connect and the ten Sfirot are tied. Even if a person performs no more than one precept, but does so with awe and love of the Holy One, blessed be He, the ten Sfirot rest on him on that account. Whoever performs even one precept properly, it is as if he observed 248 positive commandments, since there is no one commandment that does not also contain all 248 POSITIVE COMMANDMENTS.

End of Ra'aya Meheimna (the Faithful Shepherd)

5. A wife suspected of adultery (Sota)

A Synopsis

This section talks about the unfaithful wife, who has trespassed against the Congregation of Yisrael and also against her husband, and therefore against Malchut and Zeir Anpin. We learn why the woman is taken to the priest, not for judgment but only for testing by means of water and the Holy Name. Rabbi Elazar wonders why people do not pay attention to the Torah, and Rabbi Shimon tells about how God brought the people to the waters of Marah to test them to see if they had become defiled with the Egyptians. After they were acquitted the Holy Name rested with them. The rabbis talk about dust and about the bitter water and the holy sea. They talk about the consequences to the wife of having been found faithful or guilty. We hear of how important it is for a woman to keep her hair covered so that the whole family will be blessed.

60. אִישׁ אִישׁ כִּי תִשְׂטֶה אִשְׁתּוֹ וְגוֹ'. מַאי הַאי לְגַבֵּי הַאי. אֶלָּא כְּמָה דִּכְתִיב לִמְעוֹל מַעַל בַּיְיָ'. ר' אֶלְעָזָר אָמַר, אִישׁ אִישׁ, מַאי אִישׁ אִישׁ, דְּהָא בְּחַד סַגֵּי, אֶלָּא הָא אוּקְמוּהָ, אֲבָל אִישׁ אִישׁ, מַשְׁמַע דְּאִיהוּ אִישׁ, וְקַיֵּים קְרָא דִּכְתִיב, שְׁתֵה מַיִם מִבּוֹרֶךָ וְגוֹ'. כְּדֵין הוּא אִישׁ בְּעָלְמָא, אִישׁ לְגַבֵּי אִתְּתֵיה. וּמָעֲלָה בוֹ מָעַל, הָא בְּחַד סַגֵּי, אֲמַאי תְּרֵי. אֶלָּא חַד לְעֵילָּא וְחַד לְתַתָּא. חַד לִכְנֶסֶת יִשְׂרָאֵל, וְחַד לְבַעְלָהּ. בְּגִין כָּךְ וְהֵבִיא הָאִישׁ אֶת אִשְׁתּוֹ.

60. "If any man's wife goes aside..." (Bemidbar 5:12). HE ASKS: What is the connection between the two, MEANING WHY IS THE PORTION OF SOTA (LIT. 'A WIFE SUSPECTED OF ADULTERY') NEXT TO THE PASSAGES ABOUT TRESPASSING? HE RESPONDS: It is written THERE: "To do a trespass against Hashem" (Ibid. 6) and it is written here BY A SOTA: "AND COMMIT A TRESPASS AGAINST HIM" (IBID. 12). THEY ARE THE SAME SUBJECT; THEREFORE, THEY ARE NEXT TO EACH OTHER. Rabbi Eleazar quoted, "Any man's (lit. 'man man')." Why say it twice, when once would have sufficed? HE RESPONDS: That was already explained, yet "man man" means a man who is a man, that is, who fulfills the words: "Drink water out of your own cistern" (Mishlei 5:15) AND DOES NOT COVET ANOTHER WOMAN. Then he is an ordinary man, a man to his wife. "And commit (trespassed) a trespass against him." HE ASKS: One trespass would have

-86-

sufficed, so why say "TRESPASS" twice? HE RESPONDS: It refers to one TRESPASS above and one below, MEANING one against the Congregation of Yisrael, WHICH IS MALCHUT, and one against her husband, ZEIR ANPIN. Therefore, "then shall the man bring his wife TO THE PRIEST" (Ibid. 15).

61. אֲמַאי אֶל הַכֹּהֵן. רָזָא דְמִלָּה, בְּגִין דְּכַהֲנָא שׁוּשְׁבִינָא אִיהוּ דְמַטְרוֹנִיתָא. הָכָא אִית לְאִסְתַּכְּלָא, הָא כְּתִיב וְשָׁחַט אֶת בֶּן הַבָּקָר, וְשָׁחַט אַחֲרָא, וְלָאו כַּהֲנָא, דְּכַהֲנָא אָסִיר לֵיהּ בְּדִינָא, בְּגִין דְּלָא יַפְגִּים הַהוּא אֲתָר דְּאָחִיד בֵּיהּ, וְאַתְּ אֲמַרְתְּ, וְהֵבִיא הָאִישׁ אֶת אִשְׁתּוֹ אֶל הַכֹּהֵן, לְמֵידָן דִּינָהָא. אֶלָּא וַדַּאי כַּהֲנָא לְדָא חֲזֵי, בְּגִין דְּאִיהוּ שׁוּשְׁבִינָא לְמַטְרוֹנִיתָא, וְכָל נְשֵׁי עָלְמָא מִתְבָּרְכָן בכנ"י, וע"ד אִתְּתָא דִלְתַתָּא מִתְבָּרְכָא בְּשֶׁבַע בְּרָכוֹת, דַּאֲחִידַת בָּהּ בִּכְנֶסֶת יִשְׂרָאֵל, וְכַהֲנָא קָאִים לְאַתְקְנָא מִלֵּי דְמַטְרוֹנִיתָא, וּלְעַיְּינָא בְּכָל מַה דְּאִצְטְרִיךְ, בְּגִין כָּךְ כַּהֲנָא לְדָא, וְלָא אַחֲרָא.

61. HE INQUIRES: Why BRING HIS WIFE "to the priest" AND NOT TO THE JUDGE? HE RESPONDS: the secret of it is that since the priest is the attendant of the Matron, MEANING THAT HE PREPARES MALCHUT FOR UNION WITH ZEIR ANPIN, IT IS THEREFORE SUITABLE FOR HIM TO RESTORE THE BLEMISH OF THE SOTA THAT REACHES ALL THE WAY TO MALCHUT. We have to examine this verse, which says: "And he shall kill the bullock" (Vayikra 1:5), IN WHICH "he" refers to someone other than the priest. A priest is prohibited TO ACT in judgment, in order not to impair the source to which he is connected, MEANING CHESED. Yet you say that the man should bring his wife to the priest to judge her trial! It must be that only the priest is suitable for this task, because he is the attendant of the Matron, and all the women in the world are blessed from the Congregation of Yisrael. Therefore, the woman below is blessed DURING HER MARRIAGE CEREMONY with seven blessings, since she is attached to the Congregation of Yisrael, WHICH CONTAINS THE SEVEN SFIROT – CHESED, GVURAH, TIFERET, NETZACH, HOD, YESOD AND MALCHUT. The priest has to arrange the things of the Matron, WHICH IS MALCHUT, and see to all her needs. Therefore, only the priest is suitable for this and no other.

62. וְאִי תֵּימָא דְּאִיהוּ עָבֵיד דִּינָא, לָאו הָכִי, אֶלָּא לְאַסְגָּאָה שְׁלָמָא

בְּעָלְמָא קָא אִשְׁתָּדַּל בְּהַאי, וּלְאַסְגָּאָה חֶסֶד. דְּאִי הַהִיא אִתְּתָא
אִשְׁתְּכַחַת זַכָּאָה, כַּהֲנָא אַסְגֵּי שְׁלָמָא בְּהוּ, וְלֹא עוֹד אֶלָּא דְּמִתְעַבְּרָא
בִּבְרָא דְּכַר, וְאִתְעֲבֵיד שְׁלָמָא עַל יְדֵיהּ. וְאִי לָא אִשְׁתְּכַחַת זַכָּאָה, אִיהוּ
לָא עָבֵיד דִּינָא, אֶלָּא הַהוּא שְׁמָא קַדִּישָׁא דְּאִיהִי קָא מְשַׁקְּרַת בֵּיהּ,
הוּא עָבֵיד דִּינָא, וְהוּא בָּדִיק לָהּ.

62. You might say that THE PRIEST is carrying judgment, WHICH IS
CONTRADICTORY TO HIS GRADE OF CHESED. HE RESPONDS: It is not so.
It is only to try to increase peace in the world and enhance Chesed that he
strives to do so. If the wife is cleared of the accusation, the priest increases
peace between them, THE WIFE AND HER HUSBAND, and not only that but
she will also conceive a son. Through him, peace is achieved. If she is not
cleared in her trial, it is not THE PRIEST who passes judgment, but rather the
Holy Name, to which she was false, passes judgment on her and tests her.

63. תָּא חֲזֵי, כַּהֲנָא לָא עָיֵיל גַּרְמֵיהּ לְהַאי, אֶלָּא כַּד הִיא יָהֲבַת גַּרְמָהּ
קַמֵּיהּ, לְזַכָּאָה זִמְנָא, וּתְרֵין שָׁאִיל לָהּ, כֵּיוָן דְּאִיהִי בַּעְיָא לְאִשְׁתַּכְּחָא
זַכָּאָה, כְּדֵין כַּהֲנָא עָבֵיד עוֹבָדָא, בְּגִין לְאַסְגָּאָה שְׁלָמָא.

63. Come and see, The priest did not get involved here, except at the time
she presented herself to him, TO GIVE HER TO DRINK, SO she would be
acquitted. He questions her once and again and if she wishes to clarify her
innocence, only then does THE PRIEST take action to promote peace
BETWEEN HER AND HER HUSBAND.

64. כַּהֲנָא כָּתִיב שְׁמָא קַדִּישָׁא חַד זִמְנָא בְּאֹרַח מֵישָׁר, לְבָתַר כָּתַב לֵיהּ
לְמִפְרַע אַתְוָון סְרִיטִין בִּטְהִירִין, דִּינָא בְּדִינָא, רַחֲמֵי בְּרַחֲמֵי, רַחֲמֵי
בְּדִינָא, וְדִינָא בְּרַחֲמֵי. אִשְׁתְּכַחַת זַכָּאָה, אַתְוָון רַחֲמֵי אִשְׁתְּכָחוּ, וְדִינִין
סַלְּקִין. לָא אִשְׁתְּכַחַת כִּדְקָא יָאוּת, רַחֲמֵי סַלְּקִין, וְדִינִין אִשְׁתְּאָרוּ,
וּכְדֵין דִּינָא אִתְעֲבֵיד.

64. The priest writes the Holy Name once, the regular way, YUD HEI VAV
HEI, and then backwards HEI VAV HEI YUD. The letters, WHICH WERE

-88-

BLOTTED IN THE WATER, were sketched by the uppermost lights, IN FOUR MANNERS: judgment with judgment, mercy with mercy, mercy with judgment, judgment with mercy. If she is cleared, the letters of mercy remain and THE LETTERS of judgment are gone. If she is guilty, the letters of mercy are gone and the letters of judgment remain. And then her sentence is carried out.

65. ר׳ אֶלְעָזָר פָּתַח וְאָמַר, וַיָבֹאוּ מָרָתָה וְלֹא יָכְלוּ לִשְׁתּוֹת מַיִם מִמָּרָה כִּי מָרִים הֵם, הָא אוּקְמוּהָ. אָמַר, תַּוְוהְנָא אֵיךְ בְּנֵי עָלְמָא לָא מִסְתַּכְּלִין וְלָא מִשְׁתַּדְּלִין בְּמִלִּין דְּאוֹרַיְיתָא, הָכָא אִית לְאִסְתַּכְּלָא, אֲמַאי כְּתִיב הָכָא שָׁם שָׂם לוֹ חֹק וּמִשְׁפָּט וְשָׁם נִסָּהוּ.

65. Rabbi Elazar opened the discussion, saying, "And when they came to Marah, they could not drink the waters of Marah, for they were bitter (Heb. *marim*)" (Shemot 15:23). This has been explained, but I wonder why people do not observe and study Torah. This verse requires observation, as it is written here: "There he made for them a statute and an ordinance, and there he tested them" (Ibid. 25).

66. אֲבָל וַדַּאי רָזָא דְּמִלָּה, דְּהָכָא עַל מַיָּא הֲוָה, בְּגִין דְּמִצְרָאֵי הֲווֹ אָמְרֵי, דִּבְנַיְיהוּ דְּיִשְׂרָאֵל הֲווֹ מִנַּיְיהוּ, וַהֲווֹ כַּמָּה בְּיִשְׂרָאֵל דְּחַשְׁדִין לְאִנְתְּתַיְיהוּ בְּדָא. עַד דְּקוּדְשָׁא בְּרִיךְ הוּא מָטָא לוֹן לְהַאי אֲתָר, וּבָעֵי לְמִבְדַּק לוֹן, מַה כְּתִיב וַיָבֹאוּ מָרָתָה וְגוֹ׳. וַיִצְעַק אֶל יְיָ׳ וְגוֹ׳.

66. HE RESPONDS: The hidden meaning is that here, THE MIRACLE occurred on water, since the Egyptians used to claim that they fathered the babies of Yisrael, and there were indeed many men of Yisrael who suspected their wives of that until the Holy One, blessed be He, brought them to this place, MARAH, to test them. It is written here: "And when they came to Marah... And he cried to Hashem..."

67. אָמַר קוּדְשָׁא בְּרִיךְ הוּא לְמֹשֶׁה, מֹשֶׁה מַה אַתְּ בָּעֵי, הָא כַּמָּה חֲבִילִין קַיְימִין גַּבַּיְיכוּ הָכָא, וַאֲנָא בָּעֵינָא לְמִבְדַּק הָכָא נְשִׁיהוֹן דְּיִשְׂרָאֵל, כְּתוֹב שְׁמָא קַדִּישָׁא, וּרְמֵי לְמַיָּא, וְיִבָּדְקוּן כֻּלְּהוֹן, נְשֵׁי

וְגוּבְרִין, וְלָא יִשְׁתְּאַר לַעַז עַל בָּנַי. וְעַד דְּיִבָּדְקוּן כֻּלְּהוּ הָכָא, לָא אַשְׁרֵי שְׁמִי עֲלַיְיהוּ, מִיַּד וַיּוֹרֵהוּ יְיָ' עֵץ וַיַּשְׁלֵךְ אֶל הַמַּיִם, דָּא שְׁמָא קַדִּישָׁא, הַהוּא דַּהֲוָה כּוֹתֵב כַּהֲנָא לְמִבְדַּק נְשֵׁיהוֹן דְּיִשְׂרָאֵל, כְּדֵין, שָׁם שָׂם לוֹ חֹק וּמִשְׁפָּט וְשָׁם נִסָּהוּ.

67. The Holy One, blessed be He, said to Moses, 'What do you want? There are many battalions OF PROSECUTORS wishing to denounce you here and I wish to examine the wives of Yisrael here. Write the Holy Name and throw it into the water and let all OF YISRAEL be tested, women and men, so there should not remain any slander about my children. As long as they are not all checked, I will not let my Name dwell on them'. Immediately, "Hashem showed him a tree, which when he had cast it into the waters" (Ibid.). THE TREE refers to the Holy Name that the priest used to write in order to test the wives of Yisrael. Therefore, "there he made for them a statute and an ordinance, and there he tested them."

68. וְאִי תֵּימָא נְשֵׁיהוֹן דְּיִשְׂרָאֵל יָאוֹת, אִינּוּן אֲמַאי. אֶלָּא אוֹף אִינּוּן בַּעְיָין, דְּלָא אִסְתַּאֲבוּ בִּנְשֵׁיהוֹן דְּמִצְרָאֵי. וּנְשֵׁיהוֹן דְּיִשְׂרָאֵל לָא אִסְתַּאֲבוּ בְּמִצְרָאֵי, כָּל אִינּוּן שְׁנִין דַּהֲווֹ בֵּינַיְיהוּ, וְכֻלְּהוּ נָפְקוּ גּוּבְרִין וְנוּקְבִין זַכָּאִין, וְאִשְׁתְּכָחוּ זַרְעָא דְּיִשְׂרָאֵל קַדִּישִׁין, זַכָּאִין, כְּדֵין קוּדְשָׁא בְּרִיךְ הוּא אַשְׁרֵי שְׁמֵיהּ בֵּינַיְיהוּ, וְעַל דָּא עַל מַיָּא וַדַּאי, שָׁם שָׂם לוֹ חֹק וּמִשְׁפָּט וְשָׁם נִסָּהוּ אוֹף הָכָא, בְּמַיָּא בָּדִיק כַּהֲנָא לְאִתְּתָא, וּבִשְׁמָא קַדִּישָׁא.

68. You may say that it was appropriate for the wives of Yisrael TO HAVE BEEN TESTED BECAUSE OF THE SUSPICION OF THE EGYPTIANS, but why WERE THE MEN OF YISRAEL TESTED? HE RESPONDS: It is because they too had to be tested to see if they were defiled with the wives of the Egyptians. The women of Yisrael were not defiled with the Egyptians all the years that they resided among them. Both men and women came out innocent. Therefore, the seed of Yisrael was pronounced holy and worthy. Only then did the name of the Holy One, blessed be He, dwell among them. Hence, surely it is through waters, "there he made for them a statute and an ordinance, and there He tested them." Here too, the priest tested the woman with water and the Holy Name.

69. וּמִן הֶעָפָר אֲשֶׁר יִהְיֶה בְּקַרְקַע הַמִּשְׁכָּן. מַאן הֶעָפָר. הָא תָּנֵינָן,
כְּתִיב הַכֹּל הָיָה מִן הֶעָפָר וְהַכֹּל שָׁב אֶל הֶעָפָר הַכֹּל הָיָה מִן הֶעָפָר,
אֲפִילוּ גַּלְגַּל חַמָּה, כָּ"שׁ בַּ"נ דְּאִשְׁתְּכָחוּ מִנֵּיהּ.

69. "And of the dust that is on the floor of the tabernacle" (Bemidbar 5:17).
HE ASKS: What is the role of that dust? HE RESPONDS: We learned that it
is written: "All are of the dust and all return to dust" (Kohelet 3:20).
Everything originates in dust, even the sphere of the sun, and certainly man
that originates in it.

70. א"ר יוֹסֵי, אִלּוּ כְּתִיב וּמִן הֶעָפָר וְלָא יַתִּיר, הֲוֵינָא אָמַר הָכִי. אֲבָל
כֵּיוָן דִּכְתִיב וּמִן הֶעָפָר אֲשֶׁר יִהְיֶה בְּקַרְקַע הַמִּשְׁכָּן, מַשְׁמַע דְּאַחֲרָא
הוּא. אֶלָּא כְּתִיב יִתֵּן כֶּעָפָר חַרְבּוֹ, אִלֵּין מָארֵיהוֹן דְּקַיְסְטִין
וּבְלִיסְטְרָאִין, מָארֵי דְּדִינָא קַשְׁיָא. מַשְׁמַע דִּכְתִיב בְּקַרְקַע הַמִּשְׁכָּן,
דַּאֲחִידָן לְתַתָּא. וְעַל דָּא יִקַּח הַכֹּהֵן וְנָתַן אֶל הַמָּיִם.

70. Rabbi Yosi said: If it would have merely said, "And of the dust" and
nothing else, I would have agreed THAT THE EXPLANATION IS FROM THE
DUST, WHICH IS MALCHUT. But since it says, "And of the dust that is on
the floor of the tabernacle," it indicates that it is another kind OF DUST. It
must refer to what is meant by: "His sword makes them as dust (also: 'He
shall make his sword as dust')" (Yeshayah 41:2). These are the purveyors of
weaponry and stone projectiles, the advocates of harsh judgment. That is the
indication of: "on the floor of the tabernacle," MEANING THE ENDING OF
MALCHUT CALLED TABERNACLE. THAT REFERS TO THE LITIGANTS
attached at the bottom TO ITS ENDING PART, MALCHUT OF MALCHUT,
ACCORDING TO THE HIDDEN MEANING OF: "SIN CROUCHES AT THE
DOOR" (BERESHEET 4:7). Therefore "shall the priest take, and put it into
the water" (Bemidbar 5:17), BECAUSE HE SHOULD THROW FROM THE
DUST INTO THE WATERS.

71. מֵי הַמָּרִים הַמְאָרְרִים, אִלֵּין מֵי יַמָּא, דְּאִינּוּן מְרִירִין. מַאי הוּא. דָּא
שְׁמָא קַדִּישָׁא, בְּשַׁעֲתָא דְּאִשְׁתְּכַח בְּדִינָא, כְּדֵין אִקְרוּן מֵי הַמָּרִים
הַמְאָרְרִים. וּבְג"כ מַיָּא דְּיַמָּא דִּלְתַתָּא כֻּלְּהוֹן מְרִירִין.

71. "The bitter water that causes the curse" (Ibid. 18) refers to the sea water that was bitter. What is it, THE SEA WATER? It is the Holy Name, NAMELY MALCHUT THAT IS THE SEA when it is in a state of Judgment. At that time, it is called "the bitter water that causes the curse." Therefore, the water of the lower sea, THAT IS THE BRANCH TO MALCHUT, is bitter, all of it.

‎72. ת״ח, הַאי יַמָּא קַדִּישָׁא כַּמָּה נַהֲרִין מְתִיקִין עָאלִין בְּגַוֵּוהּ, וּבְגִין דְּאִיהִי דִּינָא דְּעָלְמָא, מֵימוֹי מְרִירָן, בְּגִין דְּאָחִיד בָּהּ מוֹתָא לְכָל בְּנֵי עָלְמָא. וְאע״ג דְּאִינּוּן מְרִירָן, כַּד מִתְפַּשְּׁטִין מְתִיקִין אִינּוּן. לְזִמְנִין מַיִין דְּיַמָּא מְרִירָן. לְזִמְנִין יַמָּא דְּבָלַע לְכָל שְׁאַר מֵימִין, וְאִקְרֵי יַמָּא דְקַפָּא, וּבָלַע כָּל אִינּוּן אַחֲרָנִין, וְשָׁאִיב לוֹן בְּגַוֵּויהּ, וְלָא נִיגְרִין לְבַר. לְזִמְנִין שָׁארָן מַיָּיא, וְנַגְדִין מֵהַהוּא יַמָּא, כָּל מַה דְּנָגִיד לְתַתָּאֵי. וּבְכַמָּה גְּוָונִין קַיְימָא הַאי יַמָּא. הַמַּיִם הַמְאָרֲרִים, בְּשַׁעֲתָא דְּאָתֵי חִיוְיָא וְאָטִיל זוּהֲמָא, כְּדֵין הַמַּיִם הַמְאָרֲרִים וְעַל דָּא כַּהֲנָא עָבֵיד עוֹבָדָא לְתַתָּא, וְאוֹמֵי אוֹמָאָה, וְאִתְעֲבֵיד דִּינָא.

72. Come and see this holy sea, WHICH IS MALCHUT. How many sweet rivers, WHICH ARE THE SFIROT OF ZEIR ANPIN, enter it. Because it is the Judgment of the world, its waters are bitter, since death of the whole world is involved with it, AS IT IS WRITTEN: "HER FEET GO DOWN TO DEATH" (MISHLEI 5:5). Although they are bitter, they are sweet when they spread out. Sometimes the waters of the sea are bitter, THAT IS, ON THE SIDE OF DEATH ATTACHED TO MALCHUT. Sometimes, THE WATERS OF the sea envelop all the other waters. It is called the frozen sea and it swallows all these other WATERS and sucks them in, so that they do not leak out. Sometimes, water breaks open and from that sea everything flows to the lower beings. That sea takes many shapes. When the snake soils it with filth, THEY ARE CALLED the waters that cause the curse. Therefore, the priest acted below by intoning the vow of incantation, and Judgment was accomplished.

‎73. ת״ח, אִי אִתְּתָא אִשְׁתְּכַחַת זַכְיָיתָא, אֵלֵּין מַיִין עָאלִין בְּגַוֵּוהּ, וְאִתְהַפְּכָן מְתִיקָן, וְנַקָּאן גַּרְמָהּ, וְקַיְימִין בְּגַוֵּוהּ, עַד דְּמִתְעַבְּרָא. כֵּיוָן דְּמִתְעַבְּרָא, הֲווֹ מְשַׁפְּרֵי בִּשְׁפִירֵי לְעוּבָּרָא דִּמְעָהָא, וְנָפִיק בְּרָא שַׁפִּירָא,

נְקִי בְּלָא מוּמָא דְּעָלְמָא. וְאִי לָאו, אִינּוּן מַיָּין עַיְילִין בְּגַוָּוהּ, וְאָרְחָא רֵיחָא דְּזוּהֲמָא, וְאִינּוּן מַיָּין מִתְהַפְּכִין לְחִוְיָא בִּמְעָהָא, בְּמַה דְּקִלְקְלָה אִתְפְּסַת, וְאִתְחֲזֵי קְלָנָא לְכֹלָּא, וְהָא אוּקְמוּהָ חַבְרַיָּיא.

73. Come and see, If the wife was acquitted, these waters entered her and turned out to be sweet. They cleansed her and stayed there until she conceived. As soon as she became pregnant, the waters would beautify the embryo within her, which would result in a handsome and clean child, thoroughly unblemished. If she was not CLEARED, then these waters entered her and she got the offensive odor OF THE SNAKE, and these waters would turn into a snake within her. The impairment that she caused affected her. THAT IS: "HER BELLY SHALL SWELL, AND HER THIGH SHALL FALL AWAY" (BEMIDBAR 5:21). And her shame is apparent to all, as our friends have explained.

74. ת"ח, כָּל אִינּוּן נְשֵׁי עָלְמָא, בְּאַתְרַיְיהוּ קַיְימֵי וְאִתְדָּנוּ, וְע"ד הַהוּא אֲתָר מַמָּשׁ דְּאִינְהוּ קַיְימֵי, בֵּיהּ אִתְדָּנוּ. זַכָּאָה חוּלָקֵהוֹן דְּיִשְׂרָאֵל, דְּקוּדְשָׁא בְּרִיךְ הוּא אִתְרָעֵי בְּהוּ, וּבָעֵי לְדַכְּאָה לְהוּ.

74. Come and see, All the wives in the world are then judged wherever they are, FROM THESE WATERS THAT THE SOTA DRANK. Therefore, from that exact spot from where they stem, MALCHUT OF WHICH THE WOMEN ARE BRANCHES, they are judged BECAUSE MALCHUT JUDGES THEM. Praised is the lot of Yisrael whom the Holy One, blessed be He, favored and wished to purify.

75. ר' חִזְקִיָּה פָּתַח, אֶשְׁתְּךָ כְּגֶפֶן פּוֹרִיָּה וְגוֹ', מַה גֶּפֶן לָא מְקַבֵּל עֲלֵיהּ אֶלָּא מִדִּידֵיהּ, כַּךְ אִתְּתָא דְּיִשְׂרָאֵל, קַיְימָא בְּהַאי גַּוְונָא, דְּלָא מְקַבְּלָא עֲלָהּ אֶלָּא הַהוּא בַּר זוּגָהּ. כְּשַׁפְנִינָא דָּא, דְּלָא מְקַבְּלָא אֶלָּא הַהוּא בַּר זוּגָהּ. וְע"ד כְּגֶפֶן פּוֹרִיָּה בְּיַרְכְּתֵי בֵיתֶךָ. מַהוּ פּוֹרִיָּה. כד"א פּוֹרָה רָאשׁ. פּוֹרִיָּה: פּוֹרַחַת, דְּאַפִּיקַת עֲנָפִים לְכָל סִטְרָא. וְאָן. בְּיַרְכְּתֵי בֵיתֶךָ, וְלָאו לְבַר בְּשׁוּקָא, בְּגִין דְּלָא תֵּיתֵי לְשַׁקְרָא בִּבְרִית עִלָּאָה.

75. Rabbi Chizkiyah opened the discussion with the verse: "Your wife shall be like a fruitful vine..." (Tehilim 128:3). Just as a grapevine does not crossbreed with other kinds but just of its own sort, a wife in Yisrael stands in the same ranks in that she will not accept anyone except her mate, like the dove that accepts only her mate. Therefore, "like a fruitful vine in the recesses of your house." What meaning is indicated by "fruitful (Heb. *poriyah*)"? It refers to that which is said: "that bears (Heb. *poreh*) gall" (Devarim 29:17). Fruitful means that it blooms and sprouts branches in every direction. And where does it take place? "In the recesses of your house" and not out in the marketplace, because she will not be false to the supernal covenant.

76. וּשְׁלמֹה אָמַר, הָעוֹזֶבֶת אַלוּף נְעוּרֶיהָ וְאֶת בְּרִית אֱלֹהֶיהָ שָׁכֵחָה. מַאן בְּרִית אֱלֹהֶיהָ. הַהוּא אֲתָר דְּאִקְרֵי בְּרִית. וְהִיא אִתְקַשְׁרָא בֵּיהּ, בְּגִין כָּךְ בְּיַרְכְּתֵי בֵיתֶךָ.

76. And Solomon said: "Who forsakes the friend of her youth, and forgets the covenant of her Elohim" (Mishlei 2:17). What is "the covenant of her Elohim"? It refers to the place of the covenant, THAT IS YESOD, where she was attached. Therefore, it is written: "In the recesses (thighs) of your house."

77. א"ר חִזְקִיָּה, תּוּנְבָּא לֵיתֵי עַל הַהוּא בַּר נָשׁ, דְּשָׁבַק לְאִנְתְּתֵיהּ דְּתִתְחֲזֵי מִשַּׂעֲרָא דְּרֵישָׁהּ לְבַר. וְדָא הוּא חַד מֵאִנּוּן צְנִיעוּתָא דְּבֵיתָא. וְאִתְּתָא דְּאַפִּיקַת מִשַּׂעֲרָא דְּרֵישָׁהּ לְבַר, לְאִתְתַּקְּנָא בֵּיהּ, גָּרִים מִסְכְּנוּתָא לְבֵיתָא. וְגָרִים לִבְנָהָא דְּלָא יִתְחַשְׁבוּן בְּדָרָא. וְגָרִים מִלָּה אַחֲרָא דְּשַׁרְיָא בְּבֵיתָא. מַאן גָּרִים דָּא. הַהוּא שַׂעֲרָא דְּאִתְחֲזֵי מֵרֵישָׁהּ לְבַר. וּמָה בְּבֵיתָא הַאי, כ"ש בְּשׁוּקָא, וכ"ש חֲצִיפוּתָא אַחֲרָא. ובג"כ אֶשְׁתְּךָ כְּגֶפֶן פּוֹרִיָּה בְּיַרְכְּתֵי בֵיתֶךָ.

77. Rabbi Chizkiyah said a shudder shall envelop any man that allows his wife to let the hair of her head be seen, which is one of the household modesties. A wife who exposes her hair outside to show her beauty causes destitution to visit upon the house. She causes her sons to be undistinguished in that generation and she incurs sickness upon the house, THAT IS LEPROSY. What is the root of all these? It is the hairs of her head that were seen outside. This is impudence if this happens within the house, and certainly even more so if it is in a public place. Therefore, it is written: "YOUR WIFE SHALL BE like a fruitful vine in the recesses of your house."

78. אָמַר ר' יְהוּדָה, שַׂעֲרָא דְּרֵישָׁא דְּאִתְּתָא דְּאִתְגַּלְיָיא, גָּרִים שַׂעֲרָא אַחֲרָא לְאִתְגַּלְיָיא, וּלְאַפְגְּמָא לָהּ. בְּגִין כָּךְ, בַּעְיָא אִתְּתָא דַּאֲפִילוּ טְסִירֵי דְּבֵיתָא, לָא יֶחֱמוּן שַׂעֲרָא חַד מֵרֵישָׁא, כ"ש לְבַר.

78. Rabbi Yehuda said: The hairs on the head of a woman that were exposed cause another kind of hair to be exposed, MEANING THE POWERS OF THE OTHER SIDE THAT PERMEATE THE HAIR and impair her. Therefore, a woman should be careful that none of her hair is visible even to the beams of her house, and all the more so outside.

79. ת"ח, כְּמָה בִּדְכוּרָא שַׂעֲרָא הוּא חוּמְרָא דְּכֹלָּא, הָכִי נָמֵי לְנוּקְבָּא. פּוּק חָמֵי, כַּמָּה פְּגִימוּ גָּרִים הַהוּא שַׂעֲרָא דְּאִתְּתָא. גָּרִים לְעֵילָּא, גָּרִים לְתַתָּא, גָּרִים לְבַעְלָהּ דְּאִתְלַטְיָיא, גָּרִים מִסְכְּנוּתָא, גָּרִים מִלָּה אַחֲרָא בְּבֵיתָא, גָּרִים דְּיִסְתְּלַק חֲשִׁיבוּתָא מִבְּנָהָא. רַחֲמָנָא לִישֵׁזְבוּן, מֵחֲצִיפוּ דִּלְהוֹן.

79. Come and see: Just like by a man, the hair causes the harshest things, BECAUSE THEY ARE JUDGMENTS, so it is by a woman. Look how many misfortunes the hair of a woman causes, they incur above and they incur below. They cause her husband to be cursed and they incur poverty. They cause another thing in the house, MEANING LEPROSY. They prevent her sons from achieving positions of importance. Let the Merciful One save us from their impudence.

80. וע"ד, בַּעְיָא אִתְּתָא לְאִתְכַּסְיָיא, בְּזִיוְוָתֵי דְּבֵיתָא. וְאִי עַבְדַת כֵּן מַה כְּתִיב, בָּנֶיךָ כִּשְׁתִלֵי זֵיתִים. מַהוּ כִּשְׁתִלֵי זֵיתִים. מַה זַיִת דָּא, בֵּין בְּסִתְוָוא, בֵּין בְּקַיְיטָא, לָא אִתְאֲבִידוּ טַרְפּוֹי, וְתָדִיר אִשְׁתְּכַח בֵּיהּ חֲשִׁיבוּת יַתִּיר עַל שְׁאַר אִילָנִין. כָּךְ בְּנָהָא יִסְתַּלְּקוּן בַּחֲשִׁיבוּ עַל שְׁאַר בְּנֵי עָלְמָא. וְלֹא עוֹד אֶלָּא דְּבַעְלָהּ מִתְבָּרֵךְ בְּכֹלָּא, בְּבִרְכָאן דִּלְעֵילָּא,

בְּבִרְכָאן דִּלְתַתָּא, בְּעוּתְרָא, בִּבְנִין, בִּבְנֵי בְּנִין. הה"ד הִנֵּה כִּי כֵן יְבוֹרַךְ
גָּבֶר יְרֵא יְיָ'. וּכְתִיב יְבָרֶכְךָ ה' מִצִּיּוֹן וּרְאֵה בְּטוּב יְרוּשָׁלַיִם כֹּל יְמֵי חַיֶּיךָ
וּרְאֵה בָנִים לְבָנֶיךָ שָׁלוֹם עַל יִשְׂרָאֵל.

80. Therefore, a woman should be covered even in the inside corners of her home. If she adheres to this, it is written: "Your children like olive plants" (Tehilim 128:3). What does it mean "like olive plants"? Just as an olive tree does not lose its leaf cover in winter or summer and always has more value than the rest of the trees, so should her sons elevate in respect over the rest of the people. Her husband will also be blessed in everything, with the blessings above and with the blessings below, with wealth, children and grandchildren. This is what is meant by: "Behold, thus shall the man be blessed who fears Hashem. Hashem shall bless you out of Zion: and you shall see the good of Jerusalem all the days of your life. And you shall see your children's children, and peace upon Yisrael" (Ibid. 4-5).

A Synopsis
Elijah continues the discussion about the laws of sota and about the jealousy of the evil inclination He says that when Yisrael desecrates the Torah God sends them into exile, through which experience they become cleansed and purified and refined. At the last redemption Yisrael will be tested like they were at the waters of Marah. Elijah says that in the future the children of Yisrael will leave the exile with mercy because they will taste from the Tree of Life that is the book of the Zohar.

רעיא מהימנא

81. אֵלִיָּהוּ, קוּם אַפְתַּח עַמִּי בְּפִקּוּדִין, דְּאַנְתְּ הוּא עוֹזֵר לִי, בְּכָל סִטְרָא.
דְּהָא עֲלָךְ אִתְּמַר בְּקַדְמֵיתָא, פִּנְחָס בֶּן אֶלְעָזָר בֶּן אַהֲרֹן הַכֹּהֵן. וּבֶן
אַהֲרֹן וַדַּאי אִיהוּ אָח דִּילִי, אָח לְצָרָה יִוָּלֵד.

Ra'aya Meheimna (the Faithful Shepherd)

81. Elijah, stand up and start talking with me about the precepts, since you are my help in everything. About you, it was first mentioned, "Pinchas, the son of Elazar, the son of Aaron the priest" (Bemidbar 25:11), AND PINCHAS

IS ELIJAH. "The son of Aaron" assuredly is his brother, as "a brother is born for adversity" (Mishlei 17:17).

82. פָּתַח וְאָמַר, פִּקּוּדָא לָדוּן בְּדִינֵי סוֹטָה, הה״ד וְעָבַר עָלָיו רוּחַ קִנְאָה וְקִנֵּא וְגוֹ'. וַדַּאי רוּחַ טוּמְאָה מִתְּרֵין סִטְרִין אִשְׁתְּכַח, חַד בְּשִׁקְרָא, וְחַד בִּקְשׁוֹט. בְּגִין דָּא, בְּרוּחַ שִׁקְרָא וְקִנֵּא אֶת אִשְׁתּוֹ, וְהִיא לֹא נִטְמָאָה. וְתִנְיָינָא, וְעָבַר עָלָיו וְגוֹ', וְקִנֵּא אֶת אִשְׁתּוֹ וְהִיא נִטְמָאָה.

82. He opened the discussion saying, It is a commandment to discuss the laws of a Sota, as written: "And the spirit of jealousy came upon him, and he be jealous..." (Bemidbar 5:14). Surely, a spirit of uncleanness exists on both sides, one false and one true. Therefore, in the spirit of falseness, "And he be jealous of his wife, and she be not defiled" (Ibid.) and the second: "And the spirit of jealousy came upon him...and she be defiled" (Ibid.).

83. וְכִי אִית קוּשְׁטָא בְּרוּחַ מְסָאֲבָא. אֶלָּא בְּבַר נָשׁ מִסִּטְרָא דְּאִילָנָא דְּטוֹב וָרָע, תַּמָּן יֵצֶר הָרָע, נָחָשׁ. בְּזִמְנָא דְּאִית לב״נ אִתְּתָא שַׁפִּירָא, בְּכָל עוֹבָדִין טָבִין, דְּאִתְּמַר בָּהּ אֵשֶׁת חַיִל עֲטֶרֶת בַּעְלָהּ. יֵצֶר הָרָע אִית לֵיהּ קִנְאָה, כְּגַוְונָא דְּאַשְׁכַּחְנָא דְּקַנֵּי אָדָם עַל אִנְתְּתֵיהּ, עַד דְּפַתֵּי לָהּ, וְגָרַם לָהּ מִיתָה. וּלְזִמְנִין שַׁלִּיט עָלָהּ בְּחוֹבִין, וּמְסָאֵב לָהּ, וְהָא אִתְעֲבֵידַת נְבֵלָה.

83. HE ASKS: Could there possibly be any truth in a spirit of uncleanness? HE RESPONDS: It is because in a man, who stems from the tree of good and evil, there exists the Evil Inclination, the snake. When a man has a beautiful wife, WHICH IS THE SOUL, in all her good deeds, it is said, "A virtuous woman is a crown to her husband" (Mishlei 12:4). The Evil Inclination is jealous, as we have found that THE SNAKE was jealous of Adam because of his wife, so it seduced her and caused her to die. Sometimes it dominates her through sins and defiles her, and she becomes a carcass.

84. וְיֵצֶר הָרָע, מִסִּטְרָא דִּימִינָא, דִּילֵיהּ, דַּרְגָּא דְּיִשְׁמָעֵאל, אִתְקְרֵי נָחָשׁ. וּמִסִּטְרָא דִּשְׂמָאלָא, דַּרְגֵּיהּ דְּעֵשָׂו סָמָאֵ״ל, אִתְקְרֵי כֶּלֶב, מְמָנָא דְּגֵיהִנָּם דְּצוֹוַח הַב הַב, הֲדָא הוּא דִכְתִיב לַעֲלוּקָה שְׁתֵּי בָנוֹת הַב הַב,

וּבִרְעוּתָא דִּילֵיהּ לְמֵיכַל נִשְׁמָתָא מְסָאֲבָא, בְּנוּרָא דִּילֵיהּ, גֵּיהִנָּם. וְעֲבַר
עֲלָיו רוּחַ קִנְאָה וְקִנֵּא אֶת אִשְׁתּוֹ בְּקִשּׁוּט, וְהִיא נִטְמָאָה.

84. The Evil Inclination on its right side, that is the rank of Ishmael, is
called the snake. From the left side, which is the rank of Esau, who is
Samael, it is called a dog that is appointed over Gehenom - that barks - hav
hav (arf arf), as written: "The leech has two daughters, crying, Give, give
(Heb. *hav, hav*)" (Mishlei 30:15). It wishes to burn the soul that was made
unclean with its fire in Gehenom. That is what is meant by: "And the spirit
of jealousy came upon him, and he be jealous of his wife" truthfully, "and
she be defiled." SOMETIMES, HE FALSELY ACCUSES HER BECAUSE SHE
WAS NOT DEFILED.

85. וּבְגִינָהּ אִתְּמַר, וּבַת אִישׁ כֹּהֵן, דָּא מִיכָאֵל, כִּי תֵחֵל לִזְנוֹת אֶת
אָבִיהָ הִיא מְחַלֶּלֶת בָּאֵשׁ תִּשָּׂרֵף. וְתַמָּן אִתּוֹקְדַת הַהִיא זוּהֲמָא,
וְאִתְלַבְּנַת אִיהִי מִנֵּיהּ, כַּכֶּסֶף דְּאִתְלַבַּן בְּנוּרָא, וְהַהִיא עוֹפֶרֶת דְּזוּהֲמָא
אִתּוֹקַד, וְאִתְעֲבֵיד עָפָר, וְאִתְאֲבִיד.

85. And for her, it was said, "And the daughter of any priest," who is
Michael, WHICH DENOTES CHESED, AND THE SOUL IS HIS DAUGHTER.
When she "profanes herself by playing the harlot, she profanes her father:
she shall be burnt with fire" (Vayikra 21:9). There the filth is destroyed and
she purifies herself of it, just as silver that purifies in fire - and lead, which
is the refuse, is burnt, becomes dust and is lost.

86. כְּגַוְונָא דָּא בְּיִשְׂרָאֵל, כַּד אִינּוּן מְחַלְּלִין אוֹרַיְיתָא, קוּדְשָׁא בְּרִיךְ
הוּא יֵיעוּל לוֹן בְּגָלוּתָא דִּבְנֵי עֵשָׂו וּבְנֵי יִשְׁמָעֵאל, תְּחוֹת שִׁעְבּוּדָא
דִּלְהוֹן, דְּדַרְגַּיְיהוּ כֶּלֶ"ב וְנָחָ"שׁ, וְאִתְדָּנוּ תַּמָּן, וּבְהוֹן יִתְבָּרְרוּ וְיִתְלַבְּנוּ
וְיִצּוֹרְפוּ כִּצְרוֹף הַכֶּסֶף וְכִבְחוֹן הַזָּהָב, הה"ד וּצְרַפְתִּים כִּצְרֹף אֶת הַכֶּסֶף
וּבְחַנְתִּים כִּבְחֹן אֶת הַזָּהָב, עַד דְּיִתְקַיַּים בְּהוּ, אִם יִהְיוּ חֲטָאֵיכֶם כַּשָּׁנִים
כַּשֶּׁלֶג יַלְבִּינוּ.

86. It is the same with Yisrael. When they desecrate the Torah, the Holy
One, blessed be He, sends them into exile among the children of Esau and

the children of Ishmael under their servitude, whose rank is of the dog and the snake, and they are punished there. Through them, they become cleared and purified and refined like the refinement of silver and the trying of gold. This is what is said: "And will refine them as silver is refined, and will try them as gold is tried" (Zecharyah 13:9) until this would hold true about them: "Though your sins be like scarlet, they shall be as white as snow" (Yeshayah 1:18).

87. וְאִילָנָא דְּטוֹב וָרַע, בְּגִינֵיהּ אִתְּמַר, וַיּוֹרֵהוּ יְיָ' עֵץ וַיַּשְׁלֵךְ אֶל הַמַּיִם וַיִּמְתְּקוּ הַמָּיִם וְגוֹ'. בְּגִין דַּהֲווֹ יִשְׂרָאֵל עִם עֵרֶב רַב, כֻּלְּהוּ הֲווֹ אִילָנָא דְּטוֹב וָרַע, וְעַל דָּא, חֶצְיוֹ מָתוֹק מִסִּטְרָא דִּימִינָא. וְחֶצְיוֹ מַר, מִסִּטְרָא דִּשְׂמָאלָא. וּבְזִמְנָא דְּעֵרֶב רַב הֲווֹ מַחֲטִיאִין לוֹן לְיִשְׂרָאֵל, הֲוֵי כְּאִילוּ הֲווֹ כֻּלְּהוּ מִסִּטְרָא דְּרַע. וּמַיָּא אִתְהַדְרוּ כֻּלְּהוּ מְרִירִין, כְּהַהוּא עֵץ מַר בְּמַיָּא, הה"ד וַיָּבֹאוּ מָרָתָה וְלֹא יָכְלוּ לִשְׁתּוֹת מַיִם מִמָּרָה כִּי מָרִים הֵם.

87. It is written of the Tree of Good and Evil: "And Hashem showed him a tree, which when he had cast it into the waters, the waters were made sweet..." (Shemot 15:25). Since Yisrael were INTERMINGLED with the mixed multitudes, they were all of the Tree of Good and Evil. Therefore, it is half sweet from the right side and half bitter from the left side. When the mixed multitude caused Yisrael to sin, it was as if all were on the Evil Side. CONSEQUENTLY, the waters returned to their bitter state like the tree that was THROWN into the water. This is what is meant by: "And when they came to Marah, they could not drink of the waters of Marah, for they were bitter" (Shemot 15:23).

88. וְהַאי עֵץ מַר, אִיהוּ כְּגַוְונָא דְּנִסְיוֹנָא דְּסוֹטָה, אִי סָטַת תְּחוֹת בַּעְלָהּ, אִינוּן מַיִין דְּאַשְׁקְיָין לָהּ אִתְהַדְרוּ מְרִירִין, וּבְהוֹן וְצָבְתָה בִּטְנָהּ וְנָפְלָה יְרֵיכָהּ, וְאִי לָא סָטַת מַה כְּתִיב, וְנִקְּתָה וְנִזְרְעָה זָרַע, וְאוֹלִידַת בַּר. אוֹף הָכָא וַיִּמְתְּקוּ הַמָּיִם.

88. The bitter tree THAT HE THREW INTO THE WATER was similar to the test of a wife suspected of adultery. If she indeed deviated from her husband, the waters which she had to drink turned bitter, and because of them, "her belly shall swell, and her thigh shall fall away" (Bemidbar 5:27). If she did not deviate, it is written: "Then she shall be free, and shall conceive seed" (Ibid.

28) and give birth to a son. Here too, "the waters were made sweet."

89. כְּגַוְונָא דָא, יִתְעֲבֵיד לְנַסְּאָה לוֹן לְיִשְׂרָאֵל בְּפוּרְקָנָא בַּתְרַיְיתָא, הה"ד יִתְבָּרְרוּ וְיִתְלַבְּנוּ וְיִצָּרְפוּ רַבִּים, דְּאִינּוּן מִסִּטְרָא דְּטוֹב, וְקַיְימִין בְּנִסְיוֹנָא. וְהִרְשִׁיעוּ רְשָׁעִים אִינּוּן מִסִּטְרָא דְּרַע, וְיִתְקַיֵּים בְּהוֹן וְאֶל אַדְמַת יִשְׂרָאֵל לֹא יָבֹאוּ וְקָטִיל לוֹן.

89. In the same manner, Yisrael will be tested in the last redemption. This is what is meant by: "Many shall purify themselves, and make themselves white" (Daniel 12:10), who are from the good side and who pass the test. "But the wicked shall do wickedly" (Ibid.), because they are from the Evil Side and by them, it will be fulfilled: "Neither shall they enter into the land of Yisrael" (Yechezkel 13:9). And he kills them.

90. וְהַמַּשְׂכִּילִים יָבִינוּ, מִסִּטְרָא דְּבִינָה, דְּאִיהוּ אִילָנָא דְּחַיֵּי, בְּגִינַיְיהוּ אִתְּמַר, וְהַמַּשְׂכִּילִים יַזְהִירוּ כְּזוֹהַר הָרָקִיעַ בְּהַאי חִבּוּרָא דִּילָךְ דְּאִיהוּ סֵפֶר הַזֹּהַר, מִן זוֹהֲרָא דְּאִימָא עִלָּאָה תְּשׁוּבָה. בְּאִלֵּין לָא צָרִיךְ נִסְיוֹן, וּבְגִין דַּעֲתִידִין יִשְׂרָאֵל לְמִטְעַם מֵאִילָנָא דְּחַיֵּי, דְּאִיהוּ הַאי סֵפֶר הַזֹּהַר, יִפְּקוּן בֵּיהּ מִן גָּלוּתָא בְּרַחֲמֵי. וְיִתְקַיֵּים בְּהוֹן, יְיָ' בָּדָד יַנְחֶנּוּ וְאֵין עִמּוֹ אֵל נֵכָר.

90. "But the wise shall understand" (Daniel 12:10), since they are from the side of Binah, which is the Tree of Life. For them, it was said, "And they who are wise shall shine like the brightness of the firmament" (Ibid. 3) with your composition, OF RABBI SHIMON BAR YOCHAI, which is the book of the Zohar, from the light of the supernal Ima CALLED repentance. They do not require a test and, because Yisrael in the future will taste from the Tree of Life, which is this book of the Zohar, they will leave the exile with mercy. It will hold true about them that "so Hashem did lead him, and there was no strange El with him" (Devarim 32:12).

6. The Tree of Life and the Tree of Knowledge of Good and Evil

A Synopsis

Elijah talks about the time to come when the children of Yisrael
will get all their sustenance solely from the Tree of Life, and when
the Tree of Knowledge of Good and Evil will no longer apply to
them at all. He says that the ignorant will have to learn what is
prohibited and permissible, and that they will discern no difference
between the exile and the days of Messiah since they will not taste
from the Tree of Life. At the last redemption God will differentiate
between the ignorant and the Torah scholars.

91. וְאִילָנָא דְּטוֹב וָרָע, דְּאִיהוּ אִיסוּר וְהֶיתֵּר טוּמְאָה וְטָהֲרָה, לָא
שַׁלְטָא עַל יִשְׂרָאֵל יַתִּיר, דְּהָא פַּרְנָסָה דִּילָן לָא לִיהֱוֵי, אֶלָּא מִסִּטְרָא
דְּאִילָנָא דְּחַיֵּי, דְּלֵית תַּמָּן לָא קַשְׁיָא מִסִּטְרָא דְּרַע, וְלָא מַחֲלוֹקֶת מֵרוּחַ
הַטּוּמְאָה, דִּכְתִיב וְאֶת רוּחַ הַטּוּמְאָה אַעֲבִיר מִן הָאָרֶץ.

91. The Tree of Knowledge of Good and Evil, prohibition or permission,
purity or impurity, will no longer apply to Yisrael, since our sustenance will
be solely from the side of the Tree of Life, where there are no contradictions
stemming from the Evil Side, nor any strife nor difference stemming from
the unclean spirit, as written: "And also I will cause...the unclean spirit to
pass out of the land" (Zecharyah 13:2).

92. דְּלָא יִתְפַּרְנְסוּן ת"ח מֵעַמֵּי הָאָרֶץ, אֶלָּא מִסִּטְרָא דְּטוֹב, דְּאָכְלִין
טָהֲרָה כָּשֵׁר הֶיתֵּר, וְלָא מֵעֵרֶב רַב, דְּאָכְלִין טוּמְאָה פָּסוּל אִיסוּר,
דְּאִינּוּן מְסָאֲבִין, דִּמְסָאֲבִין גַּרְמַיְיהוּ בנשג"ז. בְּגִין דְּאִינּוּן בְּנוֹי דְּלִילִית,
דְּאִיהִי, נשג"ז חַזְרִין לְשָׁרָשֵׁיהוּ. וְעָלַיְיהוּ אִתְּמַר, כִּי מִשֹּׁרֶשׁ נָחָשׁ יֵצֵא
צֶפַע.

92. The Torah scholars will not need to be sustained by the ignorant, just
from the good side by eating of the clean, kosher and permissible. They will
not need to get it from the mixed multitudes, who eat the unclean, unfit and
prohibited, and who are themselves defiled by defiling themselves with a
woman during menstruation, a maidservant, a gentile woman or a prostitute.
They are the children of Lilit, who is a menstruate woman, a maidservant, a
gentile woman and a prostitute, and they return to their roots. About them, it

is written: "For out of the serpent's root shall come forth a viper" (Yeshayah 14:29).

93. וּבְזִמְנָא דְּאִילָנָא דְּטוֹב וָרָע שַׁלְטָא, דְּאִיהוּ חוּלִין דְּטַהֲרָה, וְחוּלִין דְּטוּמְאָה. אִינּוּן חֲכָמִים דְּדָמְיָין לְשַׁבָּתוֹת וי"ט, לֵית לוֹן אֶלָּא מַה דְּיָהֲבִין לוֹן אִינּוּן חוּלִין. כְּגַוְונָא דְּיוֹם הַשַׁבָּת, דְּלֵית לֵיהּ, אֶלָּא מַה דִּמְתַקְּנִין לֵיהּ בְּיוֹמֵי דְחוֹל.

93. During the period that the Tree of Good and Evil dominates, that pertains to purity and impurity of worldly things, these sages – who are similar to the Shabbatot and holidays in that they have only what is given to them by the worldly PEOPLE – are like the Shabbat that has nothing except what was prepared for it during the weekdays.

94. וּבְזִמְנָא דְּשַׁלְטָא אִילָנָא דְּחַיֵּי, אִתְכַּפְיָיא אִילָנָא דְּטוֹב וָרָע, וְלָא יְהֵא לע"ה, אֶלָּא מַה דְּיָהֲבִין לוֹן תַּלְמִידֵי חֲכָמִים, וְאִתְכַּפְיָין תְּחוֹתַיְיהוּ, וּכְאִלּוּ לָא הֲווֹ בְּעָלְמָא.

94. During the time that the Tree of Life dominates, the Tree of Good and Evil is subdued. The common people will not have anything except for what the Torah scholars will hand out to them and they, COMMON PEOPLE, will become subdued under them as if they didn't exist.

95. וְהָכִי אִיסוּר וְהֶיתֵּר, טוּמְאָה וְטַהֲרָה, לָא אִתְעַבָּר מע"ה. דְּמִסְטְרַיְיהוּ לֵית בֵּין גָּלוּתָא לִימוֹת הַמָּשִׁיחַ אֶלָּא שִׁעְבּוּד מַלְכִיּוֹת בִּלְבַד דְּאִינּוּן לָא טַעֲמִין מֵאִילָנָא דְּחַיֵּי, וְצָרִיךְ לוֹן מַתְנִיתִין בְּאִיסּוּר וְהֶיתֵּר טוּמְאָה וְטַהֲרָה. אֶלָּא יְהוֹן מְבוּזִין קֳדָם ת"ח, כְּגַוְונָא דַּחֲשׁוֹכָא קַמֵּי נְהוֹרָא, דְּעֶרֶב רַב אִינּוּן ע"ה אִינּוּן חֲשׁוּכִין. וְלָא אִתְקְרִיאוּ יִשְׂרָאֵל, אֶלָּא עַבְדִּין זְבִינִין לְיִשְׂרָאֵל, בְּגִין דְּאִינּוּן כִּבְעִירִין. וְהָא אוּקְמוּהָ.

95. Thus, prohibition and permission, purity and impurity will not pass away from the common people. From their aspect, there will be no apparent

difference between the exile and the days of Messiah, except for the delivery from servitude of Yisrael to the empires alone because they will not taste from the Tree of Life WHEN IT WILL BE REVEALED IN THE DAYS OF MESSIAH, and they will need to learn MISHNAH, about what is prohibited and permissible, what is unclean and clean. They will be shamed in front of a Torah scholar like darkness before light, since the mixed multitudes are like beasts, who are ignorant, who are darkness and were not even called Yisrael, just slaves sold to Yisrael, as was already explained.

96. וְיִשְׂרָאֵל אִתְקְרִיאוּ אָדָם, וּמְנָלַן דְּאִית בְּהוֹן בְּעִירָא וְאָדָם. הה"ד וְאַתֵּן צֹאנִי צֹאן מַרְעִיתִי אָדָם אַתֶּם. וְאַתֵּן צֹאנִי צֹאן מַרְעִיתִי, אִינּוּן ע"ה, טָבִין, מִסִּטְרָא דְּטוֹב. אָדָם אַתֶּם, ת"ח.

96. Yisrael are called men. How do we know that YISRAEL are composed of both beast and man? It is written: "But you, my flock, the flock of my pasture, are men" (Yechezkel 34:31). "But you, my flock, the flock of my pasture": These are those who are ignorant of Torah but are good and stem from the good side. "Are men" refers to the Torah scholars.

97. וּבִקְרָא דָּא נָמֵי רָמִיז לֵיהּ, לוּ עַמִּי שׁוֹמֵעַ לִי יִשְׂרָאֵל וְגוֹ'. בָּתַר דְּאָמַר עַמִּי, אֲמַאי קָאָמַר יִשְׂרָאֵל. אֶלָּא עַמִּי: ע"ה. יִשְׂרָאֵל: ת"ח. וּבְגִינַיְיהוּ אִתְּמַר וּבְנֵי יִשְׂרָאֵל יוֹצְאִים בְּיָד רָמָה.

97. It is also alluded to in this verse, AS IT IS WRITTEN: "Oh that my people would hearken to me, Yisrael..." (Tehilim 81:14). After mentioning "my people," why say "Yisrael"? Because "my people" refers to common people and Yisrael alludes to the Torah scholars. For them, it is mentioned: "And the children of Yisrael went out with a high hand" (Shemot 14:8).

98. כְּגַוְונָא דְּפָלִיג לוֹן קוּדְשָׁא בְּרִיךְ הוּא בְּטוּרָא דְּסִינַי, הָכִי פָּלִיג לוֹן בְּפוּרְקָנָא בַּתְרַיְיתָא, דְּיִשְׂרָאֵל דְּאִתְּמַר בְּהוֹן, וַחֲמוּשִׁים עָלוּ בְּנֵי יִשְׂרָאֵל מֵאֶרֶץ מִצְרָיִם. מִסִּטְרָא דְּאִילָנָא דְּחַיֵּי, דְּאִינּוּן נ' שְׁנִין דְּיוֹבְלָא. אִתְּמַר בְּהוֹן, הֵמָּה יַעֲלוּ בָהָר. וּבְהוֹן וַיִּסַּע מַלְאַךְ הָאֱלֹהִים הַהֹלֵךְ לִפְנֵי מַחֲנֵה יִשְׂרָאֵל. וְלוֹן אִתְּמַר וָאֶשָּׂא אֶתְכֶם עַל כַּנְפֵי נְשָׁרִים, דְּאִינּוּן עֲנָנֵי כָבוֹד.

וְאָבִיא אֶתְכֶם אֵלָי. וּבְנֵי יִשְׂרָאֵל יוֹצְאִים בְּיָד רָמָה, הָכִי יָפִיק לת"ח, בְּכָל הַאי יְקָר.

98. As the Holy One, blessed be He, divided them at Mount Sinai, so He will divide them at the last redemption, because it says about Yisrael: "And the children of Yisrael went up armed (Heb. *chamushim*) out of the land of Egypt" (Shemot 13:18). *CHAMUSHIM* MEANING from the side of the Tree of Life, THAT IS ZEIR ANPIN, which are the fifty (Heb. *chamishim*) years of Jubilee, WHICH IS BINAH, SINCE ZEIR ANPIN RECEIVES THEM FROM BINAH. About them, it says, "They shall come up to the mountain" (Shemot 19:13) and: "And the angel of Elohim, who went before the camp of Yisrael, removed" (Shemot 14:19). And to them, it says: "I bore you on eagles' wings" (Shemot 19:4), which refers to the clouds of glory, "and brought you to myself" (Ibid.) AND ALSO "and the children of Yisrael went out with a high hand." So he will bring out the Torah scholars with all that honor.

99. וּכְגַוְונָא דְּאִתְּמַר בע"ה מִסִּטְרָא דְּטוֹב, וַיִּתְיַצְּבוּ בְּתַחְתִּית הָהָר. הָכִי יְהוֹן בְּמַפְּקָנָא בַּתְרַיְיתָא, תְּחוֹת ת"ח, כְּעַבְדָּא דְּאָזִיל לְרַגְלַיָּא דְּסוּסְיָא דְּמָארֵיה. וּכְגַוְונָא דְּאָמַר לוֹן בְּתַחְתִּית הָהָר, אִם תְּקַבְּלוּ תּוֹרָתִי מוּטָב, וְאִם לָאו שָׁם תְּהֵא קְבוּרַתְכֶם. הָכִי יֵימָא בְּמַפְּקָנוּ פוּרְקָנָא בַּתְרַיְיתָא, אִם תְּקַבְּלוּן עֲלֵיכוֹן ת"ח בְּמַפְּקָנוּ דְּגָלוּתָא, כְּאָדָם דְּרָכִיב עַל סוּסְיָא, וְעַבְדָּא דִּמְשַׁמֵּשׁ לֵיהּ מוּטָב. וְאִם לָאו תַּמָּן תְּהֵא קְבוּרַתְכֶם, בְּגָלוּתָא.

99. It is mentioned by those who are ignorant of Torah yet are of the good side: "And they stood at the foot of the mountain" (Ibid. 17). So will they be at the last redemption, under Torah scholars, like a slave that follows along the horse's footsteps of his lord. Just as it was called out to them at the foot of the mountain: 'If you accept the Torah, well, but if not, there will be your burial place', so he will tell them at the last redemption, 'If you will accept upon yourselves a Torah scholar during the redemption from the exile like a horse rider with his attendant servant, it is best, but if not, there in exile shall be your burial.'

7. The mixed multitudes

A Synopsis

We learn from Elijah that no new converts will be accepted during the days of Messiah. Moses asks Elijah to do his utmost not to delay the redemption, since Moses is waiting in the prison of the grave due to the sins of his people. He says that the Torah scholars are suffering and the mixed multitudes are prospering, and adjures Elijah to tell these things to God.

100. וְעֶרֶב רַב כְּגַוְונָא דְּאִתְּמַר בְּהוֹן, וַיַּרְא הָעָם וַיָּנֻעוּ וַיַּעַמְדוּ מֵרָחוֹק. הָכִי יְהוֹן רְחִיקִין מִן פּוּרְקָנָא, וְיֶחֱמוּן לת״ח, וּלְעַמָּא קַדִּישָׁא בְּכָל הַאי יְקָר, וְאִינּוּן רְחִיקִין מִינַּיְיהוּ. וְאִי בָּעוּ לְאִתְחַבְּרָא בַּהֲדַיְיהוּ מַה כְּתִיב בְּהוּ, לֹא תִגַּע בּוֹ יָד כִּי סָקוֹל יִסָּקֵל אוֹ יָרֹה יִיָּרֶה. בְּהַהוּא זִמְנָא יִתְקַיַּים בְּהוּ בְּיִשְׂרָאֵל, יְיָ' בָּדָד יַנְחֶנּוּ וְאֵין עִמּוֹ אֵל נֵכָר, וְהָא אוּקְמוּהָ אֵין מְקַבְּלִין גֵּרִים לִימוֹת הַמָּשִׁיחַ. וּרְשָׁעִים בַּחֹשֶׁךְ יִדָּמּוּ, אִינּוּן עֵרֶב רַב. ובג״ד אָמַר נְבִיאָה עֲלַיְיהוּ, וְאֶל אַדְמַת יִשְׂרָאֵל לֹא יָבֹאוּ.

100. The mixed multitudes are as it is written of them: "And when the people saw it, they were shaken, and they stood afar off" (Shemot 20:18). They will be far from the redemption and they will watch the Torah scholars and the holy nation in all this glory, but they will be far from them. If they wish to join with them, it is written: "No hand shall touch him, but he shall surely be stoned, or shot through" (Shemot 19:13). During that period, it will come true for Yisrael: "So Hashem did lead him, and there was no strange El with him" (Devarim 32:12). It was already explained that no new converts will be accepted during the days of Messiah. "And the wicked shall be silent in darkness" (II Shmuel 2:9): these are the mixed multitudes. Therefore, the prophet proclaimed about them: "Neither shall they enter into the land of Yisrael" (Yechezkel 13:9).

101. אָמַר אֵלִיָּהוּ, רַעֲיָא מְהֵימְנָא, הָא שַׁעֲתָא אִיהִי לְסַלְּקָא לְעֵילָּא, בְּאוּמָאָה אִימָּא אַנְתְּ, דְּהָא בְּגִינָךְ אֲנָא בָּעֵי לְסַלְּקָא. דְּיָהִיב לִי קוּדְשָׁא בְּרִיךְ הוּא רְשׁוּ, לְאִתְגַּלְיָיא לָךְ בְּבֵית אֲסוּרִים דִּילָךְ, בְּקִבוּרָה דִּילָךְ, וּלְמֶעְבַּד עִמָּךְ טִיבוּ, דְּאַנְתְּ מְחוֹלָל בְּחוֹבִין דְּעַמָּא. הה״ד וְהוּא מְחוֹלָל מִפְּשָׁעֵינוּ.

101. Elijah said TO THE FAITHFUL SHEPHERD: Faithful Shepherd, it is time to rise up, AND BRING THE FULL REDEMPTION. You intone a solemn oath ON ME, MEANING MAKE ME SWEAR THAT I SHOULD HASTEN THE REDEMPTION. For your sake, I wish to rise, since the Holy One, blessed be He, gave me permission to reveal myself to you in your prison, in your place of burial, and do you good because you are desecrated through the sins of the people. LIKE IN A PRISON, HE IS AMONG THEM. This is the meaning of: "But he was wounded because of our transgressions" (Yeshayah 53:5).

102. א״ל רַעְיָא מְהֵימְנָא, בְּאוֹמָאָה עֲלָךְ בִּשְׁמָא דִּידוֹ״ד, לָא תְּאַחַר בְּכָל יְכוֹלְתָּךְ, דְּהָא אֲנָא בְּצַעֲרָא סַגִּי. וַיִּפֶן כֹּה וָכֹה וַיַּרְא כִּי אֵין אִישׁ, עוֹזֵר לִי, לְאַפְּקָא לִי מֵהַאי צַעֲרָא, בְּהַאי קְבוּרָה דְּאִתְּמַר עָלַי, וַיִּתֵּן אֶת הָרְשָׁעִים קִבְרוֹ, וְלָא אִשְׁתְּמוֹדְעָן בִּי, וַאֲנִי חָשִׁיב בְּעֵינַיְיהוּ בֵּין עֵרֶב רַב רְשִׁיעַיָּיא, כְּכֶלֶב מֵת דְּסָרַח בֵּינַיְיהוּ, דְּחָכְמַת סוֹפְרִים תִּסְרַח בֵּינַיְיהוּ, בְּכָל קַרְתָּא וְקַרְתָּא, וּבְכָל אֲתַר דְּיִשְׂרָאֵל מְפוּזָרִין בֵּינַיְיהוּ בֵּין מַלְכְּוָון. וְאִתְהַדְּרוּ אִינּוּן עֵרֶב רַב רַעְיָין עַל יִשְׂרָאֵל, עָאנָא דְּקוּדְשָׁא בְּרִיךְ הוּא, דְּאִתְּמַר בְּהוּ וְאַתֵּן צֹאנִי צֹאן מַרְעִיתִי אָדָם אַתֶּם, וְלֵית לוֹן יְכוֹלֶת לְמֶעְבַּד טִיבוּ עִם ת״ח.

102. The Faithful Shepherd said to him: I intone on you solemnly the name of Yud Hei Vav Hei, that you will do your utmost not to delay THE REDEMPTION, since I am EXISTING in great distress. FOR ABOUT ME, IT IS WRITTEN: "And he looked this way and that, and when he saw that there was no man" (Shemot 2:12) to help me, to take me out of this distress, from this grave, since it says about me, "For they made his grave among the wicked" (Yeshayah 53:9). They do not recognize me but regard me as one of the evil mixed multitudes, like a dead dog that has caused a stench among them. The wisdom of the scribes shall become vapid (stinking) among them in each and every city, and in all places where Yisrael are scattered throughout their kingdoms. The mixed multitudes become the shepherds of Yisrael, who are the flock of the Holy One, blessed be He, as it is said about them: "But you, my flock, the flock of my pasture, are men" (Yechezkel 34:31). And they have no ability to do good with the Torah scholars.

103. וְאַנְשֵׁי חַיִל וְיִרְאֵי חֵטְא מְסוֹבְבִים מֵעִיר לָעִיר וְלֹא יְחוֹנָנוּ, וּמַחֲרִימִין עֵרֶב רַב בֵּינַיְיהוּ. וְלֹא יַהֲבִין לוֹן בְּאַתְרִין סַגִּיאִין אֶלָּא דָּבָר קָצוּב, דְּלָא יְהֵא תְּקוּמָה לְנְפִילוּ דִּלְהוֹן, וַאֲפִילוּ חַיֵּי שָׁעָה. וְכָל חֲכָמִים וְאַנְשֵׁי חַיִל וְיִרְאֵי חֵטְא בְּצַעֲרָא בְּדוֹחֲקָא בִּיגוֹנָא, חֲשִׁיבִין כְּכַלְבִּים. בָּנִים הַמְסוּלָאִים בַּפָּז אֵיכָה נֶחְשְׁבוּ לְנִבְלֵי חֶרֶשׂ בְּרֹאשׁ כָּל חוּצוֹת. דְּלָא אַשְׁכָּחוּ אַכְסַנְיָא בֵּינַיְיהוּ.

103. Able and sin-fearing men go about from one city to another and find no grace, and the mixed multitudes excommunicate them from among them. In many places, they are only given a meager sum so they are unable to rise from their fall, even temporarily. All the sages, able men and those who fear sin LIVE in distress and gloom and are treated like dogs. "The precious sons of Zion, comparable to fine gold, how are they esteemed as earthen pitchers" (Eichah 4:2), in the streets, unable to find accommodation among them.

104. וְאִינוּן עֵרֶב רַב, אִינוּן עֲתִירִין, בְּשַׁלְוָה, בְּחֶדְוָוא, בְּלָא צַעֲרָא, בְּלָא יְגוֹנָא כְּלָל, גַּזְלָנִין מָארֵי שׁוֹחַד, דְּאִינוּן דַּיָּינִין רֵישֵׁי עַמָּא. כִּי מָלְאָה הָאָרֶץ חָמָס מִפְּנֵיהֶם, עֲלַיְיהוּ אִתְּמַר הָיוּ צָרֶיהָ לְרֹאשׁ. בְּאוֹמָאָה עֲלָךְ זִמְנָא תִּנְיָינָא, בְּחַי יְיָ' צְבָאוֹת אֱלֹהֵי יִשְׂרָאֵל יוֹשֵׁב הַכְּרוּבִים, דְּכָל אַלֵּין מִלִּין לָא יִפְּלוּן מִפּוּמָךְ, בְּכָל יְכָלְתָּךְ לְמַלְּלָא בְּהוֹן קַמֵּי קוּדְשָׁא בְּרִיךְ הוּא, וּלְאַחֲזָאָה דּוֹחֲקָא דִּלְהוֹן.

ע"כ רעיא מהימנא

104. Meanwhile the mixed multitudes are wealthy, live in peace, in happiness, without pain, without any sorrow – robbers, bribe takers, who are the judges, the elite of their people, "for the earth is filled with violence through them" (Beresheet 6:13). About them, it is written: "Her adversaries have become the chief" (Eichah 1:5). THE FAITHFUL SHEPHERD SAID TO ELIJAH: With a solemn oath on you, the second time, upon the life or name of Hashem Tzva'ot, the Elohim of Yisrael, who is enthroned upon the Cherubs, that all these words will not fail from your mouth; with all your might, tell them before the Holy One, blessed be He, to show their distress.

End of Ra'aya Meheimna (the Faithful Shepherd)

8. "Why, when I came, there was no man"

A Synopsis
Rabbi Elazar talks about the quorum of ten people required in the synagogue.

105. אִישׁ כִּי יַפְלִיא לִנְדּוֹר וְגוֹ'. רַבִּי אֶלְעָזָר פָּתַח, מַדוּעַ בָּאתִי וְאֵין אִישׁ וְגוֹ'. מַדוּעַ בָּאתִי. כַּמָּה חֲבִיבִין אִינּוּן יִשְׂרָאֵל קַמֵּי קוּדְשָׁא בְּרִיךְ הוּא, דִּבְכָל אֲתַר דְּאִינּוּן שַׁרְיָין, קוּדְשָׁא בְּרִיךְ הוּא אִשְׁתְּכַח בֵּינַיְיהוּ, בְּגִין דְּלָא אַעֲדֵי רְחִימוּתָא דִּילֵיהּ מִנְּהוֹן, מַה כְּתִיב, וְעָשׂוּ לִי מִקְדָּשׁ וְשָׁכַנְתִּי בְּתוֹכָם. וְעָשׂוּ לִי מִקְדָּשׁ סְתָם, דְּכָל בֵּי כְּנִישְׁתָּא דְּעָלְמָא מִקְדָּשׁ אִקְרֵי. וְהָא אוּקְמוּהָ. וּשְׁכִינְתָּא אַקְדִּימַת לְבֵי כְּנִישְׁתָּא.

105. "When either man...shall pronounce a special vow..." (Bemidbar 6:2): Rabbi Elazar opened the discussion saying, "Why, when I came, there was no man..." (Yeshayah 50:2). "Why, when I came": How beloved are Yisrael before the Holy One, blessed be He! Wherever they reside, the Holy One, blessed be He, is among them, since he does not remove his love from them. It is written: "And let them make me a sanctuary: that I may dwell among them" (Shemot 25:8). "And let them make me a sanctuary" IS a generic SANCTUARY, since every synagogue in the world is called a sanctuary, as has been explained. "THAT I MAY DWELL (HEB. *SHACHANTI*) AMONG THEM," since the Shechinah comes early to the synagogue.

106. זַכָּאָה הַהוּא ב"נ דְּאִשְׁתְּכַח מֵאִינּוּן עֲשָׂרָה קַדְמָאָה בְּבֵי כְּנִישְׁתָּא, בְּגִין דְּבְהוּ אִשְׁתְּלִים מַה דְּאִשְׁתְּלִים, וְאִינּוּן מִתְקַדְּשֵׁי בְּקַדְמֵיתָא בִּשְׁכִינְתָּא. וְהָא אִתְּמַר. וְהָא בַּעְיָא דְּיִשְׁתְּכְחוּ עֲשָׂרָה בְּזִמְנָא חֲדָא בְּבֵי כְּנִישְׁתָּא. וְלָא יֵיתוּ פְּסָקֵי פְּסָקֵי, דְּלָא יִתְעַכַּב שְׁלִימוּ דְּשַׁיְיפִין, דְּהָא בַּר נָשׁ בְּזִמְנָא חַד עָבֵד לֵיהּ קוּדְשָׁא בְּרִיךְ הוּא, וְאַתְקִין לֵיהּ כַּחֲדָא כָּל שַׁיְיפֵי, הה"ד הוּא עָשְׂךָ וַיְכוֹנְנֶךָ.

106. Praised is the person who is among the first ten in the synagogue, because they complete the required fulfillment; THAT IS - THE CONGREGATION WHOSE QUORUM IS NOT LESS THAN TEN. They are the first to be sanctified

by the Shechinah, as we have already learned. It is necessary that all ten be at the synagogue at the same time in unison and not come little by little, in order not to delay the perfection of the limbs, SINCE ALL TEN ARE LIKE PARTS OF ONE BODY IN WHICH THE SHECHINAH DWELLS since man was formed in one instant by the Holy One, blessed be He, and He had all his limbs and organs prepared together. This is what is meant by: "Has he not made you, and established you?" (Devarim 32:6).

107. ת״ח, כֵּיוָן דב״נ אִשְׁתְּלִימוּ שַׁיְיפוֹי, בְּהַהוּא זִמְנָא אַתַּקָּן לְכָל שַׁיְיפָא וְשַׁיְיפָא כַּדְקָא יָאוֹת. כְּגַוְונָא דָא, כֵּיוָן דִשְׁכִינְתָּא אַקְדִּימַת לְבֵי כְּנִישְׁתָּא, בַּעְיָין עַשְׂרָה דְיִשְׁתַּכְּחוּן תַּמָּן כַּחֲדָא, וְיִשְׁתְּלִים מַה דְיִשְׁתְּלִים. וּלְבָתַר דְאִתַּקָּן כֹּלָּא. וּבַמֶּה הִיא תִּיקוּנָא דְכֹלָּא. כד״א בְּרָב עָם הַדְרַת מֶלֶךְ, וע״ד עַמָּא דְאַתְיָין לְבָתַר כֵּן, כֻּלְּהוּ תִּיקוּנָא דְגוּפָא.

107. Come and see, as soon as the limbs of man were perfected, concurrently every INDIVIDUAL part was constructed appropriately. Similarly, since the Shechinah hastens to the synagogue, there is a requirement to have a complete quorum of ten together. Then, whatever is necessary is completed, SINCE IT IS NOT CONSIDERED A CONGREGATION WITH LESS THAN TEN, WHO CORRESPOND TO THE TEN SFIROT OF MALCHUT. AS LONG AS THERE ARE NOT TEN TOGETHER, NONE IS COMPLETED. After that everything is established, THAT IS THE ESTABLISHING OF THE WHOLE CONGREGATION. What is it that establishes everything? It is as it is written: "In the multitude of people is the king's glory" (Mishlei 14:28). Therefore, the people who follow later, AFTER THE FIRST TEN, all still establish the body even more. THAT IS TO SAY, THE ESTABLISHING OF THE CONGREGATION, SINCE AN INCREASED NUMBER OF PEOPLE INCREASES THE GLORY OF THE KING.

108. וְכַד אָתַת אַקְדִּימַת שְׁכִינְתָּא, וּבְנֵי נָשָׁא לָא אַתְיָין כַּחֲדָא כַּדְקָא יָאוֹת. קוּדְשָׁא בְּרִיךְ הוּא קָארֵי מַדּוּעַ בָּאתִי וְאֵין אִישׁ. מַאי וְאֵין אִישׁ. דְלָא מִתַתְקְנֵי שַׁיְיפֵי, וְלָא אִשְׁתְּלִים גוּפָא. דְּכַד גוּפָא לָא אִשְׁתְּלִים, אֵין אִישׁ. ובג״כ, וְאֵין אִישׁ דַּיְיקָא. ות״ח, בְּשַׁעֲתָא דְגוּפָא אִשְׁתְּלִים לְתַתָּא, קְדוּשָׁה עִלָּאָה אַתְיָא וְעָאל בְּהַאי גוּפָא, וְאִתְעֲבֵיד תַּתָּאָה,

כְּגַוְונָא דִּלְעֵילָא מַמָּשׁ. וּכְדֵין, כֹּלָּא בַּעְיָין דְּלָא יִפְתְּחוּן פּוּמָא בְּמִילֵי דְעָלְמָא. בְּגִין דְּהָא קַיְימֵי יִשְׂרָאֵל בִּשְׁלִימוּ עִלָּאָה, וּמִתְקַדְּשֵׁי בִּקְדוּשָׁה עִלָּאָה, זַכָּאָה חוּלָקֵהוֹן.

108. When the Shechinah preceded and came, and the people have not yet formed a quorum OF TEN, as required, the Holy One, blessed be He, calls out, "Why, when I came, there was no man." What is: "There was no man"? It is that the parts were not completed and the body was not whole, TO BE CALLED A CONGREGATION. If the body is not whole, there is no man, MEANING EVEN THE INDIVIDUAL LIMBS THAT ALREADY CAME ARE NOT COMPLETED. Therefore, "there was no man" is precisely that. Come and see: When the body is completed below, WHEN THERE ARE TEN MEN TOGETHER, the supreme holiness comes and enters that body, and the lower resumes the likeness of the upper TEN SFIROT. All must refrain from worldly talk, since Yisrael are now in a state of lofty unison and are sanctified with supreme sanctity. Blessed is their lot.

109. אִישׁ כִּי יַפְלִיא וְגוֹ'. מַאי כִּי יַפְלִיא. דְּאִתְפְּרַשׁ מִשְּׁאַר בְּנֵי עָלְמָא, לְאִתְקַדְּשָׁא כְּגַוְונָא דִּלְעֵילָא, וּלְאִשְׁתַּכְּחָא שְׁלִים. בְּשַׁעְתָּא דְּבַר נָשׁ אָתֵי לְאִתְדַּכְּאָה, מְדַכִּין לֵיהּ. בַּר נָשׁ דְּבָעֵי לְאִתְקַדְּשָׁא, מְקַדְּשִׁין לֵיהּ. וּפַרְסֵי עֲלֵיהּ קְדוּשָׁה דִּלְעֵילָא, קְדוּשָׁה דְּאִתְקְדַּשׁ בָּהּ קוּדְשָׁא בְּרִיךְ הוּא.

109. "When either man...shall pronounce..." HE ASKS: What is "shall pronounce"? HE RESPONDS: IT MEANS he is separated from the rest of the people to become holy, in the likeness of above, and be whole. If a person comes to be cleansed, he is cleansed, and a person who wishes to be sanctified is sanctified. They envelop him in supernal holiness, the same holiness with which the Holy One, blessed be He, was sanctified.

9. Death and the punishment by beating in the grave

A Synopsis

Rabbi Aba tells us how a person assumes he will live forever, until he gets ill and undergoes judgment, at which time all his actions stand as evidence for or against him. We hear what happens as soon as he is in the grave and we hear about all the trials he has to face. Rabbi Aba says that King David said one should bless God now while he is still alive and before it is too late.

110. ר' אַבָּא פָּתַח, לְדָוִד בָּרְכִי נַפְשִׁי אֶת יְיָ' וְכָל קְרָבַי אֶת שֵׁם קָדְשׁוֹ. כַּמָּה אִית לֵיהּ לְבַר נָשׁ לְאִסְתַּכְּלָא וּלְמִנְדַּע בְּפוּלְחָנָא דְּמָארֵיהּ, דְּהָא בְּכָל יוֹמָא וְיוֹמָא כָּרוֹזָא קָארֵי וְאָמַר, עַד מָתַי פְּתָאיִם תְּאֵהֲבוּ פֶתִי וְגוֹ'. שׁוּבוּ בָּנִים שׁוֹבָבִים אֶרְפָּא מְשׁוּבוֹתֵיכֶם. וְלֵית מַאן דְּיַרְכִּין אוּדְנֵיהּ, אוֹרַיְיתָא קָא מַכְרְזָא קַמַּיְיהוּ, וְלֵית מַאן דְּיַשְׁגַּח.

110. Rabbi Aba opened the discussion saying, "Of David, Bless Hashem, my soul: and all that is within me bless his Holy Name" (Tehilim 103:1). How much a person should observe and know how to serve his Master, since every single day the proclamation goes forth and says, "How long, you simple ones, will you love being simple?" (Mishlei 1:22). "Return, faithless children, and I will heal your relapses" (Yirmeyah 3:22), but none pays attention. The Torah proclaims before them, yet nobody is attentive.

111. תָּא חֲזֵי, בַּר נָשׁ אָזִיל בְּהַאי עָלְמָא, וְהוּא חָשִׁיב דְּדִילֵיהּ הוּא תָּדִיר וְיִשְׁתָּאַר בְּגַוֵּיהּ לְדָרֵי דָּרִין, עַד דְּאִיהוּ אָזִיל בְּעָלְמָא, יָהֲבִין לֵיהּ בְּקוּלָרָא, עַד דְּאִיהוּ יָתִיב דַּיְינִין לֵיהּ בְּקִינְפוֹן עִם שְׁאָר בְּנֵי דִּינָא. אִי אִשְׁתְּכַח לֵיהּ סַנֵּיגוֹרָא, הָא אִשְׁתְּזִיב מִן דִּינָא. הה"ד אִם יֵשׁ עָלָיו מַלְאָךְ מֵלִיץ אֶחָד מִנִּי אָלֶף לְהַגִּיד לְאָדָם יָשְׁרוֹ וַיְחֻנֶּנּוּ וַיֹּאמֶר וְגוֹ'. מַאן הוּא סַנֵּיגוֹרָא. אִלֵּין עוֹבָדִין דְּכַשְׁרָן, דְּקַיְימֵי עֲלֵיהּ דב"נ בְּשַׁעְתָּא דְּאִצְטְרִיךְ לֵיהּ.

111. Come and see, a person walks about in this world and thinks that it belongs to him forever, and he will remain here for generations to come.

While he walks about, he is placed in binding chains, MEANING THAT HE GETS ILL AND IS TIED TO HIS BED. While he remains in this state, he is judged together with other litigants. If he gets a good advocate, he is saved from punishment, as it is written: "If there be an angel over him, an interpreter, one among a thousand, to declare to man what is right: then he is gracious to him, and says..." (Iyov 33:23). Who is that good advocate? These are the good deeds that stand by for a man in time of need.

112. וְאִי לָא יִשְׁתְּכַח עָלֵיהּ סַנֵּיגוֹרָא, הָא אִתְחַיָּיב מִן דִּינָא לְאִסְתַּלְּקָא מִן עָלְמָא. בְּהַהִיא שַׁעֲתָא כַּד אִיהוּ שָׁכִיב בְּקוֹלְרָא דְּמַלְכָּא, עַד דְּזָקִיף עֵינוֹי, חָמָא דְּאַתְיָין לְגַבֵּיהּ תְּרֵין, דְּכַתְבִין קַמֵּיהּ כָּל מַה דְּעָבִיד בְּהַאי עָלְמָא. וְכָל מַה דְּאָפִיק מִן פּוּמָא, וְיָהִיב דִּינָא עַל כֹּלָּא וְכַתְבִין קַמֵּיהּ. הה"ד כִּי הִנֵּה יוֹצֵר הָרִים וּבוֹרֵא רוּחַ וּמַגִּיד לְאָדָם מַה שֵּׂחוֹ וְגוֹ'. וְהוּא אוֹדֵי עֲלַיְיהוּ.

112. If there is no good advocate for him, he is found guilty in judgment and is required to pass away from this world. During that period while he lays bound in the chains of the King, in raising his eyes, he sees how two come to him. They write all that he did in this world and every word that emerged from his lips. He gives accounts about everything and it is recorded before him. This is what it says, "For, lo, he that forms the mountains, and creates the wind, and declares to man what is his thought..." (Amos 4:13). And he admits all these things.

113. מַאי טַעֲמָא, בְּגִין דְּהַהוּא עוֹבָדָא דְּאִיהוּ עָבִיד, סַלְקָא וְקַיְימָא עָלֵיהּ לְאַסְהֲדָא בֵּיהּ, וְקַיְימִין לְאַסְהֲדָא עָלֵיהּ, וְכֻלְּהוּ נַחְתִּין וְאִתְרְשִׁימוּ קַמֵּיהּ, וְקַיְימֵי קַמֵּיהּ, וְלָא מִתְעַבְּרָן מִנֵּיהּ, עַד שַׁעֲתָא דְּאִתְדָּן בְּהוּ בְּהַהוּא עָלְמָא. ת"ח, כָּל אִינּוּן מִלִּין דְּעָבֵיד ב"נ בְּהַאי עָלְמָא, כֻּלְּהוּ זְמִינִין וְקַיְימֵי לְאַסְהֲדָא בֵּיהּ, וְלָא אִתְאֲבִידוּ מִנֵּיהּ. וּבְשַׁעֲתָא דְּמַפְּקֵי לֵיהּ לְקִבְרָא, כֻּלְּהוּ מִתְעַתְּדָן וְאַזְלֵי קַמֵּיהּ. וּתְלַת כָּרוֹזֵי מַכְרְזֵי. חַד קַמֵּיהּ, וְחַד מִימִינֵיהּ, וְחַד מִשְּׂמָאלֵיהּ. וְאַמְרֵי הָא פְּלַנְיָּיא דְּמָרִיד בְּמָארֵיהּ. מָרִיד לְעֵילָּא, מָרִיד לְתַתָּא, מָרִיד בְּאוֹרַיְיתָא, מָרִיד בְּפִיקוּדוֹי. חָמוּ עוֹבָדוֹי, חָמוּ מִלּוֹי, טַב לֵיהּ דְּלָא אִבְרֵי.

113. What is the reason THAT HE ADMITS ALL HIS DEEDS? It is because the action he did ascends and stands by to give testimony. ALL DEEDS stand by UP ABOVE to give testimony about him. They all descend to be recorded before him and do not move away, until the time he is tried for them in that world. Come and see, all these things that were done by this man in this world, are all ready to testify about him, and they are not removed from him. When he is taken to his grave, they all gather and go in front of him. Three proclamations are proclaimed, one in front, one on his right and one on his left. They say that this is so-and-so who rebelled against his Master, rebelled above, rebelled below, rebelled against the Torah, revolted against the precepts. See his actions and watch his speeches! He would have been better off not to have been created.

114. עַד דְּמָטֵי לְגַבֵּי קִבְרָא, כֻּלְּהוּ מֵתִין אִתְרַגְזוּן מִדּוּכְתַּיְיהוּ עֲלֵיהּ, וְאַמְרֵי וַוי וַוי דְּדָא אִתְקְבַר בְּגַוָּון. עוֹבָדוֹי וּמִלּוֹי אַקְדְמָן וְעָאלִין לְקִבְרָא, וְקַיְימֵי עֲלֵיהּ דְּהַהוּא גוּפָא, וְרוּחֵיהּ אָזְלָא וְשָׁאט, וּמִתְאַבְּלָא עַל גּוּפָא. כֵּיוָן דב"נ אִתְטְמַר בְּבֵי קִבְרֵי, דּוּמָ"ה קָדִים וְנָפִיק תְּחוֹת יְדֵיהּ, תְּלָתָא בֵּי דִינָא, דִּי מְמָנָן עַל דִּינָא דְקִבְרָא, וּתְלַת שַׁרְבִיטֵי דְּאֶשָׁא בִּידַיְיהוּ, וְדַיְינִין רוּחָא וְגוּפָא כַּחֲדָא. וַוי עַל הַהוּא דִּינָא, וַוי עַל עוֹבָדוֹי.

114. Until they arrive at the cemetery, and all the dead rage in their places and say, Woe, woe that this one is buried among us. His actions and speech precede him into the grave and remain over that body. His spirit goes and wanders and mourns over the body. As soon as a person is covered in his grave, THE ANGEL Dumah hastens to come out with three courts under his jurisdiction appointed for the punishment in the grave. Three wands of fire are in their hands, and the spirit is on trial together with the body. Woe to that punishment and woe to his deeds.

115. בְּשַׁעֲתָא דְּאִיהוּ תָּפִיס בְּקוּלְרָא דְּמַלְכָּא, וְאִתְּדָן דִּינֵיהּ, וְאִשְׁתְּלִים, דְּלָא אִשְׁתְּכַח עֲלֵיהּ סַנֵיגוֹרְיָא. וְסַנְטִירָא דְּמַלְכָּא נָחִית, וְקָאִים קַמֵּיהּ, לְרַגְלוֹי, וְחַד סַיְיפָא שְׁנָנָא בִּידֵיהּ.

115. During the time he is held in the chains of the King, MEANING WHILE

HE IS SICK AND BOUND TO HIS BED, his trial takes place and was completed WITH A GUILTY VERDICT, because no good advocate is available for him. The King's minister, THE ANGEL OF DEATH, descends and stands at his feet, with a sharp sword in his hand.

116. זָקִיף ב"נ עֵינוֹי, וְחָמֵי כֹּתְלֵי בֵּיתָא דְּמִתְלַהֲטָן בְּאֶשָּׁא מִנֵּיהּ אַדְהָכִי חָמֵי לֵיהּ קַמֵּיהּ כּוּלֵּיהּ מָלֵי עַיְינִין, לְבוּשֵׁיהּ אֶשָּׁא דְּלָהִיט קַמֵּיהּ דְּבַר נָשׁ. הָכִי הוּא וַדַּאי, דְּהָא כַּמָה בְּנֵי נָשָׁא חָמוּ מַלְאָכָא בְּשׁוּקָא, וְקַיְימֵי קַמֵּיהּ, וּשְׁאַר בְּנֵי נָשָׁא לָא חָמָאן לֵיהּ.

116. The person lifts his eyes and sees FIRST the walls of the house radiant with fire. At the same time, he sees him, full with eyes, dressed in burning fire STANDING in front of the man. AND THOUGH OTHERS WHO STAND THERE DO NOT SEE HIS PRESENCE, it is certainly so. The proof is that some people see an angel in the marketplace and stand before him, but the rest do not perceive him.

117. וְאִי תֵּימָא, הָא כְּתִיב עוֹשֶׂה מַלְאָכָיו רוּחוֹת וְגוֹ'. הֵיךְ יָכִיל לְאִתְחֲזָאָה בְּאַרְעָא. אֶלָּא הָא מִלָּה דָּא, הָא אוּקְמוּהָ, דְּכֵיוָן דְּנָחִית מַלְאָכָא לְאַרְעָא, אִתְלָבַּשׁ בְּגוּפָא, וְאִתְחֲזֵי לְמַאן דְּאִתְחֲזֵי, בְּהַהוּא לְבוּשָׁא דְּאִתְלָבַּשׁ בֵּיהּ. וְאִי לָאו, לָא יָכִיל לְמִסְבַּל לֵיהּ עָלְמָא וּלְאִתְחֲזָאָה. כ"ש וְכָל שֶׁכֵּן הַאי דְּכָל בְּנֵי עָלְמָא צְרִיכִין לֵיהּ.

117. If you ask: Doesn't it say, "Who makes the winds his messengers (angels)..." (Tehilim 104:4)? How is it possible to see them on earth? HE RESPONDS: We already explained this. When the angel descends to earth, he is dressed in a physical body and he is seen to whoever needs to perceive him in that garment he donned. If he didn't PUT ON THAT GARMENT, the people could not bear it that he should be visible. All the more so with this one, THE ANGEL OF DEATH, whom all people need.

118. תְּלַת טִפִּין בְּחַרְבֵּיהּ וְכוּ', וְהָא אוּקְמוּהָ חַבְרַיָּא. כֵּיוָן דְּחָמֵי לֵיהּ, אִזְדַּעְזַע כָּל גּוּפֵיהּ וְרוּחֵיהּ, וְלִבֵּיהּ לָא שָׁכִיךְ, בְּגִין דְּאִיהוּ מַלְכָּא דְּכָל גּוּפָא. וְרוּחָא דִּילֵיהּ אַזְלָא בְּכָל שַׁיְיפֵי גוּפָא, וְאִשְׁתְּאִיל מִנַּיְיהוּ, כְּבַר

נָשׁ דְּאִשְׁתְּאִיל מֵחַבְרֵיה, לְמֵהַךְ לַאֲתָר אַחֲרָא. כְּדֵין הוּא אוֹמֵר וַוי עַל מַה דְּעָבַד, וְלָא מְהַנְיָיא לֵיה, אֶלָּא אִי אַקְדִּים אַסְוָותָא דִּתְשׁוּבָה, עַד לָא מָטָא הַהִיא שַׁעֲתָא.

118. There are three drops on his sword, as the friends have already explained. When he sees him, his entire body and spirit tremble and his heart does not rest, being the king of the entire body. Then his spirit travels throughout his organs and takes leave from them like a man who takes leave from his friend to go elsewhere. He then declares: Woe, what have I done, but it is of no use to him unless he preempts it with the healing powers of repentance before that moment arrives.

119. דָּחִיל הַהוּא ב"נ, וּבָעֵי לְאִתְטַמְּרָא וְלָא יָכִיל. כֵּיוָן דְּחָמֵי דְּלָא יָכִיל, הוּא פָּתַח עֵינוֹי, וְאִית לֵיה לְאִסְתַּכְּלָא בֵּיה, וְאִסְתַּכַּל בֵּיה בְּעַיְינִין פְּקִיחִין. וּכְדֵין הוּא מָסִיר גַּרְמֵיה וְנַפְשֵׁיה. וְהַהוּא שַׁעֲתָא, הוּא עִידָן דְּדִינָא רַבָּא, דְּב"נ אִתְּדָן בֵּיה בְּהַאי עָלְמָא. וּכְדֵין רוּחָא אַזְלָא בְּכָל שַׁיְיפֵי גוּפָא, וְאִשְׁתְּאִיל מִנַיְיהוּ, וְשָׁאט בְּכָל שַׁיְיפִין, וְאִזְדַּעְזְעָא לְכָל סִטְרִין וְכָל שַׁיְיפֵי גוּפָא כֻּלְּהוּ מִזְדַּעְזְעָן.

119. The person shudders with fear and wishes to hide but cannot. When he realizes that he is powerless, he opens his eyes and he has to look at him with his eyes open. He then gives his life and soul. That is the moment of the greatest judgment that a person is judged in this world. The spirit then passes through all the limbs of the body and takes leave of them. It then wanders through all the organs and shakes all over, and all the organs tremble.

120. כַּד מָטָא רוּחָא לְכָל שַׁיְיפָא וְשַׁיְיפָא, וְאִשְׁתְּאִיל מִנֵּיה. נָפַל זִיעָא עַל הַהוּא שַׁיְיפָא, וְרוּחָא אִסְתָּלִיק מִנֵּיה. וּמִיַּד מִית הַהוּא שַׁיְיפָא. וְכֵן בְּכֻלְּהוּ.

120. When the spirit arrives at each limb to take leave, sweat develops on that limb. The spirit is removed, and immediately that limb dies, and so on with all THE LIMBS.

121. כֵּיוָן דְּמָטֵי רוּחָא לְמֵיפַק, דְּהָא אִשְׁתְּאֵיל מִכָּל גּוּפָא, כְּדֵין שְׁכִינְתָּא קַיְימָא עֲלֵיהּ. וּמִיַּד פַּרְחָא מִן גּוּפָא. זַכָּאָה חוּלָקֵיהּ דְּמַאן דְּאִתְדְּבַק בָּהּ, וַוי לְאִינוּן חַיָּיבַיָּא דִּרְחִיקִין מִנָּה, וְלָא מִתְדַּבְּקִין בָּהּ.

121. As soon as the spirit is ready to depart, because it has already taken leave of all THE LIMBS OF the body, the Shechinah rests on it. Immediately, THE SPIRIT flies from the body. Praised is the lot of the person who is attached to her, THE SHECHINAH. Woe to those wicked who are far from her and are not attached to her.

122. וְכַמָּה בֵּי דִינָא אַעֲבַר בַּר נָשׁ כַּד נָפַק מֵהַאי עָלְמָא. חַד הַהוּא דִּינָא עִלָּאָה דְּקָאֲמָרָן, כַּד נָפִיק רוּחָא מִן גּוּפָא. וְחַד דִּינָא, כַּד עוֹבָדוֹי וּמִלּוֹי אָזְלִין קַמֵּיהּ, וְכָרוֹזֵי מַכְרְזֵי עֲלוֹי. וְחַד דִּינָא, כַּד עָיֵיל לְקִבְרָא וְחַד דִּינָא דְקִבְרָא. וְחַד דִּינָא דְתוֹלַעְתָּא. וְחַד דִּינָא דְגֵיהִנָּם. וְחַד דִּינָא דְרוּחָא דְּאָזְלָא וְשָׁאט בְּעָלְמָא, וְלָא אַשְׁכַּח אֲתָר, עַד דְּיִשְׁתַּלִּימוּ עוֹבָדוֹי. וַדַּאי שִׁבְעָה עִדָּנִין יַחְלְפוּן עֲלוֹי. בְּגִין כַּךְ בָּעֵי בַּר נָשׁ, כַּד אִיהוּ אִשְׁתְּכַח בְּהַאי עָלְמָא, לְדַחֲלָא מִן מָארֵיהּ, וּלְאִסְתַּכְּלָא בְּכָל יוֹמָא וְיוֹמָא בְּעוֹבָדוֹי, וְיֵיתוּב מִנַּיְיהוּ קַמֵּי מָרֵיהּ.

122. How many trials does a person have to pass when he departs from this world! One is the supreme judgment that we have already explained when the spirit leaves the body. One is the trial at the moment when his actions and speeches proceed in front of him and declare proclamations about him. There is another, the trial when he is placed in his grave; one in the grave, and one the trial of the worms THAT EAT HIS FLESH. Another is the trial of Gehenom and one is the trial of spirit that wanders through the world and finds no rest until his deeds are perfected. Seven definite periods pass over him. Therefore, a man should fear his Master, examine his actions every day and repent to his Master for them while he is still alive in this world.

123. כַּד אִסְתָּכַּל דָּוִד מַלְכָּא בְּאִינוּן דִּינִין דְּבַר נָשׁ, כַּד אִסְתַּלָּק מֵהַאי עָלְמָא, אַקְדִים וְאָמַר, בָּרְכִי נַפְשִׁי אֶת יְיָ, עַד דְּלָא תִּפּוֹק מֵעָלְמָא, הַשְׁתָּא דְּאַנְתְּ אִשְׁתְּכַחַת עִם גּוּפָא. וְכָל קְרָבַי אֶת שֵׁם קָדְשׁוֹ, אַתּוּן

שַׁיְיפֵי דְּמִשְׁתַּתְּפֵי בְּרוּחָא, הַשְׁתָּא דְּאִשְׁתְּכָחַת עִמְּכוֹן, אַקְדִּימוּ לְבָרְכָא שְׁמָא קַדִּישָׁא, עַד לָא יִמְטֵי זִמְנָא, דְּלָא תֵּיכְלוּן לְבָרְכָא לֵיהּ, וּלְאוֹדָאָה עֲלַיְיכוּ.

123. When King David examined the trials of a person whom he departs from this world, he first said "Bless Hashem, my soul" (Tehilim 103:1) before it departs the world, now while it is still in the body, "and all that is within me bless his Holy Name" – you, the limbs that are attached to the spirit, now while THE SPIRIT is still with you, hasten to bless the Holy Name, before the time arrives when you will no longer be able to bless him and thank him for you.

10. The Nazirite

A Synopsis

Rabbi Aba wonders why someone who has made the vow of a Nazirite to be sanctified with holiness is not allowed to eat grapes. Rabbi Shimon answers that wine and strong drink and grapes are all attached to the same aspect, that is of the Left Column, and it is inappropriate for a Nazirite to do anything of the left side.

124. ת"ח אִישׁ כִּי יַפְלִיא לִנְדּוֹר נֶדֶר, נָזִיר דְּאַקְדִּים בְּהַאי עָלְמָא, לְאִתְקַדְּשָׁא בִּקְדוּשָׁה דְּמָארֵיהּ מִיַּין וְשֵׁכָר יַזִּיר חוֹמֶץ יַיִן וְגוֹ'. הָכָא אִית לְאִסְתַּכְּלָא, כֵּיוָן דְּאָסִיר לֵיהּ חַמְרָא, עֲנָבִים לָמָּה. דְּהָא בְּכַהֲנֵי כְּתִיב יַיִן וְשֵׁכָר אַל תֵּשְׁתְּ וְגוֹ', יָכוֹל עֲנָבִים נַמֵי. לָא. בַּעֲנָבִים שָׁרֵי. הָכָא לַנָּזִיר, מ"ט אָסַר לֵיהּ עֲנָבִים.

124. Come and see: "When either man...shall pronounce a special vow of a Nazirite..." (Bemidbar 6:2), MEANING he hastened while in this world, to be sanctified with the holiness of his Master. Thus, "he shall abstain from wine and strong drink, and shall drink no vinegar of wine..." (Ibid. 3). Here we should deliberate. Just because he is forbidden to drink wine, why should grapes BE FORBIDDEN TO HIM, seeing that of the priest it says, "Do not drink wine or strong drink" (Vayikra 10:9), but he may eat grapes. So why is a Nazirite different? Why are grapes forbidden to him?

125. אֶלָּא, עוֹבָדָא דָא, וּמִלָּה דָא, רָזָא עִלָּאָה הוּא, לְאִתְפָּרְשָׁא מִן דִּינָא בְּכֹלָּא. וְהָא יְדִיעָא הַהוּא אִילָנָא דְּחָב בֵּיהּ אָדָם קַדְמָאָה, עֲנָבִים הֲווֹ. וְדָא הוּא רָזָא דְּמִלָּה, דְּהָא יַיִן וְשֵׁכָר וַעֲנָבִים, בְּסִטְרָא חַד אִתְאַחֲדוּ. יַיִן לְעֵילָּא וְאוּקְמוּהָ. שֵׁכָר לִשְׂמָאלָא, דְּהָא שֵׁכָר מִיַּין נָפְקָא. עֲנָבִים דְּכָנִישׁ כֻּלְּהוּ לְגַבַּיְיהוּ, וְדָא הוּא אִילָנָא דְּחָב בֵּיהּ אָדָם קַדְמָאָה. בְּג"כ כֹּלָּא בְּחַד סִטְרָא אִתְאֲחָד. וְאִי תֵּימָא דְּהַאי נָזִיר שָׁבִיק מְהֵימְנוּתָא עִלָּאָה. לָאו הָכִי, אֶלָּא לָא אִתְחֲזֵי בֵּיהּ עוֹבָדָא מִסְּטַר שְׂמָאלָא כְּלוּם.

125. HE RESPONDS: This procedure and prohibition is of the highest secret, THAT THE NAZIRITE IS to isolate himself entirely from Judgment MORE SO

-118-

THAN A PRIEST. It is known that the tree by which Adam sinned was a grapevine. That is the secret of it, that wine and strong drink and grapes are attached to the same aspect, WHICH IS OF THE LEFT COLUMN; wine above, TO THE LEFT COLUMN OF BINAH, THAT IS REFERRED TO THERE AS THE PRESERVED WINE as explained. Strong drink is to the left OF ZEIR ANPIN, since strong drink is produced from wine. SO TOO THE LEFT COLUMN OF ZEIR ANPIN IS DRAWN FROM THE LEFT COLUMN OF BINAH. Grapes gather everything to them, SINCE THEY ARE MALCHUT THAT RECEIVES FROM EVERYTHING ABOVE, and that is the tree by which Adam sinned. Consequently, all of them are connected to the same side, THE LEFT OF BINAH, OF ZEIR ANPIN AND OF MALCHUT. If you say that this Nazirite has abandoned the supreme Faith, BY NOT RECEIVING FROM THE SUPERNAL BINAH, ZEIR ANPIN AND MALCHUT, it is not so. It is just not appropriate for him to do anything of the left side.

11. "Let the hair grow" – "And let them shave"

A Synopsis

Rabbi Shimon continues by saying that the Nazirite must not cut his hair or shave because the roots of hair exist from the right side, and he is entirely isolated from judgment. After he comes back from isolation the priest must atone for him so that the Nazirite can again be allowed wine and strong drink and grapes. Rabbi Shimon says that Samson was punished because he took a gentile woman for a wife.

126. ת״ח, דְּהָכִי אוֹלִיפְנָא מִסִּפְרָא דְּרַב הַמְנוּנָא סָבָא, וְהָכִי הוּא. כְּתִיב גַּדֵּל פֶּרַע שְׂעַר רֹאשׁוֹ, בָּעֵי דְּיִתְרְבֵּי שְׂעַר רֵישֵׁיה וְדִיקְנֵיה, וְיִתְפְּרַשׁ מִיַּיִן וְשֵׁכָר וַעֲנָבִים, בְּגִין דְּכֻלְּהוּ סְטַר שְׂמָאלָא, וְלָא תַּלְיָין שַׂעֲרָא. יַיִן אִימָּא עִלָּאָה. שֵׁכָר סִטְרָא דַּאֲחִידוּ בֵּיה לֵיוָאֵי וְנַפְקֵי מִיַּיִן עִלָּאָה וְלָא תָּלֵי שַׂעֲרָא. ובג״כ כַּד סְלִיקוּ לֵיוָאֵי לְהַהוּא אֲתָר, בָּעֵיין לְאַעְבְּרָא כָּל שַׂעֲרָא דִּלְהוֹן, כד״א וְהֶעֱבִירוּ תַעַר עַל כָּל בְּשָׂרָם.

126. Come and see what I have learned from the book of Rav Hamnuna Saba (the elder). It is written: "And shall let the locks of the hair of his head grow" (Bemidbar 6:5). He must allow the hair on his head and beard to grow, and abstain from wine, strong drink and grapes, since they all pertain to the left side, but the hairs do not originate IN THEM. Wine is supernal Ima, while strong drink is of the left, to which the Levites are connected and stem from the uppermost wine, MEANING FROM SUPERNAL IMA and the hairs have no involvement WITH THEM. Therefore, when the Levites ascend to this place, TO THE LEFT, they must shave all their hair, as is said; "And let them shave all their flesh" (Bemidbar 8:7).

127. עֲנָבִים אִימָּא תַּתָּאָה, דְּכָנִישׁ יַיִן וְשֵׁכָר לְגַוֵּוּה, וְעַל דָּא אִתְפְּרַשׁ מִכָּל סְטַר שְׂמָאלָא, דְּלָא לְאַחֲזָאָה עוֹבָדָא דִּילְהוֹן לְגַבֵּיה. עֲנָבִים דָּא לָא תָּלֵי שַׂעֲרָא וְדִיקְנָא. דְּהָא נוּקְבָא בַּעְיָיא לְסַפְּרָא שַׂעֲרָא, כַּד אַתְיָא לְאִזְדַּוְּוגָא בְּדְכוּרָא, וְהָא דִּיקְנָא לָא אִשְׁתְּכַח בָּה. בג״כ הוּא תָּלֵי שַׂעֲרָא דְּרֵישָׁא וְדִיקְנָא, וְרָזָא דְּמִלָּה נְזִיר אֱלֹהִים אִקְרֵי, וְלָא נְזִיר יְיָ׳, פְּרִישׁ מְדִינָא כֹּלָּא.

-120-

127. Grapes pertain to the lower mother, MALCHUT, who gathers wine and strong drink to her. Therefore, THE NAZIRITE isolates himself from the entire left, FROM WINE AND STRONG DRINK AND GRAPES, so that none of its consequences are manifest in him. There are no hair and beard coming out of the grapes THAT ARE MALCHUT, since the female, WHICH IS MALCHUT, needs to cut her hair, THAT IS, BODY HAIR when she comes to have intercourse with the male, ZEIR ANPIN. And she has no beard. Therefore, THE NAZIRITE THAT IS FROM THE RIGHT WHERE THE ROOTS OF HAIR IS, IS OPPOSITE. The hair of the head and beard hang down, AND IT IS FORBIDDEN TO SHAVE THEM. The secret of this is that he is called "a Nazirite to Elohim" (Shoftim 13:7). HE IS ISOLATED FROM THE NAME ELOHIM THAT IS THE LEFT, and it is not 'Nazirite to Hashem', WHICH IS THE RIGHT, SINCE HE is isolated entirely from Judgment. "NAZIRITE" MEANS ONE WHO SEPARATES HIMSELF.

128. תח, עַל דָּא כְּתִיב, וְכִפֶּר עָלָיו מֵאֲשֶׁר חָטָא עַל הַנֶּפֶשׁ וְגוֹ'. עַל נַפְשׁוֹ לָא כְּתִיב, אֶלָּא עַל הַנֶּפֶשׁ סְתָם. וּמַאי אִיהוּ. דָּא עֲנָבִים, דְּאִקְרֵי נֶפֶשׁ. וע"ד כְּתִיב חָטָא, בְּגִין דְּסִטְרָא דִּילֵיהּ יַיִן וְשֵׁכָר הוּא, וְגָרַע מִנֵּיהּ אֲתַר דִּינָא. חָטָא, מַאי חָטָא. אֶלָּא גָּרַע דִּינָא שֶׁל הַנֶּפֶשׁ.

128. Come and see, about this is written: "And make atonement for him, for that he sinned by the dead (lit. 'Nefesh')..." It is not written: 'his Nefesh', but simply "the Nefesh." What is that? These are grapes, MEANING MALCHUT, that are referred to as Nefesh. Hence a sin is mentioned, MEANING HE SINNED AGAINST MALCHUT, the aspect of which is that of wine and strong drink, AS MALCHUT IS BUILT MAINLY FROM THE LEFT. AND THE NAZIRITE took the place of Judgment, THAT IS, THE ILLUMINATION FROM THE LEFT, from it. HE ASKS, Why IS THIS CONSIDERED a sin? HE REPLIES: It is because HE SINNED BY depriving the Judgment from the Nefesh, MEANING THE ILLUMINATION OF ITS CHOCHMAH THAT IS DRAWN TOGETHER WITH THE JUDGMENTS OF THE LEFT.

129. אִי הָכִי, אֲמַאי וְכִפֶּר עָלָיו. בְּגִין דְּהַשְׁתָּא קָא אַתְיָא לְאִתְחַבְּרָא בַּהֲדַיְיהוּ, וְלָא מְקַבְּלָן לֵיהּ הָנֵי אַתְרֵי, עַד דְּיִמָּלֵךְ בְּכַהֲנָא, וִיכַפֶּר עָלֵיהּ, בְּגִין דְּאִיהוּ שָׁדֵי לוֹן לְבַר בְּקַדְמֵיתָא, כֵּיוָן דְּהַשְׁתָּא אָתֵי לְגַבַּיְיהוּ, בָּעֵי לְאִתְחַבְּרָא תִּקּוּנָא דְּכַפָּרָה, וִיקַבְּלוּן לֵיהּ, וְדָא הוּא רָזָא דְּמִלָּה.

129. HE ASKS: If so, THAT A NAZIRITE ADHERES SO MUCH TO THE RIGHT, why IS IT WRITTEN FOLLOWING THAT: "And make atonement for him"? HE ANSWERS: Because he comes forth now, AFTER COMPLETING HIS ABSTENTION PERIOD, to adhere with them, WITH THE THREE ASPECTS OF THE LEFT COLUMN, AND TO BE ALLOWED WINE, STRONG DRINK AND GRAPES. These places do not accept him until he takes counsel with the priest who will atone for him, since originally he expelled them, BY ABSTAINING, and now that he returns to them he needs to adhere to correction by atonement, so they will accept him. That is the mystical explanation of this.

130. וְאִי תֵּימָא, שִׁמְשׁוֹן נְזִיר אֱלֹהִים הֲוָה, אֲמַאי אִתְעֲנָשׁ. אֶלָּא שַׁפִּיר הוּא מִלָּה, דְּבָעַל בַּת אֵל נֵכָר. וַהֲוָה לֵיהּ לְאִתְחַבְּרָא בְּדִידֵיהּ, בְּמָה דְּאִתְחֲזֵי לֵיהּ. וְהוּא דַּהֲוָה קַדִּישׁ, אַעֲרַב הַהִיא קְדוּשָׁה בְּבַת אֵל נֵכָר, וְשָׁבִיק אַתְרֵיהּ, דְּאִתְחֲזֵי לְהַהִיא קְדוּשָׁה, וּבג"כ אִתְעֲנָשׁ.

130. If you wonder about Samson, who was a Nazirite to Elohim, why was he punished? HE REPLIES: It was proper for him, MEANING HE DESERVED THE PUNISHMENT because he joined in marriage with a gentile woman, MEANING DELILAH. He should have joined with his own kind, with what was appropriate for him, but he, who was holy, mingled that holiness with a daughter of a foreign El and abandoned his appropriate state of holiness. Therefore, he was punished.

131. וְאִית מַאן דְּאָמַר, דְּלֵית לֵיהּ חוּלָקָא בְּהַהוּא עָלְמָא. מ"ט בְּגִין דְּאָמַר תָּמוּת נַפְשִׁי עִם פְּלִשְׁתִּים, וּמָסַר חוּלָקֵיהּ בְּחוּלָקָא דִּפְלִשְׁתָּאֵי, דִּימוּת נַפְשֵׁיהּ עִמְּהוֹן בְּהַהוּא עָלְמָא. כָּךְ הֲווֹ מַכְרִזֵי עַל נְזִירָא, לֵךְ לֵךְ אָמְרִין נְזִירָא, סְחוֹר סְחוֹר, לְכַרְמָא לָא תִּקְרַב. וְהָא אוּקְמוּהָ חַבְרַיָּיא.

131. Some say that he has no part in that world. Why is that? It is because he said, "Let my Nefesh die with the Philistines" (Shoftim 16:30) and he passed his lot with the lot of the Philistines, so that his Nefesh will die with them in that world. This is the way they used to proclaim to the Nazirite: 'Go all around - that you may not come near the vineyard'. The friends have already explained it.

12. Holy - Pure

A Synopsis
Rabbi Shimon talks about the secret of hair in relation to holiness.

132. לֵיוָאֵי מַה כְּתִיב בְּהוּ, וְכֹה תַעֲשֶׂה לָהֶם לְטַהֲרָם הַזֶּה עֲלֵיהֶם מֵי חַטָּאת וְהֶעֱבִירוּ תַעַר עַל כָּל בְּשָׂרָם. כֵּיוָן דְּעַבְרֵי שַׂעֲרָא, וְעַבְדֵי כּוּלֵּי הַאי, כְּדֵין אִקְרֵי לֵיוָאֵי טָהוֹר, וְלָא קָדוֹשׁ. אֲבָל הַאי נָזִיר בְּגִין דְּאִתְפְּרַשׁ מֵהַאי סִטְרָא, אִקְרֵי קָדוֹשׁ וְלָא טָהוֹר. בְּגִין כָּךְ כְּתִיב, כָּל יְמֵי נֶדֶר נִזְרוֹ וְגוֹ' אֲשֶׁר יַזִּיר לַיְיָ' קָדוֹשׁ יִהְיֶה וְגוֹ'.

132. Here is what is written about the Levites: "And thus shall you do to them, to cleanse them: Sprinkle water of purifying on them, and let them shave all their flesh" (Bemidbar 8:7). As soon as they shave their hair and fulfill all this, the Levites are considered pure but not holy. But as soon as the Nazirite isolates from the side OF THE LEFT, he is considered holy and not pure. Thus, it is written: "All the days of his vow of his separation...during which he separates himself to Hashem, he shall be holy" (Bemidbar 6:5).

133. גַּדֵּל פֶּרַע שְׂעַר רֹאשׁוֹ, מִשּׁוּם הָא דִּכְתִיב, וּשְׂעַר רֵאשֵׁהּ כַּעֲמַר נְקֵא, דִּבְהַאי דָּמֵי לְגַוְונָא דִּלְעֵילָּא. אָמַר ר' יְהוּדָה בַּר רַב, בְּשַׂעֲרֵי מַמָּשׁ אִשְׁתְּמוֹדַע דְּאִיהוּ קַדִּישָׁא, דִּכְתִיב קְווּצוֹתָיו תַּלְתַּלִּים.

133. "And shall let the locks of the hair of his head grow" (Ibid.). It is because it is written: "And the hair of whose head was like pure wool" (Daniel 7:9). By this, he is similar to the higher, SINCE HIS HAIR DRAWS CHASSADIM AND WITHOUT JUDGMENT, SINCE HE IS WHOLLY OF THE RIGHT. Rabbi Yehuda ben Rav said: With his hair alone, it is apparent that he is holy, as it is written ABOUT THE HOLY ONE, BLESSED BE HE: "His locks are wavy" (Shir Hashirim 5:11).

134. תָּאנֵי ר' שִׁמְעוֹן, אִלְמָלֵי יַדְעֵי בְּנֵי נָשָׁא, מַאי קָאַמְרֵי בְּהַאי שַׂעֲרָא, וּבְרָזָא דִּילֵיהּ, כְּמָה דְּאִיהוּ בְּרָזָא דְּרָזִין, אִשְׁתְּמוֹדְעָן לְמָארֵיהוֹן, בְּחָכְמְתָא עִלָּאָה. עַד כָּאן רָזֵי דְּאוֹרַיְיתָא, מִכָּאן וּלְהָלְאָה

סִתְרֵי תוֹרָה, סַחְרָה וְאֶתְנַנָּהּ קֹדֶשׁ לַיְיָ׳.

134. Rabbi Shimon taught, If people would know what is spoken about this hair and its secret meaning, as it is ABOVE in the utmost secrecy, they would have distinguished themselves to their Master with the highest wisdom. Up to here have been the secrets of the Torah; from now on Sitrei Torah: "And her merchandise and her hire shall be holiness to Hashem" (Yeshayah 23:18).

1. The foreword to the Idra Raba

A Synopsis

Rabbi Shimon tells the friends what he wishes to reveal to them and invites them to a new understanding. He is anguished over the question of whether to reveal secrets, until Rabbi Aba reassures him that the friends all fear God. Rabbi Shimon tells the rabbis that this is a time to act for God because people have forsaken His Torah. He talks about the talebearer who is not settled in his mind and is not trustworthy to receive secrets and he contrasts this to a faithful spirit who is stable and conceals matters. When Rabbi Shimon begins to reveal secrets, the place shakes and the friends tremble.

1. תַּנְיָא, אָמַר ר"ש לְחַבְרַיָּיא, עַד אֵימַת נֵיתִיב בְּקַיְּימָא דְּחַד סַמְכָא. כְּתִיב עֵת לַעֲשׂוֹת לַיְיָ׳ הֵפֵרוּ תּוֹרָתֶךָ. יוֹמִין זְעִירִין, וּמָארֵי דְּחוֹבָא דְּחִיק. כָּרוֹזָא קָארֵי כָּל יוֹמָא, וּמְחַצְדֵּי חַקְלָא זְעִירִין אִינּוּן. וְאִינְהוּ בְּשׁוּלֵי כַּרְמָא. לָא אַשְׁגְּחָן, וְלָא יַדְעִין, לְאָן אֲתָר אַזְלִין כְּמָה דְּיָאוֹת.

1. We were taught that Rabbi Shimon said to the friends: How long will we remain upheld by one pillar, MEANING IN THE SENSE OF THE FORMLESS WORLD (HEB. *TOHU*), IN WHICH THE SEVEN LOWER SFIROT WERE IN A SINGLE STACK, THE ONE ABOVE THE OTHER. RABBI SHIMON WISHED TO REVEAL TO THEM THE MEANING OF THE GRADES IN THE WORLD OF CORRECTION, WHICH CONSIST OF THREE PILLARS, THE HIDDEN MEANING OF THE THREE COLUMNS – RIGHT, LEFT AND CENTRAL. It is written: "It is time to act for Hashem: they have made void your Torah" (Tehilim 119:126). The days are few and the sin-master, MEANING THE PROSECUTOR, applies pressure. Every day the proclamation resounds FOR REPENTANCE and the reapers of the field are few, MEANING THOSE WHO DESERVED THE CROP OF THE SUPERNAL FIELD, MALCHUT, WHICH ARE THE UNDERSTANDINGS OF THE SECRETS OF TORAH. They, EVEN THOSE WHO UNDERSTOOD, are LOCATED at the end of the vineyard, WHICH IS MALCHUT. Even they do not pay attention and do not know where they are going.

2. אִתְכְּנָשׁוּ חַבְרַיָּיא לְבֵי אִדְּרָא, מְלוּבָּשִׁין שִׁרְיָין סַיְיפֵי וְרוּמְחֵי בִּידֵיכוֹן, אִזְדְּרָזוּ בְּתִקּוּנֵיכוֹן. בְּעֵיטָא, בְּחָכְמְתָא. בְּסוּכְלְתָנוּ. בִּדְעָתָא.

בְּחֵיזוּ. בִּידִין. בְּרַגְלִין. אַמְלִכוּ עֲלֵיכוֹן לְמַאן דִּבְרְשׁוּתֵיה חַיֵּי וּמוֹתָא. לְמִגְזַר מִלִּין דִּקְשׁוֹט. מִלִּין דְּקַדִּישֵׁי עֶלְיוֹנִין צַיְיתֵי לְהוּ, וַחֲדָאן לְמִשְׁמַע לְהוּ, וּלְמִנְדַּע לְהוּ.

2. Gather, friends, to the chamber, dressed in shields with swords and lances in your hands, WHICH IS THE SECRET OF THE UNIFICATIONS TO DESTROY THE KLIPOT. Hurry with your corrections, MEANING HURRY TO RESTORE THE THREE COLUMNS: CHOCHMAH, BINAH, DA'AT, CHESED, GVURAH, TIFERET, NETZACH, HOD AND YESOD with counsel, with wisdom, with understanding, with knowledge, with appearance, with hands, WHICH IS THE SECRET OF CHESED, GVURAH AND TIFERET and with legs, WHICH IS THE SECRET OF NETZACH, HOD AND YESOD. Appoint as King over you he who has the authority of life and death to decree truthful words, words to which the supernal holy beings will listen, and will be glad to hear and to know them.

3. יָתִיב ר״ש וּבְכָה, וְאָמַר וַוי אִי גְּלֵינָא, וַוי אִי לָא גְּלֵינָא. חַבְרַיָּיא דַּהֲוָה תַּמָּן אִשְׁתְּקוּ. קָם ר׳ אַבָּא וְא״ל, אִי נִיחָא קַמֵּיה דְּמָר לְגַלָּאָה, הָא כְּתִיב סוֹד יְיָ׳ לִירֵאָיו, וְהָא חַבְרַיָּיא אִלֵּין דַּחֲלִין דְּקוּדְשָׁא בְּרִיךְ הוּא אִינּוּן, וּכְבַר עָאלוּ בְּאִדְרָא דְּבֵי מַשְׁכְּנָא, מִנְּהוֹן עָאלוּ, מִנְּהוֹן נָפְקוּ.

3. Rabbi Shimon sat down and wept. He said: Woe if I do reveal and woe if I do not reveal. IF HE DOES NOT REVEAL, THE NEW UNDERSTANDINGS IN THE TORAH WILL GET LOST, AND IF HE DOES REVEAL, PERHAPS SOMEONE WHO IS NOT WORTHY OF THE HIDDEN MEANINGS OF THE TORAH MIGHT HEAR. The friends that were there kept silent. Finally, Rabbi Aba stood up and said to him: If my lord is graceful enough to reveal, behold it says, "The secret of Hashem is with them that fear him" (Tehilim 25:14). These friends fear the Holy One, blessed be He. They have already gained entry to the chamber of residence. WE HAVE LEARNED THAT some of them entered THIS GREAT CHAMBER and some of them exited, BUT NOT ALL SINCE THREE FRIENDS PASSED AWAY.

4. תָּאנָא, אִתְמָנוּ חַבְרַיָּיא קַמֵּיה דר״ש, וְאִשְׁתְּכָחוּ, רַבִּי אֶלְעָזָר בְּרֵיה.

וְר' אַבָּא. וְר' יְהוּדָה. וְרִבִּי יוֹסֵי בַּר יַעֲקֹב. וְר' יִצְחָק. וְר' חִזְקִיָּה בַּר רַב.
וְר' חִיָּיא. וְר' יוֹסֵי. וְר' יֵיסָא. יְדִין יָהֲבוּ לְר"ש, וְאֶצְבְּעָן זַקְפוּ לְעֵילָא.
וְעָאלוּ בְּחַקְלָא בֵּינֵי אִילָנֵי וְיָתְבוּ. קָם ר"ש וְצַלֵּי צְלוֹתֵיה, יָתִיב
בְּגַוַוייהוּ וְאָמַר, כָּל חַד יְשַׁוֵּי יְדוֹי בְּתוּקְפֵיה. שַׁוּוּ יְדַייהוּ, וְנָסִיב לוֹן .
פָּתַח וְאָמַר אָרוּר הָאִישׁ אֲשֶׁר יַעֲשֶׂה פֶסֶל וּמַסֵּכָה מַעֲשֵׂה יְדֵי חָרָשׁ וְשָׂם
בַּסֵּתֶר וְעָנוּ כָל הָעָם וְאָמְרוּ אָמֵן.

4. We have learned that the friends were counted who were present before Rabbi Shimon. The following were present: Rabbi Elazar, his son, Rabbi Aba, Rabbi Yehuda, Rabbi Yosi bar Ya'akov, Rabbi Yitzchak, Rabbi Chizkiyah bar Rav, Rabbi Chiya, Rabbi Yosi and Rabbi Yesa. They stretched their hands to Rabbi Shimon with the fingers straightened upward. They entered the field among the trees and sat down. Rabbi Shimon stood up and prayed his prayer, sat down among them and said: Let everyone place his hands in his bosom. Each one placed his hands IN HIS OWN BOSOM AND RABBI SHIMON accepted them. He opened the discussion saying, "Cursed be the man that makes any carved or molten idol, an abomination of Hashem, the work of the hands of a craftsman, and sets it up in secret. And all the people" – ALL THE FRIENDS – "shall answer and say, 'Amen' " (Devarim 27:15).

5. פָּתַח ר"ש וְאָמַר, עֵת לַעֲשׂוֹת לַיְיָ', אֲמַאי עֵת לַעֲשׂוֹת לַיְיָ'. מִשּׁוּם
דְּהֵפֵרוּ תּוֹרָתֶךָ. מַאי הֵפֵרוּ תּוֹרָתֶךָ, תּוֹרָה דִּלְעֵילָא. דְּאִיהִי מִתְבַּטְּלָא אִי
לָא יִתְעֲבִיד בְּתִקּוּנוֹי דָּא. וּלְעַתִּיק יוֹמִין אִתְּמַר. כְּתִיב אַשְׁרֶיךָ יִשְׂרָאֵל
מִי כָמוֹךָ. וּכְתִיב, מִי כָמוֹךָ בָּאֵלִים יְיָ'.

5. Rabbi Shimon opened the discussion with the verse: "It is time to act for Hashem: THEY HAVE MADE VOID YOUR TORAH" (TEHILIM 119;126), WHICH MEANS why is this a time to act for Hashem? Because "they have made void your Torah." What does "they have made void your Torah" mean? MEANING: They have made void the Torah above, WHICH IS THE SECRET OF ZEIR ANPIN, because she becomes void if she is not observed with her establishments, AS THE FOLLOWING WILL EXPLAIN. THIS VERSE was said to Atik Yomin (the Ancient of Days), WHICH IS THE BEGINNING OF THE ROOT OF ALL CORRECTIONS, AS IN THE FOLLOWING

EXPLANATION. It says, "Happy are you, Yisrael: who is like you" (Devarim 33:29), BECAUSE THEY ADHERE TO THE CENTRAL COLUMN and "Who is like you, Hashem, among the Elim" (Shemot 15:11). THIS APPLIES TO ZEIR ANPIN, WHO IS THE CENTRAL COLUMN.

‎6. קָרָא לְרבִּי אֶלְעָזָר בְּרֵיה, אוֹתְבֵיה קָמֵיה, וּלְרַבִּי אַבָּא מִסִּטְרָא אַחֲרָא, וְאָמַר אֲנָן כְּלָלָא דְכוֹלָא. עַד הַשְׁתָּא אִתְתָּקְנוּ קַיָּימִין. אִשְׁתִּיקוּ, שָׁמְעֵי קָלָא, וְאַרְכּוּבָתָן דָּא לְדָא נַקְשָׁן. מַאי קָלָא. קָלָא דִכְנוּפְיָיא עִלָּאָה דְמִתְכַּנְפֵי.

6. He called on his son Rabbi Elazar and made him sit in front of him. Rabbi Aba was on the other side and said: We are all inclusive, SINCE THE SOUL OF RABBI ELAZAR WAS OF CHOCHMAH AND THAT OF RABBI ABA WAS BINAH, AND RABBI SHIMON HIMSELF WAS DA'AT THAT UNIFIES CHOCHMAH AND BINAH TO EACH OTHER. THAT IS WHY HE SAID THAT THEY WERE ALL INCLUSIVE, SINCE CHOCHMAH, BINAH AND DA'AT INCLUDE ALL THE GRADES. Until now the pillars were constructed, MEANING THAT TO THIS POINT THEY WERE INVOLVED IN CORRECTING THE THREE COLUMNS, ALSO CALLED THREE PILLARS. They were silent. They heard a sound and their knees were knocking together BECAUSE OF FEAR. What was the sound? That was the sound of the friends above who were gathering, MEANING THE CHARIOTS OF THE HOLY ONE, BLESSED BE HE.

‎7. חֲדֵי ר״ש וְאָמַר, יְיָ' שָׁמַעְתִּי שִׁמְעֲךָ יָרֵאתִי הָתָם יָאוֹת הֲוָה לְמֶהֱוֵי דָחִיל. אֲנָן בַּחֲבִיבוּתָא תַּלְיָיא מִלְתָא, דִכְתִיב וְאָהַבְתָּ אֵת יְיָ' אֱלֹהֶיךָ, וּכְתִיב מֵאַהֲבַת יְיָ' אֶתְכֶם, וּכְתִיב אָהַבְתִּי אֶתְכֶם וְגוֹ'.

7. Rabbi Shimon rejoiced and said, "Hashem, I have heard the report of you, and I was afraid" (Chavakuk 3:2). It was true there that he feared SINCE HIS ROOT WAS FROM THE LEFT COLUMN, BUT as for us WHO ARE UNITED WITH THE CENTRAL COLUMN, it comes from love, MEANING CHASSADIM, THAT ARE THE ASPECT OF LOVE, as it is written: "And you shall love Hashem your Elohim" (Devarim 6:5), and: "Because Hashem loved you" (Devarim 7:8) and also: "I have loved you... " (Malachi 1:2).

8. ר"ש פָּתַח וְאָמַר, הוֹלֵךְ רָכִיל מְגַלֶּה סוֹד וְנֶאֱמַן רוּחַ מְכַסֶּה דָבָר. הוֹלֵךְ רָכִיל, הַאי קְרָא קַשְׁיָא, אִישׁ רָכִיל מִבָּעֵי לֵיהּ לְמֵימַר, מַאן הוֹלֵךְ. אֶלָּא מַאן דְּלָא אִתְיֵישַׁב בְּרוּחֵיהּ, וְלָא הֲוֵי מְהֵימָנָא, הַהוּא מִלָּה דְּשָׁמַע, אָזִיל בְּגַוֵּויהּ כְּחֵיזְרָא בְּמַיָא, עַד דְּרָמֵי לֵיהּ לְבַר. מ"ט. מִשּׁוּם דְּלֵית רוּחֵיהּ רוּחָא דְּקִיּוּמָא. אֲבָל מַאן דְּרוּחֵיהּ רוּחָא דְּקִיּוּמָא, בֵּיהּ כְּתִיב, וְנֶאֱמַן רוּחַ מְכַסֶּה דָבָר. וְנֶאֱמַן רוּחַ, קִיּוּמָא דְּרוּחָא. בְּרוּחָא תַּלְיָיא מִלְּתָא. וּכְתִיב, אַל תִּתֵּן אֶת פִּיךָ לַחֲטִיא אֶת בְּשָׂרֶךָ.

8. Rabbi Shimon opened the discussion saying, "A talebearer (lit. 'goer') reveals secrets: but he that is of a faithful spirit conceals the matter" (Mishlei 11:13). This verse is difficult, but it should have said 'tale-man'. What is a TALE goer? HE REPLIES: It refers to someone who is not settled in mind and not trustworthy. Whatever he has heard goes within him like a board in the water THAT DOES NOT SINK UNTIL it is expelled outside, MEANING TO SAY HE HAS NO REST UNTIL HE REVEALS WHATEVER HE HEARD TO SOMEONE ELSE. What is the reason? It is because his spirit is not stable, SETTLED. Of him who has a stable spirit, it says "But he that is of a faithful spirit conceals the matter." A faithful spirit MEANS a stable spirit. It all depends on the spirit. It is also written: "Do not let your mouth cause your flesh to sin" (Kohelet 5:5).

9. וְלֵית עָלְמָא מִתְקַיְּימָא אֶלָּא בְּרָזָא. וְכִי אִי בְּמִלֵּי עָלְמָא אִצְטְרִיךְ רָזָא. בְּמִלִּין רָזִין דְּרָזַיָּיא דְּעַתִּיק יוֹמִין, דְּלָא אִתְמַסְרָאן אֲפִילוּ לְמַלְאָכִין עִלָּאִין עאכ"ו. אר"ש, לִשְׁמַיָּא לָא אֵימָא דְּיַצִּיתוּן, לְאַרְעָא לָא אֵימָא דְּתִשְׁמַע, דְּהָא אֲנַן קִיּוּמֵי עָלְמִין. תָּנָא רָזִין דְּרָזִין, כַּד פָּתַח ר"ש בְּרָזֵי דְּרָזִין, אִזְדַּעְזַע אַתְרָא, וְחַבְרִין אִתְחַלְחָלוּ.

9. The world is preserved only through secrecy and if, in worldly things, secrecy is a prerequisite, it is so much more certain that the mysteries of mysteries of Atik Yomin are not even passed on to the angels above. Rabbi Shimon said: To the heavens, I don't say to listen. To the earth I don't say to hear, since we maintain the worlds. THAT IS TO SAY, MOSES AND ISAIAH MADE THE HEAVENS AND EARTH WITNESSES TO PUNISH THE CHILDREN

OF YISRAEL IF THEY DO NOT MAINTAIN THE WORLDS, THAT THE HEAVENS WILL NOT GIVE ITS RAIN NOR THE EARTH ITS CROPS. BUT RABBI SHIMON WAS SPEAKING TO THE RIGHTEOUS, WHO MAINTAIN THE WORLD AND HAVE NO NEED FOR WITNESSES. We have learned of the mysteries of mysteries. When Rabbi Shimon began with the secrets of secrets, the place shook and the friends trembled.

2. "And these are the kings"

A Synopsis
Rabbi Shimon begins by saying that the friends are blessed and that to them are revealed the inner secrets of the Torah that have not even been revealed to the angels. The topic at hand here is the mention of the kings of Edom that reigned before the children of Yisrael came along and had any king. The secret of this alludes to the supernal worlds and the time before His corrections were maintained; all those kings of Edom died. Rabbi Shimon ends by talking about the creation of the Torah.

10. גַּלֵּי בְּרָזָא וּפָתַח וְאָמַר, כְּתִיב וְאֵלֶּה הַמְּלָכִים אֲשֶׁר מָלְכוּ בְּאֶרֶץ אֱדוֹם לִפְנֵי מְלָךְ מֶלֶךְ וְגוֹ'. זַכָּאִין אַתּוּן צַדִּיקַיָּיא, דְּאִתְגְּלֵי לְכוֹן רָזֵי דְרָזִין דְּאוֹרַיְיתָא, דְּלָא אִתְגַּלְיָין לְקַדִּישֵׁי עֶלְיוֹנִין, מַאן יַשְׁגַּח בְּהַאי, וּמַאן יִזְכֶּה בְּהַאי, דְּהַהוּא סַהֲדוּתָא עַל מְהֵימְנוּתָא דְכֹלָּא. צְלוֹתָא בִּרְעוּתָא יְהֵא, דְּלָא יִתְחֲשַׁב לְחוֹבָא לְגַלָּאָה דָּא. וּמַה יֵימְרוּן חַבְרַיָּיא, דְּהַאי קְרָא קַשְׁיָא הוּא, דְּהָא לָא הֲוָה לֵיהּ לְמִכְתַּב הָכִי, דְּהָא חֲזֵינָן כַּמָּה מְלָכִים הֲווֹ, עַד דְּלָא יֵיתוּן בְּנֵי יִשְׂרָאֵל, וְעַד לָא יְהִי מַלְכָּא לִבְנֵי יִשְׂרָאֵל וּמַה אִתְחֲזֵי הָכָא, וּבְדָא אִתְּעָרוּ חַבְרַיָּיא. אֶלָּא רָזָא דְרָזִין הוּא, דְּלָא יַכְלִין בְּנֵי נָשָׁא לְמִנְדַּע וּלְאִשְׁתְּמוֹדַע וּלְמִרְחַשׁ בְּדַעְתַּיְיהוּ בְּהַאי.

10. He revealed in secret and opened the discussion with the verse: "And these are the kings that reigned in the land of Edom, before there reigned any king..." (Beresheet 36:31). Blessed are you, righteous, to whom were revealed the inner secrets of the Torah, which are not revealed to the most holy beings up high, MEANING THE ANGELS. Who will be attentive to this and who will deserve this, THE VERSE: "AND THESE ARE THE KINGS..." That is evidence about overall faith. May the prayer be accepted that it will not be considered a sin to reveal this. What will the friends say, since this verse is difficult, since it was unnecessary to write this because we could see how many kings Edom had before the children of Yisrael came along, and prior to the children of Yisrael having a king? What is shown to us here? It is a high secret and men are incapable of knowing and understanding and contemplating this, SINCE IT ALLUDES TO THE SUPERNAL WORLDS.

11. תָּאנָא, עַתִּיקָא דְּעַתִּיקִין, טְמִירָא דִּטְמִירִין, עַד לָא זַמִּין תִּקּוּנוֹי, וְעָטוּרֵי עָטוּרִין, שֵׁירוּתָא וְסִיּוּמָא לָא הֲוָה. וַהֲוָה מַגְלִיף וּמְשַׁעֵר בֵּיהּ. וּפָרִיס קַמֵּיהּ חַד פַּרְסָא, וּבָהּ גָּלִיף וְשִׁיעֵר מַלְכִּין.

11. We have learned about the most Ancient of ancients, the most hidden of hidden, before he prepared his constructions and the crowns of crowns. THE PREPARATION OF THE VESSELS AND READYING THEM TO RECEIVE THE LIGHTS ARE CALLED CONSTRUCTIONS. THE LIGHTS THEMSELVES ARE CALLED CROWNS, DERIVED FROM THE VERSE: "THE CROWN WITH WHICH HIS MOTHER CROWNED HIM" (SHIR HASHIRIM 3:11). There did not yet exist a beginning nor an end, WHICH ARE UPPER CHOCHMAH, THE BEGINNING OF REVELATION, AND LOWER CHOCHMAH, THE END OF REVELATION. He was carving and estimating the limits of it, MEANING OF REVEALING THE BEGINNING AND THE END. He laid out a boundary and in it he marked and measured kings.

12. וְתִקּוּנוֹי לָא אִתְקְיָימוּ, הה"ד וְאֵלֶּה הַמְּלָכִים אֲשֶׁר מָלְכוּ בְּאֶרֶץ אֱדוֹם לִפְנֵי מְלָךְ מֶלֶךְ לִבְנֵי יִשְׂרָאֵל. מַלְכָּא קַדְמָאָה, לִבְנֵי יִשְׂרָאֵל קַדְמָאָה. וְכֻלְּהוּ דְּגָלִיפוּ בִּשְׁמָהָן אִתְקְרוּן. וְלָא אִתְקְיָימוּ, עַד דְּאָנַח לְהוּ, וְאַצְנַע לְהוּ, וּלְבָתַר זִמְנָא הוּא אִסְתְּלַק בְּהַהוּא פַּרְסָא, וְאִתְתָּקַּן בְּתִקּוּנוֹי.

12. His constructions were not maintained. This is what is written: "And these are the kings that reigned in the land of Edom, before there reigned any king over the children of Yisrael," MEANING BEFORE the first king that reigned over the first children of Yisrael. All that were recorded were called by their names but did not survive so eventually he abandoned them and hid them; he was elevated by that boundary and established with His own corrections.

13. וְתָאנָא, כַּד סָלִיק בִּרְעוּתָא, לְמִבְרֵי אוֹרַיְיתָא טְמִירְתָא תְּרֵי אַלְפֵי שְׁנִין, וְאַפְּקָהּ, מִיַּד אָמְרָה קַמֵּיהּ, מַאן דְּבָעֵי לְאַתְקְנָא וּלְמֶעְבַּד, יְתַקֵּן בְּקַדְמֵיתָא תִּקּוּנוֹי.

13. We have learned that when his wish came to pass, THE WISH OF THE EMANATOR, to create the Torah, she was hidden for 2,000 years and he produced her, MEANING CREATED HER. She immediately said to him: Whoever wishes to restore and accomplish, let him first tend to his own constructions.

3. The most ancient among the ancients

A Synopsis

Rabbi Shimon tells what the Hidden Book revealed about the most ancient among the ancients, and of how the illuminating light of the whiteness of the skull in the head of Arich Anpin is the legacy of the righteous in the World to Come.

14. תָּאנָא בְּצְנִיעוּתָא דְּסִפְרָא, עַתִּיקָא דְּעַתִּיקִין, סִתְרָא דְּסִתְרִין טָמִיר דִּטְמִירִין, אִתְתָּקַּן וְאִזְדְּמַן, כְּחַד סָבָא דְּסָבִין, עַתִּיק מֵעַתִּיקִין, טָמִיר מִטְמִירִין, וּבְתִיקּוּנוֹי יְדִיעַ וְלָא יְדִיעַ. מָארֵי דְּחִוָּור כְּסוּ, וְחֵיזוּ בּוּסִיטָא דְּאַנְפּוֹי, יָתִיב עַל כּוּרְסְיָיא דִּשְׁבִיבִין, לְאַכְפְּיָיא לוֹן.

14. We have learned from Tz'niuta Desafra (the hidden book) about the most ancient among the ancient, the most concealed of concealed, the most hidden of the hidden, who in his corrections was corrected and came, like the oldest among the old, most ancient of the ancients, the most hidden of the hidden, who in his constructions is known yet unknown. He is dressed in white and has a radiant WHITE countenance. HE resides on the throne of fiery sparks, in order to subdue them.

15. אַרְבַּע מְאָה אַלְפֵי עָלְמִין, אִתְפְּשַׁט חִוָּורָא דְּגוּלְגַּלְתָּא דְּרֵישׁוֹי. וּמִנְהִירוּ דְּהַאי חִיוָּורָא, יַרְתֵּי צַדִּיקַיָּיא לְעָלְמָא דְּאָתֵי, ד׳ מְאָה עָלְמִין, הה״ד אַרְבַּע מֵאוֹת שֶׁקֶל כֶּסֶף עוֹבֵר לַסּוֹחֵר.

15. Throughout 400,000 worlds, the whiteness of the skull in the head, ARICH ANPIN, spreads. The illuminating light of this whiteness is the legacy of the righteous in the World to Come, consisting of four hundred worlds. This is what is written: "four hundred shekels of silver, current money with the merchant" (Beresheet 23:16).

4. The skull

A Synopsis

Rabbi Shimon describes the skull of Arich Anpin in which are 130 million worlds, and he describes the flow of dew to Zeir Anpin and by which the dead wake up in the World to Come. He talks about that dew that sustains the Supreme Holy Ones and about the manna that sustains the righteous in the future. We learn how the whiteness of this skull radiates light in thirteen directions and how the dew flows to Zeir Anpin. The white illumination for the rest of the lower skulls (the crowns in the grades of the three worlds Briyah, Yetzirah and Asiyah) is drawn from the skull of Zeir Anpin.

16. בְּגוּלְגַּלְתָּא, יַתְבִין תְּלֵיסַר אַלְפֵי רִבּוֹא עָלְמִין, דְּנַטְלִין עֲלוֹי רַגְלִין, וְסָמְכִין עֲלוֹי. וּמֵהַאי גוּלְגַּלְתָּא נָטִיף טַלָּא, לְהַהוּא דִּלְבַר, וּמַלְיָיא לְרֵישֵׁיה בְּכָל יוֹמָא, דִּכְתִיב שֶׁרֹאשִׁי נִמְלָא טָל.

16. In the skull, WHICH IS KETER OF ARICH ANPIN, reside 13,000 x 10,000 (130 million) worlds that move on feet and are supported by them. From this skull, dew drops flow DAILY to the exterior one, ZEIR ANPIN, and fill the head every single day, as is written: "For my head is filled with dew" (Shir Hashirim 5:2).

17. וּמֵהַהוּא טַלָּא דְּאַנְעַר מֵרֵישֵׁיה, הַהוּא דְּאִיהוּ לְבַר, יִתְעֲרוּן מֵתַיָּיא לְעָלְמָא דְּאָתֵי. דִּכְתִיב כִּי טַל אוֹרוֹת טַלֶּךָ, אוֹרוֹת נְהוֹרָא דְּחַוַורְתָּא דְּעַתִּיקָא. וּמֵהַהוּא טַלָּא, מִתְקַיְימִין קַדִּישֵׁי עֶלְיוֹנִין. וְהוּא מָנָא דְּטַחֲנֵי לְצַדִּיקַיָּיא לְעָלְמָא דְּאָתֵי. וְנָטִיף הַהוּא טַלָּא לְחַקְלָא דְּתַפּוּחִין קַדִּישִׁין. הה"ד, וַתַּעַל שִׁכְבַת הַטָּל וְהִנֵּה עַל פְּנֵי הַמִּדְבָּר דַּק מְחוּסְפָּס. וְחֵיזוּ הַהוּא טַלָּא חִוָּור. כְּהַאי גַּוְונָא דְּאַבְנִין דִּבְדוֹלְחָא, דְּאִתְחַזְיָיא כָּל גַּוְונִין בְּגַוֵּיה. הה"ד וְעֵינוֹ כְּעֵין הַבְּדֹלַח.

17. From that dew, which is outside, and which ZEIR ANPIN shakes off from his head, the dead wake up TO LIFE in the World to Come, as it is written: "For your dew is as the dew on herbs (also: 'of lights')" (Yeshayah 26:19). THIS IS BECAUSE THIS DEW IS the illumination of the white light of Atika,

MEANING THE WHITENESS OF THE SKULL THAT IS NAMED ATIKA, and from that dew the supreme holy beings are sustained. That is the manna that is ground for the righteous in the future to come. That dew flows to the field of holy apple trees, THE MALCHUT, as it says, "And when the layer of dew was gone up, behold, upon the face of the wilderness there lay a fine flaky substance" (Shemot 16:14). The appearance of that dew is white like the crystal stones that appear to contain all the colors within them, as is written: "And its color was like the color of crystal" (Bemidbar 11:7).

18. הַאי גּוּלְגַּלְתָּא. חִוּוֹרָא דִּילֵיהּ, אַנְהִיר לִתְלֵיסַר עִיבָר גְּלִיפִין בְּסַחֲרָנוֹי. לְאַרְבַּע עִיבָר בְּסִטְרָא חַד, וּלְאַרְבַּע עִיבָר בְּסִטְרָא דָּא, בְּסִטְרָא דְּאַנְפּוֹי. וּלְאַרְבַּע עִיבָר בְּסִטְרָא דָּא, לְסִטְרָא דְּאַחוֹרָא. וְחַד לְעֵילָא דְּגוּלְגַּלְתָּא.

18. The whiteness of this skull, KETER OF ARICH ANPIN, radiates light to the thirteen directions engraved around it, four directions on this side OF THE FACE, four directions on that side of its face, ON THE RIGHT AND LEFT OF THE SKULL ON THE SIDE AGAINST THE FRONT FACE, and four directions on the back side. One DIRECTION is on top of the skull, IN THE CENTER BETWEEN RIGHT AND LEFT.

19. וּמֵהַאי אִתְפְּשַׁט אוֹרְכָּא דְּאַנְפּוֹי, לִתְלַת מְאָה וְשַׁבְעִין רִבּוֹא עָלְמִין. וְהַהוּא אִתְקְרֵי אֶרֶךְ אַפִּים. וְהַאי עַתִּיקָא דְּעַתִּיקִין אִתְקְרֵי אֲרִיכָא דְּאַנְפִּין. וְהַהוּא דִּלְבַר אִתְקְרֵי זְעֵיר אַנְפִּין. לָקֳבְלֵיהּ דְּעַתִּיקָא סָבָא, קֹדֶשׁ קָדָשִׁים דְּקֻדְשַׁיָּא. וּזְעֵיר אַנְפִּין כַּד אִסְתַּכַּל לְהַאי, כֹּלָּא דִּלְתַתָּא אִתְתְּקַן, וְאַנְפּוֹי מִתְפַּשְׁטִין וַאֲרִיכִין בְּהַהוּא זִמְנָא, אֲבָל לָא כָּל שַׁעֲתָא כְּמָה דְּעַתִּיקָא.

19. From this, the length of the face OF ARICH ANPIN spreads unto the 370 x 10,000 worlds. This is referred to as longsuffering (lit. 'of a long face'). THEREFORE, this most ancient Atika is called Arich Anpin, WHICH IS ARAMAIC FOR LONG FACE. That one outside, THE ONE THAT COATS FROM THE NAVEL DOWNWARD OF ARICH ANPIN, WHERE IT IS CONSIDERED AS THE EXTERIOR OF THE BODY, is called Zeir Anpin, corresponding to the

old Atika, the Holy of Holies of the Holies, WHICH IS ARICH ANPIN. When Zeir Anpin gazes at ARICH ANPIN, all below get restored and its face spreads and lengthens during that period. This is ONLY in periods OF FAVOR but not all the time like Atika, WHICH IS ARICH ANPIN.

20. וּמֵהַאי גּוּלְגַּלְתָּא, נָפִיק חַד עִיבָר חִיוָר לְגוּלְגַּלְתָּא דִּזְעֵיר אַנְפִּין, לְתַקְּנָא רֵישֵׁיה. וּמֵהַאי לִשְׁאַר גּוּלְגַּלְתִּין דִּלְתַתָּא, דְּלֵית לוֹן חוּשְׁבָּנָא. וְכָל גּוּלְגַּלְתָּא יָהֲבִין אֲגַר חִיוַּרְתָּא לְעַתִּיק יוֹמִין. כַּד עָאלִין בְּחוּשְׁבָּנָא תְּחוֹת שַׁרְבִיטָא. וְלָקֳבֵיל דָּא, בֶּקַע לַגוּלְגּוֹלֶת לְתַתָּא, כַּד עָאלִין בְּחוּשְׁבָּנָא.

20. From this skull, WHICH IS KETER OF ARICH ANPIN, emanates one white side FROM THE THIRTEEN WHITENESSES OF THE SKULL to the skull of Zeir Anpin, WHICH IS HIS KETER, to construct his head, MEANING TO ESTABLISH FOR HIM THE FIRST THREE SFIROT THAT ARE REFERRED TO AS THE HEAD. FROM THE SKULL OF ZEIR ANPIN IS DRAWN THE WHITE ILLUMINATION for the rest of the lower skulls, REFERRING TO THE CROWNS IN THE GRADES OF BRIYAH, YETZIRAH AND ASIYAH that are without number. Each skull pays a fee for THE ILLUMINATING OF the whiteness to Atik Yomin, when they are accounted under the scepter, and the half shekel per skull THAT THE CHILDREN OF YISRAEL GIVE in their census down below is parallel to this.

5. Membrane of air and the concealed brain

A Synopsis

We learn about the membrane that covers the brain that is the concealed Chochmah of Arich Anpin. The brains of Zeir Anpin spread out to 32 paths because the membrane is detached from Him.

21. בְּחַלָלָא דְגוּלְגַּלְתָּא, קְרוּמָא דַאֲוִירָא דְחָכְמְתָא עִלָּאָה סְתִימָה דְּלָא פָסַק. וְהַאי לָא שְׁכִיחַ, וְלָא אִתְפְּתַח. וְהַאי קְרוּמָא אִתְחַפְיָיא עַל מוֹחָא דְאִיהוּ חָכְמְתָא סְתִימָאָה. וּבְגִינֵי כַּךְ אִתְכַּסְיָא הַאי חָכְמְתָא בְּהַהוּא קְרוּמָא, דְּלָא אִתְפַּתְּחָא.

21. In the hollow space of the skull, there exists a tissue made of air of concealed upper Chochmah that is not detachable. THAT IS TO SAY, IN THE CRACKS OF THE SKULL THERE IS THE BRAIN OF AIR OF SUPERNAL CHOCHMAH AND UNDERNEATH THE BRAIN OF AIR, THERE IS AN UNBROKEN MEMBRANE. It is not common THAT IT BE BROKEN and it never opens. This membrane covers the brain, which is concealed Chochmah OF ARICH ANPIN. IN ARICH ANPIN THERE ARE THREE HEADS, BESIDES THE ONE HEAD THAT IS ATIK. THESE ARE THE SKULL AND THE UPPER CONCEALED CHOCHMAH, WHICH IS REFERRED TO AS THE BRAIN OF AIR THAT IS IN THE CRACKS OF THE SKULL, WHICH IS THE SECOND HEAD. THE LOWER CONCEALED CHOCHMAH IS IN THE HOLLOW OF THE SKULL, WHICH IS THE THIRD HEAD. THE MEMBRANE IS LOCATED UNDERNEATH THE BRAIN OF AIR AND ABOVE THE CONCEALED CHOCHMAH, AND COVERS THE CONCEALED CHOCHMAH SO IT SHOULD NOT RADIATE ITS ILLUMINATION TO THE OUTSIDE OF THE MEMBRANE. THIS IS WHY THIS CHOCHMAH WAS COVERED WITH THE MEMBRANE THAT IS IMPENETRABLE.

22. וְהַאי מוֹחָא, דְּאִיהוּ הַאי חָכְמְתָא סְתִימָאָה. שָׁקִיט וְאִשְׁתְּכִיךְ בְּאַתְרֵיה, כַּחֲמַר טַב עַל דּוּרְדְּיֵיה, וְהַיְינוּ דְּאַמְרֵי סָבָא דְעַתּוֹי סָתִים, וּמוֹחֵיה סָתִים וְשָׁכִיךְ.

22. This brain, which is the concealed Chochmah, THAT IS THE THIRD HEAD OF ARICH ANPIN, is still and quiet in its location like fine wine above its sediments. That is why they say an old person's mind is vague and his brain is veiled and not agitated.

-138-

23. וְהַאי קְרוּמָא אִתְפְּסַק מִזְּעֵיר אַפִּין, וּבְגִינֵי כַּךְ מוֹחֵיה אִתְפְּשַׁט
וְנָפִיק לִתְלָתִין וּתְרֵין שְׁבִילִין, הַה"ד וְנָהָר יוֹצֵא מֵעֵדֶן. מ"ט. מִשׁוּם
דְּקְרוּמָא אִתְפְּסַק, דְּלָא מְחַפְיָא עַל מוֹחָא. וְהַיְינוּ דְּתָנֵינָן בְּרֵישׁוּמֵי
אַתְוָון, תָּי"ו רָשִׁים רִישׁוּמָא לְעַתִּיק יוֹמִין דְּלֵית דִּכְוָותֵיה.

23. That membrane is detached from Zeir Anpin. Therefore, his brain spread out to 32 paths. It is written: "And a river went out of Eden" (Beresheet 2:10). Why so? Because the membrane gets broken and does not cover the brain. We have learned that from the letters' impressions, like THAT Tav, impressed upon Atik Yomin, ARICH ANPIN, the incomparable.

6. Pure wool

A Synopsis

Rabbi Shimon talks about the thousands of groups of hairs in the skull of the head, every strand of which glows in 410 worlds. A well spring glows and flows from these strands to the strands of Zeir Anpin, and the brain of Zeir Anpin gets constructed from these, after which it flows to the 32 paths of wisdom. Rabbi Shimon says that a person's character is revealed from his hair. From the parting of the hair Rabbi Shimon deduces a parting into 613 ways of the Torah, meaning the 613 precepts.

24. תָּאנָא, בְּגוּלְגַּלְתָּא דְּרֵישָׁא, תַּלְיָין אֶלֶף אַלְפִּין רִבּוֹא, וְשִׁבְעַת אַלְפִין, וַחֲמֵשׁ מְאָה קוֹצֵי דְּשַׂעֲרֵי, חִוָּור וְנָקִי, כְּהַאי עַמְרָא כַּד אִיהוּ נָקִי, דְּלָא אִסְתְּבַּךְ דָּא בְּדָא. דְּלָא לְאַחֲזָאָה עִרְבּוּבְיָה בְּתִקּוּנוֹי. אֶלָּא כֹּלָּא עַל בּוּרְיֵיהּ, דְּלָא נָפִיק נִימָא מִנִּימָא, וְשַׂעֲרָא מִשַּׂעֲרָא.

24. We have learned that in the skull of the head – THAT IS, IN KETER OF ARICH ANPIN – there are thousands of thousands of tens of thousands, seven thousand and five hundred groups of hairs. They are clean and white like wool that is clean and free of knots, untangled, so as not to appear tangled, but everything is in its place and not even minutely intrusive, without one hair over another hair.

25. וְכָל קוֹצָא וְקוֹצָא, אִית בֵּיה אַרְבַּע מְאָה וְעֶשֶׂר נִימֵי דְּשַׂעֲרֵי, כְּחוּשְׁבַּן קָדוֹ״שׁ. וְכָל נִימָא וְנִימָא לָהֵיט בְּאַרְבַּע מְאָה וְעֶשֶׂר עָלְמִין. וְכָל עָלְמָא וְעָלְמָא סָתִים וְגָנִיז, וְלֵית דְּיָדַע לוֹן, בַּר אִיהוּ. וְלָהֵיט לְאַרְבַּע מְאָה וְעֶשֶׂר עִיבַר.

25. Every individual lock OF HAIR has 410 bundles of hair, as the numerical value of *Kadosh* (Eng. 'holy'). Each hair strand glows in 410 worlds, AS THE NUMERICAL VALUE OF KADOSH. Each world is concealed and hidden, and is entirely unknown except to itself. It glows to 410 directions, ALSO THE NUMERICAL VALUE OF KADOSH. THIS IS THE SECRET MEANING OF THE THREE RECITED HOLINESSES: 'HOLY, HOLY, HOLY'.

26. וּבְכָל נִימָא וְנִימָא, אִית מַבּוּעַ דְּנָפְק מְמוֹחָא סְתִימָאָה, וְנָהִיר וְנָגִיד

בְּהַהוּא נִימָא, לְנִימִין דִּזְעֵיר אַנְפִּין. וּמֵהַאי מִתְקַן מוֹחֵיהּ. וּכְדֵין, נָגִיד הַהוּא מוֹחָא, לִתְלָתִין וּתְרֵין שְׁבִילִין.

26. Each individual strand of hair has a wellspring that emanates from a concealed brain, THAT IS THE THIRD HEAD OF ARICH ANPIN. It glows and flows from these strands to the strands of Zeir Anpin, and the brain OF ZEIR ANPIN is constructed from these, MEANING IT RECEIVES THE FIRST THREE SFIROT. Then the brain OF ZEIR ANPIN flows to the 32 paths OF CHOCHMAH.

27. וְכָל קוֹצָא וְקוֹצָא מִתְלַהֲטָן, וְתַלְיָין. מִתְתַּקְּנָן בְּתִקּוּנָא יָאָה, בְּתִקּוּנָא שַׁפִּירָא. מְחַפְּיָין עַל גּוּלְגַּלְתָּא. מִתְתַּקְּנֵי קוֹצֵי דְּנִימִין, מֵהַאי סִטְרָא, וּמֵהַאי סִטְרָא, עַל גּוּלְגַּלְתָּא. וְתָאנָא, כָּל נִימָא וְנִימָא, אִיהִי מְשִׁיכָא מִמַּבּוּעִין סְתִימִין, דְּנָפְקִין מִמּוֹחָא סְתִימָאָה.

27. All individual tips, WITHIN EACH GROUP OF HAIR, glow and hang; they are nicely arranged and cover the skull. Groups of hair strands are well established on each side over the skull – THAT IS ON THE RIGHT, THE LEFT AND THE MIDDLE. We have learned that each individual bunch OF HAIR is a continuous flow of the sealed wellsprings that emanate from the concealed brain, WHICH IS THE THIRD HEAD OF ARICH ANPIN.

28. וְתָאנָא, מִשַּׂעֲרוֹי דב"נ, אִשְׁתְּמוֹדַע מַאי הוּא, אִי דִּינָא אִי רַחֲמֵי. מִכַּד עַבְרִין עֲלוֹי אַרְבְּעִין שְׁנִין. וַאֲפִילוּ כַּד אִיהוּ עוֹלֵם, בִּשְׂעָרֵיהּ בְּדִיוּקְנֵיהּ וּבְגִבִּינֵי עֵינוֹי.

28. We have learned that a person's character is revealed from his hair, whether he is harsh or compassionate, that is, after the age of forty. Even in his youth, IT IS ALSO APPARENT in his hair and his shape and eyelashes.

29. קוֹצִין דְּשַׂעֲרֵי, תַּלְיָין בְּתִקּוּנֵי נַקְיֵי כַּעֲמַר נָקֵא עַד כַּתְפוֹי. עַד כַּתְפוֹי ס"ד. אֶלָּא עַד רֵישֵׁי דְּכַתְפוֹי, דְּלָא אִתְחֲזֵי קוּדְלָא. מִשּׁוּם דִּכְתִיב כִּי פָנוּ אֵלַי עוֹרֶף וְלֹא פָנִים. וְשַׂעֲרָא סָלִיק אֲבַתְרוֹי דְּאוּדְנִין, דְּלָא לְחַפְּיָא עֲלוֹי, דִּכְתִיב לִהְיוֹת אָזְנֶיךָ קַשֻּׁבוֹת.

29. The locks of hair hang to his shoulders, neat as refined wool. Do you think covering his shoulders? It is just to the top of his shoulders covering the back part of his neck, since it is written: "They turned their back to me, and not their face" (Yirmeyah 2:27). The hairs are tucked behind the ears, in order not to cover THE EARS, as it is written: "Let your ears be attentive" (Tehilim 130:2) .

30. שַׂעֲרָא דְּנָפִיק מִבָּתַר אוּדְנוֹי, כּוּלֵיה בְּשִׁקּוּלָא. לָא נָפִיק דָּא מִן דָּא, תִּקּוּנָא שְׁלִים. תִּקּוּנָא יָאֶה. תִּקּוּנָא שַׁפִּירָא. תָּאִיב לְמֶחֱמֵי. תִּיאוּבְתָּא וְחֶדְוָותָא דְּצַדִּיקַיָּיא, דְּאִינּוּן בִּזְעֵיר אַפִּין, לְמֶחֱמֵי וּלְאִתְדַּבְּקָא בְּתִקּוּנוֹי. דְּעַתִּיקָא סְתִימָאָה דְּכֹלָּא.

30. The hairs showing behind the ears are equally long with none intruding on each other. That is a perfect form, a proper form, a beautiful form, lovely to behold. The yearning and joy of the righteous that are in Zeir Anpin is to observe and cling to the form of the ancient one, which is completely concealed, WHICH IS ARICH ANPIN.

31. י"ג נִימִין דְּשַׂעֲרִין, קַיְימֵי מֵהַאי סִטְרָא, וּמֵהַאי סִטְרָא דְּגוּלְגַּלְתָּא, לָקֳבֵיל אַנְפּוֹי. וּבְאִינּוּן שָׁרְיָין שַׂעֲרֵי לְאִתְפַּלְּגָא. לֵית שְׂמָאלָא בְּהַאי עַתִּיקָא סְתִימָאָה, כֹּלָּא יְמִינָא. אִתְחֲזֵי וְלָא אִתְחֲזֵי. סָתִים וְלָא סָתִים. וְהַאי בְּתִקּוּנֵיהּ, כ"ש בֵּיה.

31. There are thirteen locks, MEANING BUNDLES, of hairs on each side of the skull, WHICH IS KETER OF ARICH ANPIN, against his face. With them, the hairs begin to part. THE ASPECT OF left does not exist in this concealed Atik, ARICH ANPIN. It is totally of the right, seen yet not seen, concealed though unconcealed. All this is a reflection of its form, and more on its own self.

32. וְעַל הַאי, תָּאִיבוּ בְּנֵי יִשְׂרָאֵל לְצָרְפָא בְּלִבְּהוֹן, דִּכְתִיב הֲיֵשׁ יְיָ' בְּקִרְבֵּנוּ אִם אָיִן. בֵּין זְעֵיר אַנְפִּין דְּאִקְרֵי יְיָ', וּבֵין אָרִיךְ אַנְפִּין דְּאִקְרֵי אַיִ"ן. אֲמַאי אִתְעֲנָשׁוּ. מִשּׁוּם דְּלָא עַבְדוּ בְּחֲבִיבוּתָא, אֶלָּא בְּנִסְיוֹנָא. דִּכְתִיב וְעַל נַסּוֹתָם אֶת יְיָ' לֵאמֹר הֲיֵשׁ יְיָ' בְּקִרְבֵּנוּ אִם אָיִן.

32. The children of Yisrael were longing to test this AND TO EXAMINE in their hearts, as is written: "Is Hashem among us, or not?" (Shemot 17:7), MEANING between Zeir Anpin called Hashem and Arich Anpin called naught. HE THEN ASKS: IF SO, why were they punished? HE RESPONDS: Because they did not do so out of love, but simply testing, as it is written: "And because they tempted Hashem, saying, 'Is Hashem among us, or not?'"

33. בְּפַלְגוּתָא דְשַׂעֲרֵי, אָזִיל חַד אָרְחָא דְנָהִיר לְמָאתָן וְשַׁבְעִין עָלְמִין. וּמִנֵּיה נָהִיר אָרְחָא דז״א, דְּנְהִירִין בֵּיה צַדִּיקַיָּיא לְעָלְמָא דְאָתֵי. הֲה״ד וְאוֹרַח צַדִּיקִים כְּאוֹר נוֹגַהּ הוֹלֵךְ וָאוֹר עַד נְכוֹן הַיּוֹם. וּמִן הַהוּא אָרְחָא אִתְפְּרָשָׁא לְשִׁית מֵאָה וּתְלֵיסַר אוֹרְחִין דְּאוֹרַיְיתָא, דְּפָלִיג בִּזְעֵיר אַפִּין. דִּכְתִיב בֵּיה כָּל אָרְחוֹת יְיָ׳ חֶסֶד וֶאֱמֶת וְגוֹ׳.

33. In the parting of the hair TO RIGHT AND LEFT OF THE SKULL, a path passes BETWEEN THEM that radiates light to 270 worlds. From this illuminates the path AT THE PLACE WHERE THE HAIR PARTS, of Zeir Anpin with which the righteous illuminate in the World to Come. This is what is written: "But the path of just men is like the gleam of sunlight, that shines ever more brightly until the height of noonday" (Mishlei 4:18). From that path OF ZEIR ANPIN, there is a parting into 613 ways of the Torah, which part in Zeir Anpin, MEANING THE 613 PRECEPTS of which it is written: "All the paths of Hashem are mercy and truth... " (Tehilim 25:10).

7. The will of the forehead

A Synopsis
The forehead of the skull of Arich Anpin is described as being the will of all wills, or desire, and Rabbi Shimon says that when this forehead is revealed the prayers of Yisrael are accepted. Of all his students only Rabbi Elazar seems to know that this happens during the time of the Minchah prayer of Shabbat, when anger is soothed and goodwill exists. Rabbi Shimon reveals that this forehead spreads out into 270,000 candles that illuminate from the supernal Eden, and only Zeir Anpin can grasp the supernal Eden and its paths of wisdom.

‎34. מִצְחָא דְגוּלְגַּלְתָּא, רָצוֹן אִקְרֵי. דְּהָא רַעֲוָין דְּרַעֲוִין אִתְגְּלֵי בְּהַהוּא מִצְחָא לָקֳבֵל דָּא לְתַתָּא. כְּתִיב וְהָיָה עַל מִצְחוֹ תָּמִיד לְרָצוֹן וְגוֹ' וְהַהוּא מִצְחָא דְאִקְרֵי רָצוֹן, הוּא גְּלוּיָיא דְּכָל רֵישָׁא וְגוּלְגַּלְתָּא, דְּמִתְכַּסְיָיא בְּאַרְבַּע מְאָה וְעֶשֶׂר עָלְמִין.

34. The forehead of the skull OF ARICH ANPIN is referred to as desire (will), because the will of all wills appears on that forehead. Corresponding to this, it is written below: "It shall always be upon his forehead, that they may be accepted (desired)... " (Shemot 28:38). That brow that is called desire is the revelation OF THE LIGHTS of the whole head and skull, which are concealed in 410 worlds.

‎35. וְכַד אִתְגַּלְיָא, אִתְקַבְּלָא צְלוֹתְהוֹן דְּיִשְׂרָאֵל. אֵימָתַי אִתְגַּלְיָא. שָׁתִיק ר"ש. שָׁאַל תִּנְיָינוּת אֵימָתַי. אר"ש לר' אֶלְעָזָר בְּרֵיהּ, אֵימָתַי אִתְגַּלְיָא. א"ל בְּשַׁעֲתָא דִּצְלוֹתָא דְּמִנְחָה דְּשַׁבַּתָּא. א"ל מ"ט. א"ל, מִשּׁוּם דְּהַהִיא שַׁעֲתָא בְּיוֹמֵי דְחוֹל, תַּלְיָא דִּינָא לְתַתָּא בִּזְעֵיר אַפִּין. וּבְשַׁבַּתָּא אִתְגַּלְיָא מִצְחָא דְאִתְקְרֵי רָצוֹן. בְּהַהִיא שַׁעֲתָא אִשְׁתְּכִיךְ רוּגְזָא. וְאִשְׁתְּכַח רַעֲוָא, וּמִתְקַבְּלָא צְלוֹתָא. הה"ד, וַאֲנִי תְפִלָּתִי לְךָ יְיָ' עֵת רָצוֹן. וְעֵת רָצוֹן מֵעַתִּיק יוֹמִין, לְגַלָּאָה מִצְחָא. ובג"כ אִתְתָּקַּן הַאי קְרָא, לְמֵימְרֵיהּ בִּצְלוֹתָא דְּמִנְחָה בְּשַׁבַּתָּא. אר"ש לר' אֶלְעָזָר בְּרֵיהּ, בְּרִיךְ בְּרִי לְעַתִּיק יוֹמִין, רַעֲוָא דְּמִצְחָא תִּשְׁכַּח בְּשַׁעֲתָא דְּתִצְטָרִיךְ לֵיהּ.

35. When THIS FOREHEAD is revealed, the prayers of Yisrael are accepted. When is it revealed? Rabbi Shimon remained silent, IN ORDER THAT ONE OF THE FRIENDS WOULD RESPOND. He asked again: When? THEY DIDN'T ANSWER HIM. Rabbi Shimon asked his son Rabbi Elazar: When will THE FOREHEAD be revealed? He said to him: During the time of the Minchah prayer of Shabbat. RABBI SHIMON asked him: What is the reason THAT THE BROW IS REVEALED DURING MINCHAH OF SHABBAT? RABBI ELAZAR responded: Because during this time in the weekdays, Judgment hangs below in Zeir Anpin, SINCE ISAAC, WHO IS THE SECRET OF THE LEFT COLUMN OF ZEIR ANPIN, WAS THE AUTHOR OF THE MINCHAH PRAYER. AND JUDGMENTS COME FORTH FROM THE ILLUMINATION OF CHOCHMAH ON THE LEFT. But on Shabbat, IT IS REVERSED, SINCE the brow OF ARICH ANPIN is revealed that is called desire. At that moment, anger is soothed and goodwill (lit. 'desire') abides, and the prayer is accepted. This is what is mean by: "But as for me, let my prayer be unto you, Hashem, in an acceptable time (lit. 'time of desire')" (Tehilim 69:14), since the time of goodwill is from the Ancient of Days, so as to reveal the brow. For this reason, it was decided that this verse be mentioned in the Minchah prayer of Shabbat. Rabbi Shimon said to his son Rabbi Elazar: Blessed shall you be my son, before the Ancient of Days. You should find goodwill from the brow when you will need it.

36. ת״ח, בִּשְׁאָר דִּלְתַתָּא, כַּד אִתְגְּלֵי מִצְחָא אִשְׁתְּכַח חוּצְפָּא, הה״ד וּמֵצַח אִשָּׁה זוֹנָה הָיָה לָךְ מֵאַנְתְּ הִכָּלֵם. וְהָכָא כַּד אִתְגְּלֵי מִצְחָא, חֲבִיבוּתָא וְרַעֲוָא שְׁלִים אִשְׁתְּכַח, וְכָל רוּגְזִין אִשְׁתְּכָכוּ וּמִתְכַּפְיָין קַמֵּיהּ.

36. Come and see for the rest down below. When the brow is revealed, you find insolence. This is what is written: "And you did have a harlot's forehead, you did refuse to be ashamed" (Yirmeyah 3:3). But here IN ARICH ANPIN when the forehead is revealed, love and goodwill are found there, and all kinds of anger are silenced and subdued before it.

37. מֵהַאי מִצְחָא דִּלְתַתָּא, נָהֲרִין אַרְבַּע מְאָה בָּתֵּי דִינִין. כַּד אִתְגַּלְיָיא הַאי עֵת רָצוֹן, כֻּלְּהוּ מִשְׁתַּכְחִין קַמֵּיהּ, הֲדָא הוּא דִּכְתִיב דִּינָא יְתִיב. וְתָאנָא, שַׂעֲרָא לָא קָאִים בְּהַאי אֲתָר, מִשּׁוּם דְּמִתְגַּלְיָיא, וְלָא אִתְכַּסְּיָיא אִתְגַּלְיָא, דְּיִסְתַּכְּלוּן מָארֵי דְדִינָא, וְיִשְׁתַּכְּכוּן. וְלָא אִתְעֲבִידוּ.

37. From this brow below, four hundred courts of judgment illuminate, WHICH ARE THE SECRET OF CHOCHMAH AND BINAH, TIFERET AND MALCHUT THAT ARE DRAWN FROM THE LEFT COLUMN OF IMA TO ZEIR ANPIN, OF WHICH EACH IS A HUNDRED IN NUMBER. When this time of goodwill is revealed IN THE FOREHEAD OF ARICH ANPIN, everything is silenced in his presence. This is what is said: "They sat in judgment (also: 'judgment is seated')" (Daniel 7:10), MEANING IT REMAINS IN PLACE AND THE SENTENCE IS NOT CARRIED OUT. We have learned that there are no hairs at that location IN THE BROW because it is revealed and does not get concealed, LIKE IN THE SKULL THAT IS FILLED WITH HAIRS. It is revealed in order that the litigants should reflect and quiet down and THE TRIALS will not be carried out.

38. תָּאנָא, הַאי מִצְחָא אִתְפְּשַׁט בְּמָאתָן וְשַׁבְעִין אַלְפִּין נְהִירִין בּוּצִינִין דְּנַהֲרִין מֵעֵדֶן עִלָּאָה. דְּתַנְיָא, אִית עֵדֶן דְּנָהִיר לְעֵדֶן. עֵדֶן עִלָּאָה לָא אִתְגַּלְיָיא, וְהוּא סָתִים בִּסְתִּימָא וְלָא מִתְפָּרְשָׁא לְאָרְחִין כִּדְקָאמְרָן. וְהַאי עֵדֶן דִּלְתַתָּא, מִתְפָּרַשׁ בִּשְׁבִילוֹי, לִתְלָתִין וּתְרֵין שְׁבִילִין.

38. We have learned that this forehead spreads out into 270,000 light candles that illuminate from the supernal Eden; EDEN MEANING CHOCHMAH. We have learned that there is an Eden that illuminates on Eden. The most supernal Eden, WHICH IS THE CONCEALED CHOCHMAH OF ARICH ANPIN, is not revealed, but is superbly concealed, MEANING WITH A SURROUNDING MEMBRANE OF AIR. It does not divide into paths, as we have explained. THAT IS, ITS ILLUMINATION DOES NOT ESCAPE, and that Eden below parts into 32 paths OF CHOCHMAH.

39. וְאע"ג דְּמִתְפָּרַשׁ הַאי עֵדֶן בִּשְׁבִילוֹי, לֵית דְּיָדַע לֵיהּ, בַּר הַאי זְעֵיר אַפִּין. וְעֵדֶן דִּלְעֵילָּא, לֵית דְּיָדַע לֵיהּ, וְלָא שְׁבִילוֹי, בַּר הַהוּא אֲרִיךְ אַנְפִּין. הה"ד אֱלֹהִים הֵבִין דַּרְכָּהּ וְהוּא יָדַע אֶת מְקוֹמָהּ. אֱלֹהִים הֵבִין דַּרְכָּהּ, דָּא עֵדֶן דִּלְתַתָּא, דְּיָדַע זְעֵיר אַפִּין. וְהוּא יָדַע אֶת מְקוֹמָהּ, דָּא עֵדֶן דִּלְעֵילָּא, דְּיָדַע עַתִּיק יוֹמִין, סְתִימָאָה דְּכֹלָּא.

39. Through this Eden BELOW, BINAH divides into its paths, TO THE 32 PATHS OF CHOCHMAH. There is no one to grasp it except Zeir Anpin.

Nobody grasps the Eden above nor its paths besides Arich Anpin. This is what is written: "And Elohim understands its way, and he knows its place" (Iyov 28:23). "Elohim understands its way" refers to the Eden below, which Zeir Anpin knows, BUT NO OTHER BUT HE BESTOWS HER TO THE MALCHUT. "And he knows its place" refers to the Eden above, WHICH IS CONCEALED CHOCHMAH OF ARICH ANPIN that the Ancient of Days knows, the most concealed of all. IT DOES NOT BESTOW IT BELOW.

8. The opening of the eyes

A Synopsis

Rabbi Shimon says that the eyes of the white head are different from other eyes in that they have no membrane cover and no eyelid, because they never sleep. Everything that comes down on us with compassion has no cover over the eye. We hear a description of the three whitenesses in the right eye and the three whitenesses in the left eye, and how they illuminate, rising and descending. The eye of Arich Anpin is never closed and it consists of two eyes reconstituted into one; he watches over everyone and keeps everyone safe. Rabbi Shimon says that the righteous will see this eye of Arich Anpin in the future with a spirit of wisdom. He tells how the hidden book reveals that everything gets illuminated from the ever-attentive watch of the lower eye of Zeir Anpin that receives light from the eye above. The eyes of Zeir Anpin are not always open; these eyes open upon some people in judgment if they are not righteous. We learn that the name of the Atik is the most concealed of all and is only mentioned openly in the Torah in one place. Rabbi Yehuda tells about the throne of Atik Yomin.

40. עֵינוֹי דְּרֵישָׁא חִוָּורָא, מִשְׁתַּנְּיִין מִשְּׁאַר עַיְינִין, לֵית כְּסוּתָא עַל עֵינָא. וְלֵית גְּבִינִין עַל עֵינָא. מ"ט. דִּכְתִיב הִנֵּה לֹא יָנוּם וְלֹא יִישָׁן שׁוֹמֵר יִשְׂרָאֵל. יִשְׂרָאֵל דִּלְעֵילָּא. וּכְתִיב אֲשֶׁר עֵינֶיךָ פְּקוּחוֹת. וְתָאנָא, כָּל מַה דְּאָתֵי בְּרַחֲמֵי, לֵית כְּסוּתָא עַל עֵינָא, וְלֵית גְּבִינִין עַל עֵינָא. כ"ש רֵישָׁא חִוָּורָא, דְּלָא בָּעֵא מִידִי.

40. The eyes of the white head, THAT IS, KETER OF ARICH ANPIN, THAT IS CALLED THE SKULL are different from other eyes. There is no membrane cover and no eyelid over the eye. What is the reason? It is because it is written: "Behold, he who keeps Yisrael shall neither slumber nor sleep" (Tehilim 121:4), MEANING HE WHO KEEPS Yisrael above, WHICH IS ZEIR ANPIN, WHOM THE EYES OF ARICH ANPIN KEEP. It is written: "Your eyes are open" (Yirmeyah 32:19) WITHOUT A MEMBRANE COVER, and we learn that everything that descends upon us with compassion has no cover on the eye and has no eyelid over the eye. All the more so the white head that needs none.

41. אָמַר ר' שִׁמְעוֹן לְר' אַבָּא לְמַאי הִיא רְמִיזָא. א"ל לְנוּנֵי יַמָּא, דְּלֵית

כְּסוּתָא עַל עֵינָא, וְלֵית גְּבִינִין עַל עֵינָא, וְלָא נַיְימִין, וְלָא בָּעְיָין נְטוּרָא
עַל עֵינָא. כ״ש עַתִּיקָא דְּעַתִּיקָא, דְּלָא בָּעֵי נְטוּרָא. וְכ״ש דְּאִיהוּ מַשְׁגַּח
לְכֹלָּא, וְכֹלָּא מִתְּזָן בֵּיהּ וְלָא נָאִים. הה״ד, הִנֵּה לֹא יָנוּם וְלֹא יִישָׁן
שׁוֹמֵר יִשְׂרָאֵל, יִשְׂרָאֵל דִּלְעֵילָּא.

41. Rabbi Shimon remarked to Rabbi Aba: What is this alluding to? He
replied to him: To fish of the sea that have no eyelids or covering
membranes. They do not sleep and require no protection over their eyes,
BECAUSE MERCY FLOWS ON THEM. All the more so the most Ancient of
all that requires no sentinel, since he is the one that takes care of everything,
and all take their sustenance from him. He does not sleep. That is what is
meant by: "Behold, he who keeps Yisrael shall neither slumber nor sleep,"
FOR IT GUARDS Yisrael above, WHICH IS ZEIR ANPIN.

42. כְּתִיב הִנֵּה עֵין יְיָ' אֶל יְרֵאָיו. וּכְתִיב עֵינֵי יְיָ' יְיָ' הֵמָּה מְשׁוֹטְטִים בְּכָל
הָאָרֶץ. לָא קַשְׁיָא, הָא בִּזְעֵיר אַפִּין. הָא בַּאֲרִיךְ אַנְפִּין. וְעכ״ד תְּרֵי
עַיְינִין אִינוּן וְאִתְחַזְרוּ לְחַד, עֵינָא דְּאִיהִי חִוָּור בְּגוֹ חִוָּור וְחִוָּור דִּכְלִיל
כָּל חִוָּור.

42. It is written: "Behold, the eye of Hashem is upon those who fear him"
(Tehilim 33:18), WHICH MEANS ONE EYE. It is written: "The eyes of
Hashem, they rove to and fro through the whole earth" (Zechariah 4:10),
WHICH MEANS TWO EYES. HE REPLIES: It is no contradiction. Here in Zeir
Anpin, THERE ARE TWO EYES, but here in Arich Anpin, THERE IS ONE
EYE. In spite of all this, there are two eyes that turn into one, which is white
within the white, and the white is inclusive of all that is white.

43. חִוָּורָא קַדְמָאָה, נָהִיר וְסָלִיק, וְנָחִית לְאַסְתַּכְּלָא, דְּצָרִיר בִּצְרוֹרָא.
תָּאנָא, בָּטַשׁ הַאי חִוָּורָא, וְאַדְלִיק ג' בּוֹצִינֵי, דְּאִקְרוּן: הוֹד. וְהָדָר.
וְחֶדְוָה. וְלַהֲטִין בְּחֶדְוָותָא בִּשְׁלֵימוּתָא.

43. The original whiteness illuminates, ascends and descends to look on
THAT which is bounded in a bundle. We have learned that whiteness struck
and lit three candles called glory, majesty and joy, and they all glow in
perfect happiness.

44. חִוָּורָא תִּנְיָינָא, נָהִיר, וְסָלִיק וְנָחִית, וּבָטַשׁ וְאַפִּיק ג' בּוֹצִינִין אַחֲרָנִין, דְּאִקְרוּן נֶצַח וָחֶסֶד וְתִפְאֶרֶת, וְלָהֲטִין בִּשְׁלֵימוּתָא בְּחֶדְוָותָא.

44. The second whiteness illuminates. It ascends and ITS LIGHT descends. It stamps and produces three other candles called Netzach, Chesed and Tiferet which glow in perfect happiness.

45. חִוָּורָא תְּלִיתָאָה, לָהִיט וְנָהִיר, וְנָחִית וְסָלִיק, וְנָפִיק מִסְתִּימוּתָא דְּמוֹחָא, וּבָטַשׁ בְּבוֹצִינָא אֶמְצָעִיתָא, שְׁבִיעָאָה. וְאַפִּיק אָרְחָא לְמוֹחָא תַּתָּאָה, וּמִתְלַהֲטָן כֻּלְּהוּ בּוֹצִינִין דִּלְתַתָּא. אָמַר ר"שׁ יָאוּת הוּא, וְעַתִּיק יוֹמִין יִפְקַח עֵינָא דָּא עֲלָךְ, בְּשַׁעֲתָא דְּתִצְטְרִיךְ לֵיהּ.

45. The third whiteness glows and radiates light. It exits the cover of the brain, and it stamps the center candle in the seventh. It creates a path to ILLUMINATE to the lower brain, ZEIR ANPIN, and all candles below, IN ZEIR ANPIN, glow. Rabbi Shimon said: It is beautiful. May the Ancient of Days open His eyes over you when you need Him.

46. תָּאנָא חִוָּור בְּגוֹ חִוָּור. וְחִוָּור דְּכָלִיל כָּל חִוָּור. חִוָּורָא קַדְמָאָה, נָהִיר, וְסָלִיק. וְנָחִית לְתַתָּא לִתְלַת בּוֹצִינֵי דְּלִסְטַר שְׂמָאלָא, וְלָהֲטִין וְאַסְחָן בְּהַאי חִוָּורָא, כְּמַאן דְּאַסְחֵי גוּפֵיהּ בְּבוּסְמִין טָבִין, וּבְרֵיחִין, עַל מַה דַּהֲווֹ עֲלוֹי בְּקַדְמֵיתָא.

46. We have learned that of white is within white. The white includes all that is white. HE EXPLAINS: The first white shine, ascends and descends downward to the three candles on the left side. They glow and bathe in this white, as someone who bathes his body with good perfumes and pleasant fragrances to clean what he went through before.

47. חִוָּורָא תִּנְיָינָא, נָחִית, וְסָלִיק, וְנָהִיר לִתְלַת בּוֹצִינֵי, דְּלִסְטַר יְמִינָא, וְלָהֲטִין וְאַסְחִין בְּהַאי חִוָּורָא, כְּמַאן דְּאַסְחֵי בְּבוּסְמִין טָבִין וּבְרֵיחִין, עַל מַה דַּהֲווֹ עֲלוֹי בְּקַדְמֵיתָא.

47. The second white descends and ascends and illuminates to the three candles of the right side. They glow and bathe in the white OF THE RIGHT EYE as one that bathes himself in fine perfumes and fragrances, to cleanse what he went through before.

48. חִוָּוְרָא תְּלִיתָאָה, נָהִיר וְסָלִיק וְנָחִית, וְנָפִיק נְהִירוּ דְּחִוָּוְרָא, דִּלְגוֹ לְגוֹ מִן מוֹחָא, וּבָטַשׁ בְּשַׂעֲרָא אוּכְמָא, כַּד אִצְטְרִיךָ. וּבְרֵישָׁא. וּבְמוֹחָא דְּרֵישָׁא. וְנָהִיר לִתְלַת כִּתְרִין דְּאִשְׁתָּאֲרוּ, כְּמָה דְּאִצְטְרִיךָ לְגַלָּאָה. אִי נִיחָא קַמֵּי עַתִּיק סְתִימָא דְּכֹלָּא.

48. The third white illuminates rising and descending. THROUGH IT, white light emanates from the innermost part of the brain and beats on the black hair OF ZEIR ANPIN as needed, and also on the head and the brain in the head OF ZEIR ANPIN. It illuminates the remaining three Sfirot, WHICH ARE CHOCHMAH, BINAH AND DA'AT. UNTIL NOW, NOTHING IS REVEALED EXCEPT FOR CHESED, GVURAH, TIFERET, NETZACH, HOD AND YESOD. THEY BECOME REVEALED as revelation is necessary, if the concealed Atik wishes TO HAVE IT REVEALED.

49. וְתָאנָא לָא סָתִים הַאי עֵינָא. וְאִינּוּן תְּרֵין וְאִתְחֲזָרוּ לְחַד. כֹּלָּא הוּא יְמִינָא. לֵית בֵּיהּ שְׂמָאלָא. לָא נָאִים וְלָא אַדְמִיךָ, וְלָא בָּעֵי נְטִירוּתָא. לֵית מַאן דְּאָגִין עֲלֵיהּ. הוּא אַגִּין עַל כֹּלָּא, וְהוּא אַשְׁגַּח עַל כֹּלָּא. וּמֵאַשְׁגָּחוּתָא דְּהַאי עֵינָא מִתְזָנָן כֻּלְּהוּ.

49. We have learned that this eye OF ARICH ANPIN is not closed, and they are two EYES reconstituted into one. All of it is right and it contains no left, since it does not slumber or sleep and it requires no guarding. There is no one that is capable of shielding it. It keeps everyone else safe and watches over all. From the watchful guardianship of that eye, everyone is sustained.

50. תָּאנָא, אִי עֵינָא דָּא אַסְתִּים רִגְעָא חֲדָא, לָא יַכְלִין לְקַיְּימָא כֻּלְּהוּ, בְּג"כ אִקְרֵי עֵינָא פְּקִיחָא. עֵינָא עִלָּאָה. עֵינָא קַדִּישָׁא. עֵינָא דְּאַשְׁגָּחוּתָא. עֵינָא דְּלָא אַדְמִיךָ וְלָא נָאִים. עֵינָא דְּהוּא נְטוּרָא דְּכֹלָּא.

עֵינָא דְהוּא קִיּוּמָא דְּכֹלָּא. וְעַל הַאי כְּתִיב טוֹב עַיִן הוּא יְבוֹרָךְ, אַל תִּקְרֵי יְבוֹרָךְ אֶלָּא יְבָרֵךְ. דְּהַאי אִתְקְרֵי טוֹב עַיִן, וּמִנֵּיהּ מְבָרֵךְ לְכֹלָּא.

50. We have learned that if that one eye OF ARICH ANPIN is closed for even a split second, no existence would be possible. Therefore, it is called an open eye, a supernal eye, a holy eye, an ever-attentive eye, an eye that does not slumber or sleep, an eye that is vigilant of everything, an eye that is the preservation of everything in existence. About this eye, it is written: "He that has a generous eye shall be blessed" (Mishlei 22:9). Do not read it as "shall be blessed," but rather 'shall bless', since that is considered one of a goodly eye. From it, everyone gets blessed.

51. וְתָאנָא, לֵית נְהִירוּ לְעֵינָא תַּתָּאָה, לְאִסְתַּחֲאָה מֵאַדְמִימוּתָא מֵאוּכְמוּתָא בַּר כַּד חֲזֵי מֵהַאי נְהוֹרָא חִוּוֹרָא דְעֵינָא עִלָּאָה דְּאִקְרֵי טוֹב עַיִן. וְלֵית דְּיָדַע כַּד נָהִיר עֵינָא עִלָּאָה דָא קַדִּישָׁא וְאַסְחֵי לְעֵינָא תַּתָּאָה דָא. בַּר אִיהוּ.

51. We have learned that there is no light to this lower eye OF ZEIR ANPIN to wash away the redness and blackness, except when it sees the white light of the upper eye OF ARICH ANPIN, which is referred to as one at a goodly eye. No one knows when this upper holy eye OF ARICH ANPIN illuminates and bathes the lower eye OF ZEIR ANPIN, except for it.

52. וְזִמְנִין צַדִּיקַיָּיא, זַכָּאֵי עֶלְיוֹנִין, לְמֶחֱמֵי דָא בְּרוּחָא דְחָכְמְתָא, הה"ד כִּי עַיִן בְּעַיִן יִרְאוּ. אֵימָתַי. בְּשׁוּב יְיָ' צִיּוֹן. וּכְתִיב אֲשֶׁר עַיִן בְּעַיִן נִרְאָה אַתָּה יְיָ'. וְאִלְמָלֵא עֵינָא טָבָא עִלָּאָה, דְּאַשְׁגַּח וְאַסְחֵי לְעֵינָא תַּתָּאָה, לָא יָכִיל עָלְמָא לְמֵיקָם רִגְעָא חֲדָא.

52. The righteous and the most meritorious will see in the future this EYE OF ARICH ANPIN with a spirit of wisdom. This is what is written: "For they shall see eye to eye" (Yeshayah 52:8). When WILL THIS HAPPEN? When "Hashem returning to Zion" (Ibid.). It is further written: "That you Hashem are seen eye to eye" (Bemidbar 14:14). If not for the uppermost good eye OF ARICH ANPIN that is ever-attentive and bathes the lower eye OF ZEIR

ANPIN, the universe could not exist even for a moment.

53. תָּאנָא בְּצְנִיעוּתָא דְּסִפְרָא, אַשְׁגָּחוּתָא דְעֵינָא תַּתָּאָה, כַּד אַשְׁגַּח נְהִירוּ עִלָּאָה בֵּיהּ, וְעָיֵיל הַהוּא נְהִירוּ דְעִלָּאָה בְּתַתָּאָה. דְּמִנֵּיהּ נָהִיר כֹּלָּא הה"ד אֲשֶׁר עַיִן בְּעַיִן נִרְאָה אַתָּה יְיָ'.

53. We have learned in the hidden book that everything is illuminated from the ever-attentive watch of the lower eye, when the light of the above EYE is attentive to it and the light of the above EYE enters the lower EYE OF ZEIR ANPIN. This is what is written: "That you Hashem are seen eye to eye."

54. כְּתִיב הִנֵּה עֵין יְיָ' אֶל יְרֵאָיו. וּכְתִיב עֵינֵי ה' הֵמָּה מְשׁוֹטְטִים בְּכָל הָאָרֶץ. זָכוּ, עֵינֵי יְיָ' אֶל יְרֵאָיו, עֵינָא דִּלְעֵילָא. לָא זָכוּ, עֵינֵי יְיָ' הֵמָּה מְשׁוֹטְטוֹת, עֵינָא דִּלְתַתָּא.

54. It is written: "Behold, the eye of Hashem is upon those who fear him" (Tehilim 33:18) and it is also written: "The eyes of Hashem, they rove to and fro through the whole earth" (Zechariah 4:10). MEANING: If they merit, "the eye of Hashem is upon those who fear him": that is, the upper eye OF ARICH ANPIN. If they have no merit, "the eyes of Hashem, they rove to and fro": THAT IS the lower eye OF ZEIR ANPIN.

55. דְּתַנְיָא, מִפְּנֵי מָה זָכָה יוֹסֵף דְּלָא שַׁלְטָא בֵּיהּ עֵינָא בִּישָׁא, מִפְּנֵי שֶׁזָּכָה לְאִשְׁתַּגְּחָא בְּעֵינָא טָבָא עִילָּאָה, הה"ד בֵּן פּוֹרָת יוֹסֵף בֵּן פּוֹרָת עֲלֵי עָיִן. אַמַּאי הוּא בֵּן פּוֹרָת. עֲלֵי עָיִן. כְּלוֹמַר עַל סִבַּת עַיִן דְּאִשְׁתְּגַח בֵּיהּ.

55. We have learned that the reason Joseph merited that no evil eye would have any domination over him is because he gained the merit to be watched by the upper good eye OF ARICH ANPIN. This is what it means in, "Joseph is a fruitful bough, a fruitful bough by a well" (Beresheet 49:22), MEANING why is he "a fruitful bough"? BECAUSE NO EVIL EYE WAS DOMINATING HIM BECAUSE OF "a well (Heb. ayin)," meaning to say due to the eye (Heb. ayin) OF THE HIGH ONE OF ARICH ANPIN that was watchful of him.

‏56. וּכְתִיב טוֹב עַיִן הוּא יְבוֹרָךְ, מ״ט. כִּי נָתַן מִלַּחְמוֹ לַדָּל. מ״ט אִקְרֵי חַד. ת״ח, בְּעֵינֵיה דִּתַתָּאָה אִית עֵינָא יְמִינָא, וְאִית עֵינָא דִּשְׂמָאלָא. וְאִינּוּן תְּרֵי, בִּתְרֵי גְּוָונֵי. אֲבָל הָכָא, לֵית עֵינָא שְׂמָאלָא. וְתַרְווַיְיהוּ בְּדַרְגָּא חַד סַלְקֵי, וְכֹלָּא יְמִינָא. וּבְגִינֵי כַּךְ, עֵינָא חַד, וְלָא תְּרֵין.‏

56. It is written: "He that has a generous eye shall be blessed." What is the reason? "For he gives of his bread to the poor" (Mishlei 22:9). He further inquires: What is the reason that it is referred to as one EYE? IT DID NOT SAY, 'HE THAT HAS GENEROUS EYES SHALL BE BLESSED'. HE RESPONDS: Come and see, in the lower eye OF ZEIR ANPIN, there exists a right eye and a left eye. They are two, in two SPECIFIC senses, THE RIGHT BEING CHASSADIM AND THE LEFT BEING THE ILLUMINATION OF CHOCHMAH. However, here IN ARICH ANPIN, there exists no left eye. Both are considered in one level, everything being right, THE MEANING OF WHITE WITHIN WHITE. Therefore, IT IS WRITTEN AS one eye: "GENEROUS EYE SHALL BE BLESSED" and not two, BECAUSE HE WHO "GIVES OF HIS BREAD TO THE POOR" MERITS THE BLESSING OF THE UPPER EYE OF ARICH ANPIN, WHICH IS ONE EYE.

‏57. וְתָאנָא, עֵינָא דָּא, דְּהוּא עֵינָא דְּאַשְׁגָּחוּתָא. פְּקִיחָא תָּדִיר. חַיְיכָאן תָּדִיר. וְחַדָּאן תָּדִיר, דְּלָא הֲוֵי הָכִי לְתַתָּאָה, דְּכְלִילָן בְּסוּמָקָא וּבְאוּכְמָא וּבְחִוְוָרָא, בג׳ גְּוָונֵי, וְלָא הֲוָה תָּדִיר פְּקִיחָא דְּלֵיה עֵינֵיה בִּגְבִינֵי דִמְכַסָּאן עַל עֵינָא. וע״ד כְּתִיב, עוּרָה לָמָּה תִישַׁן יְיָ׳. פְּקַח יְיָ׳ עֵינֶיךָ.‏

57. We have learned that this eye OF ARICH ANPIN, the ever-attentive eye, is always open, always smiling, always happy. That is not the case below, IN ZEIR ANPIN, that ARE combined in red, black, and white, in three colors. They are not continuously open, since it has eyelids over the eyes that cover the eye. Therefore, it is written: "Awake, why sleep you, Hashem?" (Tehilim 44:24). "Open, Hashem, your eyes, and see" (II Melachim 19:16), WHICH MEANS THEY ARE NOT ALWAYS OPEN.

‏58. כַּד אִתְפְּקַח, אִית לְמַאן דְּאִתְפְּקַח לְטָב. וּלְמַאן דְּלָא אִתְפְּקַח לְטָב. וַוי לְמַאן דְּאִתְפְּקַח וְעֵינָא אִתְעָרַב בְּסוּמָקָא, וְסוּמָקָא אִתְחֲזֵי לְקַבְלֵיה,‏

וּמְכַסְיָא עֵינָא. מַאן יִשְׁתְּזִיב מִנֵּיהּ. אֲבָל עַתִּיק יוֹמִין, טָבָא דְּעֵינָא.
חִוֵּור בְּגוֹ חִוֵּור. חִוֵּור דְּכָלִיל כָּל חִוּוּרֵי. זַכָּאָה חוּלָקֵיהּ, לְמַאן דְּיִשְׁגַּח
עֲלֵיהּ, חַד חִוֵּור מִנַּיְיהוּ. וְעַ"ד וַדַּאי כְּתִיב טוֹב עַיִן הוּא יְבוֹרָךְ. וּכְתִיב
בֵּית יַעֲקֹב לְכוּ וְנֵלְכָה בְּאוֹר יְיָ'.

58. When THE EYES OF ZEIR ANPIN opened, there were some upon whom the eyes opened for good and some upon whom the eyes did not open for good. Woe to the one TO WHOM THE EYES opened and the eye is blended with red, WHICH IS THE COLOR OF JUDGMENT. This red appears before him and covers the eye. Who could be saved from it? MEANING TO SAY THAT WHOEVER HAS NO MERIT, THE LEFT ILLUMINATES UPON HIM WITHOUT THE RIGHT, THE SECRET MEANING OF THE RED COLOR, DURING WHICH TIME ALL HARSH JUDGMENTS ARE DRAWN FROM IT. However, the Ancient of Days, MEANING ARICH ANPIN, has a good eye that is white within white, and a white containing all whites. Praiseworthy is the lot of the person who has one of the whites watchful over him. About this, it is most certainly written: "He that has a generous eye shall be blessed." It is also written: "O house of Jacob, come, and let us continue to go in the light of Hashem" (Yeshayah 2:5), MEANING, LET US WALK UNDER THE SUPERVISION OF THE LIGHT OF HASHEM, WHO IS OF A BENEFICENT EYE, AS MENTIONED.

59. תָּאנָא, שְׁמֵיהּ דְּעַתִּיקָא סָתִים מִכֹּלָּא, וְלָא מִתְפָּרֵשׁ בְּאוֹרָיְיתָא, בַּר
מִן אֲתָר חַד, דְּאוֹמֵי זְעֵיר אַפִּין לְאַבְרָהָם, דִּכְתִיב בִּי נִשְׁבַּעְתִּי נְאֻם יְיָ'.
נְאֻם דִּזְעֵיר אַפִּין. וּכְתִיב, בְּךָ יְבָרֵךְ יִשְׂרָאֵל, יִשְׂרָאֵל דִּלְעֵילָא. וּכְתִיב
יִשְׂרָאֵל אֲשֶׁר בְּךָ אֶתְפָּאָר, לְיִשְׂרָאֵל קָאָמַר דָּא. וְתָנֵינָן עַתִּיק יוֹמִין
אָמְרוֹ וְהַאי וְהַאי שַׁפִּיר.

59. We have learned that the name of Atik THAT IS ARICH ANPIN IS the most concealed of all, and is not mentioned openly in the Torah except for one place, that Zeir Anpin swore to Abraham, as is written: "By Myself have I sworn, says Hashem" (Beresheet 22:16). That is the speech of Zeir Anpin, WHEN SWEARING BY ATIK. It is also written: "By You shall Yisrael bless" (Beresheet 48:20), meaning Yisrael of above. IF SO, "BY YOU SHALL YISRAEL BLESS" IS ADDRESSED TO ATIK THAT IS ARICH ANPIN. It is also written: "Yisrael, in whom I will be glorified" (Yeshayah 49:3). He said this to Yisrael and we learn that Ancient of Days said this TO ZEIR ANPIN, WHO IS YISRAEL ABOVE. Both are good, SINCE BOTH EXPLANATIONS HOLD TRUE.

60. תַּנְיָא, כְּתִיב חָזֵה הֲוֵית עַד דִּי כּוֹרְסָוָון רְמִיו וְעַתִּיק יוֹמִין יְתִיב. כּוֹרְסָוָון רְמִיו, מַאן הוּא. אָמַר לְרַבִּי יְהוּדָה, קוּם בְּקִיוּמָךְ וְאַתְקִין כֻּרְסְיָיא דָּא.

60. We have learned that it is written: "As I looked, thrones were placed, and an ancient of days did sit" (Daniel 7:9). HE ASKS: What is the meaning of "thrones were placed"? He told Rabbi Yehuda: Rise in your place and prepare this throne.

61. א"ר יְהוּדָה, כְּתִיב כּוֹרְסְיֵיה שְׁבִיבִין דִּינוּר. וְעַתִּיק יוֹמִין יְתִיב עַל הַאי כֻּרְסְיָיא. מ"ט. דְּתַנְיָא אִי עַתִּיק יוֹמִין לָא יָתִיב עַל הַאי כֻּרְסְיָיא, לָא יָכִיל לְאַתְקַיְּימָא עָלְמָא, מִקַּמֵּי הַהוּא כּוּרְסְיָיא. כַּד יְתִיב עַתִּיק יוֹמִין עֲלֵיה אִתְכַּפְיָיא לְהַהוּא כּוּרְסְיָיא, וּמַאן דְּרָכִיב שַׁלִּיט. בְּעִידָנָא דְּנָטִיל מֵהַאי כֻּרְסְיָיא, וְיָתִיב עַל כּוּרְסְיָיא אַחֲרָא, כּוּרְסְיָיא קַדְמָאָה רְמִיו, דְּלָא שַׁלְטָא אֶלָּא אִיהוּ דְּרָכִיב בֵּיה עַתִּיק יוֹמִין. א"ר שִׁמְעוֹן לר' יְהוּדָה, יִתְּתַּקַּן אָרְחָךְ, וְיֵיתֵי בָּךְ מֵעַתִּיק יוֹמִין.

61. Rabbi Yehuda said: It is written: "His throne was fiery flames" (Ibid.) and ancient of days did sit upon this throne. What is the reason THAT HE SITS ON A FIERY THRONE? We have learned if Atik Yomin would not have been sitting on this throne, the world would have no possibility of existence because of this throne. When Atik Yomin sits on it, this throne is subdued and whoever rides it reigns. During the periods that He leaves this throne and sits on another throne, the first throne gets discarded, since dominion is only to the throne upon which Atik Yomin rides. Rabbi Shimon told Rabbi Yehuda: Let your path be readied and let THE ILLUMINATION OF ATIK YOMIN enter you.

9. The nose

A Synopsis

This section describes the nose of Arich Anpin, from which emanates life, the light of life of the resurrection of the dead, and the spirit of life called forgiveness that blows to Zeir Anpin. Rabbi Yosi informs us that during the time of Messiah all people will know God and will not need to learn wisdom from one another. During that time Atik Yomin will emanate a spirit that awakens the spirits below, the holy Sfirot of Zeir Anpin. The spirits of everyone will consist of omniscience, wisdom, understanding, counsel, might, knowledge and the fear of God. We are told that the nose of Arich Anpin is life with all its aspects, both in this world and in the World to Come.

62. וְת"ח כְּתִיב אֲנִי יְיָ' רִאשׁוֹן וְאֶת אַחֲרוֹנִים אֲנִי הוּא. כֹּלָּא הוּא, וְהוּא סָתִים מִכָּל סִטְרוֹי. חוֹטָמָא. תָּאנָא, בְּחוֹטָמָא אִשְׁתְּמוֹדַע פַּרְצוּפָא.

62. Come and see that it is written: "I Hashem, the first; and with the last, I am he" (Yeshayah 41:4). He is everything, MEANING ARICH ANPIN. He is concealed from all sides. The nose, WHAT IS IT? We have learned that the countenance is known through the nose, SINCE YOU CAN'T GIVE EVIDENCE ON THE FACIAL SHAPE UNLESS THROUGH THE NOSE.

63. וְתָא חֲזֵי מַה בֵּין עַתִּיקָא, לִזְעֵיר אַפִּין. דָּא מָארֵיהּ דְּחוֹטָמָא מֵחַד נוּקְבָּא חַיִּין, וּמֵחַד נוּקְבָּא חַיִּין דְּחַיִּין. הַאי חוֹטָמָא. הוּא פַּרְדַּשְׁקָא, דְּבֵיהּ נָשִׁיב רוּחָא דְּחַיֵּי, לִזְעֵיר אַפִּין. וְקָרֵינָן לֵיהּ סְלִיחָה. וְהוּא נַחַת רוּחַ, אִתְבַּסְּמוּתָא דְרוּחָא.

63. Come and see what is the difference between Atik and Zeir Anpin. Atik has a nose. From one opening IS BESTOWED life and from one opening IS BESTOWED the life of life, MEANING THE LIGHT OF LIFE OF THE RESURRECTION OF THE DEAD. This nose is a window through which blows the spirit of life to Zeir Anpin, and it is called forgiveness, SINCE THE SPIRIT OF LIFE IS THE ILLUMINATION OF CHOCHMAH, AND FROM CHOCHMAH COMES THE FORGIVENESS OF SINS. That is satisfaction to the spirit, the soothing of the spirit.

64. דְּרוּחָא דְּנָפִיק מֵאִינּוּן נוּקְבֵי, חַד רוּחָא נָפִיק לִזְעֵיר אַפִּין. לְאִתְּעָרָא לֵיהּ בְּגִנְתָּא דְּעֵדֶן. וְחַד רוּחָא דְּחַיֵּי, דְּבֵיהּ זַמִּין לִזְמַנָּא לִבְרֵיהּ דְּדָוִד, לְמִנְדַּע חָכְמְתָא. וּמֵהַהוּא נוּקְבָּא, אִתְּעַר וְנָפִיק רוּחָא מִמּוֹחָא סְתִימָאָה, וְזַמִּין לְאַשְׁרָאָה עַל מַלְכָּא מְשִׁיחָא, דִּכְתִיב וְנָחָה עָלָיו רוּחַ יְיָ׳ רוּחַ חָכְמָה וּבִינָה רוּחַ עֵצָה וּגְבוּרָה רוּחַ דַּעַת וְיִרְאַת יְיָ׳. הָא הָכָא ד׳ רוּחִין, וְהָא רוּחָא חֲדָא אָמְרֵינָן. אֲמַאי תְּלַת. קוּם רִבִּי יוֹסֵי בְּקִיּוּמָךְ.

64. Since the spirit flows from these openings OF THE NOSE, one spirit goes out to Zeir Anpin to awaken him in the Garden of Eden. One spirit of life FLOWS FROM IT, with which the offspring of David will be summoned to learn wisdom in the future, BECAUSE THESE TWO SPIRITS OF THE NOSTRILS ARE CONSIDERED YESOD AND MALCHUT. THEREFORE, FROM THE SPIRIT OF YESOD, THE RIGHT NOSTRIL, THERE WILL BE A FLOW TO ZEIR ANPIN. FROM THE SPIRIT OF MALCHUT, WHICH IS IN THE LEFT NOSTRIL, THERE WILL BE A FLOW TO THE SON OF DAVID, THE SECRET OF MALCHUT. From this LEFT opening a spirit rises and flows out from the concealed brain, WHICH IS CHOCHMAH OF ARICH ANPIN, which will dwell on King Messiah, as is written: "And the spirit of Hashem shall rest upon him, the spirit of wisdom and understanding, the spirit of counsel and might, the spirit of knowledge and of the fear of Hashem" (Yeshayah 11:2). HE INQUIRES: There are here IN THE VERSE four spirits. Since we speak of one spirit, WHICH FLOWS FROM THE LEFT OF THE OPENING OF ARICH ANPIN, what do we mean with the three? Rise, Rabbi Yosi, from your place AND ANSWER THIS.

65. קָם ר׳ יוֹסֵי וְאָמַר. בְּיוֹמוֹי דְּמַלְכָּא מְשִׁיחָא, לָא יֵימְרוּן חַד לְחַד, אַלִּיף לִי חָכְמְתָא, דִּכְתִיב וְלֹא יְלַמְּדוּ עוֹד אִישׁ אֶת רֵעֵהוּ וְגוֹ׳, כִּי כֻלָּם יֵדְעוּ אוֹתִי לְמִקְּטַנָּם וְעַד גְּדוֹלָם. וּבְהַהוּא זִמְנָא, יִתְּעַר עַתִּיק יוֹמִין, רוּחָא דְּנָפִיק מִמּוֹחָא סְתִימָאָה דְּכֹלָּא, וְכַד יִשְׁלוֹף דָּא, כָּל רוּחִין דִּלְתַתָּא יִתְּעֲרוּן עִמֵּיהּ. וּמַאן אִינּוּן. אִינּוּן כִּתְרִין קַדִּישִׁין דִּזְעֵיר אַפִּין. וְאִינּוּן שִׁיתָא רוּחִין אַחֲרָנִין, דְּהָכִי אִינּוּן דִּכְתִיב רוּחַ חָכְמָה וּבִינָה רוּחַ עֵצָה וּגְבוּרָה רוּחַ דַּעַת וְיִרְאַת יְיָ׳.

65. Rabbi Yosi stood up and said: During the times of King Messiah, one will not say 'teach me wisdom' to the other, as it is written: "And they shall teach no more every man his neighbor...for they shall all know me, from the least of them to the greatest of them" (Yirmeyah 31:33). During that period, Atik Yomin will awaken a spirit emanating from the brain that is concealed to all, WHICH IS CHOCHMAH OF ARICH ANPIN. When he imparts all this, all the spirits below will awaken with him. Who are they, THE SPIRITS BELOW? They are the holy Sfirot of Zeir Anpin, which are another six spirits like it. It is written ABOUT THEM: "The spirit of wisdom and understanding, the spirit of counsel and might, the spirit of knowledge and of the fear of Hashem," WHICH ARE THE ASPECTS OF CHESED, GVURAH, TIFERET, NETZACH, HOD AND YESOD IN ZEIR ANPIN.

66. דְּתָנֵינָן, כְּתִיב וַיֵּשֶׁב שְׁלֹמֹה עַל כִּסֵּא יְיָ׳. וּכְתִיב שֵׁשׁ מַעֲלוֹת לַכִּסֵּא. וּמַלְכָּא מְשִׁיחָא זַמִּין לְמֵיתַב בְּשִׁבְעָה. שִׁיתָא אִינּוּן וְרוּחָא דְּעַתִּיק יוֹמִין דְּעָלַיְיהוּ, הָא שִׁבְעָה. כְּמָה דְּאִתְּמַר. אָ"ל ר"ש, רוּחָךְ יָנוּחַ לְעָלְמָא דְּאָתֵי.

66. As we have learned, it is written: "Then Solomon sat on the throne of Hashem" (I Divrei Hayamim 29:23) and also: "The throne had six steps" (I Melachim 10:19), CORRESPONDING TO CHESED, GVURAH, TIFERET, NETZACH, HOD AND YESOD. King Messiah will sit in the future on A THRONE OF seven LEVELS. Six are CORRESPONDING TO CHESED, GVURAH, TIFERET, NETZACH, HOD AND YESOD, and together with the spirit of Atik Yomin upon them, THAT FLOWS FROM THE LEFT OPENING OF HIS NOSE AS MENTIONED, there are seven, as we were taught. Rabbi Shimon said: May your spirit rest in the World to Come.

67. ת"ח, כְּתִיב כֹּה אָמַר יְיָ׳ מֵאַרְבַּע רוּחוֹת בֹּאִי הָרוּחַ וְגוֹ׳. וְכִי אַרְבַּע רוּחֵי עָלְמָא, מַאי עַבְדֵּי הָכָא. אֶלָּא אַרְבַּע רוּחֵי יִתְעֲרוּן. ג׳ אִינּוּן. וְרוּחָא דְּעַתִּיקָא סְתִימָא אַרְבַּע, וְהָכִי הֲווֹ. דְּכַד יִפּוֹק דָּא, נָפְקִין עִמֵּיה תְּלָתָא, דִּכְלִילָן בְּגוֹ תְּלָתָא אַחֲרָנִין.

67. Come and see that it is written: "Thus says Adonai Elohim; Come from the four winds, O breath (also: 'wind')..." (Yechezkel 37:9). HE ASKS: What are the four winds of the world doing here? HE RESPONDS: Four spirits (winds) will awaken. They are actually three, MEANING THE THREE TIMES IT SAYS "SPIRIT" IN THE VERSE: "THE SPIRIT OF WISDOM AND UNDERSTANDING..." With the spirit of Atik who is concealed, FROM THE NOSE, there are altogether four. So they are. When the one SPIRIT OF THE NOSE emanates, three other SPIRITS that are comprised of three others go along with it. IT SAYS "SPIRIT" THREE TIMES AND EACH SPIRIT HAS TWO ASPECTS, MEANING "THE SPIRIT OF WISDOM AND UNDERSTANDING, THE SPIRIT OF COUNSEL AND MIGHT, AND THE SPIRIT OF KNOWLEDGE AND OF THE FEAR OF HASHEM."

68. וְזַמִּין קוּדְשָׁא בְּרִיךְ הוּא לְאַפָּקָא חַד רוּחָא דְּכָלִיל מִכָּלְּהוּ. דִּכְתִיב מֵאַרְבַּע רוּחוֹת בֹּאִי הָרוּחַ. אַרְבַּע רוּחוֹת בֹּאִי לָא כְּתִיב כָּאן, אֶלָּא מֵאַרְבַּע רוּחוֹת בֹּאִי. וּבְיוֹמֵי דְּמַלְכָּא מְשִׁיחָא, לָא יִצְטָרְכוּן לְמֵילַף חַד לְחַד, דְּהָא רוּחָא דִּלְהוֹן דְּכָלִיל מִכָּל רוּחִין יְדִיעַ כֹּלָּא. חָכְמָה וּבִינָה עֵצָה וּגְבוּרָה דַּעַת וְיִרְאַת יְיָ'. מִשּׁוּם רוּחָא דְּכָלִילָא מִכָּל רוּחֵי. בְּג"כ כְּתִיב, מֵאַרְבַּע רוּחוֹת, דְּאִינּוּן אַרְבַּע דִּכְלִילָן בְּשִׁבְעָה דַּרְגִּין עִלָּאִין דַּאֲמָרָן. וְתָאנָא, דְּכֻלְּהוּ כְּלִילָן בְּהַאי רוּחָא דְּעַתִּיקָא דְּעַתִּיקִין, דְּנָפִיק מִמּוֹחָא סְתִימָאָה לְנוּקְבָּא דְּחוֹטָמָא.

68. The Holy One, blessed be He, will produce one spirit that is comprised of all THE SEVEN SPIRITS MENTIONED ABOVE, since it is written: "Come from the four winds, O wind." 'Come the four winds' is not written here, but "Come from the four winds," WHICH MEANS COME O WIND, WHICH IS MADE FROM THE FOUR WINDS THAT ARE SIX, AS MENTIONED. In the days of King Messiah, there will be no need to teach one another, since their spirit will be comprised of all spirits, and will know everything, wisdom, understanding, counsel, might, knowledge, and fear of Hashem, because THEIR spirit encompasses all spirits. This is why it is written: "From the four spirits," since they are four that are included in the seven higher levels, as we have said. We have learned that all are comprised within this spirit of the most Ancient of all, THAT IS ARICH ANPIN, that emanates from the concealed brain, WHICH IS HIS CHOCHMAH to the nostril of his nose, WHICH IS THE SECRET OF HIS MALCHUT.

69. וְת"ח, מַה בֵּין חוֹטָמָא לְחוֹטָמָא. חוֹטָמָא דְּעַתִּיק יוֹמִין חַיִּין מִכָּל

סְטְרוֹי. חוֹטָמָא דִזְעֵיר אַפִּין, כְּתִיב, עָלָה עָשָׁן בְּאַפּוֹ וְאֵשׁ מִפִּיו תֹּאכֵל
וְגוֹ'. עָלָה עָשָׁן בְּאַפּוֹ, וּמֵהַהוּא עָשָׁן דָלִיק נוּר, כַּד סָלִיק תְּנָנָא לְבָתַר.
גֶּחָלִים בָּעֲרוּ מִמֶּנוּ. מַהוּ מִמֶּנוּ. מֵאוֹתוֹ עָשָׁן.

69. Come and see the difference between one nose and another nose,
MEANING BETWEEN THE NOSE OF ARICH ANPIN AND THE NOSE OF ZEIR
ANPIN. It is that the nose of the Ancient of Days, ARICH ANPIN, is life with
all its aspects, BOTH LIFE IN THIS WORLD AND LIFE OF THE WORLD TO
COME, AS MENTIONED. It is written of the nose of Zeir Anpin: "There
went up a smoke out of his nostrils, and fire out of his mouth..." (II Shmuel
22:9). "There went up a smoke out of his nostrils" and from that smoke, a
fire is lit. When the smoke later rises, "coals were kindled by it" (Ibid.).
What is meant by "by it"? It is by that smoke, SINCE FROM THE SMOKE A
FIRE IS LIT, AS MENTIONED.

‎70. תָּאנָא, כַּד הֲוָה רַב הַמְנוּנָא סָבָא בָּעֵי לְצַלָּאָה צְלוֹתֵיה, אָמַר לְבַעַל
הַחוֹטָם אֲנִי מִתְפַּלֵּל, לְבַעַל הַחוֹטָם אֲנִי מִתְחַנֵּן. וְהַיְינוּ דִכְתִיב וּתְהִלָּתִי
אֶחֱטָם לָךְ, הַאי קְרָא לְעַתִּיק יוֹמִין אֲמָרוּ.

70. We have learned that when Rav Hamnuna Saba (the elder) wished to say
his prayer, he said, To the nose master I pray, the nose master I beseech.
MEANING TO ARICH ANPIN WHO HAS A NOSE (HEB. *CHOTEM*). That is
the meaning of what is written: "and for my praise will I refrain (Heb.
echetam) for you" (Yeshayah 48:9). This verse was said to Atik Yomin,
WHO IS ARICH ANPIN, WHOSE NOSE IS LIFE IN EVERY ASPECT.

‎71. תָּנָא, אוֹרְכָא דְחוֹטָמָא, תְּלַת מְאָה וע"ה עָלְמִין, אִתְמַלְּיָין מִן
הַהוּא חוֹטָמָא. וְכֻלְּהוּ מִתְדַּבְּקָן בִּזְעֵיר אַפִּין. הַאי תּוּשְׁבַּחְתָּא דְתִקּוּנָא
דְחוֹטָמָא הוּא. וְכָל תִּקּוּנֵי דְעַתִּיק יוֹמִין, אִתְחֲזוּן וְלָא אִתְחֲזוּן, אִתְחֲזוּן
לְמָארֵי מְדִין, וְלָא אִתְחֲזוּן לְכֹלָּא.

71. We have learned, the length of the nose is such that 375 worlds are filled
from that nose, and all are attached to Zeir Anpin. That is the praise of the
form of the nose. All the constructions of the Ancient of Days are seen yet
are not seen, they are seen to those who sit on the seat of judgment but not
seen to everyone.

10. The thirteen Corrections of the beard

A Synopsis

Rabbi Shimon tells what he learned in the Hidden Book about the most hidden and concealed precious supreme beard of Arich Anpin; that beard is the universal faith within which flow thirteen springs. He describes the thirteen Corrections of the beard. The thirteen Corrections that depend on the precious beard are available in the universe in the seventh month during the ten days of repentance.

72. פָּתַח ר"ש וְאָמַר, וַוי מַאן דְּאוֹשִׁיט יְדוֹי בְּדִיקְנָא יַקִּירָא עִלָּאָה, דְּסָבָא קַדִּישָׁא, טָמִיר וְסָתִים מִכֹּלָּא דִּיקְנָא דְּהַהִיא תּוּשְׁבַּחְתָּא. דִּיקְנָא דְּסָתִים וְיַקִּיר מִכָּל תִּקּוּנוֹי. דִּיקְנָא דְּלָא יַדְעִין עִלָּאִין וְתַתָּאִין. דִּיקְנָא דְּהִיא תּוּשְׁבַּחְתָּא דְּכָל תּוּשְׁבָּחִין. דִּיקְנָא דְּלָא הֲוֵי בַּר נָשׁ נְבִיאָה וְקַדִּישָׁא דְּיִקְרַב לְמֶחֱמֵי לֵיהּ. דִּיקְנָא דְּהִיא תַּלְיָיא בְּשַׂעֲרוֹי עַד טַבּוּרָא דְּלִבָּא. חִוָּורָא כְּתַלְגָּא יַקִּירָא דִּיקִירִין. טְמִירָא דִּטְמִירִין. מְהֵימְנוּתָא דִּמְהֵימְנוּתָא דְּכֹלָּא.

72. Rabbi Shimon began by saying: Woe to the person that extends his hand to the precious supreme beard of the holy old man, WHO IS ARICH ANPIN, who is hidden and concealed from all. The beard of that praise, the beard concealed and most precious of any of His forms OF ARICH ANPIN, the beard THAT IS not known to the higher and lower beings, the beard that is the praise of all praises, the beard which could be neither approached nor seen by any prophet or holy man, the beard that hangs by its hair to the center of the heart is white as snow, most precious of all, most concealed of anything concealed, the faith of universal Faith.

73. תָּאנָא, בְּצִנִיעוּתָא דְּסִפְרָא, דְּהַאי דִּיקְנָא מְהֵימְנוּתָא דְּכֹלָּא, נָפִיק מֵאוּדְנוֹי, וְנָחִית סוֹחֲרָנֵיהּ דְּפוּמָא קַדִּישָׁא, וְנָחִית וְסָלִיק וְחָפֵי, בְּתִקְרוּבְתָּא דְּבוּסְמָא טָבָא, חִוָּורָא דִּיקִירָא. וְנָחִית בְּשִׁקּוּלָא, וְחָפֵי עַד טַבּוּרָא. הוּא דִּיקְנָא יַקִּירָא, מְהֵימָנָא שְׁלֵימָא, דְּנַגְדִין בֵּיהּ י"ג נְבִיעִין, מַבּוּעִין דִּמְשַׁח רְבוּת טָבָא, בִּתְלַת עֲשַׂר תִּקּוּנִין מִתְתַּקְּנָא.

73. We have learned in the hidden book that that beard, which is the universal Faith, starts UNDERNEATH his ears and descends down around the holy mouth. It lowers and proceeds upward to cover with offering of fine fragrance the white and the precious, MEANING IT COVERS THE SKIN OF THE FACE OF ARICH ANPIN, WHICH IS WHITE, and at the same time lowers and covers up to the center OF THE HEART. This is the precious beard, the perfect faith, within which flow thirteen springs that stream forth from the goodly anointing oil. In thirteen Corrections it is established.

74. תִּקּוּנָא קַדְמָאָה. מִתְתַּקַּן שַׂעֲרָא מִלְּעֵילָא, וְשָׁארֵי מֵהַהוּא תִּקּוּנָא דִּשְׂעַר רֵישֵׁיה, דְּסָלִיק בְּתִקּוּנוֹי לְעֵילָא מֵאוּדְנוֹי, וְנָחִית מִקַּמֵּי פִּתְחָא דְּאוּדְנִין, בְּחַד חוּטָא בְּשִׁקּוּלָא טָבָא, עַד רֵישָׁא דְּפוּמָא.

74. The first Correction OF THE THIRTEEN CONSTRUCTIONS OF THE BEARD: The hairs are formed above and originate from that style of the hair on the head that ascends, in form, above his ears and descends in front of the opening of the ears with one strand in good measure to the beginning of the mouth. THE EXPLANATION FOLLOWS.

75. תִּקּוּנָא תִּנְיָינָא. מִתְתַּקַּן שַׂעֲרָא מֵרֵישָׁא דְּפוּמָא, עַד רֵישָׁא אָחֳרָא דְּפוּמָא, בְּתִקּוּנָא שָׁקִיל.

75. The second Correction: The hair gets shaped from one corner of the mouth to the other corner end of the mouth in a symmetrical form.

76. תִּקּוּנָא תְּלִיתָאָה. מֵאֶמְצָעִיתָא דִּתְחוֹת חוֹטָמָא, מִתְּחוֹת תְּרֵין נוּקְבִין, נָפִיק חַד אוֹרְחָא, וְשַׂעֲרָא אִתְפְּסַק בְּהַהוּא אָרְחָא, וּמַלְיָא מֵהַאי גִּיסָא, וּמֵהַאי גִּיסָא שַׂעֲרָא, מִתְקּוּנָא שְׁלִים סוֹחֲרָנֵיה דְּהַהוּא אוֹרְחָא.

76. The third Correction: From underneath the center of the nose, below the two openings OF THE NOSE, one path follows out. The hairs cease from that path and it is full of hair on both sides OF THIS PATH, in perfect shape, surrounding this path.

77. תִּקּוּנָא רְבִיעָאָה. מִתְתַּקַּן שַׂעֲרָא תְּחוֹת פּוּמָא, מֵרֵישָׁא חֲדָא

לְרֵישָׁא חֲדָא, בְּתִקּוּנָא שְׁלִים.

77. The fourth Correction: The hair underneath the mouth from one point to the other point forms in a harmoniously perfect shape. THAT IS THE ONE CALLED THE BEARD ON THE POINTED END OF THE CHIN.

78. תִּקּוּנָא חֲמִישָׁאָה. תְּחוֹת פּוּמָא נָפִיק אָרְחָא אַחֲרָא, בְּשִׁקּוּלָא דְּאָרְחָא דִּלְעֵילָא, וְאִלֵּין תְּרֵין אָרְחִין רְשִׁימִין עַל פּוּמָא, מִכָּאן מִכָּאן.

78. The fifth Correction: Underneath the mouth goes forth another path counterbalancing IN CONFORMITY the upper path, UNDER THE NOSE. Those two paths are distinguished on both sides of the mouth, THE UPPER PATH ABOVE THE MOUTH AND THE LOWER PATH UNDERNEATH THE MOUTH.

79. תִּקּוּנָא שְׁתִיתָאָה. מִתְתַּקֵּן שַׂעֲרָא, וְסָלִיק וְנָפִיק מִלְרַע לְעֵיל לְרֵישָׁא דְּפוּמָא. וְחָפֵי תִּקְרוֹבְתָּא דְּבוּסְמָא טָבָא, עַד רֵישָׁא דְּפוּמָא דִּלְעֵילָא. וְנָחִית שַׂעֲרָא לְרֵישָׁא דְּפִתְחָא דְּאוֹרְחָא תַּתָּאָה דְּפוּמָא.

79. The sixth Correction: The hairs are shaped upwards and go forth from the lower to the upper point of the mouth and cover the precious offering of fine fragrances to the top of the mouth above. The hair descends FROM THERE to the starting point of the lower opening BELOW the mouth.

80. תִּקּוּנָא שְׁבִיעָאָה. פָּסִיק שַׂעֲרָא, וְאִתְחֲזָן תְּרֵין תַּפּוּחִין, בְּתִקְרוֹבְתָּא דְּבוּסְמָא טָבָא, שַׁפִּירָן וְיָאָן לְמֶחֱזֵי. בְּגִינֵיהוֹן אִתְקַיָּים עָלְמָא, הֲה"ד בְּאוֹר פְּנֵי מֶלֶךְ חַיִּים.

80. The seventh Correction: The hairs stop FROM GROWING and two parts of the faces are visible, THAT IS - THE RIGHT FACE AND THE LEFT FACE, WITHOUT THE HAIR, with an offering of good and pleasant smells, good and pleasing in appearance. The universe exists because of them and this is what is written: "In the light of the king's countenance is life" (Mishlei 16:15).

‏81. תִּקּוּנָא תְּמִינָאָה. נָפִיק חַד חוּטָא דְּשַׂעֲרֵי סוֹחֲרָנֵי דְּדִיקְנָא, וְתַלְיָין בְּשִׁקּוּלָא עַד טַבּוּרָא.

81. The eighth Correction: One thread of hair goes around the beard and hangs in balance to the navel.

‏82. תִּקּוּנָא תְּשִׁיעָאָה. מִתְעָרֵי וּמִתְעָרְבִין שַׂעֲרֵי דִיקְנָא, עִם אִינּוּן שַׂעֲרֵי דְּתַלְיָין בְּשִׁקּוּלָא, וְלָא נַפְקֵי דָּא מִן דָּא.

82. The ninth Correction: THE HAIR is roused, and the beard gets blended with the hairs that hang IN THE THROAT AND ARE balanced, MEANING IN EQUAL MEASURE, and do not extrude from one another.

‏83. תִּקּוּנָא עֲשִׂירָאָה. נַחְתִּין שַׂעֲרֵי תְּחוֹת דִיקְנָא, וְחַפְיָין בְּגְרוֹנָא תְּחוֹת דִיקְנָא.

83. The tenth Correction: The hair descends under the beard and covers the throat that is under the beard.

‏84. תִּקּוּנָא חַד סַר. דְּלָא נָפְקִין נִימָא מִן נִימָא, וּמִתְשַׁעֲרָן בְּשִׁיעוּרָא שְׁלִים.

84. The eleventh Correction: No hair grows out of another hair and all are measured in precise perfect measure.

‏85. תִּקּוּנָא תְּרֵיסַר. דְּלָא תַּלְיָין שַׂעֲרֵי עַל פּוּמָא, וּפוּמָא אִתְפְּנֵי מִכָּל סִטְרוֹי. וְיָאָן שַׂעֲרֵי סְחוֹר סְחוֹר לֵיהּ.

85. The twelfth Correction: No hair hangs over the mouth and the mouth opening is clear OF ALL HAIR from all sides. And all around it, the hair looks nice.

‏86. תִּקּוּנָא תְּלֵיסַר. דְּתַלְיָין שַׂעֲרָן בְּתְחוֹת דִיקְנָא, מִכָּאן וּמִכָּאן, בִּיקָרָא יָאָה, בִּיקָרָא שַׁפִּירָא. מְחַפְיָין עַד טַבּוּרָא. לָא אִתְחֲזֵי מִכָּל אַנְפֵּי

תִּקְרוּבָא דְּבוּסְמָא, בַּר אִינּוּן תַּפּוּחִין שַׁפִּירִין חִוְּורִין, דְּמַפְּקִין חַיִּין לְעָלְמָא, וּמַחֲזַיָּין חֶדוּ לִזְעֵיר אַפִּין.

86. The thirteenth Correction: The hair hangs underneath the beard from each side, MEANING THE WHOLE AREA OF THE HAIR UNDER THE BACK OF THE BEARD, with a pleasing glory, a handsome glory, covering to the center OF THE HEART. So the fragrant offering is not seen by anyone, save this beautifully white face that bestows life to the universe and shows joy to Zeir Anpin.

87. בִּתְלֵיסַר תִּקּוּנִין אִלֵּין, נַגְדִּין וְנָפְקִין תְּלֵיסַר מַבּוּעִין דִּמְשַׁח רְבוּת, וְנַגְדִּין לְכָל אִינּוּן דִּלְתַתָּא. וּנְהִרִין בְּהַהוּא מִשְׁחָא. וּמְשִׁיחִין מֵהַהוּא מִשְׁחָא, דְּבִתְלֵיסַר תִּקּוּנִין אִלֵּין. בִּתְלֵיסַר תִּקּוּנִין אִלֵּין אִתְרְשִׁים דִּיקְנָא יַקִּירָא, סְתִימָאָה דְּכֹלָּא, דְּעַתִּיק דְּעַתִּיקִין. מִתְּרֵי תַּפּוּחִין שַׁפִּירָן דְּאַנְפּוֹי, נְהִירִין אַנְפּוֹי דִּזְעֵיר אַנְפִּין, וְכָל חֵיזוּר וְשׁוּשַׁן דְּאִשְׁתַּכְּחָן לְתַתָּא, נְהִירִין וּמִתְלַהֲטִין מֵהַהוּא נְהוֹרָא דִּלְעֵילָּא. תִּקּוּנִין תְּלֵיסַר אִלֵּין, אִשְׁתַּכְּחוּ בְּדִיקְנָא, וּבִשְׁלֵימוּת דִּיקְנָא בְּתִקּוּנוֹי, אִתְקְרֵי בַּר נָשׁ נֶאֱמָן. דְּכָל דְּחָמֵי דִּיקְנֵיהּ, תָּלֵי בֵּיהּ מְהֵימְנוּתָא.

87. With these thirteen Corrections flow forth thirteen springs of anointing oil which reach all those below. They illuminate from this oil and anoint with that oil that is comprised of these thirteen sets. With these thirteen Corrections, the concealed glorious beard of the most Ancient One becomes distinguished, THAT IS ARICH ANPIN. From the two precious circles of His face, the face of Zeir Anpin brightens up and every knob and flower, MEANING ALL VARIOUS GRADES, that exist below brighten and glow from that light above. These thirteen Corrections occur in the beard and with the perfection of the beard through its shapes, man is called faithful, since everyone who sees his beard ascribes faith to him.

88. תָּאנָא בְּצְנִיעוּתָא דְּסִפְרָא, תְּלֵיסַר תִּקּוּנִין אִלֵּין דְּתַלְיָין בְּדִיקְנָא יַקִּירָא, בִּשְׁבִיעָאָה מִשְׁתַּכְּחֵי בְּעָלְמָא, וּמִתְפַּתְּחֵי בִּתְלֵיסַר תַּרְעֵי דְּרַחֲמֵי. וּמַאן דְּאוֹשִׁיט יְדֵיהּ לְאוּמָאָה, כְּמַאן דְּאוֹמֵי בִּתְלֵיסַר תִּקּוּנֵי דִּיקְנָא.

הַאי בַּאֲרִיךְ אַפִּין. בִּזְעֵיר אַפִּין בְּכַמָּה. אָמַר לְרִבִּי יִצְחָק, קוּם בְּקִיּוּמָךְ, וְסַלְסֵל בְּסַלְסְלָא דְּתִקּוּנָא דְּמַלְכָּא קַדִּישָׁא הֵיאַךְ יִתְתַּקְנוּן.

88. We have learned in the concealed book these thirteen Corrections that depend on the precious beard exist in the world in the seventh MONTH THAT IS - IN THE TEN DAYS OF REPENTANCE, and open up by the thirteen gates of mercy. Whoever extends his hand to swear BY HIS BEARD, it is as if he swears by the thirteen Corrections of the beard. That applies for Arich Anpin, WHICH COMPRISES THE THIRTEEN CORRECTIONS OF THE BEARD. How many in Zeir Anpin? HOW MANY CORRECTIONS EXIST IN HIS BEARD? RABBI SHIMON told Rabbi Yitzchak: Stand up in your place and trim the forms of the Holy King, ARICH ANPIN. How did they get established?

11. The first Correction

A Synopsis

Rabbi Yitzchak draws a distinction between the rough hairs and the smooth hairs, the latter of which draw Chochmah to the brain of Zeir Anpin. He says that hairs must not bond to neighboring hairs, and that hair on the head must be long so that Chochmah can enter through the hair to the spinal cord that gets nourishment from the brain. We hear that all the hairs of the hair and beard of Arich Anpin are white as snow, while the beard of Zeir Anpin is black. Thirteen measures of mercy stem from the ancient Holy One, and corresponding to these there are thirteen measures in Zeir Anpin. We learn that if the thirteen Corrections of the beard of Arich Anpin had not existed neither the upper grades nor the lower grades would exist; children, longevity and sustenance depend on those Corrections.

89. קָם רִבִּי יִצְחָק, פָּתַח וְאָמַר, מִי אֵל כָּמוֹךְ נוֹשֵׂא עָוֹן וְגוֹ', יָשׁוּב יְרַחֲמֵנוּ וְגוֹ', תִּתֵּן אֱמֶת לְיַעֲקֹב וְגוֹ'. תָּאנָא, תְּלֵיסַר מְכִילָן אִתְחֲזוּן הָכָא, וְכֻלְּהוּ נָפְקִין מִתְּלֵיסַר מַבּוּעִין דִּמְשַׁח רְבוּת דְּתִיקּוּנֵי דִּיקְנָא קַדִּישָׁא, עַתִּיקָא דְּעַתִּיקִין. טְמִירָא דְּטְמִירִין. תָּנָא, תִּקּוּנָא דְּדִיקְנָא טָמִיר וְסָתִים, טָמִיר וְלָא טָמִיר. סָתִים וְלָא סָתִים. בְּתִקּוּנוֹי יְדִיעַ וְלָא יְדִיעַ.

89. Rabbi Yitzchak stood up and opened the discussion saying, "Who is El like you, who pardons iniquity...he will again have compassion upon us... You will show truth to Jacob..." (Michah 7:18-20). We have learned that thirteen shapes appear here IN THIS SCRIPTURAL VERSE - all emanate from the thirteen springs of the anointing oil of the THIRTEEN Corrections of the holy beard of the most Ancient One, the concealed of all that is concealed, ARICH ANPIN. We have learned that the beard shapes are hidden and veiled, concealed yet not concealed, covered and not covered, known through its shapes, aware but not clearly, MEANING TO SAY, HE IS REVEALED AND KNOWN TO THOSE WORTHY OF HIM. TO THOSE WHO ARE NOT WORTHY OF HIM, HE IS HIDDEN AND NOT KNOWN.

90. תִּקּוּנָא קַדְמָאָה. הָא תָּנֵינָן, דְּכָל שַׂעֲרָא וְשַׂעֲרָא וְכָל נִימָא וְנִימָא לָא מִתְדַּבְּקָא לְחַבְרָתֵּהּ. וְשָׁארוּ נִימִין דְּדִיקְנָא לְאַתְקָּנָא, מִתְקַנָא

דִּשְׂעַר רֵישָׁא.

90. We have already learned the first principle that every single hair, however minute and insignificant, does not bond to its neighboring hair. The fine hairs of the beard begin to form according to the form of the hair in the head, MEANING THEY BEGIN AT THE SIDES OF THE HEAD.

91. הָכָא אִית לְאִסְתַּכְּלָא, אִי כָּל נִימִין דִּשְׂעַר רֵישָׁא, וְנִימִין דְּדִיקְנָא יַקִּירָא עִלָּאָה, בְּחַד נִימָא אִתְכְּלָלוּ, אֲמַאי אִלֵּין אֲרִיכִין, וְאִלֵּין לָא אֲרִיכִין. אֲמַאי נִימִין דְּדִיקְנָא לָא אֲרִיכִין כּוּלֵי הַאי, וְקַשְׁיָין. וְאִלֵּין דְּרֵישָׁא לָא קַשְׁיָין, אֶלָּא שְׁעִיעִין.

91. Here we have to scrutinize to see whether all the minute hairs of the head and the minute hairs of the glorious supreme beard are all included in one hair, MEANING THAT THEY ARE OF ONE LEVEL AND FLOW FROM ONE ROOT - FROM THE MEMBRANE OF AIR - IF SO, why are these HAIRS OF THE HEAD long, and these HAIRS OF THE BEARD not so long? Why are the fine hairs of the beard not very long, but rough, and those of the head are not so rough, but rather smooth?

92. אֶלָּא, כָּל נִימִין שְׁקִילִין דְּרֵישָׁא וְדִיקְנָא. דְּרֵישָׁא אֲרִיכִין עַל כַּתְפִין, לְמֵיגַד לְרֵישָׁא דִּזְעֵיר אַפִּין, מֵהַהוּא מְשִׁיכָא דְּמוֹחָא, לְמוֹחָא דִּילֵיהּ. וּבְגִינֵי כַּךְ לָא הֲווֹ קַשְׁיָין. וע"ד אִתְחֲזָן לְמֶהֱוֵי רְכִיכֵי.

92. HE ANSWERS: All the hairs of the head and beard are in measure, EACH ACCORDING TO ITS PARTICULAR ASPECT. Those of the head are long to the shoulders to reach the top of Zeir Anpin, from the inspiration of his own brain to the brain OF ZEIR ANPIN. Therefore, they are not rough but rather soft.

93. תָּאנָא, מַאי דִּכְתִיב, חַכְמוֹת בַּחוּץ תָּרֹנָּה. וּלְבַסּוֹף כְּתִיב, בָּרְחֹבוֹת תִּתֵּן קוֹלָהּ. הַאי קְרָא לָאו רֵישֵׁיהּ סֵיפֵיהּ, וְלָאו סֵיפֵיהּ רֵישֵׁיהּ. אֶלָּא חַכְמוֹת בַּחוּץ תָּרֹנָּה, כַּד נָגִיד מִמּוֹחָא סְתִימָאָה דְּאַרִיךְ אַפִּין, לְמוֹחָא

-169-

דְּזְעֵיר אַפִּין, בְּאִינּוּן נִימִין. כְּאִילּוּ מִתְחַבְּרָאן לְבַר, תְּרֵין מוֹחִין,
וְאִתְעֲבֵיד חַד מוֹחָא, בְּגִין דְּלֵית קִיּוּמָא לְמוֹחָא תַּתָּאָה, אֶלָּא בְּקִיּוּמָא
דְּמוֹחָא עִלָּאָה. וְכַד נָגִיד מֵהַאי לְהַאי, כְּתִיב תִּתֵּן קוֹלָהּ חַד.

93. We have learned that it is written: "Wisdoms cry aloud in the street" (Mishlei 1:20) and at the end it is written: "She utters her voice in the squares" (Ibid.). The beginning of this verse does not suit the end and its conclusion does not complement its beginning, AS IT BEGINS TO SPEAK IN THE PLURAL FORM "WISDOMS" AND CONCLUDES BY SAYING, "HER VOICE" IN SINGULAR FORM. HE ANSWERS: When it says, "Wisdoms cry aloud in the street" EXPRESSING IT IN PLURAL FORM, it refers to when Chochmah flows forth from the concealed brain of Arich Anpin through the hair strands, OF THE HEAD HAIR, to the brain of Zeir Anpin. It is as if externally IN ZEIR ANPIN, WHICH IS OUTSIDE ARICH ANPIN, two brains joins, CHOCHMAH OF ARICH ANPIN AND CHOCHMAH OF ZEIR ANPIN. They integrate into one brain, since the lower brain, IN ZEIR ANPIN, has no existence of its own without the upper brain OF ARICH ANPIN. THAT IS WHY IT IS EXPRESSED IN PLURAL "WISDOMS" AS THERE ARE TWO CHOCHMOT. After drawing one from the other, MEANING AFTER CHOCHMAH OF ZEIR ANPIN HAS RECEIVED FROM THE CONCEALED BRAIN, it is written: "She utters her voice," SINCE it is one CHOCHMAH, CHOCHMAH OF ZEIR ANPIN.

94. וּבְגִין דְּנָגִיד מִמּוֹחָא לְמוֹחָא בְּאִינּוּן נִימִין אִינּוּן לָא אִשְׁתְּכְחוּ
קַשִׁישִׁין. מ"ט. מִשּׁוּם דְּאִי אִשְׁתְּכָחוּ קַשִׁישִׁין, לָא נָגִיד חָכְמְתָא לְמוֹחָא
בְּהוֹן. בְּגִינֵי כָּךְ, לֵית חָכְמְתָא נָפְקָא מִבַּר נָשׁ דְּאִיהוּ קַשְׁיָא וּמָארֵי
דְּרוּגְזָא. דִּכְתִיב דִּבְרֵי חֲכָמִים בְּנַחַת נִשְׁמָעִים. וּמֵהָכָא אוֹלִיפְנָא, מַאן
דְּשַׂעֲרוֹי דְּרֵישֵׁיהּ קַשִׁישָׁן, לָאו חָכְמְתָא מִתְיַשְּׁבָא עֲמֵיהּ.

94. Because CHOCHMAH is drawn from the brain OF ARICH ANPIN to the brain OF ZEIR ANPIN through these strands of hair OF THE HEAD HAIR, they are not rough. What is the reason? It is because if they would have been rough, Chochmah could not be drawn through them to the brain OF ZEIR ANPIN. This is the reason that Chochmah does not emanate from a person who has harsh and angry character, as it is written: "The words of wise men heard in quiet" (Kohelet 9:17). We learn from here that wisdom does not settle on a man whose head hair is rough.

95. וע"ד אִינּוּן אֲרִיכֵי, לְמֵיתֵי תּוֹעַלְתָּא לְכֹלָּא. מַאי לְכֹלָּא. לְמֵיעַל עַל חוּטָא דְּשִׁדְרָה, דְּמִתְשַׁקְיָין מִן מוֹחָא. ובג"ד לָא תָּלֵי שַׂעֲרָא דְּרֵישָׁא עַל שַׂעֲרָא דְּדִיקְנָא. דְּשַׂעֲרָא דְּרֵישָׁא תָּלֵי וְסָלִיק עַל אוּדְנִין לַאֲחוֹרוֹי, וְלָא תָּלֵי עַל דִּיקְנָא, מִשּׁוּם דְּלָא אִצְטְרִיךְ לְאִתְעָרְבָא אִלֵּין בְּאִלֵּין. דְּכֻלְּהוּ מִתְפָּרְשָׁן בְּאָרְחַיְיהוּ.

95. Therefore, THE HAIR ON THE HEAD is long to be of use for everybody. What is for everybody? THAT IS SO THAT CHOCHMAH should enter THROUGH THE HAIR to the spinal cord that gets nourishment from the brain; THEREFORE, THEY ARE LONG TO THE TOP OF THE SHOULDER, SINCE THERE IS THE LOCATION OF THE SPINAL CORD. Therefore, the hair of the head does not hang over the hair of the beard, since the hairs of the head hang and rise above the ear to the back OF THE HEAD. They do not hang on the beard, since they must not be blended the ones with the others, since each one follows its own path.

96. תָּאנָא, כֻּלְּהוּ שַׂעֲרֵי בֵּין דְּרֵישָׁא, בֵּין דְּדִיקְנָא, כֻּלְּהוּ חִוָּורֵי כְּתַלְגָּא. וְתָאנָא, אִינְהוּ דְּדִיקְנָא קַשִׁישָׁאי כֻּלְּהוּ. מ"ט. מִשּׁוּם דְּאִינּוּן תַּקִּיפָא דְּתַקִּיפִין, לְאַחֲתָא אִינּוּן י"ג מְכִילָן, מֵעַתִּיק דְּעַתִּיקִין. וַהֲנֵי מְכִילָן מִקַּמֵּי אוּדְנוֹי שַׁרְיָין, וַהֲנֵי מְכִילָן סְתִימָן אִינּוּן, דְּלָא יִתְעָרְבוּן בְּאַחֲרָנִין.

96. We have learned that all hairs, either of the head or of the beard OF ARICH ANPIN, are white as snow. We have learned that those of the beard are coarse. What is the reason? It is because they are the strongest of the strong, in order to lower TO THE ONES BELOW these thirteen measures OF THE THIRTEEN CORRECTIONS OF THE BEARD of the most Ancient One of all, THAT IS ARICH ANPIN. Those THIRTEEN measures originate from the front of the ears. These THIRTEEN measures are concealed so they do not blend with others, WITH THE THIRTEEN MEASURES OF ZEIR ANPIN.

97. וְאִי תֵּימָא דְּלֵית אַחֲרָנִין כְּוָותַיְיהוּ. לָא. דְּתַנְיָא תְּלֵיסַר מְכִילָן

דְרַחֲמֵי מֵעַתִּיקָא קַדִּישָׁא: מִי אֵל כָּמוֹךָ, חַד. נוֹשֵׂא עָוֹן, תְּרֵי. וְעוֹבֵר עַל
פֶּשַׁע, תְּלַת. לִשְׁאֵרִית נַחֲלָתוֹ, אַרְבַּע. לֹא הֶחֱזִיק לָעַד אַפּוֹ, חָמֵשׁ. כִּי
חָפֵץ חֶסֶד הוּא, שִׁית. יָשׁוּב יְרַחֲמֵנוּ, שְׁבְעָה. יִכְבּוֹשׁ עֲוֹנוֹתֵינוּ, תְּמַנְיָא.
וְתַשְׁלִיךְ בִּמְצוּלוֹת יָם כָּל חַטֹּאתָם, תִּשְׁעָה. תִּתֵּן אֱמֶת לְיַעֲקֹב, עֲשָׂרָה.
חֶסֶד לְאַבְרָהָם, חַד סָר. אֲשֶׁר נִשְׁבַּעְתָּ לַאֲבוֹתֵינוּ, תְּרֵיסָר. מִימֵי קֶדֶם,
תְּלֵיסַר. לָקֳבֵיל דָּא, אֵל רַחוּם וְחַנּוּן וְגוֹ', אִינּוּן לְתַתָּא.

97. If you say that there are no others like them, it is not so. We have learned that the thirteen measures of mercy stem from the ancient Holy One: "who is El like you" (Michah 7:18) is one; "who pardons iniquity" (Ibid.) is two; "and forgives the transgressions" (Ibid.) is three; "of the remnant of His heritage" (Ibid.) is four; "He does not maintain His anger for ever" (Ibid.) is five; "because he delights in mercy" (Ibid.) is six; "He again will have compassion upon us" (Ibid. 19) is seven; "He will suppress our iniquities" (Ibid.) is eight; "and you will cast all their sins into the depths of the sea" (Ibid.) is nine; "You will show truth to Jacob" (Ibid. 20) is ten; "loyal love to Abraham" (Ibid.) is eleven; "as you have sworn to our fathers" (Ibid.) is twelve and "from days of old" (Ibid.) is thirteen. Corresponding to these, THERE ARE THIRTEEN MEASURES IN ZEIR ANPIN, WHICH ARE: "El, merciful and gracious, slow to anger..." (Shemot 34:6), which are below IN ZEIR ANPIN.

98. וְאִי תֵּימָא, מֹשֶׁה אֵיךְ לָא אָמַר אִלֵּין עִלָּאִין. אֶלָּא, מֹשֶׁה לָא
אִצְטְרִיךְ, אֶלָּא לְאֲתָר דְּדִינָא אִשְׁתְּכַח, וּבַאֲתָר דְּדִינָא אִשְׁתְּכַח, לָא
בָּעֵי הָכִי לְמֵימָר. וּמֹשֶׁה לָא אָמַר, אֶלָּא בְּעִידָנָא דְּיִשְׂרָאֵל חָאבוּ, וְדִינָא
הֲוָה תַּלְיָיא, וּבְגִינֵי כַּךְ לָא אָמַר מֹשֶׁה, אֶלָּא בַּאֲתָר דְּדִינָא אִשְׁתְּכַח.
אֲבָל בְּהַאי אֲתָר, סִדּוּרָא דְּשֻׁבְחָא דְּעַתִּיק יוֹמִין מְסַדֵּר נְבִיאָה.

98. You may wonder why Moses did not say all these THIRTEEN MEASURES of the above IN ARICH ANPIN, WHICH ARE, "WHO IS EL LIKE YOU..." BUT SAID RATHER THE "EL, MERCIFUL AND GRACIOUS," WHICH ARE THE THIRTEEN MEASURES OF ZEIR ANPIN. HE ANSWERS: It is because Moses required only the place where there is Judgment, WHICH IS ZEIR ANPIN, and where there is Judgment one must not speak of this, THE THIRTEEN MEASURES OF ARICH ANPIN. Moses said that only when

Yisrael were sinful and Judgment was impending OVER THEM. Therefore, Moses did not say THE THIRTEEN MEASURES OF MERCY, only in the place where Judgment was dwelling, MEANING IN ZEIR ANPIN. However, for the place where it is the order of prayer OF THE THIRTEEN MEASURES to the Ancient of Days, MEANING "WHO IS EL LIKE YOU...," the prophet sets THEM in order.

99. וְאִינּוּן תְּלֵיסָר תִּקּוּנִין דְּדִיקְנָא עִלָּאָה קַדִּישָׁא, טְמִירָא דְּטְמִירִין, תַּקִּיפִין, לְתַבְּרָא וּלְאַכְפְּיָיא כָּל גִּזְרֵי דִּינִין. מַאן חָמֵי דִּיקְנָא עִלָּאָה קַדִּישָׁא, טְמִירָא דְּטְמִירִין דְּלָא אַכְסִיף מִנֵּיהּ. וּבְג״כ, כָּל שַׂעֲרוֹי קְשִׁישִׁין, וְתַקִּיפִין בְּתִקּוּנוֹי.

99. These thirteen Corrections of the holy upper beard OF ARICH ANPIN are among the hidden most hidden, and strong, so as to break and subdue all verdicts. He who saw the beard of the uppermost holy, most hidden among the concealed, must not be ashamed before it. Due to that, all its hairs are coarse and strong in their shapes.

100(1). וְאִי תֵּימָא, אִי הָכִי הָא שַׂעֲרֵי דִּלְתַתָּא, אִינּוּן אוּכְמֵי, אֲמַאי לָא הֲווֹ כְּדָא. דְּתָנֵינָא כְּתִיב, קְווּצּוֹתָיו תַּלְתַּלִּים שְׁחוֹרוֹת כָּעוֹרֵב. וּכְתִיב, וּשְׂעַר רֵישֵׁיהּ כַּעֲמַר נְקֵא. לָא קַשְׁיָא, הָא בְּדִיקְנָא עִלָּאָה, הָא בְּדִיקְנָא תַּתָּאָה. וע״ד, כַּד אִתְיְיהִיבַת אוֹרַיְיתָא לְיִשְׂרָאֵל, אִתְיְיהִיבַת בְּאֵשׁ שְׁחוֹרָה עַל גַּבֵּי אֵשׁ לְבָנָה.

100a. You might say, If so, the hairs below OF ZEIR ANPIN are black. Why then were these not like those OF ARICH ANPIN WHICH ARE WHITE? Because we have learned that it is written: "His locks are wavy, and black as a raven" (Shir Hashirim 5:11), "And the hair of whose head was like the pure wool" (Daniel 7:9), MEANING WHITE. THE SCRIPTURES SEEM TO CONTRADICT EACH OTHER. HE REPLIES: That is no problem. WHERE IT SAYS, "LIKE THE PURE WOOL," it refers to the supernal beard OF ARICH ANPIN and WHERE IT SAYS, "BLACK AS A RAVEN," it refers to the beard below IN ZEIR ANPIN. Thus, when the Torah was given to Yisrael, it was conveyed in black fire over white fire.

100)(2). וְעִקְּרָא דְמִלָּה מִשּׁוּם דְּהָנֵי שַׂעֲרֵי בְּגִין דְּמִמּוֹחָא אִשְׁתְּכָחוּ לְאִתְמַשְׁכָא לְמוֹחָא דִּלְתַתָּא וְאִינוּן לְעֵילָא מִן דִּיקְנָא דִיקְנָא בִּלְחוֹדוֹי הוּא. וְכָל תִּקּוּנוֹי בִּלְחוֹדֵיהוֹן אִשְׁתְּכָחוּ. דִּיקְנָא בִּלְחוֹדוֹי. וְשַׂעֲרֵי בִּלְחוֹדַיְיהוּ.

100b. The essence of it is that these hairs are from the brain, flowing to the lower brain OF ZEIR ANPIN. They are above the hair of the beard; the beard is separate and the hairs OF THE HEAD are separate.

101. תִּקּוּנָא קַדְמָאָה תִּקּוּנָא דְּשָׁארֵי מֵרֵישָׁא דְּשַׂעֲרֵי דְּרֵישָׁא. וְתָאנָא, כָּל תִּקּוּנֵי דִיקְנָא לָא אִשְׁתְּכַח אֶלָּא מִמּוֹחָא דְרֵישָׁא, וְהָכָא לָא פָּרִישׁ הָכִי, דְּהָא לָא הֲוֵי. אֶלָּא תִּקּוּנָא דָא, דְּנָחִית מִן רֵישָׁא דְּשַׂעֲרֵי דְּרֵישָׁא, הָכִי אִשְׁתְּכַח.

101. The first Correction OF THE BEARD HAIR is the Correction that starts at the top of the head-hair, MEANING AT THE SIDES OF THE HEAD THAT ARE THE BEGINNING OF THE HEAD-HAIR UPWARDS, WHICH IS THE SECRET OF THEIR MALCHUT. We have learned that all the Corrections of the beard are only affected through the brain of the head. Here, BY THE FIRST CORRECTION, he does not explain it that way, SINCE HE SAYS THAT IT IS IN THE SIDES OF THE HEAD, because it is not caused FROM THE BRAIN IN THE HEAD, BUT RATHER FROM THE SIDES OF THE HEAD. Therefore, the first Correction is such that it descends from the top of the head-hair AND NOT FROM THE CONCEALED BRAIN.

102. וּמֵהַאי דִּיקְנָא אִשְׁתְּמוֹדַע, כָּל מַה דַּהֲוֵי בְּרֵישָׁא, דְּאֶלֶף עָלְמִין דְּחַתִּימִין בְּעִזְקָא דְּדַכְיָא. עִזְקָא, דְּכָלִיל כָּל עִזְקִין.

102. From THE COMPOSITION OF this beard, everything that is in the head becomes known. That is the thousand worlds sealed with the pure ring, the ring that is composed of all rings. THAT IS THE SECRET OF THE CONCEALED WISDOM IN THE HEAD OF ARICH ANPIN.

103. אוֹרְכָּא דְּכָל שַׂעֲרָא, דְּנָחִית מִקַּמֵּי אוּדְנוֹי, לָא הֲוֵי אֲרִיכָא. וְלָא

אִתְדְּבַּק דָּא בְּדָא, וְלָא נַחְתִּין. אִלֵּין שַׂעֲרִין. מִכַּד נַגְדִין אִתְמַשְׁכָן
וְתַלְיָין.

103. The length of each hair that descends in front of the ears is not long, MEANING TO SAY THAT CHOCHMAH ALLUDED TO AS LENGTH BECOMES REVEALED THERE AND THE HAIRS do not cleave to each other. THE HAIRS ARE SHORT and do not fall down. When they grow big, THESE HAIRS flow and hang UPWARD.

104. וְשֵׁירוּתָא דְּתִקּוּנָא קַדְמָאָה, תְּלָתִין וְחַד קוֹצֵי, שְׁקִילָן, אִתְמַשְׁכָן
עַד רֵישָׁא דְּפוּמָא. וּתְלַת מְאָה וְתִשְׁעִין נִימִין אִשְׁתַּכְּחָן בְּכָל קוֹצָא
וְקוֹצָא.

104. At the start of the first Correction, there are 31 groups of hair THAT ARE even, extending to the top of the mouth, and 390 strands are contained in each individual group.

105. תְּלָתִין וְחַד קוֹצֵי שְׁקִילִין, דַּהֲווּ בְּתִקּוּנָא קַדְמָאָה תַּקִּיפִין,
לְאַכְפַּיָיא לְתַתָּא, כְּחוּשְׁבַּן אֵ״ל. מַהוּ אֵ״ל. תַּקִּיף יָכוֹל. וּבְכָל קוֹצָא
וְקוֹצָא, מִתְפַּרְשִׁין תְּלָתִין וְחַד עָלְמִין, תַּקִּיפִין שָׁלְטִין, לְאַכְפַּיָא,
וְאִתְפָּשְׁטוּ לְ״א בְּהַאי סְטָר, וְלְ״א בְּהַאי סְטָר. וְכָל עָלְמָא וְעָלְמָא מִנֵּיהּ,
מִתְפְּרַשׁ לְאֶלֶף עָלְמִין דִּכְסִיפִין לְעִדּוּנָא רַבָּא. וְכֹלָּא סְתִים בְּרֵישָׁא
דְּדִיקְנָא, דְּכָלִיל תַּקִּיפָא, וּכְלִילָן בְּהַאי אֵ״ל. וְעִם כָּל דָּא, הַאי אֵ״ל
אִתְכַּפְיָיא לְרַחֲמֵי, דְּרַחֲמֵי דְּעַתִּיק יוֹמִין, וְאִתְכְּלַל וְאִתְפָּשַׁט בֵּיהּ.

105. HE EXPLAINS THE MATTERS IN THE GENERAL SENSE OF THE CORRECTION AND GOES ON TO SAY: The 31 locks that are EQUALLY even, which are in the first Correction, are coarse, so as to subordinate JUDGMENTS below. They are of the numerical value of El. What is the meaning of El? IT IS a mighty EL, capable OF SUBDUING EVERYTHING. In every lock OF THE ASPECT OF ITS ENTIRETY, there is a division into 31 mighty dominating worlds, to subdue. They then spread out, 31 on this side and 31 on this SIDE OF THE FACE, and each individual world of it divides to a thousand desirable worlds of great delight. All this is concealed at the top of the beard – that is, contains harsh JUDGMENT. ALL are contained in this NAME El and, despite all this, this NAME El is submissive to the compassionate mercy of Atik Yomin. It is contained and spread in it.

106. אֲמַאי עַד פּוּמָא. מִשׁוּם דִּכְתִּיב דִּינָא יְתִיב וְסִפְרִין וְגוֹ'. מַאי דִּינָא יְתִיב. יְתִיב לְאַתְרֵיהּ דְּלָא שַׁלְטָא. הה״ד פֶּלֶא יוֹעֵץ אֵל גִּבּוֹר. אֵל דְּהוּא גִּבּוֹר, וְאִתְבְּסַם בְּדִיקְנָא קַדִּישָׁא דְּעַתִּיק יוֹמִין. וְרָזָא דִּכְתִּיב, מִי אֵל כָּמוֹךְ בְּעַתִּיק יוֹמִין אִתְּמַר, בְּתִקּוּנָא קַדְמָאָה דְּדִיקְנָא קַדִּישָׁא עִלָּאָה.

106. HE ASKS: Why DOES THE FIRST CORRECTION EXTEND UNDER THE EARS to the mouth? HE REPLIES: IT IS because it is written: "Sat in judgment, and the books..." (Daniel 7:10). What is the meaning of "sat in judgment," MEANING THAT JUDGMENT sits in its position and does not reign? This is what is written: "Wonderful, counselor, mighty El" (Yeshayah 9:5), meaning El who is mighty, WHICH IS ALLUDED TO IN THE 31 LOCKS OF HAIR, AS MENTIONED ABOVE. He is filled with the aroma of the holy beard of Atik Yomin. The secret of this is written: "Who is El like you" and refers to Atik Yomin, to the first Correction of the most holy beard.

107. עָלְמָא קַדְמָאָה, דְּנָפִיק מִתִּקּוּנָא קַדְמָאָה, שַׁלִּיט וְנָחִית. וְסָלִיק לְאַלַף אַלְפִין וְרִבּוֹא רִבְבָן מָארֵי תְּרִיסִין. וּמִנֵּיהּ מִתְאַחֲדִין, בְּקִסְטָא בְּעִזְקָא רַבָּא.

107. The first world, which extends from this first Correction, dominates and descends and ascends to a thousand of thousands and ten thousand of tens of thousands of shielded beings who hold to it through the measure of a great ring.

108. עָלְמָא תִּנְיָינָא. דְּנָפִיק מֵהַאי תִּקּוּנָא. שַׁלִּיט וְנָפִיק, וְנָחִית וְסָלִיק, לְשַׁבְעָה וְחַמְשִׁין אֶלֶף דַּרְגִּין, מָארֵי דִיבָבָא. וּמִתְאַחֲדָן מִנֵּיהּ, לְאִכְפַּיְיא בְּקוֹדְלָא בְּחִיוָּרָא.

108. The second world emerging from this Correction is dominant and leaves to descend BELOW. It rises to 57,000 levels of wailing beings which hold to it, so as to surrender to the white part of the back of its neck, MEANING IN THE FLESH OF THE BACK OF THE NECK.

109. עָלְמָא תְּלִיתָאָה. דְּנָפִיק מֵהַאי תִּקּוּנָא שַׁלִּיט וְנָחִית, וְסָלִיק לצ״ו אַלְפִין מָארֵי דִּילָלָה, וּמִתְאַחֲדָן מִנֵּיהּ בְּבוּצִינָא קְמוּרָא, וּמֵהַאי תִּקּוּנָא, מִתְכַּפְיָין כֻּלְּהוּ, וּמִתְבַּסְּמָן בִּמְרִירָא דְּדִמְעִין, דְּמִתְבַּסְּמִין בְּיַמָּא רַבָּא.

109. The third world emerging from this Correction dominates and descends DOWNWARD and rises to 96,000 lamenting beings. They hold to it via the concealed candle. From this Correction, all are subdued and are filled with the fragrant bitterness of tears that are firmly established in the great sea.

110. מַאן חָמֵי תִּקּוּנָא דָא, דְּדִיקְנָא קַדִּישָׁא, עִלָּאָה, יַקִּירָא, דְּלָא אַכְסִיף מִנֵּיהּ. מַאן חָמֵי יַקִּירוּתָא דְּקוֹצִין דְּשַׂעֲרֵי דְּתַלְיָין מֵהַאי סָבָא. יָתִיב בְּעִיטְרָא דְּעִטְרִין, עִטְרִין דְּכָל עִטְרִין. עִטְרִין דְּלָא אִתְכְּלִילוּ בְּעִטְרִין. עִטְרִין דְּלָא כִּשְׁאָר עִטְרִין. עִטְרִין, דְּעִטְרִין דִּלְתַתָּא מִתְאַחֲדָן מִנְּהוֹן. ובג״כ, הָנֵי תִּקּוּנִין, אִינוּן תִּקּוּנִין דִּלְתַתָּא מִנְּהוֹן מִתְאַחֲדִין.

110. Who saw this Correction of the holy beard, the supernal, the precious, and did not become ashamed by it? Who saw the glory of the locks of the hair hanging from this old one, who is sitting adorned with crowns, THAT ARE THE THIRTEEN CORRECTIONS OF THE BEARD REFERRED TO AS CROWNS? These are the crowns of all crowns, SINCE THE BEARD CORRECTIONS OF ZEIR ANPIN ARE DRAWN FROM THE BEARD CORRECTIONS OF ARICH ANPIN. THEY ARE THE CROWNS OF ALL CROWNS. They are crowns that were not contained in the crowns OF ZEIR ANPIN, MEANING TO SAY, THEY DO NOT DESCEND TO BE CLOTHED IN THEM. They are crowns unlike the rest of the crowns of ZEIR ANPIN, BECAUSE THE CROWNS OF ARICH ANPIN ARE LIKE CLEAN WOOL AND THE CROWNS OF ZEIR ANPIN ARE BLACK LIKE A RAVEN. They are the crowns to which the lower crowns, OF ZEIR ANPIN, hold, BECAUSE THE BEARD CORRECTIONS OF ZEIR ANPIN RECEIVE FROM THE THIRTEEN CORRECTIONS OF THE BEARD IN ARICH ANPIN. That is why these

Corrections WERE ESTABLISHED, so the lower Corrections OF ZEIR ANPIN would be able to hold to them.

111. תִּקּוּנֵי דְּאִתְתְּקַן, דְּאִצְטְרִיךְ לְאִתְבָּרְכָא, מַאן דְּבָעֵי בִּרְכָה. דְּכָל תִּקּוּנִין דְּאִתְתְּקַן בְּקַבְלֵיהוֹן, בִּרְכָאן מִשְׁתַּכְּחִין לְקַבְלֵיהוֹן וְאִתְעָבֵיד מַה דְּאִתְעָבֵיד. כֹּלָּא כָּלִיל בְּהָנֵי תִּקּוּנִין. כֹּלָּא זַקְפָן לְקַבְלֵיהּ תִּקּוּנִין דְּמַלְכָּא תַּקִּיפָא, עַתִּיקָא, סְתִימָא דְּכֹלָּא. וְכֻלְּהוּ אִתְבַּסְּמָן מִתִּקּוּנִין אִלֵּין.

111. The Corrections were formed, since it is necessary to bless the one who requires a blessing. There are blessings for all the Corrections that were formed BELOW, and whatever needs to be done is accomplished, WHETHER IT IS A BLESSING FOR CHILDREN, LONGEVITY OR SUSTENANCE. Everything is included and contained in these Corrections and all straighten THEIR STATURE in accord with the Corrections of the ancient forceful King who is concealed by all. All are firmly established from these Corrections.

112. תָּאנָא. אִי עַתִּיק דְּעַתִּיקִין, קַדִּישָׁא דְּקַדִּישִׁין, לָא אִתְתְּקַן בְּאִלֵּין תִּקּוּנִין, לָא אִשְׁתְּכָחוּ עִלָּאִין וְתַתָּאִין. וְכֹלָּא הֲוֵי כֹּלָּא הֲוֵי. וְתַנְיָא, עַד כַּמָּה זְהִירִין אִלֵּין תִּקּוּנֵי דְּדִיקְנָא. עַד תְּלֵיסַר, וְכָל זִמְנָא דִּתְלֵיסַר אִלֵּין מִשְׁתַּכְּחִין, זְהִירִין אִלֵּין דִּלְתַתָּא. וְכֹלָּא. בְּחוּשְׁבָּנָא דְּאִלֵּין תְּלֵיסַר, אִשְׁתְּכַח דִּיקְנָא דְּמַלְכָּא עַתִּיקָא יַקִּירָא מִכֹּלָּא. כֹּלָּא בְּחַד אִיהוּ טְמִירָא וְיַקִּירָא.

112. We have learned that if the most ancient among the ancient, the most holy among the noly THAT IS ARICH ANPIN, would not have been formed with all these Corrections, the upper and lower beings would not exist. Everything would have been as if it were not, SINCE WITHOUT THEM, THERE WOULD BE NEITHER CHILDREN, LONGEVITY NOR SUSTENANCE, NOT ABOVE AND NOT BELOW. We learn to what extent these beard Corrections illuminate, up to thirteen. As long as these thirteen exist, those below and the rest illuminate. In the account of these thirteen, there is the beard of the ancient King most precious of all. All as one are concealed and glorious.

113. וּבְגִין דְּאִיהוּ יַקִּירָא וּטְמִירָא מִכֹּלָּא, לָא אִדְכַּר בְּאוֹרַיְיתָא, וְלָא אִתְגַּלְיָיא. וּמַה דִּיקְנָא אִתְגַּלְיָיא. דִּיקְנָא דְּכַהֲנָא רַבָּא עִלָּאָה. וּמֵהַאי דִּיקְנָא, נָחִית לְדִיקְנָא דְּכַהֲנָא רַבָּא דִּלְתַתָּא. דִּיקְנָא דְּכַהֲנָא רַבָּא בִּתְמַנְיָא תִּקּוּנִין אִתְתְּקַן. וּבְגִין כַּךְ, תְּמַנְיָא תִּקּוּנִין לְכַהֲנָא רַבָּא, כַּד מְשְׁחָא נָחִית עַל דִּקְנֵיהּ, הה״ד כַּשֶּׁמֶן הַטּוֹב עַל הָרֹאשׁ יוֹרֵד עַל הַזָּקָן וְגוֹ'.

113. Since it is honored and concealed from any PROPHET, THE BEARD is not mentioned in the Torah and it is not revealed in it which beard was revealed. It is the beard of the uppermost High Priest, WHICH IS CHESED OF ZEIR ANPIN. This beard descends to the beard of the lower High Priest. The beard of the High Priest, OF ZEIR ANPIN, was formed with eight Corrections AND, TOGETHER WITH MALCHUT THAT CONTAINS THEM, THEY ARE NINE. Consequently, there are eight Corrections to the High Priest, when oil runs down on his beard, THAT IS THE EIGHT PRIESTLY GARMENTS. This is what is written: "It is like the precious ointment upon the head, running down upon the beard... " (Tehilim 133:2).

114. וּמְנָ״ל. דִּכְתִיב שֶׁבֶת אַחִים גַּם יָחַד. גַּם לְרַבּוֹת כֹּהֵן גָּדוֹל דִּלְתַתָּא. דְּכָל זִמְנָא דְּכַהֲנָא רַבָּא דִּלְתַתָּא, מְשַׁמֵּשׁ בִּכְהוּנָא רַבָּא, כְּבִיכוֹל כֹּהֵן גָּדוֹל דִּלְעֵילָא, מְשַׁמֵּשׁ בִּכְהוּנָא רַבָּא.

114. We know THAT THE HIGH PRIEST BELOW COINCIDES WITH THE HIGH PRIEST ABOVE, since it is written: "For brothers to dwell together (lit. 'also') in unity" (Ibid. 1). "Also" comes to add the High Priest below. As long as the High Priest below serves in the High Priesthood, it is as if the High Priest above performs in the High Priesthood.

115. דָּא תִּקּוּנָא חַד, דְּדִיקְנָא דְּעַתִּיקָא סְתִימָא דְּכֹלָּא. אָ״ל רִבִּי שִׁמְעוֹן, יָאוּת אַנְתְּ ר' יִצְחָק, לְמֶחֱמֵי בִּיקָרָא דְּתִקּוּנֵי דְּדִיקְנָא, וּסְבַר אַפֵּי דְּעַתִּיק יוֹמִין, עַתִּיקָא דְּעַתִּיקִין. זַכָּאָה חוּלָקָךְ, וְזַכָּאָה חוּלָקִי עִמְּכוֹן בְּעָלְמָא דְּאָתֵי.

115. That is one of the Corrections of the beard of Atik that is most concealed of all. Rabbi Shimon said to him: It is fitting for you, Rabbi Yitzchak, to see the glory of the Corrections of the beard and the countenance of Atik Yomin, the most ancient. Praiseworthy is your lot and praiseworthy is my part with you in the World to Come.

12. The second Correction

A Synopsis

Rabbi Chizkiyah leads us into the discussion of the second Correction, saying that it means "who pardons iniquity." Rabbi Shimon's face is shining like the sun, and he says that Moses was not aware when his face was glowing. Rabbi Shimon tells the friends that each of their explanations of the thirteen Corrections gets established and concealed among the Corrections of the sanctified beard above. It now appears that a different rabbi must explain each different Correction.

116. תִּקּוּנָא תִּנְיָינָא. מִתְתָּקַן שַׂעֲרָא, מֵרֵישָׁא דְפוּמָא, עַד רֵישָׁא אַחֲרָא דְפוּמָא, בְּתִקּוּנָא שָׁקִיל.

116. The second Correction: The hair gets shaped from one corner of the mouth to the other corner of the mouth evenly.

117. קוּם ר' חִזְקִיָּה, וְקָאִים בְּקִיּוּמָךְ, וְאוֹקִיר יְקָרָא דְּתִקּוּנָא דָּא דְדִיקְנָא קַדִּישָׁא. קָם ר' חִזְקִיָּה, שָׁארֵי וְאָמַר, אֲנִי לְדוֹדִי וְעָלַי תְּשׁוּקָתוֹ מִי גָרַם שֶׁאֲנִי לְדוֹדִי. מִשּׁוּם דְּעָלַי תְּשׁוּקָתוֹ.

117. Rise, Rabbi Chizkiyah. Take your position and honor the preciousness of this Correction of the holy beard. Rabbi Chizkiyah stood up and opened the discussion saying, "I am my beloved's, and his desire is towards me" (Shir Hashirim 7:11), MEANING What is the cause that I am my beloved's? It is because of his longing for me.

118. מִסְתַּכֵּל הֲוֵינָא, וְאָרוּ חָמֵית, נְהוֹרָא יַקִּירָא דְּבוּצִינָא עִלָּאָה, נָהִיר וְסָלִיק לִתְלַת מְאָה וַחֲמִשָּׁה וְעֶשְׂרִין עִיבָר. וְחַד חָשׁוֹךְ הֲוָה אִתְסְחֵי בְּהַהוּא נְהוֹרָא, כְּמַאן דְּאִתְסְחֵי בְּהַהוּא נַהֲרָא עֲמִיקָא, דְּמֵימוֹי מִתְפַּלְּגִין, וּנְהִרִין, וְנַגְדִּין לְכָל עִיבָר, מִמָּה דְּעָלוֹי. וְסָלִיק הַהוּא נְהוֹרָא, בִּשְׂפָתָא דְיַמָּא עִלָּאָה עֲמִיקָא, דְּכָל פִּתְחִין טָבִין וְיַקִּירִין, בְּהַהוּא פִּתְחָא אִתְפַּתְּחָן.

118. I was watching, and behold, I noticed the precious light of the upper candle, BINAH, lighting to 325 directions. A dark one was bathing in that light like someone who bathes in a deep river, WHICH IS BINAH, whose waters divide and flow to light up every direction IT PASSES over. That light surfaces at the shore of the uppermost deep sea, where all goodly and precious openings open up at that door.

119. אֲנָא שָׁאִיל מֵהֶם, פִּשְׁרָא דְּחָמֵית. פָּתְחוּ וְאָמְרוּ, נוֹשֵׂא עָוֹן חֲמֵיתָא. אָמַר, דָּא הוּא תִּקּוּנָא תִּנְיָינָא. יָתִיב. א"ר שִׁמְעוֹן, הָאִידָנָא אִתְבְּסָם עָלְמָא. בְּרִיךְ אַנְתְּ ר' חִזְקִיָּה, לְעַתִּיקָא דְּעַתִּיקִין.

119. I asked them the explanation of THE THINGS I have seen. They said, You saw "Who pardons iniquity" (Michah 7:18). He said: That is the second Correction. He sat. Rabbi Shimon said: Now the world is firmly established, MEANING THE MALCHUT THAT IS REFERRED TO AS THE WORLD IS FIRMLY ESTABLISHED AND SWEETENED WITH BINAH THROUGH THIS CORRECTION. Blessed are you, Rabbi Chizkiyah, to the most ancient among the ancient.

120. אָמַר ר"ש, כֻּלְּהוּ בּוּצִינִין חַבְרִין, דְּאַתְיָין בְּהַאי עִזְקָא קַדִּישָׁא. אַסְהַדְנָא עָלַי שְׁמַיָּיא עִלָּאִין דְּעֶלְאִין, וְאַרְעָא קַדִּישָׁא עִלָּאָה דְּעֶלְאָה. דַּאֲנָא חָמֵי הַשְׁתָּא, מַה דְּלָא חָמָא בַּר נָשׁ, מִיּוֹמָא דְּסָלִיק מֹשֶׁה זִמְנָא תִּנְיָינָא לְטוּרָא דְּסִינַי. דַּאֲנָא חֲמֵינָא אַנְפָּאי נְהִירִין, כִּנְהוֹרָא דְּשִׁמְשָׁא תַּקִּיפָא, דְּזַמִּין לְמֵיפַּק בְּאַסְוָותָא לְעָלְמָא. דִּכְתִּיב, וְזָרְחָה לָכֶם יִרְאֵי שְׁמִי שֶׁמֶשׁ צְדָקָה וּמַרְפֵּא בִּכְנָפֶיהָ. וְעוֹד דַּאֲנָא יָדַעְנָא דְּאַנְפָּאי נְהִירִין, וּמֹשֶׁה לָא יָדַע וְלָא אִסְתָּכַּל. הה"ד וּמֹשֶׁה לָא יָדַע כִּי קָרַן עוֹר פָּנָיו.

120. Rabbi Shimon said TO THE FRIENDS: All the luminaries, THAT IS, YOU THE friends that attend here TO BE ESTABLISHED with this holy ring, THAT IS, WITH THE THIRTEEN BEARD CORRECTIONS, LISTEN. I take upon myself as evidence the uppermost heavens and the uppermost holy earth. THAT IS THE SECRET OF THE NEW HEAVENS AND THE NEW EARTH THAT ARE PRODUCED THROUGH THE SECRETS OF THE TORAH. I now see what no human has seen since the day that Moses ascended Mount Sinai for the second time, since I perceive my face to be shining like the powerful sun that will heal the world in the future. It is written: "But to you who fear my name the sun of righteousness shall arise with healing in its wings" (Malachi 3:20). Moreover, I am aware that my face is shining, but Moses was not aware that the skin on his face was aglow, as written: "Moses knew not that the skin of his face shone" (Shemot 34:29).

121. וְעוֹד, דַּאֲנָא חָמֵי בְּעֵינַי, תְּלֵיסַר מְכִילִין גְּלִיפִין קַמָּאי, וּנְהִירִין כְּבוֹצִינִין. וְכַד אִתְפְּרִישׁ כָּל חַד מִנַּיְיהוּ מִפּוּמֵיכוֹן, אִסְתָּלִיק וְאִתְתָּקַן, וְאִתְעַטַּר וְאִתְטַמַּר בִּטְמִירוּתָא דְּתִקּוּנֵי דְּדִיקְנָא, וְכָל אַחֲרָנִין אִשְׁתָּאֲרָן. וּבְעוֹד דְּכָל חַד מִתְפָּרַשׁ בְּפוּמַיְיכוּ, נָהִיר וְאִתְעַטַּר וְיָתִיב כְּמַלְכָּא בְּגוֹ חֵילֵיהּ. וְכַד אִסְתַּיִּים לְאִתְפָּרְשָׁא, סָלִיק וְאִתְעַטַּר בְּעִטְרָא קַדִּישָׁא, וְאִתְתָּקַן וְאִתְטַמַּר, וְיָתִיב בְּתִקּוּנוֹי דְּדִיקְנָא קַדִּישָׁא, וְכֵן לְכָל חַד וְחַד. אִזְדָּרְזוּ חַבְרִין קַדִּישִׁין, דְּהָא בְּקִיּוּמָא דָּא, לָא יְהֵא עַד דְּיֵיתֵי מַלְכָּא מְשִׁיחָא.

121. Moreover, I see with my eyes thirteen measures engraved in front of me and illuminating like candles. When each one of them is explained by you, it is uplifted and formed, IN ACCORDANCE WITH THE WAY YOU EXPLAINED IT, gets adorned and is hidden in the mysteries of the beard Corrections ABOVE. All the other ones THAT YOU HAVE NOT EXPLAINED YET remain AND AWAIT THE ORDER OF YOUR EXPLANATION. As each OF THE CORRECTIONS is explained by your words, THAT CORRECTION shines and gets adorned and takes its position like a king among his legions. When the definition is completed, THAT CORRECTION rises and gets adorned with the holy crown and is formed and concealed and positioned among the Corrections of the holy beard ABOVE. So it follows with each one THAT IS DEFINED BY YOU. Make haste, sacred friends, because such support THE WORLD will never have until King Messiah comes.

122. קוֹם ר' חִזְקִיָּה תִּנְיָינוּת. וְאוֹקִיר תִּיקוּנָא תְּלִיתָאָה, דְּדִיקְנָא קַדִּישָׁא. תָּנָא, עַד לָא קָם ר' חִזְקִיָּה, קָלָא נָפַק וְאָמַר, אֵין מַלְאָךְ אֶחָד עוֹשֶׂה שְׁתֵּי שְׁלִיחוּת. אִתְרְגִּישׁ ר"ש וְאָמַר, וַדַּאי כָּל חַד וְחַד בְּאַתְרֵיהּ. וַאֲנָא, וְר' אֶלְעָזָר בְּרִי, וְר' אַבָּא, אִשְׁתְּלִים שְׁלֵימָתָא עִלָּאָה.

122. Rise, Rabbi Chizkiyah, for a second time, and honor the third Correction of the holy beard. We have learned that prior to Rabbi Chizkiyah's rise, a voice declared: One messenger does not act on two missions. Rabbi Shimon was excited and commented: Most certainly, each individual is on its own level. THAT IS TO SAY, EACH ONE HAS A LIMIT THAT PREVENTS HIM FROM ESTABLISHING WHAT IS ABOVE HIS CONCEPTION. My son Rabbi Elazar and Rabbi Aba and myself, WE have achieved the highest perfection, MEANING THAT SINCE THEY WERE IN A DEGREE OF CHOCHMAH, BINAH AND DA'AT, THEY WERE ABLE TO RESTORE WHOLLY WHAT WAS LACKING IN EACH INDIVIDUAL.

13. The third Correction

A Synopsis

Rabbi Chiya opens by telling the difference between speaking and saying, and we hear that speaking calls for both a raising of the voice and a proclamation of words. He points out several places where 'speaking' is used, and says that Moses was not even fearful when Hashem spoke to him. Rabbi Chiya tells us that the first and second Corrections of the beard came to bring about the third one, the forgiveness of transgressions.

123. קוּם ר' חִיָּיא. קָם ר' חִיָּיא, פָּתַח וְאָמַר, וָאוֹמַר אֲהָהּ יְיָ' אֱלֹהִים הִנֵּה לֹא יָדַעְתִּי דַּבֵּר כִּי נַעַר אָנֹכִי. וְכִי יִרְמְיָה לָא הֲוָה יָדַע לְמַלְּלָא, וְהָא כַּמָּה מְלוּלִין נַפְקֵי מִפּוּמוֹי, עַד לָא אָמַר דָּא. וְהוּא אָמַר מִלָּה כְּדִיבָא, דִּכְתִיב הִנֵּה לֹא יָדַעְתִּי דַּבֵּר. אֶלָּא ח"ו דְּאִיהוּ אָמַר עַל דָּא. אֶלָּא הָכִי תָּאנָא, מַה בֵּין דִּבּוּר לַאֲמִירָה. אֲמִירָה הוּא דְּלָא בָּעֵי לְאַרְמָא קָלָא, דִּבּוּר, בָּעֵי לְאַרְמָא קָלָא, וּלְאַכְרְזָא מִלִּין.

123. Rise, Rabbi Chiya. Rabbi Chiya rose. He opened the discussion with the verse: "Then said I, 'Ah, Adonai Elohim! behold, I cannot speak, for I am a child'" (Yirmeyah 1:6). HE ASKS: Did Jeremiah not know how to speak, for many words came out of his mouth before he said this? So he said a falsehood, for it is written: "Behold, I cannot speak." HE REPLIES: Heaven forbid that he said something like that, but we have learned what the difference is between speaking and saying. Saying does not require a raising of the voice, but speaking calls for a raising of voice and a proclamation of words.

124. דִּכְתִיב וַיְדַבֵּר אֱלֹהִים אֵת כָּל הַדְּבָרִים הָאֵלֶּה לֵאמֹר. וְתָאנָא, כָּל עָלְמָא שָׁמְעוּ הַהוּא דִּבּוּר, וְכָל עָלְמָא אִזְדַּעְזָעוּ. וּבְגִין כַּךְ כְּתִיב וַיְדַבֵּר, וְלָא כְּתִיב וַיֹּאמֶר. אוֹף הָכָא כְּתִיב הִנֵּה לֹא יָדַעְתִּי דַּבֵּר, לְאַכְרְזָא מִלָּה וּלְאוֹכְחָא בְּרוּחַ קֻדְשָׁא לְעָלְמָא.

124. It is written: "And Elohim spoke all these words, saying" (Shemot 20:1). We have learned that the whole world heard that speech and everyone trembled. Therefore, it says, "spoke" and is not written: 'said'. Here too it

says, "Behold, I cannot speak" to declare to the world and reprimand them with the Holy Spirit.

125. אִי הָכִי, הָא כְּתִיב וַיְדַבֵּר יְיָ׳ אֶל מֹשֶׁה לֵּאמֹר. אֶלָּא, מַאן הוּא נְבִיאָה עִלָּאָה כְּמֹשֶׁה, דְּלָא זָכָה ב״נ כְּוָותֵיהּ. דְּהוּא שָׁמַע דִּבּוּר בְּהַכְרָזָה, וְלָא דָּחִיל, וְלָא אִזְדַּעְזַע. וּשְׁאַר נְבִיאִים אִזְדַּעְזָעוּ, אֲפִילוּ בַּאֲמִירָה, וְדַחֲלִין בִּדְחִילוּ.

125. He asks: If so, here it is written: "And Hashem spoke to Moses, saying" (Shemot 6:10). Why did Jeremiah say, "behold, I cannot speak"? He responds: Is there anyone with such a high degree of prophecy as Moses, since no human deserved like him to hear a speech in a form of declaration? He was not fearful or trembling either, while other prophets were shaken even in the form of 'saying,' and were filled with fear.

126(1). וְתָאנָא, תִּקּוּנָא קַדְמָאָה דְּדִיקְנָא, וְתִנְיָינָא לְאַיְיתָאָה לִתְלִיתָאָה. דִּכְתִיב, הֶן כָּל אֵלֶּה יִפְעַל אֵל פַּעֲמַיִם שָׁלֹשׁ עִם גָּבֶר.

126a. We have learned that the first Correction of the beard and the second Correction came to bring about the third correction, as is written: "Lo, El does all these things twice or three times with a man" (Iyov 33:29).

126(2). תִּקּוּנָא תְּלִיתָאָה. מֵאֶמְצָעִיתָא דִּתְחוֹת חוֹטָמָא, מִתְּחוֹת תְּרֵין נוּקְבִין. נָפִיק חַד אָרְחָא, וְשַׂעֲרָא אִתְפְּסַק בְּהַהוּא אָרְחָא. אֲמַאי אִתְפְּסַק. מִשּׁוּם דְּהַאי אוֹרְחָא אִתְתָּקַן לְאַעְבְּרָא בֵּיהּ. וּבְגִין כַּךְ, יְתִיב תְּחוֹת נוּקְבֵי חוֹטָמָא הַאי אוֹרְחָא. וְשַׂעֲרָא לָא אִתְרַבֵּי בְּהַאי אוֹרְחָא, מִשּׁוּם דִּכְתִיב וְעוֹבֵר עַל פֶּשַׁע, לְמֵיהַב אַעְבְּרָא עַד פּוּמָא קַדִּישָׁא, דְּיֵימָא סָלַחְתִּי. תָּאנָא, כַּמָּה עַרְקִיסָאוֹת מְחַכָּאן לְהַהוּא פּוּמָא, וְלָא אִתְגְּלֵי לְחַד מִנַּיְיהוּ, דְּהָא אִסְתְּלַק וְאִתְעַטַּר, יְדִיעַ וְלָא יְדִיעַ.

126b. The third Correction is from the center under the nose. Below the two nostrils, a path emerges where the hairs do not grow on that path. What is the cause of the interruption? It is because this path was devised to carry through it the spirit of Chochmah of the nose. Therefore, this route is situated below the openings of the nose, and hairs do not grow there, since it is written: "And forgives (lit. 'passes') the transgression" (Michah 7:18) in order to give passage up to the holy mouth, so he should say, 'I have forgiven.' We have learned that numerous trial courts await that mouth, OF ARICH ANPIN, THAT HE SHOULD SAY, 'I HAVE FORGIVEN.' It does not reveal itself to any of them, because it is exalted and adorned, known yet unknown.

126(3). תָּאנָא, בְּצִנִיעוּתָא דְּסִפְרָא, מַהוּ דִּכְתִיב פֶּשַׁע. זָכוּ עוֹבֵר, לֹא זָכוּ פֶּשַׁע. הַאי בִּזְעֵיר אַפִּין.

126c. We have learned in the hidden book the meaning of what is written as transgression. If they deserve so, the transgression is passed over, but if they don't merit it, it stays a transgression. That OCCURS ONLY in Zeir Anpin, BUT NOT IN ARICH ANPIN, WHO IS ENTIRELY COMPASSIONATE.

127. מַאי בֵּין הַאי לְהַאי. בִּזְעֵיר אַפִּין, כַּד נָחִית הַהוּא אוֹרְחָא מִתְּחוֹת נוּקְבֵי חוֹטָמֵי, כְּתִיב, וַיִּחַר אַף יְיָ' בָּם וַיֵּלַךְ. מַאי וַיֵּלַךְ. דְּנָפִיק רוּחָא דְּרוּגְזָא מֵאִינּוּן נוּקְבֵי, וּמַאן דְּאַשְׁכַּח קַמֵּיהּ, אָזִיל וְלָא אִשְׁתְּכַח. הֲדָא הוּא דִכְתִיב, כִּי רוּחַ יְיָ' נָשְׁבָה בּוֹ וְאֵינֶנּוּ. בְּאָרִיךְ אַפִּין כְּתִיב, וְעוֹבֵר עַל פֶּשַׁע. וּכְתִיב, וְרוּחַ עָבְרָה וַתְּטַהֲרֵם. וְתָאנָא, הָכָא כְּתִיב, עוֹבֵר עַל פֶּשַׁע בְּהַהוּא אָרְחָא. הָתָם, וְעָבַר יְיָ' לִנְגּוֹף אֶת מִצְרָיִם.

127. HE ASKS: What is the difference between the one and the other, BETWEEN ARICH ANPIN AND ZEIR ANPIN? HE REPLIES: In Zeir Anpin, when that path descends underneath the nostrils, it says, "And Hashem was wrathful over them and he went away" (Bemidbar 12:9). This means that a spirit of anger exudes from the nostrils, and whoever happens in the way is gone and disappears. This is what is written: "A spirit of Hashem blew and he is no longer here" (Yeshayah 40:7). BUT in Arich Anpin, it says, "And he passes over the transgression" (Michah 7:18) and also: "And a spirit passed and purified them" (Iyov 37:21). We have learned that about this path here that it is written: "Passes over the transgression" and there "and Hashem passed to strike Egypt" (Shemot 12:23).

128. זַכָּאָה חוּלְקֵיהּ דְּמַאן דְּזָכֵי לְהַאי. וְדָא הוּא תִּקּוּנָא תְּלִיתָאָה,

דְּדִיקְנָא יַקִּירָא קַדִּישָׁא עִלָּאָה עַתִּיקָא דְּעַתִּיקֵי. אָמַר ר"ש, וַדַּאי
קוּדְשָׁא בְּרִיךְ הוּא יַסְגֵּי לְאוֹטָבָא לָךְ, וְיֶחֱדֵי לְאַגָּנָא עֲלָךְ.

128. Praised is the lot of the one who deserves TO RECEIVE FROM this
CORRECTION. This is the third Correction of the most holy and glorious
beard of the most ancient of the ancient. Rabbi Shimon said: Certainly, the
Holy One, blessed be He, will continue to benefit you and will be happy to
protect you.

129. וְתָאנָא, מַאי דִּכְתִיב שׂוֹשׂ אָשִׂישׂ בַּיְיָ', בְּעַתִּיק יוֹמִין אִתְּמַר. דְּהָא
הוּא חֶדְוָותָא דְּכֹלָּא. תָּאנָא, בְּשַׁעֲתָא דְּאִתְגְּלֵי הַאי אוֹרְחָא דְּדִיקְנָא
דְּעַתִּיק יוֹמִין. כֻּלְּהוּ מָארֵי דִּיבָבָא וִילָלָה, וּמָארֵיהוֹן דְּדִינָא סְתִימִין
וּשְׁתִיקִין, וְלֵית דִּיפְתַּח פִּטְרָא לְאַבְאָשָׁא. מִשּׁוּם דְּהַאי אוֹרְחָא
אִתְגַּלְיָיא לְתַקְנָא. וּמֵהַאי, מַאן דְּאָחִיד וְאַזְהַר לְשַׁתְקָאָה, לְהַאי
אוֹרְחָא רְשִׁים, דְּהוּא סִימָנָא דְּעַתִּיקָא קַדִּישָׁא.

129. We have learned that what is written: "I will greatly rejoice in
Hashem" (Yeshayah 61:10) is said about Atik Yomin, since he is the joy of
everything. We have learned that when this path of the beard of Atik Yomin
is revealed, the prosecutors and all those who lament and wail are quieted
and silenced. There exists no one to say anything bad, because this path is
revealed so as to correct. Hence, whoever grasps SOMEONE and cautions
him to silence, he impresses this path which is a sign of the holy Atik.

14. The fourth Correction

A Synopsis
The word remnant is used to explain this Correction, as in "The remnants of Yisrael shall not do iniquity."

130. תִּקּוּנָא רְבִיעָאָה, מִתְתַּקַּן שַׂעֲרָא תְּחוֹת פּוּמָא, מֵרֵישָׁא חֲדָא לְרֵישָׁא חֲדָא. הה"ד, לִשְׁאֵרִית נַחֲלָתוֹ. כד"א וְנָשָׂאתָ תְפִלָּה בְּעַד הַשְּׁאֵרִית הַנִּמְצָאָה. הַנִּמְצָאָה מַמָּשׁ. שְׁאֵרִית דִּכְתִּיב, שְׁאֵרִית יִשְׂרָאֵל לֹא יַעֲשׂוּ עַוְלָה.

130. The fourth Correction: The hair is shaped underneath the mouth from one corner to the other corner, MEANING THE BEARD ON THE POINT OF THE CHIN - this is what is written: "The remnant of His heritage" (Michah 7:18) as it says, "Wherefore send up a prayer for the remnant that are left" (II Melachim 19:4) – actually those left. "The remnant" IS LIKE what is written: "The remnants of Yisrael shall not do iniquity" (Tzefanyah 3:13).

15. The fifth Correction

A Synopsis

The fifth Correction is that God does not maintain His anger forever. We learn that whenever a path in the beard of the Atik is revealed it benefits all levels below because proper advice then becomes available to produce benefits for everyone.

131. תִּקּוּנָא חֲמִישָׁאָה. נָפִיק אוֹרְחָא אַחֲרָא מִתְּחוֹת פּוּמָא, הה"ד לֹא הֶחֱזִיק לָעַד אַפּוֹ. קָם ר' יוֹסֵי. פָּתַח וְאָמַר, אַשְׁרֵי הָעָם שֶׁכָּכָה לוֹ אַשְׁרֵי הָעָם שֶׁיְיָ' אֱלֹהָיו. אַשְׁרֵי הָעָם שֶׁכָּכָה לוֹ. מַהוּ שֶׁכָּכָה לוֹ. כד"א וַחֲמַת הַמֶּלֶךְ שָׁכָכָה, שָׁכִיךְ מֵרוּגְזֵיה.

131. The fifth Correction: Another path proceeds from underneath the mouth, as is written: "He does not maintain his anger for ever" (Michah 7:18). Rabbi Yosi rose. He opened the discussion saying, "Happy is that people, that is in such a case: happy is that people, whose Elohim is Hashem" (Tehilim 144:15). HE ASKS: "Happy is that people, that is in such a case." What is the meaning of: "in such a case (Heb. *shekachah*)." HE RESPONDS: It is as you say, "Then the king's wrath was pacified (Heb. *shachachah*)" (Ester 7:10), which means that he quieted down from his anger.

132. ד"א. שָׁכִיךְ בְּרוּגְזֵיה, הה"ד וְאִם כָּכָה אַתְּ עוֹשֶׂה לִי הָרְגֵנִי נָא הָרוֹג. דָּא הוּא דִּינָא דְּדִינָא. אַשְׁרֵי הָעָם שֶׁיְיָ' אֱלֹהָיו, רַחֲמֵי דְּרַחֲמֵי.

132. Another explanation is that he was pacified by his anger, MEANING TO SAY THAT BECAUSE OF HIS WRATH, HE QUIETED DOWN. This is what is written: "And if you deal thus (Heb. *kachah*) with me, kill me, I pray you" (Bemidbar 11:15). THUS WE FIND THAT "HAPPY IS THAT PEOPLE, THAT IS IN SUCH A CASE" is Judgment within Judgment and "happy is that people, whose Elohim is Hashem" is Mercy within Mercy.

133. ד"א, שֶׁכָּכָה, שְׁמָא דְּכָלִיל כָּל שְׁמָהָן, וקוּדְשָׁא בְּרִיךְ הוּא מַעֲבַר רוּגְזֵיה, וַאֲנַח בֵּיה לִזְעֵיר אַנְפִּין, וּמַעֲבִיר עַל כָּל אִינּוּן דִּלְבַר.

133. Another explanation: Shekachah is the general term of all the names by which the Holy One, blessed be He, QUIETS DOWN, BY passing over the anger and producing calmness in Zeir Anpin. HE CALMS DOWN and passes over THAT ANGER OF HIS to all those outside.

134. דְּתָנֵינָא, אָרְחָא, עִלָּאָה דְּדִיקְנָא קַדִּישָׁא, דְּאִיהוּ נָחִית תְּחוֹת נוּקְבֵי דְּחוֹטָמָא דְּעַתִּיקִי. וְהַאי אָרְחָא דִּלְתַתָּא. שְׁקִילָן אִינּוּן בְּכֹלָּא. דָּא לְעֵילָּא, וְדָא לְתַתָּא. לְעֵילָּא, עוֹבֵר עַל פֶּשַׁע. לְתַתָּא, לֹא הֶחֱזִיק לָעַד אַפּוֹ. וְתָנֵינָן, לֹא הֶחֱזִיק: דְּלָא אִית אֲתָר לְמֵיתַב. כְּמָה דִּלְעֵילָּא יָהִיב אַתְרָא לְאַעְבְּרָא. כַּךְ לְתַתָּא, יָהִיב אֲתָר לְאַעְבְּרָא.

134. We have learned that the upper path of the holy beard, which passes down OVER THE UPPER LIP under the two nostrils of the nose of Atik, and that path below, IN THE MIDDLE OF THE HAIR OF THE LOWER LIP, are similar in everything, the one above IN THE UPPER LIP and the one below IN THE LOWER LIP. Above, THE PATH IS REFERRED TO AS: "Forgives (lit. 'passes') the transgression" (Michah 7:18) and below, it is referred to as: "He does not maintain His anger (lit. 'nose') for ever." We have learned that "does not maintain" MEANS there is no place to sit there. As THE PATH above provides a route JUST FOR THE SPIRIT OF CHOCHMAH FROM THE NOSE to cross over it, it is also so that below it just provides a route to cross over it, THE SPIRIT OF CHOCHMAH.

135. תָּנָא, בְּכָל אֲתָר דִּבְהַאי עַתִּיקָא טְמִירָא דְּכֹלָּא אָרְחָא אִתְגַּלְיָיא, טַב לְכֻלְּהוּ דִּלְתַתָּא, דְּהָא אִתְחֲזֵי עֵיטָא לְמֶעְבַּד טַב לְכֹלָּא. מַאן דְּסָתִים וְלָא אִתְגַּלְיָיא, לֵית עֵיטָא, וְלֵית מַאן דְּיָדַע לֵיהּ, אֶלָּא הוּא בִּלְחוֹדוֹי. כְּמָה דְּעֵדֶן עִלָּאָה, לֵית דְּיָדַע לֵיהּ אֶלָּא הוּא עַתִּיקָא דְּעַתִּיקִי. וְעַל הַאי כְּתִיב, מַה גָּדְלוּ מַעֲשֶׂיךָ יְיָ' מְאֹד עָמְקוּ מַחְשְׁבוֹתֶיךָ. אר"ש יִתְתַּקְנוּן עוֹבָדָךְ לְעָלְמָא דְּאָתֵי. מֵעִם עַתִּיקָא דְּעַתִּיקִין.

135. We have learned that wherever a path is revealed, in this Atik who is concealed of all, it benefits all LEVELS below, BECAUSE THE COMPREHENSIVE MEANING OF REVEALING A PATH IS that proper advice becomes available to produce benefits for everyone. Whatever is covered and not exposed, MEANING THE PLACES COVERED FULLY WITH HAIR AND WITHOUT A PATH, it shows that there is no solution. There is no one there to comprehend except he alone AND NO OTHER LEVEL BELOW HIM. Just like in the supernal Eden, WHICH IS THE SECRET OF THE CONCEALED CHOCHMAH IN ARICH ANPIN, there exists no one to conceive it except the most Ancient among the ancient himself. About this, it is written: "Hashem, how great are your works! Your thoughts are very deep" (Tehilim 92:6). Rabbi Shimon said: Let your deeds be established by the most ancient among the ancient for the World to Come.

16. The sixth Correction

A Synopsis

Rabbi Yisa establishes this Correction as God's promise that His
faithful love (Chesed) shall never depart from us. He talks about
the inner Chesed, the light of Neshamah, and the external Chesed,
the light of Ruach. That true kindness of Atik Yomin does not
apply during the life of the body but rather to the life of the
Neshamah.

136. תִּקּוּנָא שְׁתִיתָאָה. מִתְתָּקָן שַׂעֲרָא וְסָלִיק מִלְּרַע לְעֵילָא, וְחָפֵי
תִּקְרוּבְתָּא דְּבוּסְמָא טָבָא עַד רֵישָׁא דְּפוּמָא דִּלְעֵילָא. וְנָחִית שַׂעֲרָא
לְרֵישָׁא דְּפִתְחָא דְּאָרְחָא תַּתָּאָה דְּפוּמָא.

136. The sixth Correction: The hair is shaped rising from below upward,
MEANING FROM UNDER THE LOWER LIP BY THE BOTTOM JAW TO THE
TOP OF THE HIGHER JAW. The offering of the pleasant fragrance, MEANING
THE SPREAD OF HAIRS, covers FROM BELOW THE LOWER LIP to the top of
the mouth above TO THE UPPER LIP. The hairs again descend to the top of
the opening of the lower passage of the mouth, UNDERNEATH THE LOWER
LIP. THIS MEANS THAT THEY GROW AGAIN IN THEIR FIXED POSITION IN
THE LOWER JAW. THIS IS THE SECRET OF THE BREADTH OF THE BEARD
THAT UNFOLDS IN THE LOWER JAW FROM THE EDGE OF THE JAW TO THE
TOP OF THE UPPER LIP AND UNDER THE LOWER LIP. THAT IS ALSO
CALLED THE SIDE CURL, THE CORNER OF THE BEARD.

137. קוּם ר' יֵיסָא וְאַתְקִין תִּקּוּנָא דָא. קָם ר' יֵיסָא, פָּתַח וְאָמַר, וְחַסְדִּי
מֵאִתֵּךְ לֹא יָמוּשׁ, וּכְתִיב וּבְחֶסֶד עוֹלָם רִחַמְתִּיךְ, הָנֵי קְרָאֵי קַשְׁיָין
אֲהַדְדֵי.

137. Rise, Rabbi Yesa, and establish the SIXTH Correction. Rabbi Yesa rose
and opened the discussion saying, "But my faithful love (Heb. Chesed) shall
not depart from you" (Yeshayah 54:10), and: "But with everlasting faithful
love (lit. 'Chesed of the world') will I have mercy on you" (Ibid. 8). These
two verses are contradictory to each other, BECAUSE ONE SEEMS TO SAY,
"SHALL NOT DEPART," INDICATING AN INFINITE TIME PERIOD. THE
OTHER VERSE SAYS, "CHESED OF THE WORLD," WHICH MEANS IT
APPLIES ONLY TO THE DAYS OF THE WORLD, WHICH ARE 6,000 YEARS.

138. וְלָא אַקְשׁוּ, דְּתָנֵינָן, אִית חֶסֶד וְאִית חֶסֶד. אִית חֶסֶד דִּלְגוֹ, וְאִית חֶסֶד דִּלְבַר. חֶסֶד דִּלְגוֹ, הָא דְּאָמַרָן דְּעַתִּיקָא דְּעַתִּיקִין, וְהוּא סָתִים בְּסִטְרָא דָּא דְּדִיקְנָא, דְּאִקְרֵי פְּאַת הַזָּקָן. וְלָא בָּעֵי ב"נ לְחַבְּלָא הַאי סִטְרָא, מִשּׁוּם הַאי חֶסֶד דִּלְגוֹ דְּעַתִּיק יוֹמִין. ובג"כ, בְּכֹהֵן דִּלְתַתָּא כְּתִיב בֵּיה, לֹא יִקְרְחָה קָרְחָה בְּרֹאשָׁם וּפְאַת זְקָנָם לֹא יְגַלֵּחוּ .מ"ט. בְּגִין דְּלָא לְחַבְּלָא אוֹרְחוֹי דְּחֶסֶד דְּעַתִּיקָא, דְּכֹהֵן מִסִּטְרָא דָּא קָא אָתֵי.

138. HE RESPONDS: There is no problem, since we have learned that there are various types of Chesed. There is an inner Chesed, WHICH IS THE LIGHT OF NESHAMAH, and there is the external Chesed, THE LIGHT OF RUACH. HE EXPLAINS: The inner Chesed applies to the most ancient among the ancient ones, as we said, who is concealed on this side of the beard called the side curl, the corner of the beard, WHICH IS THE SIXTH CORRECTION. Hence, a man must not destroy this side because of this Chesed within. THAT IS THE SECRET OF SIX ENDS OF THE SOUL of Atik Yomin. Referring to the priest below, it is written: "They shall not make baldness on their head, neither shall they shave off the corner of their beard" (Vayikra 21:5). What is the reason? It is in order not to destroy his paths, MEANING THE CORRECTIONS of the Chesed of the Ancient One, since the priest represents that side; THAT IS, THE ASPECT OF CHESED.

139. וְתָאנָא בְּצְנִיעוּתָא דְּסִפְרָא, בְּכֹלָּא אִצְטְרִיךְ חֶסֶד לְאִתְרַבְּאָה וּלְמִבְנֵי, וְלָא לְקַטְעָא לֵיה, וְלָא אִשְׁתְּצֵי מֵעַלְמָא. וְהַאי דִּכְתִיב וְחַסְדִּי מֵאִתָּךְ לֹא יָמוּשׁ, חֶסֶד דְּעַתִּיק יוֹמִין. וּבְחֶסֶד עוֹלָם, חֶסֶד דְּאִקְרֵי חֶסֶד עוֹלָם, וְהַאי הוּא אַחֲרָא דז"א, דִּכְתִיב אָמַרְתִּי עוֹלָם חֶסֶד יִבָּנֶה.

139. We have learned in the concealed book that Chesed must become abundant and built in any MANNER and not be trimmed, MEANING NOT TO DESTROY THE CORNER OF THE BEARD, because it does not end from the world. This is what is written: "But my Chesed shall not depart from you," which is the Chesed of Atik Yomin, WHICH IS DRAWN THROUGH THIS SIXTH CORRECTION. "Chesed of the world" refers to the Chesed called Chesed of the world. That is another CHESED of Zeir Anpin, THE ASPECT OF RUACH, as is written: "The world is built by Chesed" (Tehilim 89:3).

140. וְהַאי חֶסֶד דְּעַתִּיק דְּעַתִּיקִין, הוּא חֶסֶד דִּקְשׁוֹט. וְחֶסֶד דִּקְשׁוֹט לָאו בְּחַיֵּי גּוּפָא אִתְּמַר, אֶלָּא בְּחַיֵּי דְּנִשְׁמָתָא. וּבג"כ כְּתִיב, כִּי חָפֵץ חֶסֶד הוּא. דָּא הוּא תִּקּוּנָא שְׁתִיתָאָה דִּדְיקָנָא יַקִּירָא, דְּעַתִּיק דְּעַתִּיקֵי.

140. That Chesed of the most Ancient of all ancient ones, OF THE SIXTH CORRECTION, is true Chesed. And that true kindness does not apply to during the life of the body, WHICH IS THE ASPECT OF RUACH, MEANING ZEIR ANPIN REFERRED TO AS BODY. It applies rather to the life of the Neshamah, BECAUSE THE SIXTH CORRECTION IS SIX ENDS OF GREATNESS, WHICH IS THE SECRET OF THE LIFE OF NESHAMAH. Therefore, it is written: "Because he delights in Chesed" (Michah 7:18), since that is the sixth Correction of the precious beard of the most Ancient of all ancient ones.

17. The seventh Correction

A Synopsis
Rabbi Shimon tells us that this Correction is "Like the apple tree among the trees of the wood," and that from these apples life emanates to the world. He talks about the light of the countenance of God and says that when it shines the universe gets blessed. These apples in Arich Anpin are always glowing and white and sending out light in 370 directions. This seventh Correction is referred to as, "He will again have compassion upon us."

141. תִּקּוּנָא שְׁבִיעָאָה. פָּסִיק שַׂעֲרָא, וְאִתְחָזָן ב׳ תַּפּוּחִין בִּתְקָרוּבְתָּא דְּבוּסְמָא, שַׁפִּירָן וְיָאָן לְמֶחֱזֵי.

141. The seventh Correction: The hairs split and two apples appear in the offering of the fragrance, pleasant and beautiful in appearance, MEANING THAT BOTH SIDES OF THE FACE, WHICH ARE CLEAR OF HAIRS, EMERGE OUT OF THE HAIRS OF THE BEARD, WHICH ARE CALLED AN OFFERING OF FRAGRANCE. THEY ARE THE SOURCES OF THIS ILLUMINATION OF CHOCHMAH, ALSO CALLED FRAGRANCE, IN THE SAME SENSE AS IN THE VERSE: "AND HIS DELIGHT SHALL BE (ALSO: 'HE SHALL SMELL') IN THE FEAR OF HASHEM" (YESHAYAH 11:3).

142. פָּתַח ר״ש וְאָמַר, כְּתַפּוּחַ בַּעֲצֵי הַיַּעַר וְגוֹ׳. מַה תַּפּוּחַ זֶה כָּלִיל בִּתְלַת גְּוֵונִי, כַּךְ קוּדְשָׁא בְּרִיךְ הוּא, תְּרֵין תַּפּוּחִין כָּלִיל שִׁיתָא גְּוֵונִי, וּתְרֵין תַּפּוּחִין אִלֵּין, דְּאִינּוּן תִּקּוּנָא ז׳, אִינּוּן כְּלָלָא דְּכָל שִׁיתָא תִּקּוּנִין דַּאֲמֵינָא. וּבְגִינֵיהוֹן אִתְקַיים בְּאוֹר פְּנֵי מֶלֶךְ חַיִּים.

142. Rabbi Shimon opened the discussion saying, "Like the apple tree among the trees of the wood..." (Shir Hashirim 2:3). The Holy One, blessed be He, is like this apple that is composed of three colors, WHITE, RED AND GREEN. Two apples include six colors and these two apples, WHICH ARE THE SECRET OF THE TWO BARE SIDES OF THE FACE CLEAR OF HAIR, which are the seventh Correction, are comprised of all the PREVIOUS six Corrections that I mentioned. For their sake, this verse is fulfilled: "In the light of the king's countenance is life" (Mishlei 16:15).

143. וְתָאנָא, מֵהָנֵי תַּפּוּחִין נָפְקִין חַיִּין לְעָלְמָא, וּמְחַזְּיָין חֵידוּ לְזָעֵיר אַפִּין. כְּתִיב יָאֵר יְיָ' פָּנָיו אֵלֶיךָ. וּכְתִיב בְּאוֹר פְּנֵי מֶלֶךְ חַיִּים. בְּאוֹר פְּנֵי מֶלֶךְ אִלֵּין אִינּוּן תְּרֵין תַּפּוּחִין דְּתִקְרוֹבְתָּא דְּבוּסְמָא דַּאֲמֵינָא. יָאֵר יְיָ' פָּנָיו אֵלֶיךָ, פָּנִים דִּלְבַר, דְּכַד נָהֲרִין מִתְבָּרֵךְ עָלְמָא.

143. We have learned that from these apples, life emanates to the world, WHICH IS THE SECRET OF THE ILLUMINATION OF CHOCHMAH. They show happiness to Zeir Anpin, as is written: "Hashem make his face shine upon you" (Bemidbar 6:25) and it is also written: "In the light of the king's countenance is life." "In the light of the king's countenance" refers to the two apples of the fragrance offering, as I mentioned. "Hashem make his face shine upon you" means the external area of the face THAT IS OF ZEIR ANPIN, WHICH IS OUTSIDE OF ARICH ANPIN, because when it shines the world is blessed.

144. וְתָאנָא, כָּל זְמַן דְּהָנֵי בּוֹצִינֵי דִּלְבַר נְהִירִין, כָּל עָלְמָא מִתְבָּרֵךְ, וְלָא אִשְׁתְּכַח רוּגְזָא בְּעָלְמָא. וּמַה אִי הָנֵי דִּלְבַר כָּךְ. תְּרֵין תַּפּוּחִין דְּנָהֲרִין תְּדִירָא, דְּחַדָּאן תְּדִירָא עאכ"ו.

144. We have learned that as long that these candles on the outside illuminate, WHICH ARE MALE AND FEMALE, the whole world is blessed and there is no anger in the world. If we find it so with the external beings, it is all the more so with the two apples OF ARICH ANPIN that constantly illuminate and are always rejoicing.

145. תַּנְיָא, כַּד אִתְגַּלְיָין תְּרֵין תַּפּוּחִין אִלֵּין, אִתְחֲזֵי זְעֵיר אַפִּין בְּחֶדְוָותָא. וְכָל אִינּוּן בּוֹצִינִין דִּלְתַתָּא, בְּחֶדְוָותָא. וְכָל אִינּוּן דִּלְתַתָּא, נְהִרִין, וְכָל עָלְמִין חַדָּאן, וּשְׁלֵימִין מִכָּל שְׁלֵימוּתָא. וְכֹלָּא חַדָּאן וְנָהֲרִין. וְכָל טִיבוּ לָא פָּסִיק. כֻּלְּהוּ אִתְמַלְיָין בְּשַׁעְתָּא חֲדָא, כֻּלְּהוּ חַדָּאן בְּשַׁעְתָּא חֲדָא.

145. We have learned that when these two apples are revealed, Zeir Anpin appears happy and all those candles below, IN MALCHUT, are happy. All

those below are glowing and all the realms are rejoicing in total perfection. All are happy and shining and there is no end to all kinds of benevolence. All are satiated at once WITH ABUNDANCE and all rejoice simultaneously.

146. ת״ח, פָּנִים דִּלְבַר, אִית זְמַן דְּנַהֲרִין, וְאִית זְמַן דְּלָא נְהִרִין. וּבְגִ״כ כְּתִיב, יָאֵר יְיָ' פָּנָיו אֵלֶיךָ. יָאֵר פָּנָיו אִתָּנוּ סֶלָה. מִכְּלָל דְּלָא הֲוֵי תְּדִירָא. אֶלָּא כַּד אִתְגַּלְּיָין תַּפּוּחִין דִּלְעֵילָא.

146. Come and see the external face OF ZEIR ANPIN. There are times when they are glowing and times when they do not illuminate. Therefore, it is written: "Hashem make his face shine upon you" and also "and cause his face to shine upon us; Sela" (Tehilim 67:2). The meaning here is that he does not always illuminate; THEREFORE, WE PRAY THAT HE WOULD SHINE UPON US, SINCE IT DOES NOT ILLUMINATE IN ZEIR ANPIN except when the apples above, OF ARICH ANPIN, are revealed.

147. תָּאנָא, אִלֵּין תַּפּוּחִין דִּסְתִּימִין, נְהִירִין וְחַוּוֹרִין תְּדִירָא. וּמִנְּהוֹן נְהִירִין לִתְלַת מְאָה וְשַׁבְעִין עִיבָר. וְכָל שִׁיתָא תִּקּוּנִין קַדְמָאִין דְּבְדִיקְנָא בֵּיהּ כְּלִילָן. הֲדָא הוּא דִכְתִיב, יָשׁוּב יְרַחֲמֵנוּ. יָשׁוּב, מִכְּלָל דְּזִמְנִין טְמִירִין, וְזִמְנִין אִתְגַּלְּיָין. הָכָא, הוּא יָשׁוּב יְרַחֲמֵנוּ. וּבְהַאי דִּלְתַתָּא, הוּא וֶאֱמֶת. דָּא הוּא תִּקּוּנָא שְׁבִיעָאָה, דְּכָלִיל שִׁיתָא, בִּתְרֵין תַּפּוּחִין דִּבְעַתִּיקָא דְּעַתִּיקִין.

147. We have learned that these apples IN ARICH ANPIN, which are concealed, are always glowing and white. Light is sent to the 370 directions from them, and all the first six Corrections of the beard are included in them. This is what it says: "He will again have compassion upon us" (Michah 7:19). "Again" indicates that it is occasionally concealed and occasionally revealed. Here IN ARICH ANPIN, THIS CORRECTION IS REFERRED TO AS: "He will again have compassion upon us" and in the one below, IN THE BEARD OF ZEIR ANPIN, MEANING THE THIRTEEN MEASURES OF THE TORAH, HE IS CALLED: "And truth" (Shemot 34:6). That is the seventh Correction, which comprises the six in the two apples of the most ancient among the ancient, ARICH ANPIN.

18. The eighth Correction

A Synopsis

Rabbi Elazar begins by saying that everything including the Torah scroll depends on Mazal (constellation) but wonders whether everything is really dependent on the constellations; can anyone who is truly hallowed be dependent on the birth of planets? Rabbi Shimon says that the holy thread on which all hair depends is referred to as 'Mazal' because all the holy of Holies of Holies depend upon this constellation and the Torah scroll. Everything is dependent on the planets. All successes depend on Mazal, including all worldly things, children, longevity and sustenance.

148. תִּקּוּנָא תְּמִינָאָה. נָפִיק חַד חוּטָא דְּשַׂעְרֵי סוֹחֲרָנֵיהּ דְּדִיקָנָא, וְתַלְיָין בְּשִׁקּוּלָא עַד טַבּוּרָא. קוּם אֶלְעָזָר בְּרִי, אַתְקִין תִּקּוּנָא דָּא.

148. The eighth Correction: A thread of hairs circles the beard, which hang evenly to the center OF THE HEART. Rise, my son Elazar, and establish this Correction.

149. קָם רִבִּי אֶלְעָזָר, פָּתַח וְאָמַר, הַכֹּל תָּלוּי בְּמַזָּל, וַאֲפִילוּ ס"ת בַּהֵיכָל. מִלָּה דָּא אוּקִימְנָא בְּסִפְרָא דִּצְנִיעוּתָא, וְהָכָא אִית לְאִסְתַּכְּלָא, וְכִי הַכֹּל תָּלוּי בְּמַזָּל, וְתָנֵינָן, ס"ת קֹדֶשׁ, וְנַרְתֵּקוֹ קֹדֶשׁ, וְהַהֵיכָל קֹדֶשׁ. וּכְתִיב וְקָרָא זֶה אֶל זֶה וְאָמַר קק"ק, הָא תְּלַת אִינוּן. וס"ת. לָקָבְלֵיהוֹן, נַרְתֵּקוֹ קֹדֶשׁ, וְהַהֵיכָל קֹדֶשׁ, וְהוּא קָדַשׁ. וְהַתּוֹרָה נִתְּנָה בְּג' קְדוּשׁוֹת. בְּשָׁלֹשׁ מַעֲלוֹת, בְּיָמִים שְׁלֹשָׁה, שְׁכִינָה בְּשָׁלֹשׁ, לוּחוֹת וַאֲרוֹן וְהֵיכָל בס"ת תַּלְיָא, וְאִיהוּ תַּלְיָא בְּמַזָּל, וּכְתִיב וּמֵאוֹתוֹת הַשָּׁמַיִם אַל תֵּחָתּוּ. מַאן דְּאִיהוּ בִּקְדוּשׁוֹת הַלָּלוּ לֶהֱוֵי תַּלְיָא בְּמַזָּלָא.

149. Rabbi Elazar rose and began to speak. Everything depends on the stars (Heb. *Mazal*), even the scroll of the Torah in the sanctuary, as we have explained in the hidden book. Now here we must observe. Is everything really dependent upon the stars, since we have learned that the scroll of the Torah is holy and its coat is holy and the sanctuary is holy? It is written: "And one cried to another, and said, 'Holy, holy, holy'" (Yeshayah 6:30). We have HOLY three times and the Torah scroll corresponds to it because its

receptacle is holy, the sanctuary is holy and it is holy. The Torah was given in three grades of holiness, PRIESTS, LEVITES AND YISRAEL, in three days, AS IS WRITTEN: "BE READY BY THE THIRD DAY" (SHEMOT 19:15). The Shechinah is also in three, the tablets, the Ark and the sanctuary, and it is all dependent on the Torah scroll. You say that THE TORAH SCROLL is dependent on the stars, but behold it is written: "And be not dismayed at the signs of heaven" (Yirmeyah 10:2). Whoever is so hallowed, should he be dependent on the stars?

150. אֶלָּא הָכִי אוֹקִימְנָא בְּסִפְרָא דִּצְנִיעוּתָא, הַאי חוּטָא יַקִּירָא קַדִּישָׁא, דְּכָל שַׂעֲרֵי דְּדִיקְנָא תַּלְיָין בֵּיה, אִתְקְרֵי מַזָּל. מ״ט. מִשּׁוּם דְּכָל קָדְשֵׁי קוּדְשִׁין דְּקוּדְשַׁיָּא, בְּהַאי מַזָּלָא תַּלְיָין. וס״ת, אע״ג דְּאִיהוּ קָדוֹשׁ לָא חָל עֲלֵיה עֶשֶׂר קְדוּשִׁין עַד דְּעָיֵיל לְהֵיכָל. כֵּיוָן דְּעָיֵיל לְהֵיכָל, אִתְקְרֵי קָדוֹשׁ בְּעֶשֶׂר קְדוּשׁוֹת. כְּגַוְונָא דָּא דְּלָא אִתְקְרֵי הֵיכָל, אֶלָּא כַּד אִתְחַבְּרָן עֶשֶׂר קְדוּשׁוֹת. וְתָאנָא, הַכֹּל תָּלוּי בְּמַזָּל, דְּאִיהוּ הַאי חוּטָא יַקִּירָא קַדִּישָׁא, דְּכָל שַׂעֲרִין תַּלְיָין בֵּיה.

150. HE RESPONDS: But this is the way I have explained it in the hidden book. This precious and holy thread on which all hair hangs – THAT IS, THE TOTAL UPPER SURFACE OF THE HAIR OF THE BEARD CIRCLING THE FACE LIKE A STRING OF HAIRS, is referred to as "Mazal." What is the explanation? It is because the holy of holies, of the holies, MEANING ALL THE LEVELS AND MOCHIN THAT ARE CALLED HOLY OF HOLIES, depend upon Mazal, BECAUSE THE FLOW OF MAZAL IS CALLED THE HOLY OF HOLIES. And the Torah scroll, although it is hallowed, the ten sanctifications do not apply to ZEIR ANPIN, MEANING HE DOES NOT HAVE THE FIRST THREE SFIROT until it enters the sanctuary, WHICH IS MALCHUT. IT IS NOT PERFECTED IN THE FIRST THREE SFIROT, SAVE THROUGH ITS UNION WITH MALCHUT. Once it enters the sanctuary, NAMELY, UNITES WITH MALCHUT, it is called holy with ten sanctifications. Similarly, MALCHUT is not considered a sanctuary except when the ten sanctifications are joined with it, MEANING ONLY WHEN SHE IS IN UNITY WITH ZEIR ANPIN; THEN THERE IS IN MALCHUT TEN SANCTIFICATIONS. We have learned that everything is dependent on Mazal, SINCE ALL THE FIRST THREE SFIROT IN ZEIR ANPIN AND MALCHUT DEPEND ON MAZAL,

which is the precious and holy thread on which all hairs hang, FROM WHICH ARE RECEIVED ALL THESE SANCTIFICATIONS.

151. אֲמַאי אִקְרֵי מַזָּל. מִשּׁוּם דְּמִנֵּיהּ תַּלְיָין מַזְלֵי, וּמַזְלֵי מִנֵּיהּ עִלָּאִין וְתַתָּאִין. וּבְג״כ אִיהִי תַּלְיָיא. וּבֵיהּ תַּלְיָין כָּל מִלֵּי דְעָלְמָא עִלָּאִין וְתַתָּאִין. וַאֲפִילוּ ס״ת שֶׁבַּהֵיכָל, דְּמִתְעַטֵּר בְּעֶשֶׂר קְדוּשׁוֹת, לָא נָפִיק מִכְּלָלֵיהּ עִם שְׁאַר קְדוּשִׁין וְכֻלְּהוּ תַּלְיָין בְּהַאי. וּמַאן דְּחָמֵי לְהַאי תִּקּוּנָא, אִתְכַּבְּשָׁן חוֹבֵיהוֹן מִקַּמֵּיהּ וּמִתְכַּפְּיָין, הה״ד יִכְבּוֹשׁ עֲוֹנוֹתֵינוּ. א״ל ר״ש, בְּרִיךְ בְּרִי לְקוּדְשָׁא דְקַדִּישִׁין, עַתִּיק מִכֹּלָּא.

151. HE INQUIRES: Why is it referred to as Mazal? HE RESPONDS: All successes depend upon it, and the upper and lower beings receive success from it. It is therefore suspended, THAT IS, IT IS HANGING TO THE CHEST. All worldly things, the highest and the lowest, depend upon it, SINCE CHILDREN, LONGEVITY AND SUSTENANCE DEPEND ON NOT MERIT BUT ON MAZAL. Even the Torah scroll in the sanctuary that is adorned with ten sanctifications is not excepted from the others with ALL other sanctities, and everything depends upon this CORRECTION. Whoever is aware of this Correction, his iniquities are suppressed and subdued. This is what is written: "He will suppress our iniquities" (Michah 7:19). Rabbi Shimon told him: Blessed is my son to the Holy of Holies, the most ancient of all.

19. The ninth Correction

A Synopsis
Rabbi Aba says that the hairs that get blended with the hanging hairs are referred to as depths of the sea, since they emerge from the cords of the brain, and from this place all the complaints that demand justice for the sins of men are subdued.

152. תִּקוּנָא תְּשִׁיעָאָה. מִתְעָרְבִין שַׂעֲרֵי עִם אִינּוּן שַׂעֲרֵי דְּתַלְיָין, וְלָא נָפְקִין דָּא מִן דָּא. קוּם ר' אַבָּא, קָם ר' אַבָּא וְאָמַר, אִלֵּין שַׂעֲרֵי דְּמִתְעָרְבִין עִם אִינּוּן דְּתַלְיָין, אִקְרוּן מְצוּלוֹת יָם. מִשׁוּם דְּנַפְקֵי מִמּוֹתְרֵי מוֹחָא, וּמֵהַאי אַתְרָא רְמִיוּ, כָּל מָארֵי דְּתַבְעִין חוֹבֵי דִּבְנֵי נָשָׁא וּמִתְכַּפְיָין. אר"ש, בְּרִיךְ תְּהֵא לְעַתִּיק יוֹמִין.

152. The ninth Correction: The hairs blend with the hanging hair and do not stick out in relation to one another. Rise, Rabbi Aba. Rabbi Aba rose and said, Those hairs that are blended with the ones that are hanging are referred to as depths of the sea, since they emerge from the cords of the brain. From this place are thrown all the litigates that demand justice for the sins of men, and they are subdued. Rabbi Shimon said: Be blessed to Atik Yomin.

20. The tenth and eleventh Corrections

A Synopsis
Rabbi Yehuda talks about the fear of Hashem, and says that the tenth Correction is called "You will show truth to Jacob," while the eleventh is called "Loyal love to Abraham."

153. תִּקּוּנָא עֲשִׂירָאָה. נַחְתִּין שַׂעֲרֵי תְּחוֹת דִּיקְנָא, וְחַפְיָין בְּגְרוֹנָא תְּחוֹת דִּיקְנָא. קוּם ר' יְהוּדָה. קָם ר' יְהוּדָה פְּתַח וְאָמַר, וּבָאוּ בִּמְעָרוֹת צוּרִים וּבִמְחִלּוֹת עָפָר מִפְּנֵי פַּחַד יְיָ' וְגוֹ'. מִפְּנֵי פַחַד יְיָ', הָא אִתְיְדַע דְּמַאן דְּאִיהוּ לְבַר, פַּחַד יְיָ' אִתְקְרֵי. וּמֵהֲדַר גְּאוֹנוֹ, אִינּוּן שַׂעֲרֵי דִּתְחוֹת דִּיקְנָא, וְאִתְקְרוּן הֲדַר גְּאוֹנוֹ, תְּרֵי. תִּקּוּנָא עֲשִׂירָאָה, תִּתֵּן אֱמֶת לְיַעֲקֹב. וְחַד סָר, דְּלָא נַפְקֵי נִימָא מִן נִימָא, חֶסֶד לְאַבְרָהָם.

153. The tenth Correction: The hairs go down under the beard and cover over the throat under the beard. Rise, Rabbi Yehuda. Rabbi Yehuda rose and opened the discussion saying, "And they shall go into the holes of the rocks, and into the caves of the earth, for fear of Hashem..." (Yeshayah 2:19). "For fear of Hashem": It is well known that whoever is outside, THAT IS ZEIR ANPIN, is referred to as "fear of Hashem." "And for the glory of his majesty" (Ibid.): These are the hairs OF THE THROAT underneath the beard, which are referred to as "the glory of his majesty." There are two CORRECTIONS WITHIN THEM, the tenth Correction called: "You will show truth to Jacob" (Micah 7:20), and the eleventh CORRECTION that no hair goes out more than the other hair, MEANING THAT NO HAIR'S LENGTH IS LONGER THAN ITS NEIGHBOR'S, BUT THEY ARE ALL EQUAL IN LENGTH. THAT IS CALLED: "Loyal love to Abraham" (Ibid.).

21. The twelfth Correction

A Synopsis

Rabbi Shimon explains to Rabbi Yehuda that the hairs around the mouth of Arich Anpin are cleared away so that the inhalation of Zeir Anpin will not be interfered with, as the breath comes from the uppermost holy mouth. The breath that comes from the mouth of Arich Anpin splits up into 37,000 directions and clothes whoever is deserving of being clothed by it, "As You have sworn to our fathers."

154. תִּקּוּנָא דִּתְרֵיסַר. דְּלָא תַּלְיָין שַׂעֲרֵי עַל פּוּמָא, וּפוּמָא אִתְפְּנֵי מִכָּל סִטְרִין, וְיָאִין שַׂעֲרֵי סְחוֹר סְחוֹר לֵיהּ, בְּגִין דְּלָא אִשְׁתְּכַח טִרְחוּתָא, כְּמָה דְּאִצְטְרִיךְ.

154. The twelfth Correction: The hairs do not hang over the mouth and the mouth is clear OF ANY HAIR on all sides. The hairs are tidy round about THE MOUTH, in order that there should be no inconvenience, as it aught to be.

155. טִרְחוּתָא בְּמַאי קָא מַיְירֵי. דִּינָא. בַּאֲתַר דִּינָא טִרְחוּתָא אִשְׁתְּכַח. וְכִי שַׂעֲרֵי דְּדִיקְנָא טִרְחָא אִינּוּן, אוֹ דִּינָא אִינּוּן, וְהָא כֹּלָּא רַחֲמֵי אִתְחֲזֵי. אֶלָּא דְּלָא אִתְטְרַח בְּנִשּׁוּבָא דְּרוּחָא דִּזְעֵיר אַפִּין.

155. HE ASKS: What does he mean by this inconvenience? HE REPLIES THAT HE MEANS Judgment, because there is inconvenience in a place of Judgment. HE ASKS: Then, are the hairs of the beard IN ARICH ANPIN an inconvenience or are they Judgment, since everything in the beard seems to be of Mercy? HE REPLIES: THE REASON WHY THE MOUTH IS CLEARED OF HAIR is in order not to interfere with the inhalation of Zeir Anpin.

156. דְּתָאנָא מֵהַאי פּוּמָא קַדִּישָׁא עִלָּאָה, קֹדֶשׁ קָדָשִׁים, נָשְׁבָא רוּחָא. מַאי רוּחָא. רוּחָא דְּאִתְּרַק בֵּיהּ, דְּמִתְלַבַּשׁ בֵּיהּ זְעֵיר אַפִּין. וּמֵהַאי רוּחָא מִתְלַבְּשִׁין כָּל אִינּוּן דִּלְתַתָּא. וְכַד הַהוּא רוּחָא נָפִיק, אִתְפְּרַשׁ לִתְלָתִין וְשִׁבְעָה אֶלֶף עִיבָר. וְאִתְפְּשַׁט כָּל חַד בִּלְחוֹדוֹי לְאַתְרֵיהּ, וְכָל מַאן דְּאִתְחֲזֵי לְאִתְלַבְּשָׁא מִנֵּיהּ אִתְלַבַּשׁ. וְעַל דָּא שַׂעֲרִין לָא אִשְׁתְּכָחוּ

עַל פּוּמָא קַדִּישָׁא, מִשׁוּם דְּרוּחֵיהּ נָפִיק, וְלָא בָּעֵי מִלָּה אַחֲרָא לְאִתְעָרְבָא בֵּיהּ, וּלְקָרְבָא בַּהֲדֵיהּ.

156. We have learned from this uppermost holy mouth, WHICH IS the Holy of Holies, that the breath comes. What is breath? HE REPLIES: It is the breath that is sent to rouse in him, IN ARICH ANPIN, THAT IS DRAWN FROM THE UNKNOWN HEAD TO HIS MOUTH and in which Zeir Anpin is dressed. THE BREATH BLOWS FROM THE MOUTH OF ARICH ANPIN TO THE MOUTH OF ZEIR ANPIN AND ZEIR ANPIN BECOMES ATTIRED IN IT. From this breath, all below are clothed, BECAUSE THEY RECEIVE IT THROUGH THE MOUTH OF ZEIR ANPIN. When this breath exits FROM THE MOUTH OF ARICH ANPIN, it splits up into 37,000 directions, WHICH IS THE NUMERICAL EQUIVALENT OF *HEVEL* (ENG. 'BREATH') THAT ALLUDES TO THE AIR EXHALED FROM THE MOUTH. Each one individually spreads to its place, and whoever is deserving and is worthy to dress up in it is clothed. Therefore, there is not one hair on the holy mouth OF ARICH ANPIN, because his breath emanates THROUGH THERE. No other matter needs to be mixed up in it or approach it.

157. וְדָא הוּא טְמִירוּתָא דְּכֹלָּא, דְּלָא אִתְדְּבַק לָא לְעֵילָּא וְלָא לְתַתָּא. וְהוּא סָתִים בִּסְתִימָא דִּסְתִּימִין דְּלָא אִתְיְדַע. דָּא הוּא דְּלָא אִתְתָּקַן, וְלָא הֲוָה בֵּיהּ תִּקּוּנָא. וּבְגִין כָּךְ, רוּחַ דְּנָפִיק מֵהַהוּא דִּלְבַר, וּמִתְלַבְּשִׁין בֵּיהּ נְבִיאֵי מְהֵימְנֵי, אִתְקְרֵי פֶּה יְיָ'. אֲבָל בְּהַאי עַתִּיקָא דְּעַתִּיקִין לָא אִתְפְּרַשׁ. וְלֵית מַאן דְּיֵדַע רוּחֵיהּ בַּר אִיהוּ. וּבְגִין כָּךְ שַׂעֲרוֹי שְׁקִילִין סוּחֲרָנֵא דְּפוּמָא, וּפוּמָא אִתְפְּנֵי מִכָּל סִטְרוֹי.

157. This BREATH OF THE MOUTH is hidden from everything since it does not adhere above or below. It is concealed within that which is the most concealed and unknown, the one that was not shaped and had no Correction. Therefore, the breath that emanates from the one on the outside THAT IS ZEIR ANPIN, in which the true prophets were clothed, is referred to as the mouth of Hashem. However, in the most ancient among the ancient, ARICH ANPIN, THE MOUTH is not defined, since there exists no one who could comprehend his spirit besides himself. Therefore, his hairs are even around the mouth and the mouth itself is clear on all sides.

158. וּבְהַאי אִתְרְחִיצוּ אֲבְהָתָנָא, לְאִתְלַבְּשָׁא בְּהַאי רוּחָא, דְּמִתְפָּשֵׁט לְכַמָּה עִיבְרִין, בַּאֲתָר דְּכָל שַׂעֲרֵי שְׁקִילִין בְּסוֹחֲרָנוֹי. דִּכְתִיב אֲשֶׁר נִשְׁבַּעְתָּ לַאֲבוֹתֵינוּ. וְדָא הוּא תִּקּוּנָא קַדִּישָׁא עִלָּאָה דִּתְרֵיסָר. דְּמִכָּאן אִשְׁתְּלְשָׁלוּ י"ב תְּחוּמִין לְעֵילָא. י"ב תְּחוּמִין לְתַתָּא. י"ב תְּחוּמִין לִי"ב שִׁבְטֵי אֲבָהָתָא. הה"ד אֲשֶׁר נִשְׁבַּעְתָּ לַאֲבוֹתֵינוּ.

158. The patriarchs trusted in this, in being dressed in this breath that spreads to various directions in the place where all the hair is even around it. IT IS THROUGH THIS THAT THE BREATH BLOWS FROM THERE TO ZEIR ANPIN WITHOUT ANY INCONVENIENCE, as is written: "As you have sworn to our fathers" (Michah 7:20). That is the twelfth most holy Correction, because twelve boundaries above were lowered in succession from here, IN CHESED, GVURAH AND TIFERET of ZEIR ANPIN, twelve boundaries below IN MALCHUT, and twelve boundaries to the twelve tribes of our fathers. This is what is said: "As you have sworn to our fathers."

22. The thirteenth Correction

A Synopsis

Rabbi Shimon says that all the other Corrections are included in this thirteenth one that finalizes and completes all the rest. He tells us that the Corrections are called 'days of old', 'ancient primordial days', while the Corrections that exist in Zeir Anpin are called 'days of the world'. Rabbi Shimon says that the time during which Atik Yomin will awaken with the Corrections is referred to as 'one day', in which the beard will be glorified and it alone will be present. In the unfolding of all thirteen Corrections, Atik Yomin is known and not known, hidden and not hidden, but is known by the Corrections that spread and flow down to illuminate.

159. תִּקּוּנָא דִּתְלֵיסַר. תַּלְיָין שַׂעֲרֵי דְתָחוֹת דִּיקְנָא מִכָּאן וּמִכָּאן, בִּיקָרָא יָאֶה, וּבִיקָרָא שַׁפִּירָא, וְחַפְיָין עַד טַבּוּרָא וְלָא אִתְחַזְיָין מֵאַנְפֵּי תַּקְרוּבָא דְּבוּסְמָא, בַּר אִינּוּן תַּפּוּחִין שַׁפִּירָן חִוּוֹרִין.

159. The thirteenth Correction: The hairs hang under the beard from both sides in fine glory and splendid dignity, and cover to the navel. THAT IS THE ENTIRE BOTTOM AREA OF THE BEARD THAT IS INVISIBLE TO THE EYE. Nothing is apparent from the face of the fragrant offering except for these TWO pretty white apples, WHICH ARE THE SECRET OF THE SEVENTH CORRECTION, AS MENTIONED ABOVE.

160. א"ר שמעוֹן, זַכָּאָה חוּלָקֵיה דְּמַאן דְּאִשְׁתְּכַח בְּהַאי אִדְרָא קַדִּישָׁא עִלָּאָה דַּאֲנָן בֵּיה. זַכָּאָה חוּלָקֵיה בְּעָלְמָא דֵּין, וּבְעָלְמָא דְּאָתֵי, דַּאֲנָן יַתְבִין בִּקְדוּשָׁא עִלָּאָה, אֶשָּׁא עִלָּאָה אַסְחַר לָן וְהָא כָּל תִּקּוּנִין עִלָּאִין דְּדִיקְנָא קַדִּישָׁא אִתְתָּקָנוּ, וְאִתְעַטָּרוּ וְאַסְחֲרוּ לְדוּכְתַּיְיהוּ.

160. Rabbi Shimon said: Blessed is the lot of whoever is in this supernal *Idra Kadisha* (Eng. 'holy chamber') in which we are. Blessed is his portion in this world and the World to Come, since we dwell in uppermost holiness and supernal fire encircles us. Behold, all the entire uppermost Corrections of the holy beard were established and adorned and returned to their place.

161. וְהַאי תִּקּוּנָא דִּתְלֵיסַר, הוּא תִּקּוּנָא יָאֶה, דְּבֵיה אֲחִידָן כֹּלָּא. כֻּלְּהוּ

מִתְכַּסְפִין לְמִזְקַף רֵישָׁא לְקָבְלֵיהּ. מִנֵּיהּ תַּלְיָין כָּל אִינּוּן דִּבְזָעֵיר אַפִּין
אֲחִידָן. מִנֵּיהּ תַּלְיָין עִלָּאִין וְתַתָּאִין, וְכָל גִּנְזִין עִלָּאִין וְתַתָּאִין גְּנִיזִין
בֵּיהּ, וּבֵיהּ כְּלִילָן. וְאִיהוּ מַזָּלָא דְּמִתְזָלָא מִנֵּיהּ כֹּלָּא, דָּא הוּא תִּקּוּנָא
שְׁלֵימָתָא, דְּאַשְׁלִים לְכָל תִּקּוּנִין, דָּא אַשְׁלִים לְכֹלָּא.

161. This thirteenth Correction is an appropriate Correction in which all CORRECTIONS are included. All long and desire to raise their head towards it, MEANING TO RECEIVE FROM THEM THE FIRST THREE SFIROT, WHICH ARE REFERRED TO AS THE HEAD. All these CORRECTIONS that are attached to Zeir Anpin originate in it, MEANING THAT HIS CORRECTIONS ARE RECEIVED FROM THIS BEARD. Higher and lower beings are dependent upon it. The upper and lower treasures are concealed in it and contained within and it is the star from which everyone can benefit and have good luck. This is the perfect Correction that finalizes and completes all the other Corrections. This fulfills and completes everything, BECAUSE THIS IS THE SECRET OF MALCHUT THAT PERFECTS AND COMPLETES ALL THE SFIROT.

162. תָּאנָא, אֵלֵין תִּקּוּנִין אִקְרוּן יְמֵי קֶדֶם, יוֹמִין קַדְמָאִין דְּקַדְמָאֵי. וְאִינּוּן דְּאִשְׁתְּכָחוּ בִּזְעֵיר אַפִּין, אִקְרוּן יְמֵי עוֹלָם. וְתָאנָא, אֵלֵין יְמֵי קֶדֶם, כֻּלְּהוּ מִתְתַּקְּנָן בְּתִקּוּנָא דְּדִיקְנָא דְּעַתִּיקָא דְּעַתִּיקִין, טְמִירָא דִּטְמִירִין. וְהַאי דְּתַלְיֵיסַר כָּלִיל לְהוֹן, כְּמָה דְּאִתְּמַר. וְדָא יוֹמָא לָא אִתְכְּלִיל בַּהֲדַיְיהוּ, אֶלָּא הוּא כָּלִיל כֹּלָּא.

162. We have learned that these Corrections are called days of old, ancient primordial days. Those CORRECTIONS that are in Zeir Anpin are referred to as "days of the world" (Yeshayah 63:9). We have learned that these days of old are all formed in the Correction of the beard of the most ancient among the ancient, the most concealed among the concealed. This thirteenth CORRECTION includes them, as we have said, and this day, WHICH IS THE THIRTEENTH CORRECTION, is not included among them but rather contains and comprises all of them.

163. וּבְהַהוּא זִמְנָא דְּאִתְּעַר עַתִּיק יוֹמִין בְּתִקּוּנִין דִּלְעֵילָּא, הַהוּא אִתְקְרֵי יוֹם אֶחָד, דְּבֵיהּ זַמִּין לְאוֹקִיר דִּיקְנֵיהּ, הֲדָא הוּא דִּכְתִיב יוֹם

אֶחָד הוּא יִוָּדַע לַיְיָ'. הוּא בִּלְחוֹדוֹי יַתִּיר מִכֹּלָּא. הוּא דִּכְלִיל כֹּלָא, הוּא דְּאִתְקְרֵי בִּשְׁמָא יְדִיעָא.

163. The period during which Atik Yomin will awaken with the Corrections above THE BEARD is referred to as one day, in which the beard will be glorified, as written: "One particular day which shall be known as Hashem's" (Zecharyah 14:7). That particular day alone is more special than anything, because it contains everything and is referred to by a specific name. THAT IS ONE DAY.

164. דְּתָנֵינָן, בַּאֲתַר דְּאִית יוֹם אִית לַיְלָה דְּלֵית יוֹם בְּלָא לַיְלָה. וּמִשּׁוּם דְּהַהוּא זִמְנָא זְמַן יְהֵא הַיִּקְרָא דְּדִיקְנָא. וְהוּא בִּלְחוֹדוֹי יִשְׁתְּכַח, לָא אִתְקְרֵי לָא יוֹם וְלָא לַיְלָה. דְּלֵית יוֹם אִקְרֵי, אֶלָּא מִסִּטְרָא דִּילָן. וְלֵית לַיְלָה אִקְרֵי, אֶלָּא מִסִּטְרָא דִּילָן. וּמִשּׁוּם דְּהַאי תִּקּוּנָא כָּלִיל כֹּלָּא, לָא אִתְיְדַע וְלָא אִתְחֲזֵי מִנֵּיהּ, וּמִנֵּיהּ נָגִיד מְשַׁחָא דִּרְבוּתָא לִתְלֵיסַר עִיבָר מַבּוּעִין. לְכָל אִינּוּן דִּלְתַתָּא, דְּנַהֲרִין בְּהַהוּא מְשָׁחָא.

164. We have learned that in a place where there is day, there is night, because there is no day without night. During that period, it will be a time of the beard's glory and it alone will be present. It is called neither day nor night, since it is only called day from our perspective and it is only called night from our perspective. Because this Correction includes everything, nothing is known or apparent of it BEFORE THE TIME IT IS REFERRED TO AS ONE DAY, EXCEPT that from it the anointing oil flows to the thirteen aspects of the springs for those below that illuminate with that oil.

165. בִּתְלֵיסַר תִּקּוּנִין אִלֵּין אִתְתַּקָּנָא דִּיקְנָא קַדִּישָׁא עִלָּאָה, וְאִלֵּין תִּקּוּנִין דְּבַהַאי דִּיקְנָא, מִתְתַּקְּנָן וְנַחְתָּן לְכַמָּה עִיבָר. וְלָא אִתְחֲזוּן הֵיךְ מִתְפַּשְּׁטִין וְהֵיךְ נָפְקִין, מִכֹּלָּא אַסְתִּימוּ, וּמִכֹּלָּא אִתְטַמְּרוּ. לֵית דְּיָדַע אֲתָר לְהַאי עַתִּיקָא, בְּפַשִּׁיטוּתָא דִּלְהוֹן כֻּלְּהוֹן כְּלִילָן, כְּמָה דְּאִתְּמַר, אִתְיְדַע וְלָא אִתְיְדַע. טָמִיר וְלָא טָמִיר. עֲלֵיהּ אִתְקְרֵי, אֲנִי יְיָ' הוּא שְׁמִי וּכְבוֹדִי לְאַחֵר לֹא אֶתֵּן. וּכְתִיב הוּא עָשָׂנוּ וְלֹא אֲנַחְנוּ. וּכְתִיב וְעַתִּיק יוֹמִין יָתִיב. בְּאַתְרֵיהּ יָתִיב וְלֵית יְדִיעַ לֵיהּ. יָתִיב וְלָא שְׁכִיחַ, וּכְתִיב

אוֹדְךָ עַל כִּי נוֹרָאוֹת נִפְלֵיתִי וְגוֹ'.

165. With these thirteen Corrections, the most holy beard above is established and the Corrections of this beard are prepared and flow down TO ILLUMINATE in several directions. It is not seen how they spread and come out, BECAUSE THEY ARE totally concealed and hidden from all. There is no one who can designate a place for this Atik. In the unfolding of these CORRECTIONS, everything is included, as we said that He is known yet unknown, hidden yet not hidden, MEANING TO SAY THAT HE IS ESSENTIALLY UNKNOWN AND HIDDEN. BUT BY HIS SPREADING CORRECTIONS HE IS KNOWN. About this, it is written: "I am Hashem: that is my name: and my glory will I not give to another" (Yeshayah 42:8), and "It is he who made us, and we belong to him" (Tehilim 100:3) and, "And an ancient of days did sit" (Daniel 7:9), MEANING he stays in his place and there is no ONE who knows him. He is sitting yet not present. It is written: "I will praise you; for I am fearfully and wonderfully made..." (Tehilim 139:14).

23. When this veil is spread

A Synopsis

Rabbi Shimon describes the veil or curtain that is spread over the friends, and says that the thirteen Corrections had been awaiting their explanations, and afterwards they ascended to their places, causing great joy among the angels. At the end of correction the rabbis will again say all these holy sayings in the World to Come.

166. אָמַר ר"ש לְחַבְרַיָּיא, כַּד אִתְפְּרִיס פְּרִיסָא דָא, דְּאַתּוּן חָמָאן עֲלָנָא, אֲנָא חֲמֵינָא דְּנַחְתּוּ כֹּל תִּקּוּנִין בְּגַוָּוה, וּנְהִירוּ בְּאַתַר דָּא. וְחַד פְּרוֹכְתָּא בּוּצִינָא דְקוּדְשָׁא בְּרִיךְ הוּא, פְּרִיסָא בְּאַרְבַּע סַמְכִין, לְאַרְבַּע עִיבָר.

166. Rabbi Shimon said to the friends: When this veil that you see over us is spread, I perceive that all Corrections have entered within and brighten this area. HE EXPLAINS: And a curtain, MEANING A VEIL, which is the candle of the Holy One, blessed be He, is spread to the four pillars in the four directions.

167. סַמְכָא חַד הוּא יָתִיב מִתַּתָּא לְעֵילָא, וְחַד מַגְרוֹפְיָא בִּידֵיה. וּבְמַגְרוֹפְיָא אַרְבַּע מַפְתְּחֵי שַׁנְיָין מִכָּל סִטְרוֹי. וּמִתְאַחֲדָן פַּרְסָא, וְנַחְתִּין לָה מֵעֵילָא לְתַתָּא. וְכֵן לְסַמְכָא תִּנְיָינָא, וּתְלִיתָאָה וּרְבִיעָאָה. וּבֵין סַמְכָא לְסַמְכָא, אֲחִידָן תְּמָנֵיסָר רַגְלֵי דְסַמְכֵי וּמִתְנַהֲרִין בְּבוּצִינָא דִּגְלִיפָא בְּהַהוּא פְּרִיסָא. וְכֵן לְד' עִיבָר.

167. One pillar is situated from below upwards and a rake is in its hand, A TOOL TO CLEAN THE WASTE. In that rake are four keys, different FROM ONE ANOTHER in every direction. They latch on to the curtain and lower it from top to bottom and similarly to the second, third and fourth pillars. Between one pillar and another are attached eighteen stakes of support, which are lit up with the candle that is engraved in that particular veil. It is the same with all four directions.

168. וַחֲמֵינָא אִלֵּין תִּקּוּנִין דִּנְהַרִין עָלָה, וַהֲווֹ מְחַכָּאן מִלֵּי דְּפוּמָנָא,

לְאִתְעַטְּרָא וּלְאִסְתַּלְּקָא כָּל חַד בְּאַתְרֵיהּ. וְכַד הֲווֹ מִתְתַּקְּנָן מִפּוּמָנָא, כָּל חַד וְחַד סָלִיק וְאִתְעַטַּר וְאִתָּקַן בְּהַהוּא תִּקּוּנָא דְּאִתָּקַן הָכָא, מִכָּל פּוּמָא דְּחַד מִינָן. וּבְשַׁעֲתָא דְּחַד מִינָן פָּתַח פּוּמָא, לְתַקְּנָא בְּהַהוּא תִּקּוּנָא, הַהוּא תִּקּוּנָא הֲוָה יָתִיב וּמְחַכֶּה לְמִלָּה דְּנָפִיק מִפּוּמֵיכוֹן, וּכְדֵין סָלְקָא בְּדוּכְתֵּיהּ וְאִתְעַטַּר.

168. I saw these Correction shining on it and the words in our mouths, MEANING THE EXPLANATIONS OF THE CORRECTIONS WHICH WE HAVE EXPOUNDED UPON, were waiting to be crowned and ascend each one to its proper place. While those CORRECTIONS were established by our mouths – MEANING WHILE WE WERE EXPLAINING THEM, SINCE THAT WAY WE GAVE THEM MEANING SO THEY WERE ESTABLISHED ABOVE, each one rose. Each was crowned and established by the same Correction that each one of us has established here, by the mouth of each one of us. During the time that each one of us opened his mouth to explain a certain Correction, that Correction was awaiting the words that would come from your mouth. Following that, it would continue upward to be crowned in its place.

169. וְכָל סַמְכִין מִכָּאן וּמִכָּאן, חַדָּאן עַל דְּשַׁמְעִין מַה דְּלָא יָדְעוּ, וְצַיְּיתִין לְקָלֵיכוֹן. כַּמָּה רְתִיכִין קַיְּימִין הָכָא בְּגִינֵיכוֹן. זַכָּאִין אַתּוּן לְעָלְמָא דְּאָתֵי, דְּכֻלְּהוּ מִלֵּי דְּנָפְקֵי מִפּוּמֵיכוֹן, כֻּלְּהוּ מִלִּין קַדִּישִׁין. מִלִּין כַּשְׁרָן דְּלָא אַסְטָאן לִימִינָא וְלִשְׂמָאלָא.

169. All the pillars, MEANING THE ANGELS THAT SUPPORT THE THRONE OF MALCHUT from both sides, were joyous, since they heard and understood what they had not previously known and were listening attentively to your voice. How many Chariots were present here for your sake, MEANING THE ANGELS, ON WHOM MALCHUT RIDES. Praised are you for the World to Come, since all the words that were uttered from your mouth are holy words, honest words that do not deviate right or left BUT ARE COMING FROM THE CENTRAL COLUMN THAT CONTAINS THEM ALL.

170. קוּדְשָׁא בְּרִיךְ הוּא חַדֵּי לְמִשְׁמַע, וְצַיֵּית לְהָנֵי מִלֵּי, עַד דְּהוּא אַגְמַר דִּינָא, דִּי לְעָלְמָא דְּאָתֵי תֵּימְרוּן זִמְנָא אַחֲרָא כָּל הָנֵי מִלֵּי

קַדִּישִׁין. עֲלַיְיכוּ כְּתִיב, וְחִכֵּךְ כְּיֵין הַטוֹב וְגו', דוֹבֵב שִׂפְתֵי יְשֵׁנִים. מַאי דוֹבֵב שִׂפְתֵי יְשֵׁנִים. דַּאֲפִילוּ לְעָלְמָא דְּאָתֵי מְרַחְשָׁן שִׂפְוָותַיְכוּ אוֹרַיְיתָא קַמֵּיה.

170. The Holy One, blessed be He, is happy to hear and pays attention to these words until he finishes judging, MEANING UNTIL THE FINAL CORRECTION, because you will say for a second time all these holy words in the World to Come. About you, it is written: "And the roof of your mouth like the best wine...causing the sleepers' lips to murmur" (Shir Hashirim 7:10). What is the meaning of: "causing the sleepers' lips to murmur"? It means that your lips will be speaking of Torah in his presence even in the World to Come.

24. The formation of Zeir Anpin

A Synopsis

Here we read about the Corrections of Zeir Anpin as derived from those of Atik Yomin. Rabbi Shimon talks about His Corrections unfurling like the countenance of man, since man encompasses Zeir Anpin and Malchut. We are told how the most Ancient of ancients designed the kings that did not endure, and how He rejected them and stored them in hiding for a later period – this refers to the kings that reigned in the land of Edom, the place where all judgments exist. When the white head was formed it prepared all the corrections above and below. All the worlds had been destroyed because man had not been established and the seven kings were unable to rise and take their place; thus they ceased to exist. Rabbi Shimon says that anyone who descends from a higher level in which he first existed is considered to have died. When the seven kings had the likeness of a man installed in them they were called by other names and endured.

171. הַשְׁתָּא אִתְתָּקְנוּ וְאִתְכַּוְּונוּ דַעְתָּא, לְמִתְקַן תִּקּוּנוֹי דִּזְעֵיר אַפִּין, הֵיךְ יִתְתְּקַן, וְהֵיךְ יִתְלַבֵּשׁ בְּתִקּוּנוֹי מִתְקוּנֵי עַתִּיק יוֹמִין, קַדִּישָׁא דְּקַדִּישִׁין, טְמִירָא דִּטְמִירִין, טְמִירָא מִכֹּלָּא. דְּהַשְׁתָּא חוֹבְתָּא עֲלַיְיכוּ, לְמִגְזַר דִּינָא קוּשְׁטָאה יָאָה וְשַׁפִּירָא וּלְאַתְקְנָא כָּל תִּקּוּנִין עַל בּוּרְיֵיה.

171. Get ready and direct your minds to establish the Corrections of Zeir Anpin, how he will be constructed and don the Corrections of Atik Yomin, Holy of Holies, concealed of all concealed, hidden from all. It is now your duty to carry out and establish a splendidly beautiful and truthful judgment, and to establish all the Corrections thoroughly.

172. תִּקּוּנֵי דִּזְעֵיר אַפִּין, מִתְקוּנֵי דַּאֲרִיךְ אַפִּין אִתְתָּקְנוּ. וְאִתְפַּשְׁטוּ תִּקּוּנוֹי מִכָּאן וּמִכָּאן, כְּחֵיזוּ בַּ"נ, לְמִשְׁלְטָא בֵּיה רוּחָא דִּטְמִירָא דְּכָל טְמִירִין. בְּגִין לְמֵיתַב עַל כּוּרְסַיָּיא, דִּכְתִיב וְעַל דְּמוּת הַכִּסֵּא דְּמוּת כְּמַרְאֵה אָדָם עָלָיו מִלְמָעְלָה. כְּמַרְאֵה אָדָם: דְּכָלִיל כָּל דְּיוּקְנִין. כְּמַרְאֵה אָדָם: דְּכָלִיל כָּל שְׁמָהָן. כְּמַרְאֵה אָדָם: דְּבֵיה סְתִימִין כָּל עָלְמִין עִלָּאִין וְתַתָּאִין. כְּמַרְאֵה אָדָם: דְּכָלִיל כָּל רָזִין דְּאִתְאַמְרוּ וְאִתְתָּקְנוּ עַד דְּלָא אִבְרֵי עָלְמָא, וְאע"ג דְּלָא אִתְקָיְימוּ.

-214-

172. The Corrections of Zeir Anpin were made through the Corrections of Arich Anpin, and his Corrections unfurled from this side and that side, MEANING FROM RIGHT, LEFT AND CENTER, like the countenance of man. MAN IS INDICATIVE OF THE CENTRAL COLUMN THAT INCLUDES ALL THREE COLUMNS in order that the spirit of the concealed of all concealed, THAT IS ARICH ANPIN, will reign in him. So he will sit on the throne, WHICH IS MALCHUT, since it is written: "And upon the likeness of the throne was the likeness as the appearance of a man above upon it" (Yechezkel 1:26). "The appearance of a man," MEANING LIKE THE FACE OF A MAN, that comprises all forms, SINCE THE THREE FACES, LION, OX, EAGLE, ARE CONTAINED IN MAN'S COUNTENANCE. THAT IS FROM THE ASPECT OF MALCHUT WITHIN HIM, SINCE MAN ENCOMPASSES ZEIR ANPIN AND MALCHUT. IT IS ALSO "the appearance of a man," as it includes all the names, BECAUSE ZEIR ANPIN IS CALLED YUD HEI VAV HEI THAT INCLUDES ALL THE NAMES. IT IS ALSO "The appearance of a man" in which are sealed all the worlds above and below. IT IS ALSO, "the appearance of a man" for including the secrets that were expressed and established prior to the world's creation, MEANING BY THE SEVEN KINGS IN THE FORMLESS WORLD, even though THEY WERE DESTROYED AND did not last.

173. תָּאנָא בִּצְנִיעוּתָא דְּסִפְרָא, עַתִּיקָא דְּעַתִּיקִין עַד לָא זַמִּין תִּקּוּנוֹי, בָּאנֵי מַלְכִין, גָּלִיף מַלְכִין וּמְשַׁעֵר מַלְכִין, וְלָא הֲווֹ מִתְקַיְּימֵי, עַד דְּדָחֵי לוֹן, וְאַצְנַע לוֹן לְבָתַר זִמְנָא, הה״ד וְאֵלֶּה הַמְּלָכִים אֲשֶׁר מָלְכוּ בְּאֶרֶץ אֱדוֹם. בְּאֶרֶץ אֱדוֹם, בַּאֲתָר דְּכָל דִּינִין מִתְקַיְּימִין תַּמָּן, וְכֻלְּהוּ לָא אִתְקַיְּימוּ.

173. We have learned in the hidden book that the most ancient among the ancient, raised kings, designed kings, and measured the size of kings, but they did not last. He rejected them and stored them in hiding for a later period. This is the meaning of what is written: "And these are kings that reigned in the land of Edom" (Beresheet 36:31). "In the land of Edom" MEANS the place where all Judgments exist. None of them endured, SINCE IT SAYS BY EACH ONE: "AND...REIGNED...AND...DIED" (IBID.).

174. עַד דְּרֵישָׁא חִוְּורָא עַתִּיקָא דְּעַתִּיקִין אִתְתָּקַן. כַּד אִתְתָּקַן, תַּקִּין כָּל תִּקּוּנִין דִּלְתַתָּא, תַּקִּין כָּל תִּקּוּנִין דְּעֶלָּאִין וְתַתָּאִין. מִכָּאן אוֹלִיפְנָא,

כָּל רֵישָׁא דְעַמָּא, דְּלָא אִתְתַּקַּן הוּא בְּקַדְמֵיתָא, לֵית עַמָּא מִתְתַּקְּנָא. וְאִי אִיהוּ מִתְתַּקַּן, כֻּלְּהוּ מִתְתַּקְּנָן. וְאִי אִיהוּ לָא מִתְתַּקַּן בְּקַדְמֵיתָא, לָא יַכְלִין עַמָּא לְאִתְתַּקְּנָא.

174. Until the white head, THAT IS THE SKULL OF ARICH ANPIN, the most ancient among the ancient was formed. When it was formed, it prepared all the corrections above and below. From here we learn that unless a ruler of a nation was established first, his nation could not be settled. When he is established, everyone is. If he is not settled first, the people in his nation are unable to settle.

175. מְנָלָן. מֵעַתִּיק יוֹמִין. דְּעַד לָא אִתְתַּקַּן הוּא בְּתִקּוּנוֹי, לָא אִתְתַּקְנוּ כָּל אִינּוּן דְּבָעוּ לְאִתְתַּקְּנָא, וְכֻלְּהוּ עָלְמִין אִתְחֲרָבוּ. הה"ד, וַיִּמְלוֹךְ בֶּאֱדוֹם בֶּלַע בֶּן בְּעוֹר. וַיִּמְלוֹךְ בֶּאֱדוֹם, רָזָא יַקִּירָא הוּא. אֲתָר דְּכָל דִּינִין מִתְקַטְּרִין תַּמָּן, וְתַלְיָין, מִתַּמָּן.

175. Where DO WE HAVE THIS? From Atik Yomin. As long as he was not established, then all those that need to be formed are not established, and all the worlds were destroyed. This is what is written: "And Bela the son of Beor reigned in Edom" (Beresheet 36:32). "Reigned in Edom" is a precious secret. It is a place to which all Judgments connect and from which all Judgments impend.

176. בֶּלַע בֶּן בְּעוֹר, תָּאנָא הוּא גְּזֵרַת דִּינָא, תַּקִּיפָא דְּתַקִּיפִין, דְּבְגִינֵיהּ מִתְקַטְּרָן אֶלֶף אַלְפִין מָארֵי דְּיַבָּבָא וִילָלָה. וְשֵׁם עִירוֹ דִּנְהָבָה. מַאי דִּנְהָבָה. כְּלוֹמַר דִּין הָבָה. כד"א, לַעֲלוּקָה שְׁתֵּי בָּנוֹת הַב הַב.

176. "Bela the son of Beor": We have learned that he is the source of the heaviest verdict through whom are enjoined and linked thousands of thousands of those who wail and lament "and the name of his city was Dinhabah" (Ibid.). What is the meaning of Dinhabah? It means literally: Give justice, as it says, "The leech has two daughters, crying, 'Give (Heb. hav), give'" (Mishlei 30:15).

177. כֵּיוָן דְּסָלִיק לְאִתְיַשְּׁבָא, בֵּיה לָא קָאֵים, וְלָא הֲוָה יָכִיל לְמֵיקָם, וְכֻלְּהוּ עָלְמִין אִתְחָרְבוּ. מַאי טַעֲמָא. מִשּׁוּם דְּאָדָם לָא אִתְתָּקַּן. דְּתִקוּנָא דְּאָדָם בְּדִיּוּקְנֵיה, כָּלִיל כֹּלָּא, וְיָכִיל כֹּלָּא לְאִתְיַשְּׁבָא בֵּיה.

177. As soon as he rose to take his seat ON HIS LEVEL, he could not keep the position and was unable to withstand it. What is the reason that all the worlds were destroyed? It is because man was not established. The establishing of man in his image includes everything, and everything can settle in it AND ENDURE.

178. וּבְגִין דְּתִקוּנָא דָּא דְּאָדָם, לָא אִשְׁתְּכַח, לָא יָכִילוּ לְמֵיקָם וּלְאִתְיַשְּׁבָא, וְאִתְבְּטָלוּ. וְאִתְבְּטָלוּ ס״ד וְהָא כֻּלְּהוּ בְּאָדָם אִתְכְּלִילָן. אֶלָּא אִתְבְּטָלוּ וְאִסְתַּלָּקוּ מֵהַהוּא תִּקּוּנָא, עַד דְּיֵיתֵי תִּקוּנָא דְּאָדָם. וְכַד אָתָא הַאי דִּיּוּקְנָא, אִתְגַּלְפוּ כֻּלְּהוּ, וְאִתְחַזָּרוּ לְקִיּוּמָא אַחֲרָא. מִנְּהוֹן אִתְבְּסָמוּ, וּמִנְּהוֹן לָא אִתְבְּסָמוּ כְּלָל.

178. Since this establishing of man did not exist IN THEM, THE SEVEN KINGS were unable to rise and take their place, so they ceased to exist. HE ASKS: Could you imagine that they completely ceased to exist? Weren't all of them LATER included in man, IN ZEIR ANPIN? HE REPLIES: It simply means that they ceased and were severed from that establishment, until man's correction. When this countenance arrived, they were all engraved IN HIS FORM and reverted to a different kind of existence. Some of them were established and some were not.

179. וְאִי תֵּימָא וְהָא כְּתִיב וַיָּמָת וַיָּמָת. דְּאִתְבְּטָלוּ לְגַמְרֵי. לָאו הָכִי, אֶלָּא כָּל מַאן דְּנָחִית מִדַּרְגָּא קַדְמָאָה דַּהֲוָה בֵּיה, קָארֵי בֵּיה מִיתָה. כד״א, וַיָּמָת מֶלֶךְ מִצְרַיִם, דְּנָחַת מִדַּרְגָּא קַדְמָאָה דַּהֲוָה קָם בֵּיה. וְכֵיוָן דְּאִתְתָּקַּן אָדָם, אִתְקְרוֹן בִּשְׁמָהָן אַחֲרָנִין, וְאִתְבְּסָמוּ בְּקִיּוּמָא בֵּיה, וְקַיְימִין בְּדוּכְתַּיְיהוּ.

179. You might say that it is written: "And...died...and...died," WHICH INDICATES that they completely ceased to exist. HE REPLIES: It is not so.

Anyone that descends from a higher level in which he existed before is considered as if he died, as it is written: "The king of Egypt died" (Shemot 2:23), MEANING that he was lowered from the previous level in which he was standing, MEANING HE BECAME LEPROUS. As soon as THE IMAGE OF a man, OF THE THREE COLUMNS, was installed IN THEM they were called by other names. They were settled through him in endurance and endured in their position.

180. וְכֻלְּהוּ אִתְקְרוּן בִּשְׁמָהָן אַחֲרָנִין מִן קַדְמָאִין, בַּר הַהוּא דִּכְתִּיב בֵּיה, וְשֵׁם אִשְׁתּוֹ מְהֵיטַבְאֵל בַּת מַטְרֵד בַּת מֵי זָהָב. מ"ט. מִשּׁוּם דְּהָנֵי לָא אִתְבְּטָלוּ כִּשְׁאָר אַחֲרָנִין. מִשּׁוּם דַּהֲוָה דְכַר וְנוּקְבָּא. כְּהַאי תַּמְרָא, דְּלָא סַלְקָא אֶלָּא דְכַר וְנוּקְבָּא. וּבג"כ הַשָׁתָּא דְּאִשְׁתְּכָחוּ דְכַר וְנוּקְבָּא, לָא כְּתִיב בְּהוּ מִיתָה כְּאַחֲרָנִין, וְאִתְקְיָימוּ. אֲבָל לָא אִתְיַשְּׁבוּ, עַד דְּאִתְתְּקַן דְּיוּקְנָא דְּאָדָם, וְכֵיוָן דְּאִתְתְּקַן דְּיוּקְנָא דְּאָדָם, אִתְחֲזָרוּ וְאִתְקְיָימוּ בְּקִיּוּמָא אַחֲרָא, וְאִתְיַישְּׁבוּ.

180. All were called by different names than they had at first, except the one of whom it is written: "And his wife's name was Mehetabel, daughter of Matred, daughter of Mezehab" (Beresheet 36:39). THAT IS THE SECRET OF THE NAME OF NUMERICAL VALUE OF 45 THAT RENEWS THE MALE AND FEMALE REFERRED TO BY HADAR AND MEHETABEL. WHY WAS HE NOT CALLED BY A DIFFERENT NAME? Because these, HADAR AND MEHETABEL, were not lost like the rest OF THE SEVEN KINGS, because they were male and female. This is similar to the palm tree that does not bear fruit unless you have planted a male and female stock. Therefore, now that we found them to be male and female, the term death was not mentioned in relation to them as with the rest. They lived, but they were not COMPLETELY secure until they acquired the likeness of a man. When they were finally established with a human countenance, they returned to exist in an alternate state and were settled.

25. The skull of Zeir Anpin

A Synopsis

Rabbi Shimon explains the process whereby Arich Anpin sent the spark and the fine pure air that spread to create the skull of Zeir Anpin. Thousands of worlds reside in this skull, and dew drips into it from the white head; from that dew which he shakes off his head the dead will be restored to life. Those who awake to everlasting life will merit the white dew, and those who awake to shame and everlasting contempt will merit the dew that has a red hue in it. We read about the illumination of this skull to both sides and how it spreads to His face. When Zeir Anpin observes the face of Arich Anpin and has compassion on the world His face becomes long like that of Arich Anpin. The illumination that spreads from Zeir Anpin to those below requires that those below give dues to Atik Yomin when they are counted in the census.

181. תָּאנָא, כַּד סָלִיק בִּרְעוּתָא דְּרֵישָׁא חִוְּורָא, לְמֶעְבַּד יְקָרָא לִיקָרֵיהּ, תַּקִּין וְזַמִּין וְאַפִּיק מְבוּצִינָא דְּקַרְדִינוּתָא, חַד נִיצוֹצָא, וְסָלִיק וְאִתְפַּשַּׁט לִתְלַת מְאָה וְשַׁבְעִין עִיבָר. וְנִיצוֹצָא קַאִים, וְשָׁארֵי נָפִיק אֲוִירָא דַּכְיָא וּמִתְגַּלְגְּלָא, נָשַׁב בֵּיהּ אִתְתַּקַּן. וְנָפִיק חַד גּוּלְגַּלְתָּא תַּקִּיפָא, וְאִתְפַּשַּׁט לְאַרְבַּע סִטְרִין.

181. We have learned that when it was the wish of the white head, THE SKULL OF ARICH ANPIN, to glorify its glory, it formed and prepared and produced from the hard candle a spark which went up and spread into 370 directions. That spark is constant and pure air begins to be discharged and roll forth. It blew at it, so it was restored. A strong skull was released and spread to four directions.

182. וּבְהַאי אֲוִירָא דַּכְיָא, אִשְׁתְּאִיב נִיצוֹצָא וְאִתְאֲחַד, וְאִתְכְּלִיל בֵּיהּ. בֵּיהּ ס"ד. אֶלָּא אִתְטַמַּר בֵּיהּ. וּבְגִין כָּךְ, הַאי גּוּלְגַּלְתָּא אִתְפַּשַּׁט בְּסִטְרוֹי, וְהַאי אֲוִירָא הוּא טָמִיר דִּטְמִירִין דְּעַתִּיק יוֹמִין, בְּרוּחָא דְּגָנִיז.

182. Within fine pure air, THAT IS IN THE SKULL, the spark was sucked, and became part of it. HE ASKS: Could you imagine that it became part of it? HE REPLIES: It only means that it was hidden in it. Therefore, this skull OF

ZEIR ANPIN was spread to its sides and this air WITHIN IT, is the most hidden from Atik Yomin, with the spirit that it stored.

183. בְּהַאי גּוּלְגַּלְתָּא אִתְפְּשָׁטוּ אֶשָׁא מִסְטַר חַד, וַאֲוִירָא מִסְטַר חַד. וַאֲוִירָא דַּכְיָא קָאִים עֲלֵיה מֵהַאי סְטָר. וְאֶשָׁא דַּכְיָא קָאִים מֵהַאי סְטָר. מַאי אֶשָׁא הָכָא. אֶלָּא לָאו הוּא אֶשָׁא, אֲבָל דָּא נִיצוֹצָא דְּאִתְכְּלִיל בַּאֲוִירָא דַּכְיָא, נָהִיר לְמָאתָן וְשַׁבְעִין עָלְמִין, וְדִינָא מִסְטְרוֹי אִשְׁתְּכַח, וּבְג"ד, הַאי גּוּלְגַּלְתָּא, אִתְקְרֵי גּוּלְגַּלְתָּא תַּקִּיפָא.

183. In the skull OF ZEIR ANPIN fire unfurled from one direction and air from the other. Pure air is prevalent above it from one side and pure fire is prevalent upon it from the other side. HE ASKS: What is the fire here? HE REPLIES: It is not really composed of fire, but this spark, that is comprised in the refined air, illuminates to the 270 worlds, and Judgment emerges from its side. Therefore, this skull is referred to as the hard skull.

184. בְּגוּלְגַּלְתָּא דָא, יַתְבִין תִּשְׁעָה אַלְפֵי רִבּוֹא עָלְמִין, דְּנַטְלִין עֲלוֹי וְסַמְכִין עֲלוֹי. בְּהַאי גּוּלְגַּלְתָּא, נָטִיף טַלָּא מֵרֵישָׁא חִיוָּורָא, דְּאִתְמְלֵי מִנֵּיהּ תָּדִיר. וּמֵהַאי טַלָּא דְּאַנְעַר מֵרֵישֵׁיהּ זְמִינִין מֵיתַיָּיא לְאַחֲיָאה.

184. In this skull, nine thousand ten thousands worlds reside which ride on it and depend on it. Into this skull drips dew from the white head, MEANING FROM THE SKULL OF ARICH ANPIN, that is always filled from it. From this dew, which He shakes off from His head, the dead will be restored to life.

185. וְהוּא טַלָּא דְּאִתְכְּלִיל בִּתְרֵי גְּוָונֵי, מִסִּטְרָא דְּרֵישָׁא חִיוָּורָא, חִיוָּור בְּגַוְויֵהּ. דְּכָלִיל כֻּלְּהוּ חִיוָּורֵי אֲבָל כַּד אִתְיַישְׁבָן בְּהַאי רֵישָׁא דִּזְעֵיר אַפִּין, אִתְחֲזֵי בֵּיהּ סוּמְקָא. כְּהַאי בְּדוֹלְחָא דְּאִיהוּ חִיוָּור, וְאִתְחַזְיָיא גְּוָונָא סוּמְקָא בְּגַוְונָא חִיוָּורָא.

185. That dew is included in two aspects from the direction of the white head, THAT IS ARICH ANPIN. FIRSTLY, it is in essence white. SECONDLY, it comprises all whites. However, when THIS DEW resides on this head in Zeir

Anpin, some redness is apparent, it is like the crystal, which is in essence white but where the red color appears in the white color.

186. וּבְגִין כָּךְ כְּתִיב, וְרַבִּים מִיְשֵׁנֵי אַדְמַת עָפָר יָקִיצוּ אֵלֶּה לְחַיֵּי עוֹלָם וְאֵלֶּה לַחֲרָפוֹת לְדִרְאוֹן עוֹלָם. לְחַיֵּי עוֹלָם, בְּגִין דְּאִתְחֲזִיאוּ לְהַהוּא חִיוָּרָא, דְּאָתֵי מִסִּטְרָא דְּעַתִּיק יוֹמִין, אֲרִיכָא דְאַנְפִּין. לַחֲרָפוֹת לְדִרְאוֹן עוֹלָם, בְּגִין דְּאִתְחֲזִיאוּ לְהַהוּא סוּמָקָא דִּזְעֵיר אַפִּין. וְכֹלָּא כָּלִיל בְּהַהוּא טַלָּא, הה"ד כִּי טַל אוֹרֹת טַלֶּךָ. אוֹרוֹת: תְּרֵין. וְהַהוּא טַלָּא דְּנָטִיף, נָטִיף כָּל יוֹמָא לְחַקְלָא דְתַפּוּחִים, כִּגְוְונֵי חִיוָּרָא וְסוּמָקָא.

186. Therefore, it is written: "And many of those who sleep in the dust of the earth shall awake, some to everlasting life, and some to shame and everlasting contempt" (Daniel 12:2). "To everlasting life": These are the ones that merit this white DEW, which comes from the direction of Atik Yomin, Arich Anpin. "Some to shame and everlasting contempt" are those that deserve that red color IN THE DEW of Zeir Anpin. All is included in that dew, as is written: "For your dew is as the dew on herbs (also: 'of lights')" (Yeshayah 26:19). Lights MEANING two, since that dew drips every day to the field of apple trees, WHICH IS MALCHUT, AND CONTAINS WITHIN IT TWO LIGHTS similar to white and red.

187. הַאי גוּלְגַּלְתָּא אַנְהִיר בִּתְרֵי גְווֹנֵי, לְהַאי סְטַר וּלְהַאי סְטַר. וּמֵהַאי אֲוִירָא דַּכְיָא, אִתְפַּשַּׁט מִגּוּלְגַּלְתָּא לְאַנְפּוֹי ק"נ רִבּוֹא עָלְמִין. וּבְגִין כָּךְ אִתְקְרֵי זְעֵיר אַפִּין. וּבְשַׁעֲתָא דְּאִצְטְרִיךְ, אִתְפַּשְּׁטוּ אַנְפּוֹי וַאֲרִיכִין בְּהַהוּא זִמְנָא, בְּגִין דְּאַשְׁגַּח בְּאַנְפּוֹי דְּעַתִּיקֵי דְּעַתִּיקִין, וְחָיֵיס לְעָלְמָא.

187. This skull, OF ZEIR ANPIN, illuminates on both sides to this direction and to that direction, THAT IS REFINED AIR AND REFINED FIRE. From this refined air, spread from HIS skull to his face 150 ten thousands realms. Therefore, it is called Zeir Anpin, WHICH MEANS A SMALL FACE. When the need arises, MEANING WHEN THE LOWER GRADES ARE WORTHY, His face expands and becomes long during that period, SIMILAR TO ARICH ANPIN (LIT. 'LONG FACE') THAT IS 370 TEN THOUSAND ILLUMINATIONS. This is because He sees the face of the most ancient of the ancient and has compassion on the world.

188. וּמֵהַאי גּוּלְגַּלְתָּא, נָפִיק חַד עִיבָר, לְכָל אִינּוּן דִּלְתַתָּא. וְיָהֲבֵי אֲגַר אוֹרָאוּתָא לְעַתִּיק יוֹמִין. כַּד עָאלִין בְּחוּשְׁבָּנָא, תְּחוֹת שַׁרְבִּיטָא. וְלָקֳבֵיל דָּא. בֶּקַע לַגוּלְגַּלְת לְתַתָּא, כַּד עָאלִין בְּחוּשְׁבָּנָא. וְהַאי בֶּקַע אֲגַר אוֹרָאוּתָא, אִשְׁתְּכַח מִנֵּיהּ לְעַתִּיק יוֹמִין.

188. From this skull IN ZEIR ANPIN, a path goes out, to all those below. They give dues to Atik Yomin, when they are numbered under the wand. Corresponding to this is the "beka for every man" (Shemot 38:26) THAT IS GIVEN below when census is taken. This "beka" is the due compensation which is given to Atik Yomin.

26. The three brains of Zeir Anpin

A Synopsis

Rabbi Shimon describes the three chambers of the skull of Zeir Anpin, and the 32 paths of wisdom and the fifty gates of Binah that emanate and open from it. The central chamber is that wherein Da'at resides, and thus knowledge fills the other chambers. The three chambers permeate the entire body.

189. בַּחֲלָלֵיהּ דְּגוּלְגַּלְתָּא, ג' חַלָלִין אִשְׁתְּכָחוּ, דְּשַׁרְיָיא מוֹחָא בְּהוּ, וּקְרוּמָא דָּקִיק חַפְיָיא עֲלַיְיהוּ. אֲבָל לָא קְרוּמָא קְשִׁישָׁא סְתִימָא כְּעַתִּיק יוֹמִין. וּבְגִין דָּא, הַאי מוֹחָא אִתְפְּשַׁט וְנָהִיר לִתְלָתִין וּתְרֵין שְׁבִילִין. הה"ד וְנָהָר יוֹצֵא מֵעֵדֶן.

189. Three spaces exist in the inner space of the skull in which the brain resides, and a thin membrane covers them. It is not a heavy and thick membrane as by Atik Yomin. Therefore, this brain permeates and illuminates to 32 pathways OF CHOCHMAH, as written: "And a river went out of Eden" (Beresheet 2:10).

190. וְתָאנָא, בִּתְלַת חַלָלִין דְּגוּלְגַלְתָּא מוֹחָא שַׁרְיָיא. מֵחֲלָלָא חַד מִתְבְּקַע וּמִתְפְּשַׁט חַד מַבּוּעָא לְד' סִטְרִין, וְנָפִיק מֵהַהוּא מוֹחָא דְּשַׁרְיָיא בְּהַאי חַלָלָא, תְּלָתִין וּתְרֵין שְׁבִילִין רוּחִין דְּחָכְמְתָא.

190. We have further learned that in the three spaces of the skull resides the brain OF ZEIR ANPIN, and from a spatial cavern a spring gushes forth to four directions. From that particular brain that resides in this space, 32 pathways of the spirit of wisdom emanate.

191. מֵחֲלָלָא תִּנְיָינָא, מִתְבְּקַע וּמִתְפְּשַׁט חַד מַבּוּעָא אַחֲרָא. וּמִתְפַּתְחִין ן' תַּרְעִין. מֵאִלֵּין ן' תַּרְעִין, אִתְאַחֲדָן ן' יוֹמִין דְּאוֹרַיְיתָא. ן' שְׁנִין דְּיוֹבְלָא. ן' אֶלֶף דָּרִין, דְּזַמִּין קוּדְשָׁא בְּרִיךְ הוּא לְאָתָבָא רוּחֵיהּ לֵיהּ, וּלְשַׁרְיָיא בֵּיהּ.

191. From the second space, another spring bubbles up and spreads, WHICH IS THE SECRET OF THE LEFT COLUMN CALLED BINAH, and fifty gates

open up. From these fifty gates are united the fifty days of the Torah,
MEANING ON THE FIFTIETH DAY OF THE COUNT OF THE OMER IN WHICH
THE TORAH WAS GIVEN, the fifty years of the Jubilee, 50,000 generations
that the Holy One, blessed be He, will refresh his spirit in them and dwell in.

192. מֵחַלָלָא תְּלִיתָאָה, נָפְקִין אֶלֶף אַלְפִין אִדָּרִין וְאַכְסַדְרָאִין, דְּדַעְתָּא
שַׁרְיָיא עֲלַיְיהוּ, וְדָרֵי בְּהוּ. וְהַאי חַלָלָא שָׁרֵי מָדוֹרֵיהּ בֵּין הַאי חַלָלָא
וּבֵין הַאי חַלָלָא, וְאִתְמַלְיָין מִתְּרֵין סִטְרִין. כָּל אִינוּן אִדָּרִין. הה״ד
וּבְדַעַת חֲדָרִים יִמָּלְאוּ. וְאִלֵּין ג׳ מִתְפַּשְׁטִין בְּכָל גּוּפָא, לְהַאי סִטְרָא
וּלְהַאי סִטְרָא. וּבְאִינּוּן אָחִיד כָּל גּוּפָא וְאָחִיד בְּהוּ גּוּפָא מִכָּל סִטְרוֹי.
וּבְכָל גּוּפָא אִתְפַּשְׁטָן וְאִשְׁתַּכְּחָן.

192. From the third space, thousand of thousand chambers and foyers
emanate within which Da'at rests and resides. This space is situated
between the other two spaces, MEANING IT IS THE CENTRAL SPACE
BETWEEN THE RIGHT AND LEFT CAVERN SPACES. All these chambers are
replenished from both directions, FROM RIGHT AND LEFT, as is written:
"And by knowledge (Heb. *Da'at*) are the chambers filled" (Mishlei 24:4).
These three SPACES, WHICH ARE CHOCHMAH, BINAH AND DA'AT,
permeate the whole body to this direction and that direction. The entire
body is linked to them and the body is attached to them in all their aspects.
And they permeate and exist throughout the entire body.

27. The hair of the head of Zeir Anpin

A Synopsis

We learn about the thousands of locks of black hair on the head of Zeir Anpin, that are entangled together and are strong, some soft and some hard. They hang in curls because they flow from great springs of the three divisions of the brains. Right and left, light and darkness, mercy and judgment all depend on these curls. Where the hairs part, 613 paths separate and divide into the ways of the Torah commandments.

193. תָּאנָא, בְּגוּלְגַּלְתָּא דְּרֵישָׁא, תַּלְיָין אֶלֶף אַלְפֵי רִבּוֹא וְרִבּוֹא רִבְבָן קוֹצֵי דְּשַׂעֲרֵי אוּכְמָן, וּמִסְתַּבְּכִין דָּא בְּדָא, וּמִתְעָרְבִין דָּא בְּדָא. וְלֵית חוּשְׁבְּנָא לְנִימִין דְּכָל קוֹצָא וְקוֹצָא, דַּאֲחִידָן בֵּיהּ דַּכְיָין וּמְסָאֲבָן. וּמִכָּאן אִתְאַחֲדָן טַעֲמֵי אוֹרַיְיתָא, בְּדַכְיָא וּבִמְסָאֲבָא. בְּכָל אִינּוּן סְטְרִין דְּאִינּוּן דַּכְיָין, בְּכָל אִינּוּן סְטְרִין דְּאִינּוּן מְסָאֲבָן.

193. We have learned that in the skull of the head OF ZEIR ANPIN, thousands of thousands of ten thousands and ten thousands of ten thousands locks of black hair hang and are entangled one in the other. They blend into one another and there is no accounting of these strands that are attached to each individual lock OF HAIR, BECAUSE THEY ARE pure and defiled. From here are attached reasons and explanations of the Torah relating to defilement and purity, in all these aspects that are clean and all the aspects that are unclean.

194. יַתְבִין קוֹצֵי מִסְתַּבְּכִין וְתַקִּיפִין. מִנְהוֹן שְׁעִיעִין, וּמִנְהוֹן תַּקִּיפִין. וּבְכָל קוֹצָא וְקוֹצָא, יַתְבִין נִימִין תְּלִין עַל תְּלִין. מִתְלַהֲטָן וְתַלְיָין כְּגִיבָּר תַּקִּיף, מָארֵי נַצַּח קְרָבִין. בְּתִקּוּנָא יָאֶה בְּתִקּוּנָא שַׁפִּירָא תַּקִּיפָא רַבְרְבִין וְתַקִּיפִין. הה"ד בָּחוּר כָּאֲרָזִים.

194. The HAIR locks are situated ON THE SKULL OF ZEIR ANPIN, are entangled ONE IN THE OTHER and ARE strong. Some are soft and some are coarse. In each individual lock are situated wavy strands OF HAIR, glowing and hanging like strong mighty man victorious in battles, in a nice arrangements, a beautiful mighty arrangement. They are great and strong, as is written: "Excellent as the cedars" (Shir Hashirim 5:15).

195. מִתְתַּקְנִין קוֹצִין דְּשַׂעֲרֵי, וְתַלְיָין תַּלְיָין עַל תִּלִּין, מֵהַאי סִטְרָא לְהַאי סִטְרָא, עַל גּוּלְגַּלְתָּא. הה״ד, קְווּצוֹתָיו תַּלְתַּלִּים. וְתָאנָא יַתְבִין תְּלֵי תִּלִּין, מִשּׁוּם דְּמַשְׁכִין מִמַּבּוּעִין סַגִּיאִין, דִּתְלַת רַהֲטֵי מוֹחָא. מִמַּבּוּעָא חַלָּלָא חַד דְּגוּלְגַּלְתָּא, אִתְמַשְׁכָן שַׂעֲרֵי בִּמְשִׁיכוּתָא, וּמִתְעַבְדִּין תִּלִּין, דְּתַלְיָין מִכַּמָּה מַבּוּעִין, דְּאִתְמַשְׁכָן מֵהַאי חַלָּלָא. מֵחַלָּלָא תִּנְיָינָא, נַפְקֵי חַמְשִׁין מַבּוּעִין, וְאִתְמַשְׁכָן שַׂעֲרֵי מֵאִינּוּן מַבּוּעִין בִּמְשִׁיכוּתָא, וְאִתְעַבְדִּין תִּלִּין, דְּתַלְיָין וּמִתְעַרְבִין בְּקוֹצִין אַחֲרָנִין. מֵחַלָּלָא תְּלִיתָאָה, נַפְקֵי אֶלֶף אַלְפִין אִדְרִין וְאַכְסַדְרָאִין, וְאִתְמַשְׁכָן שַׂעֲרֵי בִּמְשִׁיכוּתָא מִכֻּלְּהוּ. ובג״כ אִינּוּן קוֹצִין, תִּלִּין עַל תִּלִּין.

195. The hair locks are shaped and hang in wavy curls from one side to the other side of the skull. This is what is written: "His locks are wavy" (Ibid. 11). We have learned that they are placed hanging in curls, because they flow forth from great springs of the three divisions of the brains. From the spring of the first space in the skull, THAT IS, CHOCHMAH OF ZEIR ANPIN, hairs are going forth continuously and are formed in curls coming from several sources that flow forth from this space. From the second space, WHICH IS BINAH OF ZEIR ANPIN, fifty sources spring forth, and the hairs carry on continuously from these sources and form waves that hang and blend in other locks. From the third space go forth thousands of thousands of rooms and chambers, and the hairs flow forth continuously from all. Therefore, these locks are curls upon curls.

196. וְכֻלְּהוּ מְשִׁיכָן דְּאִתְמַשְׁכָן מִג׳ חַלָּלִין דְּמוֹחָא דְּגוּלְגַּלְתָּא. וְכָל אִינּוּן נִימִין וְכָל אִינּוּן קוֹצֵי תַּלְיָין וְחַפְיָין לְסִטְרָא דְּאוּדְנִין. ובג״כ כְּתִיב, הַטֵּה אֱלֹהַי אָזְנְךָ וּשְׁמָע. וּבְהַאי תָּלִין, תַּלְיָין יְמִינָא וּשְׂמָאלָא, נְהוֹרָא וַחֲשׁוֹכָא, רַחֲמֵי וְדִינָא. וְכָל יְמִינָא וּשְׂמָאלָא תָּלֵי בְּהַאי, וְלָא בְּעַתִּיקָא.

196. All the transmissions that issue forth from these three spaces in the brain of the skull, and all these threads OF HAIR and all these locks hang over and cover the sides of the ears. Therefore, it is written: "O my Elohim, incline your ear, and hear" (Daniel 9:18). From these curls come out right

and left, light and darkness, Mercy and Judgment. All ASPECTS OF right and left depend on Zeir Anpin, but not on Atik THAT IS ARICH ANPIN.

197. בְּפַלְגוּתָא דְשַׂעֲרֵי, אִתְחֲזֵי חַד אוֹרְחָא דָקִיק, דְּמִתְאַחֲדָא מֵהַהוּא אָרְחָא דְּעַתִּיק יוֹמִין. וּמֵהַהוּא אָרְחָא, אִתְפָּרְשָׁן שִׁית מְאָה וּתְלֵיסָר אָרְחִין, דְּאִתְפַּלְגוּן בְּאָרְחִין דְּפִקּוּדֵי דְּאוֹרַיְיתָא. דִּכְתִיב, כָּל אָרְחוֹת יְיָ׳ חֶסֶד וֶאֱמֶת לְנוֹצְרֵי בְרִיתוֹ וְעֵדוֹתָיו.

197. When the hairs part TO RIGHT AND LEFT, a narrow path is apparent IN THE MIDDLE that join this path of Atik Yomin. From this path IN ZEIR ANPIN, 613 paths separate that divide into the ways of the Torah commandments. THAT IS TO SAY THAT EACH INDIVIDUAL COMMANDMENT OF THE 613 PRECEPTS IN THE TORAH IS FLOWING FORTH FROM THAT CENTRAL COLUMN, WHICH IS AMONG THE HAIRS IN ZEIR ANPIN, as is written: "All the paths of Hashem are mercy and truth to such as keep his covenant and his testimonies" (Tehilim 25:10).

198. תָּנָא, בְּכָל קוֹצָא וְקוֹצָא, מִתְאַחֲדָן אֶלֶף אַלְפִין מָארֵי דִיבָבָא וִילָלָה, דְּתַלְיָין בְּכָל קוֹצָא וְקוֹצָא מֵאִינּוּן תַּקִּיפִין. וּמֵאִינּוּן שְׂעִיעִין מָארֵיהוֹן דְּמִתְקְלָא, בג״כ אִית יְמִינָא וְאִית שְׂמָאלָא.

198. We have learned that in every individual hair lock are grasped thousands of thousands of those who wail and lament and hang on to each lock of rough HAIRS. From those soft hairs flow forth the balancing ones – THAT IS, THOSE WHO FOLLOW THE CENTRAL COLUMN. Therefore, there is right and left IN THE HAIR.

28. The forehead of Zeir Anpin

A Synopsis

Rabbi Shimon says that the forehead of the skull is the supervision of providence, and that it is not revealed except when it is necessary to scrutinize the deeds of the wicked; then the world at large is given to trial except when Atik Yomin wishes to have compassion on Yisrael because their prayers ascend to Him. When God is aroused to delight in the righteous, the face of Atik Yomin shines in the face of Zeir Anpin; the forehead of Arich Anpin is revealed and shines upon the forehead of Zeir Anpin – this is referred to as a period of grace, when judgment is silenced and not executed. In the countenance of man there are correspondences to the brow of Zeir Anpin, wherein the six Sfirot are revealed. When the forehead of Zeir Anpin is revealed, all is in judgment because the brow of Adam is also revealed.

199. מִצְחָא דְּגוּלְגַּלְתָּא. אַשְׁגָּחוּתָא דְּאַשְׁגָּלְיָיא. וְלָא מִתְגַּלְיָיא, בַּר הַהוּא זִמְנָא, דְּצְרִיכִין חַיָּיבַיָּא לְאִתְפַּקְדָא, וּלְעַיְּינָא בְּעוֹבָדֵייהוֹן. וְתָאנָא, כַּד אִתְגַּלְיָיא הַאי מִצְחָא, אִתְּעָרוּ כָּל מָארֵיהוֹן דְּדִינָא, וְכָל עָלְמָא בְּדִינָא אִתְמְסַר. בַּר הַהִיא שַׁעֲתָא, כַּד סָלְקוּ צְלוֹתְהוֹן דְּיִשְׂרָאֵל לְקַמֵּי עַתִּיק יוֹמִין, וּבָעֵי לְרַחֲמָא עַל בְּנוֹי, גַּלֵּי מִצְחָא דְּרַעֲוָא דְּרַעֲוִין, וְנָהִיר בְּהַאי דִּזְעֵיר אַפִּין, וְאִשְׁתְּכִיךְ דִּינָא.

199. The forehead of the skull is the supervision of providence. It is not revealed except for the period during which the wicked must be accounted AND IT IS NECESSARY to scrutinize their deeds. We have learned that when the forehead OF ZEIR ANPIN is revealed, all the plaintiffs are aroused and the world at large is given to trial, except for that particular period when the prayers of Yisrael ascend before Atik Yomin and he wishes to have compassion on his children. He reveals HIS forehead THAT IS REFERRED TO AS the Will of all Will and illuminates with that FOREHEAD of Zeir Anpin, and Judgment is soothed.

200. בְּהַאי מִצְחָא, נָפִיק חַד שַׂעֲרָא, דְּמִתְפַּשֵּׁט בֵּיה מִמּוֹחָא דְּאַפִיק חַמְשִׁין תַּרְעִין. וְכַד אִתְפַּשָּׁט, אִתְעֲבִיד מִצְחָא דְּאַשְׁגָּחוּתָא, לְחַיָּיבֵי

עָלְמָא, לְאִינּוּן דְּלָא מִתְכַּסְּפֵי בְּעוֹבָדֵיהוֹן. הה"ד, וּמֵצַח אִשָּׁה זוֹנָה הָיָה לָךְ מֵאַנְתְּ הִכָּלֵם.

200. In that forehead emerges one hair that spreads on it from the brain that produced fifty gates. When THAT HAIR expands OVER THE FOREHEAD OF ZEIR ANPIN, it becomes the supervising forehead over the wicked of the world, those who are not ashamed of their deeds. This is the meaning of: "And you did have a harlot's forehead, you did refuse to be ashamed" (Yirmeyah 3:3).

201. וְתָנֵינָא, שַׂעֲרָא לָא קָאִים בְּהַאי אֲתָר דְּמִצְחָא, בְּגִין דְּאִתְגַּלְיָיא לְאִינּוּן דְּחַצִיפִין בְּחוֹבַיְיהוּ. וְשַׁעֲתָא דְּמִתְעַר קוּדְשָׁא בְּרִיךְ הוּא לְאִשְׁתַּעְשְׁעָא עִם צַדִּיקַיָּיא, נְהִירִין אַנְפּוֹהִי דְּעַתִּיק יוֹמִין, בְּאַנְפּוֹי דִּזְעֵיר אַפִּין, וּמִתְגַּלְיָיא מִצְחֵיה, וְנָהִיר לְהַאי מִצְחָא, וּכְדֵין אִתְקְרֵי עֵת רָצוֹן. וְכָל שַׁעֲתָא וְשַׁעֲתָא דְּדִינָא תָּלֵי, וְהַאי מִצְחָא דִּזְעֵיר אַפִּין אִתְגַּלְיָיא, אִתְגַּלְיָיא מִצְחָא דְּעַתִּיקָא דְּעַתִּיקִין, וְאִשְׁתְּכִיךְ דִּינָא, וְלָא אִתְעֲבֵיד.

201. We have learned that there is no hair in that specific place in the brow, because THE FOREHEAD is revealed to those who sin with impudence. During the period that the Holy One, blessed be He, is aroused to delight in the righteous, the face of Atik Yomin shines in the face of Zeir Anpin. The forehead OF ARICH ANPIN is revealed and shines upon the forehead OF ZEIR ANPIN and it is referred to as a time of goodwill. During each individual period that Judgment impends and the forehead of Zeir Anpin is revealed, the forehead of the most ancient among the ancient ones is revealed, and Judgment is appeared and not executed.

202. תָּאנָא, הַאי מִצְחָא, אִתְפְּשַׁט בְּמָאתָן אֶלֶף סוּמָקֵי דְּסוּמָקֵי, דְּאִתְאַחֲדָן בֵּיה, וּכְלִילָן בֵּיה. וְכַד אִתְגַּלְיָיא מִצְחָא דִּזְעֵיר אַפִּין, אִית רְשׁוּתָא לְכֻלְּהוּ לְחַרְבָּא. וְכַד אִתְגַּלְיָיא מִצְחָא דְּרַעֲוָא דְּרַעֲוִין, דְּנָהִיר לְהַאי מִצְחָא, כְּדֵין כֻּלְּהוּ מִשְׁתַּכְּכִין.

202. We have learned that this brow expands in 200,000 beings most red that are attached to it and are comprised within. When the forehead of Zeir

Anpin is revealed, there is permission for all to destroy; THAT IS, TO CAUSE
DESTRUCTION. When the forehead of the Will of all wills is revealed and
shines on to this forehead, all are appeased.

203. וְתַנְיָא, עֶשְׂרִין וְאַרְבַּע בָּתֵּי דִינִין מִשְׁתַּכְּחִין בְּהַאי מִצְחָא, וְכֻלְּהוּ
אִקְרוּן נֶצַח. וּבְאַתְוָון רְצוּפִין, הוּא מֶצַח. וְאִית נֶצַח דְּאִינּוּן נְצָחִים.
וְהַיְינוּ דִּתְנָן נֶצַח נְצָחִים. וְאִינּוּן בְּמִצְחָא, וּמִתְפַּשְׁטָן מִנְּהוֹן בְּגוּפָא,
בַּאֲתָרִין יְדִיעָן.

203. We have learned that 24 courts of law exist in this brow and all are
referred to as Netzach. With the adjoining letters, MEANING THE
TRANSPOSITION OF ADJACENT LETTERS, it becomes *Metzach* (Eng.
'forehead'), SINCE THE NUN OF NETZACH EXCHANGES WITH MEM. There
is a Netzach which is Netzachim, or as we have learned Netzach Netzachim.
They exist in the forehead and expand from there into the body in certain
places.

204. תַּנְיָא, מַאי דִּכְתִיב וְגַם נֵצַח יִשְׂרָאֵל לֹא יְשַׁקֵּר וְלֹא יִנָּחֵם כִּי לֹא
אָדָם הוּא לְהִנָּחֵם. הַאי רָזָא אוֹקִימְנָא, כָּל הַהוּא נֶצַח דְּאִתְפָּשַׁט
בְּגוּפָא, זִמְנִין דְּתַלֵּי עַל עָלְמָא לְמֵידָן, וְתָב וּמִתְחָרֵט וְלָא עָבֵיד דִּינָא,
אִי תַּיְיבִין. מ"ט. מִשּׁוּם דְּקָאֵי בְּדוּכְתָּא דְּאִקְרֵי אָדָם, וְיָכִיל לְאִתְחָרְטָא.
אֲבָל אִי בְּאֲתָר דְּאִתְקְרֵי רֹאשׁ, אִתְחֲזֵי וְאִתְגַּלְיָיא הַאי נֶצַח, לָאו הוּא
עִידָן וַאֲתָר לְאִתְחָרְטָא. מ"ט. מִשּׁוּם דְּלָא הֲוָה מֵאֲתָר דְּאִקְרֵי אָדָם,
דְּהָא לָא אִתְגְּלֵי פַּרְצוּפָא וְחוֹטָמָא, אֶלָּא מִצְחָא בִּלְחוֹדוֹי. וּבַאֲתָר דְּלָא
אִשְׁתְּכַח פַּרְצוּפָא, לָא אִקְרֵי אָדָם. וּבְג"כ לָא אָדָם הוּא לְהִנָּחֵם כְּנֵצַח
דִּבְשְׁאָר תִּקּוּנֵי גוּפָא.

204. We have learned that it is written: "And also the Eternal One (Heb.
Netzach) of Yisrael will not lie nor change his mind: for he is not a man,
that He should change his mind" (I Shmuel 15:29). We have explained this
secret meaning: All the Netzach that spreads in the body, THAT IS, IN THE
SIX EXTEMITIES, sometimes causes judgment to impend on people to judge,
and then changes his mind and does not execute judgment if they repent.
What is the reason? Because he exists in a place referred to as man and is

able to change his mind. However, if it is in a place referred to as head, MEANING THE FIRST THREE SFIROT, then that Netzach is revealed; it is not the time and place to change his mind. What is the reason? It is because he is not in the place called man, WHICH IS THE SIX EXTREMITIES, SINCE the countenance OF THE FACE and nose, WHICH ARE SIX EXTREMITIES CALLED MAN, were not revealed, just the brow itself is revealed, THAT IS THE FIRST THREE SFIROT, SINCE THE FOREHEAD AND THE FACE ARE THE FIRST THREE SFIROT AND THE SIX EXTREMITIES. In the place where there is no countenance OF THE FACE, WHICH IS SIX EXTREMITIES THAT ARE IN THE FOREHEAD, it is not considered man. Therefore, "for he is not a man, that he should change his mind," as is the Netzach in other bodily Corrections, MEANING THE NETZACH IN THE SIX EXTREMITIES THAT MAKE UP MAN.

29. The eyes of Zeir Anpin

A Synopsis

Rabbi Shimon describes the eyes of Zeir Anpin, and the black eyebrows to which are attached 700,000 observing supervisors. He describes the eyelids, and how when His eyes are opened they see the watchful open eye of Arich Anpin. He describes the red, black and green hues in the eyes, and how seven types of supervision emanate from those hues. We hear the meaning of the different colors and how He watches Yisrael and the heathen nations. During the opening of Zeir Anpin's eyes there is an opening for goodness and an opening for evil, but the eye of Atik Yomin is totally tranquil and serene since there exists no judgment in it; it is an eye of compassion. Rabbi Shimon says that when the Holy of Holies wants to have mercy on Yisrael He sheds two tears to perfume the great ocean of the uppermost Chochmah, so that the children of Yisrael can bathe in the spring that emanates from great wisdom.

205. עֵינוֹי דְּרֵישָׁא, מִשְׁתַּנְיָין מִשְׁאָר עַיְינִין, שְׁרְקוּתָא דִּבְגַבְּתָא, דְּעַל רִיסֵי עַיְינִין, מְכַּחֲלָן בְּאוּכָמְתָא, תַּלְיָין תְּלִין עַל תְּלִין דְּשַׂעֲרֵי, וְאִינּוּן תִּקּוּנָא דְּעַל עַיְינִין, בְּרֵישָׁא דְּמִצְחָא, וּמִתְאַחֲדָן מִתַּרְוַויְיהוּ שְׁבַע מְאָה אַלְפֵי מָארֵי דְּאַשְׁגָּחוּתָא.

205. The eyes of the head IN ZEIR ANPIN are different from other eyes, MEANING THAN THE EYES OF ARICH ANPIN. The color in the eyebrows above the eyelids are painted with black COLOR and waves upon waves of hair hang. They are in a set above the eyes at the top of the forehead and 700,000 observing supervisors are attached from BOTH EYEBROWS.

206. בְּכְסוּתָא דְּעַיְינִין, לְהַטִּין אֶלֶף וְאַרְבַּע מְאָה רִבּוֹא, דְּמִתְאַחֲדָן בְּגְבִינִין דְּאִינְהוּ כְּסוּתָא. וְאַשְׁגָּחוּתָא דְּעֵינָא דְּעַתִּיק יוֹמִין עָלַיְיהוּ. וּבְשַׁעֲתָא דְּסַלְּקִין אִינּוּן כְּסוּתָא, אִתְחֲזֵי כְּמַאן דְּאִתְּעַר מִשְּׁנָתֵיהּ, וְאִתְפַּקְּחָן עֵינוֹי, וְחָמָאן לְעֵינָא פְּקִיחָא, וְאִתְסָחָן בְּחַד חִוּוָרָא דְּעֵינָא טָבָא, הַהוּ״ד, רוֹחֲצוֹת בֶּחָלָב. מַאי בְּחָלָב. בְּחִוּוָרָא דִּלְעֵילָא קַדְמָאָה. וּבְהַהִיא שַׁעֲתָא אִשְׁתְּכַח אַשְׁגָּחוּתָא דְּרַחֲמֵי.

206. In the cover over the eyes, THAT IS THE EYELIDS, glow 14,000,000 of those who unite in the eyelids, which are a cover. The supervision of Atik Yomin is upon them. When the cover ABOVE OVER THE EYES is removed, it seems as if he is waking up from his sleep. His eyes are opened; they see an open eye OF ARICH ANPIN, and they bathe in certain whiteness of THAT good eye. This is what is written: "Washed with milk" (Shir Hashirim 5:12). What is the meaning of: "with milk"? It is in the whiteness of the above, the original, IN THE WHITENESS OF THE EYE IN ARICH ANPIN. During that period the providence of compassion prevails.

207. וע״ד צַלֵּי דָוִד, עוּרָה לָמָה תִישָׁן יְיָ׳ הָקִיצָה. דְּיִפְקַח עֵינוֹי, וְיִתְסְחוּן בְּהַהוּא חִוּוָרָא. וְכָל זִמְנָא דְּעֵינוֹי לָאו מִתְפַּקְחָן, כָּל מָארֵיהוֹן דְּדִינִין, כַּפְיָין לְהוּ לְיִשְׂרָאֵל, וּשְׁאָר עַמִּין שַׁלְטִין עָלַייהוּ. וּבְזִמְנָא דְּיִפְקַח עֵינוֹי, יִתְסְחָן בְּעֵינָא טָבָא, וְרַחֲמֵי עַל יִשְׂרָאֵל. וְאִסְתְּחַר עֵינָא, וְעָבֵיד נוּקְמִין בִּשְׁאָר עַמִּין. הה״ד, הָעִירָה וְהָקִיצָה. הָעִירָה: לְאִתְסְחָאָה בְּהַהִיא חִוּוָרָא. הָקִיצָה: לְמֶעְבַּד נוּקְמִין לְאִינּוּן דְּכַפְיָין לוֹן.

207. About this David prayed, "Awake, why sleep you, Hashem? arise" (Tehilim 44:24), MEANING that he should open his eyes and bathe them in that whiteness THAT IS DRAWN FROM THE EYE IN ARICH ANPIN. During the entire period that his eyes do not open up, all the plaintiffs pressure Yisrael and the rest of the nations dominate over them. During the period that he will open his eyes, they will go bathed in the WHITENESS OF THE good eye and compassion is over Yisrael, as the eye travels around and executes its revenge among the rest of the nations. This is what is written: "Rouse Yourself, and awake" (Tehilim 35:23). "Rouse Yourself," MEANING to bathe in that whiteness, and "awake," MEANING to execute vengeance to those who oppress YISRAEL.

208. עֵינוֹי כַּד אִתְפַּקְחָן, אִתְחֲזוּן שַׁפִּירִין כְּהָנֵי יוֹנִים, בְּסוּמָק וְאוּכָם וְיָרוֹק, חִוּוָר לָא אִתְגְּלֵי, אֶלָּא בְּזִמְנָא דְּאִסְתַּכַּל בְּעֵינָא טָבָא, וּמִסְתַּחְאָן כָּל אִינּוּן גַּוְונִין, בְּהַהוּא חִוּוָר.

208. When the eyes OF ZEIR ANPIN open up, they look pretty like doves, in colors of red, black and green. White does not show, except during a period when he looks with a good eye OF ARICH ANPIN and all these colors bathe in the whiteness OF THE EYE IN ARICH ANPIN.

209. מֵאִינּוּן גַּוְונִין דְּמִתְגַּלְיָין, נָפְקִין שִׁבְעָה עַיְינִין דְּאַשְׁגָּחוּתָא. דְּנַפְקֵי מֵאוּכָמָא דְעֵינָא. הה"ד, עַל אֶבֶן אַחַת שִׁבְעָה עֵינָיִם. מַאן אֶבֶן אַחַת. אוּכְמְתָא דְעֵינָא.

209. From those colors that appear IN THE EYE emanate seven eyes of supervision. They emerge from the black in the eye. This is what is written: "Upon one stone are seven facets (lit. 'eyes')" (Zechariah 3:9). What is the meaning of "one stone"? It is the blackness in the eye.

210. מְסוּמָקָא, נָפְקִין שִׁבְעָה רְהִיטִין, דְּסַמְכִין לְסְטַר שְׂמָאלָא, וּמִתְלַהֲטִין בְּאֶשָׁא דִּלְסְטַר צָפוֹן, וּמִתְאַחֲדָן לְאִתְפַּשְׁטָא בְּעָלְמָא, לְגַלָּאָה אָרְחִין דְּחַיָּיבַיָּא הה"ד שִׁבְעָה אֵלֶּה עֵינֵי יְיָ' הֵמָּה מְשׁוֹטְטִים בְּכָל הָאָרֶץ.

210. From the red IN THE EYE emerge seven runners that support the left side and glow in the fire of the north side. They are attached TO THE RED COLOR in order to expand in the world to reveal the ways of the wicked. This is what is written: "Those seven...the eyes of Hashem, they rove to and fro through the whole earth" (Ibid. 4:10).

211. מִירוֹקָא, נָפְקִין שִׁבְעָה טְהִירִין דְּסַחֲרָאן לְסְטַר דָּרוֹמָא, וּמִתְאַחֲדָן לְאִתְפַּשְׁטָא בְּעָלְמָא, לְגַלָּאָה אָרְחִין וְעוֹבָדִין דִּבְנֵי נָשָׁא, בֵּין טַב בֵּין בִּיש, דִּכְתִיב כִּי עֵינָיו עַל דַּרְכֵי אִיש וְגוֹ'.

211. From the green IN THE EYE emerge seven lights that circle to the south side. They attach themselves TO THE GREEN COLOR to spread in the world and discover the ways and deeds of the people either good or bad, as written: "For his eyes are upon the ways of man" (Iyov 34:21).

212. וְכַד אִסְתְּחָאן בְּחִוָּורָא, מִשְׁתַּכְּחִין כֻּלְּהוּ לְאַשְׁגָּחָא לְכָל מָארֵי קְשׁוֹט, לְאוֹטָבָא עָלְמָא בְּגִינֵהוֹן. וְכָל אַשְׁגָחוּתָא דְּהַהוּא חִוָּורָא, הֲוֵי

לְטַב עַל יִשְׂרָאֵל. וְאַשְׁגַּח בְּסוּמְקָא לְמַאן דְּעָאקִין לְהוּ. הה"ד רָאֹה רָאִיתִי. רָאֹה: לְאוֹטָבָא לוֹן. רָאִיתִי: לְנַקְּמָא לוֹן, מִדְעָקִין לוֹן, וּבְגִין כַּךְ כְּתִיב, עוּרָה לָמָּה תִישַׁן יְיָ׳ הָקִיצָה אַל תִּזְנַח לָנֶצַח. עוּרָה, וְהָקִיצָה, תְּרֵי אַשְׁגָּחוּתָא. תְּרֵי פְּקִיחִין. תְּרֵי טָבָן. רַחֲמֵי וְנוּקְמִין.

212. When they bathe in the whiteness, all are watchful over all the truthful people to benefit the world for their sake. All the supervision of that whiteness is to benefit Yisrael. He supervises with the redness IN THE EYE TO REVENGE those who besiege YISRAEL. This is what is written: "And I have surely seen (lit. 'saw')" (Shemot 3:7): "Saw" in order to benefit Yisrael; "have...seen" in order to revenge for their sake those who besiege YISRAEL. Therefore, it is written: "Awake, why sleep you, Hashem? Arise, cast us not off for ever." "Awake" and "arise" are two supervisions, two openings OF THE EYES, two KINDS OF good, compassion and vengeance.

213. גְּוָונָא קַדְמָאָה, סוּמָקָא בְּגוֹ סוּמָקָא כָּלִיל וְסָתִים כָּל סוּמָקִין, מִקָּמֵיהּ לָא אִתְחֲזֵי. סוֹחֲרָנֵיהּ דְּהַהוּא סוּמָקָא, אַסְחַר חַד חוּטָא אוּכְמָא, וְאָקִיף לֵיהּ.

213. The first color OF THE EYE is red within red that comprises and covers all reds, SINCE ALL REDS do not appear RED in his presence. One black thread circles around this red and surrounds it.

214. גְּוָונָא תִּנְיָינָא, אוּכְמָא. כְּאַבְנָא חַד דְּנָפִיק מִתְּהוֹמָא, חַד זְמַן לְאַלְף שְׁנִים, בְּיַמָּא רַבָּא. וְכַד נָפִיק הַאי אַבְנָא, אָתֵי רִגְשָׁא וְתָקְפָא עַל יַמָּא. וְקָלֵיהּ דְּיַמָּא, וְגַלְגְּלוֹהִי אַזְלִין, וְאִשְׁתַּמְעוּ לְנוּנָא רַבָּא, דְּאִקְרֵי לִוְיָתָן. וְנָפִיק מִתְּהוֹמָא. וְהַאי אַבְנָא מִתְגַּלְגְּלָא בְּתוּקְפָא דְּיַמָּא, וְנָפִיק לְבַר. וְהִיא אוּכְמָא, דְּכָל אוּכְמִין סְתִימִין קַמֵּיהּ. וְכַךְ הִיא אוּכְמוּתָא דְּעֵינָא, אוּכְמָא, דְּכָלִיל וְסָתִים כָּל שְׁאַר אוּכְמִין. וְסוֹחֲרָנֵיהּ דְּהַהוּא אוּכְמָא, אַסְחַר חַד חוּטָא סוּמָקָא, וְאָקִיף לְהַהוּא אוּכְמָא.

214. The second color IN THE EYE is black, similar to the one stone that emerges from the depths in the great ocean once in a thousand years. When this stone emerges FROM THE DEPTHS, it is accompanied by thunderous noise and anger over the ocean. The noise of the ocean and its waves go forth and are heard by the great fish called Leviathan, and he emerges from the depths. This stone rolls in the angry sea and is expelled outwards. It is so black, that all black are obscured by comparison, MEANING THAT THEY ARE NOT RECOGNIZED AS BLACK IN COMPARISON TO IT. So is the black in the eye, for it is a black that includes and conceals all blacks, MEANING THAT THEY ARE NOT RECOGNIZABLY BLACK IN COMPARISON TO IT. A red thread circles around that black and surrounds it.

215. גְּוִוּנָא תְּלִיתָאָה. יְרוֹקָא דִּירוֹקֵי, דִּכְלִיל וְסָתִים כָּל יְרוֹקִין. וּבְסוֹחֲרָנֵיה דְּהַהוּא יְרוֹקָא, אַסְחָרוּ תְּרֵין חוּטִין. חוּטָא סוּמָקָא לִסְטַר חַד. וְחַד חוּטָא אוּכְמָא לִסְטַר חַד. וְאַקִיפִין לְהַהוּא יְרוֹקָא.

215. The third color IN THE EYE is the greenest of green that comprises and conceals all the greens. Around that green, two threads encircle a red thread to one side and a black thread to the other side, and they surround that green.

216. וְכַד אִתְגְּלֵי חִוְורָא, וְאִסְתְּחָרֵי עֵינָא, כָּל אִינּוּן גְּוְונִין לָא מִשְׁתַּכְּחִין, וּמִשְׁתַּקְעִין לְתַתָּא. לָא אִתְחֲזֵי בַּר הַהוּא חִוְורָא, דְּנָהִיר מֵעַתִּיק יוֹמִין. וּנְהִירִין מִנֵּיה כָּל אִינּוּן דִּלְתַתָּא.

216. When the white IN THE EYE is revealed and the eye is rolled AND COMES UNDER THE DOMINATION OF THE WHITE, all these OTHER colors do not exist AT THAT MOMENT. They descend downward and nothing is visible IN THE EYES besides that white color that shines from THE EYES OF Atik Yomin TO THE EYES OF ZEIR ANPIN. And all THE GRADES below are illuminated from it.

217. וְלֵית גְּוִוּנָא אִתְחַזְיָיא, בַּר הַהוּא חִוְורָא בִּלְחוֹדוֹי. וּבְגִין כָּךְ אִסְתְּלָקוּ כָּל מַארֵיהוֹן דְּסוּמָקָא וְאוּכְמָא, דְּאִינּוּן תְּאוֹמִין כַּחֲדָא. הה"ד שִׁנַּיִךְ כְּעֵדֶר הַקְּצוּבוֹת שֶׁעָלוּ מִן הָרַחְצָה שֶׁכֻּלָּם מַתְאִימוֹת. מַאי מִן הָרַחְצָה. מֵהַהוּא אַסְחוּתָא דְּעֵינָא קַדִּישָׁא עִלָּאָה. שֶׁכֻּלָּם מַתְאִימוֹת.

-236-

מִתְעָרְבָן דָּא בְּדָא, וְאִתְדַּבְּקָן דָּא בְּדָא. וּמַה דְּאָמַר שַׁנַּיִךְ כְּעֵדֶר
הַקְּצוּבוֹת, וְאַתְּ אָמְרַת שֶׁכֻּלָּם מַתְאִימוֹת. כְּלוֹמַר, חִוָּרָא דִּלְהוֹן,
כְּהַהוּא חִוָּרָא דְּעַיְינִין, כַּד אַסְחָן בְּחִוָּורְתָּא דְּעֵינָא עִלָּאָה.

217. There is not another color visible except for that white alone. Therefore, all those that have red and black, which are twins, have disappeared. THAT IS TO SAY, AND THE BLACK IS RECOGNIZED AS DISTINCT COLOR FROM RED, SINCE THE BLACK COLOR INDICATES ABOUT ITSELF, THAT IT HAS A DOUBLE BLEMISH. This is what is written: "Your teeth are like a flock of shorn ewes, which came up from the washing; all of which bear twins" (Shir Hashirim 4:2). What is the meaning of: "from the washing"? This is from the bath of the uppermost holy eye, OF ARICH ANPIN, THAT THROUGH THIS THE WHITE ALONE WILL BE DOMINANT. "All of which bear twins": They blend with each other and adhere to each other UNTIL THEY LOOK LIKE TWINS WITH NO APPARENT DIFFERENCE BETWEEN THEM. As for: "Your teeth are like a flock of shorn ewes (Heb. *ketzuvot*)," THAT SEEMS TO INDICATE THAT THERE IS A MEASURE (HEB. *KITZBAH*) AND INDIVIDUAL DISTINCTION TO EACH ONE OF THEM. Yet you say, "All of which bear twins," WHICH INDICATES THAT THERE IS NO DISTINCTION. THE EXPLANATION IS THAT THE VERSE COMES to tell us that the whiteness IN THE TEETH is like the whiteness in the eyes during the period when they are bathed in the whiteness of the supernal eye, WHICH IS THEN REFERRED TO AS "A FLOCK OF SHORN EWES." IT DOES NOT MEAN THAT THERE IS A MEASURE AND DISTINCTION BETWEEN EACH COLOR.

218. וְדָא זְמִינִין לְמִנְדַּע צַדִּיקַיָּיא, לְמֶחֱזֵי בְּרוּחָא דְּחָכְמְתָא, כְּד"א כִּי
עַיִן בְּעַיִן יִרְאוּ. אֵימָתַי בְּשׁוּב יְיָ' צִיּוֹן. וּכְתִיב אֲשֶׁר עַיִן בְּעַיִן נִרְאָה
אַתָּה יְיָ', וּכְדֵין פְּקִיחוּתָא דְּעַיְינִין לְטַב.

218. The righteous will know and perceive THIS LIGHT, THE WHITE IN THE EYE in the spirit of wisdom, as it says, "For they shall see eye to eye" (Yeshayah 52:8), NAMELY THE ILLUMINATION OF THE WHITE OF THE EYE OF ARICH ANPIN IN THE EYE OF ZEIR ANPIN. When will this happen? When "Hashem returning to Zion" (Ibid.). It is written: "That you Hashem are seen eye to eye" (Bemidbar 14:14). This is when the opening of the eyes is for the good.

219. וְאִית פְּקִיחוּתָא דְּעַיְינִין לְטַב. וְאִית פְּקִיחוּתָא דְּעַיְינִין לְבִישׁ.
כְּמָה דִּכְתִּיב פְּקַח עֵינֶיךָ וּרְאֵה שׁוֹמְמוֹתֵינוּ וְגוֹ'. וְדָא הָכָא לְטַב, וּלְבִישׁ.
וּכְתִיב עֵינֶיךָ תִרְאֶנָה יְרוּשָׁלַם נָוֶה שַׁאֲנָן אֹהֶל בַּל יִצְעָן בַּל יִסַּע
יְתֵדוֹתָיו לָנֶצַח הָא הָכָא לְטַב וּלְבִישׁ. דְּלָא אִתְעֲבֵיד דָּא בְּלָא דָא.

219. There is an opening of eyes for the good and an opening of eyes for the bad, MEANING TO SAY THAT DURING THE OPENING OF THE EYES IN ZEIR ANPIN, THERE IS AN OPENING ON ONE SIDE FOR GOODNESS AND AN OPENING ON ONE SIDE FOR EVIL. It is written: "Open your eyes, and see our desolations..." (Daniel 9:18), so we find EXISTING here AN OPENING OF EYES. This is for the good and for the bad. It is written: "Your eyes shall see Jerusalem, a quiet habitation, a tent that shall never be taken down; its pegs shall not be removed" (Yeshayah 33:20). We find here AN OPENING OF EYES for good and for bad, because they do not happen one without the other.

220. תָּנָא בְּצִנִיעוּתָא דְּסִפְרָא, מַהוּ עֵינֶיךָ תִרְאֶנָה יְרוּשָׁלַם נָוֶה שַׁאֲנָן.
וְכִי יְרוּשָׁלֵם נָוֶה שַׁאֲנָן הוּא, וְהָא כְּתִיב צֶדֶק יָלִין בָּהּ. וּבַאֲתַר
דְּאִשְׁתְּכַח צֶדֶק, לָאו שָׁקִיט, וְלָאו שַׁאֲנָן הוּא. אֶלָּא עֵינֶיךָ תִרְאֶנָה
יְרוּשָׁלַם נָוֶה שַׁאֲנָן, נָוֶה שַׁאֲנָן, לְעַתִּיק יוֹמִין אִתְּמַר, דְּהַהוּא עֵינָא
שָׁקִיט וְשַׁאֲנָן. עֵינָא דְּרַחֲמֵי, עֵינָא דְּלָא נָטִיל מֵאַשְׁגָּחוּתָא דָּא,
לְאַשְׁגָּחוּתָא אַחֲרָא. וּבְגִין כַּךְ כְּתִיב, עֵינְךָ תִרְאֶינָה חָסֵר יו"ד, וְלָא
עֵינֶיךָ. וּמַה דְּאָמַר יְרוּשָׁלַם וְלָא צִיּוֹן, הָכִי אִצְטְרִיךְ, לְאַכְפְּיָיא לְדִינָא,
דְּאִשְׁתְּכַח בָּה וּלְרַחֲמָא עֲלָהּ.

220. We have learned this in the hidden book. What is the meaning of: "Your eyes shall see Jerusalem, a quiet habitation"? Is then Jerusalem a quiet habitation? Isn't it written that "righteousness lodged in it" (Yeshayah 1:21), THAT IS THE JUDGMENTS THAT ARE REFERRED TO AS RIGHTEOUSNESS, and a place where righteousness is residing is neither tranquil nor quiet. HE REPLIES: Just as "your eyes shall see Jerusalem, a quiet habitation," HERE "a quiet habitation" refers to Atik Yomin. The eye OF ATIK YOMIN THAT IS TOTALLY WHITE is tranquil and serene, SINCE THERE IS NO JUDGMENT AT ALL FROM THERE, because it is an eye of

-238-

mercy, an eye that does not move from this providence OF MERCY to another providence OF JUDGMENT. Therefore, "Your eyes (Heb. *einecha*) shall see," is spelled without Yud (plural) instead of: '*eineicha*', SINCE THE TWO EYES OF ARICH ANPIN ARE CONSIDERED ONE AND THE MEANING IN THE VERSE IS THAT THE EYE OF ARICH ANPIN, WHICH IS A QUIET HABITATION, SHALL POUR FORTH BOUNTY AND BEHOLD JERUSALEM, WHICH IS MALCHUT. Its saying "Jerusalem" rather than 'Zion,' IN NOT SAYING, 'YOUR EYES SHALL SEE ZION' is as it should be, in order to suppress the Judgment that exists in her and have mercy on her.

221. וְתָאנָא, כְּתִיב עֵינֵי ה' אֱלֹהֶיךָ בָּה מֵרֵשִׁית הַשָּׁנָה וְעַד אַחֲרִית שָׁנָה, וּלְזִמְנָא דְּאָתֵי, יִשְׁתְּכַח בָּה עֵינָא חַד דְּרַחֲמֵי. עֵינָא דְּעַתִּיקָא דְּעַתִּיקִין הה"ד וּבְרַחֲמִים גְּדוֹלִים אֲקַבְּצֵךְ. כֵּיוָן דְּאָמַר רַחֲמִים, מַהוּ גְּדוֹלִים. אֶלָּא אִית רַחֲמֵי, וְאִית רַחֲמֵי. רַחֲמֵי דְּעַתִּיק דְּעַתִּיקִין, אִינּוּן אִקְרוּן רַחֲמִים גְּדוֹלִים. רַחֲמֵי דִּזְעֵיר אַנְפִּין, אִקְרוּן רַחֲמִים סְתָם. וּבג"כ וּבְרַחֲמִים גְּדוֹלִים אֲקַבְּצֵךְ, דְּעַתִּיק יוֹמִין.

221. We have further learned that it is written: "For the eyes of Hashem your Elohim, are always upon it, from the beginning of the year to the end of the year" (Devarim 11:12). THESE ARE THE EYES OF ZEIR ANPIN THAT HAVE IN THEM A PROVIDENCE FOR GOOD AND A PROVIDENCE FOR BAD, WHICH IS THE SECRET OF THE TWO EYES, ONE FOR MERCY AND ONE FOR JUDGMENT. In the future to come, you will find in her, MALCHUT, one eye of mercy AND NOT THE PROVIDENCE OF JUDGMENT, which is the eye of the most ancient among ancient, MEANING ARICH ANPIN. This is what is written: "But with great mercy will I gather you" (Yeshayah 54:7). HE ASKS: Since it says mercy, why does it say great? HE ANSWERS: There is Mercy and there is ZMercy. THERE IS mercy of the most Ancient among ancient and it is referred to as great Mercy, AND THERE EXISTS mercy in Zeir Anpin; this is referred to simply as mercy. Therefore, THE VERSE SAYS, "But with great mercy will I gather you," MEANING THE MERCY of Atik Yomin.

222. תָּאנָא בְּהָנֵי עַיְינִין, בִּתְרֵין גְּוָונִין מִנַּיְיהוּ, בְּסוּמָקָא וְאוּכָמָא, שָׁרָאן תְּרֵין דְּמָעִין. וְכַד בָּעֵי קוּדְשָׁא דְּקוּדְשִׁין לְרַחֲמָא עַל יִשְׂרָאֵל,

אֲחִית תְּרֵין דִּמְעִין, לְאִתְבַּסְּמָא בְּיַמָּא רַבָּא. מַאן יַמָּא רַבָּא. יַמָּא דְּחָכְמְתָא עִלָּאָה. כְּלוֹמַר דְּיִתְחַסְחוּן בְּחִוּוָרָא בְּמַבּוּעָא דְּנָפִיק מֵחָכְמְתָא רַבָּא, וּמְרַחֵם לְהוּ לְיִשְׂרָאֵל.

222. We have learned that within the eyes OF ZEIR ANPIN, the two colors in them, the red and black, reside two tears. When the Holy of Holies wishes to have mercy upon Yisrael, he drops two tears to be established in the great ocean. What is this great ocean? It is the ocean of uppermost Chochmah, meaning to say in order that they should bathe in the whiteness, in the spring that emanates from great wisdom and has mercy on Yisrael.

30. The nose of Zeir Anpin

A Synopsis

Rabbi Shimon explains the smoke that went out of the nostrils of Zeir Anpin, saying that the smoke included fire and coals of fire. The black and red smoke corresponds to anger and hot displeasure and the destroyer. We learn about the many powers existent in Zeir Anpin and how they spread in His body; they all begin to emerge from the nose until all the Gvurot are heated and wander around until they descend to the bright blade of the revolving sword. As a result of the sins of the wicked, compassion is overturned to justice, in that Atik Yomin does not appear on Zeir Anpin so Zeir Anpin activates justice. Rabbi Shimon says that the separating note between Abraham, Abraham and Jacob, Jacob indicate that the first name is incomplete and the second is complete. In Hashem, Hashem the first Yud Hei Vav Hei is whole, but the second Yud Hei Vav Hei is complete in its entirety, being Zeir Anpin during the period it receives from the thirteen Corrections of the beard in Arich Anpin. Moses brought down the thirteen measures of compassion from the Holy Atika below. Rabbi Shimon describes the two openings of the nose, the first of which emanates smoke and the second of which emanates a consuming fire. The nose must smell the sweet savor of the smoke and fire that ascend from the offering in order that it will sweeten the judgments.

223. חוֹטָמָא. תָּאנָא בְּצְנִיעוּתָא דְּסִפְרָא, חוֹטָמָא דְּזְעֵיר אַנְפִּין. בְּחוֹטָמָא אִשְׁתְּמוֹדַע פַּרְצוּפָא. בְּהַאי חוֹטָמָא אִתְפְּרָשָׁא מִלָּה דִּכְתִיב, עָלָה עָשָׁן בְּאַפּוֹ וְגוֹ'. עָלָה עָשָׁן בְּאַפּוֹ, בְּהַאי תְּנָנָא, אִתְכְּלָלוּ אֶשָׁא, וְגַחֲלֵי דְּנוּרָא. דְּלֵית תְּנָנָא בְּלָא אֶשָׁא, וְלָא אֶשָׁא בְּלָא תְּנָנָא. וְכֻלְּהוּ אִסְתְּלִיקוּ וְנָפְקֵי מֵחוֹטָמוֹי.

223. The nose OF ZEIR ANPIN: We have learned in the hidden book about the nose of Zeir Anpin. Through the nose, the facial countenance is apparent. In this nose, the subject matter of this verse is explained: "There went up a smoke out of his nostrils, AND FIRE OUT OF HIS MOUTH DEVOURED: COALS WERE KINDLED BY IT" (II Shmuel 22:9). "There went up a smoke out of his nostrils": In this smoke were included fire and coals of fire, since there is no smoke without fire and there is no fire without smoke. All rise and emerge from the nose.

224. וְתָאנָא, כַּד אִתְחַבְּרוּ תְּלַת אִלֵּין, דִּכְלִילָן בְּהַאי תְּנָנָא, דְּנָפִיק מֵחוּטָמָא. אִתְקַמַּט חוּטָמָא, וְנָשִׁיב וְנָפִיק תְּנָנָא אוּכָמָא וְסוּמָקָא. וּבֵין תְּרֵי גְּוֵונֵי. וְקָרֵינָן לֵיהּ, אַף וְחֵימָה וּמַשְׁחִית. וְאִי תֵּימָא אַף וְחֵימָה כְּתִיב, כִּי יָגֹרְתִּי מִפְּנֵי הָאַף וְהַחֵימָה, דְּאִינּוּן תְּנָנָא אוּכָמָא וְסוּמָקָא, מַשְׁחִית מנ״ל. דִּכְתִיב, לִפְנֵי שַׁחֵת יְיָ' אֶת סְדוֹם וְאֶת עֲמוֹרָה. שַׁחֵת הַמַּשְׁחִית, בְּנוּרָא דָּלִיק מוֹקְדָא.

224. We have learned that when these three joined, the ones included in the smoke that emerges from the nose, the nose gets wrinkled AND BECOMES SHORTER. THIS IMPLIES THAT CHOCHMAH, WHICH IS THE SECRET OF LENGTH, DOES NOT SHINE WITHIN IT AND THEREFORE IT IS SHORT. It exhales, and smoke that is black and red emerges, as does anything that is in between these colors. They are called anger, hot displeasure and destroyer. If you say that anger and wrath are mentioned: "For I was afraid of the anger and hot displeasure" (Devarim 9:19), which are the black and red smoke, where do we find that destroyer? HE REPLIES: It is written, "Before Hashem destroyed Sodom and Amorah" (Beresheet 13:10), for the destroyer destroyed SODOM AND AMORAH in a bonfire of consuming fire.

225. וְתָאנָא, חָמֵשׁ גְּבוּרָאן אִינּוּן, בְּהַאי זְעֵיר אַנְפִּין. וְאִסְתְּלָקוּ לְאַלְף וְאַרְבַּע מְאָה גְּבוּרָאן. וּמִתְפַּשְׁטָאן בְּחוּטָמוֹי. בְּפוּמָא. בִּדְרוֹעוֹי. בִּידִין. בְּאֶצְבְּעִין. וּבג״כ כְּתִיב, מִי יְמַלֵּל גְּבוּרוֹת יְיָ'. גְּבוּרֹת כְּתִיב הָכָא גְּבוּרוֹת, וּכְתִיב הָתָם, לְךָ יְיָ' הַגְּדוּלָה וְהַגְּבוּרָה. אֶלָּא הָכִי תָּאנָא, כַּד אִתְחַבְּרָאן כֻּלְּהוּ גְּבוּרָאן כַּחֲדָא, אִתְקְרֵי גְּבוּרָה חֲדָא.

225. We have learned that there are five Gvurot in Zeir Anpin. They amount to 1,400 Gvurot and they spread in the nose, in the mouth, in the arms, in the hands and in the fingers. Therefore, it is written: "Who can utter the mighty acts (Heb. *Gvurot*) of Hashem" (Tehilim 106:2). It is spelled Gvurot WITHOUT VAV, WHICH INDICATES THE PLURAL, and it is written there: "Yours, Hashem, is the greatness, and the power (Heb. *Gvurah*)" (I Divrei Hayamim 29:11). THAT IS ALSO WRITTEN IN SINGULAR FORM, AND YOU SAY THAT THERE ARE 1,400 GVUROT. HE REPLIES: This is how we have learned it: when all the Gvurot join together, they are referred to as one Gvurah. THEREFORE, IT SAYS GVURAH IN SINGULAR FORM.

226. וְכֻלְּהוּ גְּבוּרָאן, שַׁרְיָאן לְנַחְתָּא מֵחוֹטָמוֹי. וּמֵהַאי תַּלְיָין, אֶלֶף וְאַרְבַּע מְאָה רִבּוֹא, לְכָל חַד מִנַּיְיהוּ. וּבְהַאי תְּנָנָא דְּאַפִּיק מֵחוֹטָמוֹי, תַּלְיָין אֶלֶף וְאַרְבַּע מְאָה דְּסִטַר גְּבוּרָה דָּא. וְכֻלְּהוּ גְּבוּרָאן תַּלְיָין מֵהַאי חוֹטָמָא, דִּכְתִיב דּוֹר לְדוֹר יְשַׁבַּח מַעֲשֶׂיךָ וְגוֹ'. וְכַד שָׁארֵי גְּבוּרָה דָּא, כֻּלְּהוּ גְּבוּרָאן מִתְלַהֲטָן וְשָׁטָאן, עַד דְּנַחְתָּן לְלַהַט הַחֶרֶב הַמִּתְהַפֶּכֶת.

226. All the Gvurot begin to emerge from the nose, where there are suspended 14,000,000 to each one OF THE FIVE GVUROT IN THE NOSE. In the smoke that emerges from the nose are suspended 1,400 of this side of Gvurah. All the Gvurot are suspended from this nose, as is written: "One generation shall praise your works to another, and shall declare your mighty acts" (Tehilim 145:4). When Gvurah resides IN THIS NOSE, all the Gvurot are heated and wander around until they descend to the bright blade of the revolving sword.

227. כְּתִיב, כִּי מַשְׁחִיתִים אֲנַחְנוּ אֶת הַמָּקוֹם הַזֶּה. וּכְתִיב לִפְנֵי שַׁחֵת יְיָ אֶת סְדוֹם אֶת עֲמוֹרָה. וּכְתִיב, וַיְיָ' הִמְטִיר עַל סְדוֹם וְעַל עֲמוֹרָה. אֶלָּא הָכִי תָּאנָא, לֹא דַּיָּין לָרְשָׁעִים וְכוּ', אֶלָּא דִּמְהַפְּכֵי מִ"ד לְמִ"ה.

227. It is written: "For we will destroy this place" (Beresheet 19:13), MEANING THE ANGELS OF THE MEASURE OF JUDGMENT, yet it is written: "Before Hashem destroyed Sodom and Amorah" WHERE IT IS SAID YUD HEI VAV HEI, WHICH IS THE ATTRIBUTE OF MERCY. It is further written: "And Hashem rained upon Sodom and upon Amorah" (Ibid. 19:24), WHICH IS THE SECRET OF ZEIR ANPIN AND HIS COURT OF LAW THAT ARE REFERRED TO AS "AND HASHEM" (VAV YUD HEI VAV HEI). WHY ARE THEY MENTIONED ONCE THE MEASURE OF JUDGMENT AND ONCE A MEASURE OF MERCY? HE REPLIES: It is only because we have learned that the wicked are not content until they reverse the measure of Judgment to a measure of Mercy, SINCE THE MEASURE OF MERCY ACTIVATES WITHIN THEM JUDGMENT.

228. וְהָאֵיךְ מְהַפְּכֵי, וְהָא כְּתִיב אֲנִי יְיָ' לֹא שָׁנִיתִי. אֶלָּא בְּכָל זִמְנָא דְּעַתִּיק דְּעַתִּיקֵי, רֵישָׁא חִוּוָרָא, רְעוּ דִּרְעוּוִין, אִתְגַּלְיָין, רַחֲמִין רַבְרְבִין

אִשְׁתְּכָחוּ בְּכֹלָּא. וּבְשַׁעְתָּא דְּלָא אִתְגַּלְיָיא, כָּל דִּינִין דִּזְעֵיר אַפִּין
זְמִינִין, וְכִבְיָכוֹל רַחֲמֵי, עָבֵיד דִּינָא, הַהוּא עַתִּיקָא דְּכֹלָּא.

228. HE ASKS: How do they reverse THE MEASURE OF JUDGMENT TO A MEASURE OF MERCY, since it is written: "For I am Hashem, I do not change" (Malachi 3:6)? HE REPLIES: It is only because there exists great mercy in everything as long as Atik of Atikin, the white head THAT IS THE SECRET OF THE CROWN OF ARICH ANPIN, the Will of wills, THIS IS THE SECRET OF THE BROW OF ARICH ANPIN, are revealed. During the times they are not revealed, all the Judgments of Zeir Anpin are ready and ZEIR ANPIN, WHO IS Mercy, the most ancient of all, executes judgment.

229. דְּתַנְיָא, כַּד אִתְגַּלְיָיא עַתִּיקָא דְּעַתִּיקִין, רַעֲוָא דְּרַעֲוִין, כֻּלְּהוּ
בּוֹצִינֵי דְּאִתְקְרוּן בִּשְׁמָא דָּא, נְהִירִין. וְרַחֲמֵי אִשְׁתְּכָחוּ בְּכֹלָּא. וּבְשַׁעְתָּא
דְּלָא אִתְגְּלֵי טְמִירָא דִּטְמִירִין, וְלָא אִתְנַהֲרָן אִלֵּין בּוֹצִינֵי. מִתְעָרִין
דִּינִין, וְאִתְעֲבֵיד דִּינָא. מַאן גָּרִים לְהַאי דִּינָא. רַעֲוָא דְּרַעֲוִין דְּלָא
אִתְגְּלֵי, וּבְג"כ מְהַפְּכִין חַיָּיבַיָּא רַחֲמֵי לְדִינָא. וּמָה דְּאָמַר הָכָא, מֵאֵת
יְיָ' מִן הַשָּׁמָיִם. בִּזְעֵיר אַפִּין אִתְּמַר. וּמִשְׁמַע דִּכְתִיב מִן הַשָּׁמַיִם, אֵשׁ
וּמַיִם. רַחֲמֵי וְדִינָא. לְאַפְּקָא מַאן דְּלֵית בֵּיהּ דִּינָא כְּלָל.

229. We have learned that when the most ancient among the ancient is revealed, Will of all wills, all the candles referred to by the name OF ATIK illuminate, and compassion exists all over. During the time that the most hidden does not reveal himself and the candles, HIS SFIROT, are not illuminating, judgments are awakened and justice is executed. Who caused this justice? The Will of all wills that did not reveal himself; therefore, the wicked overturn Mercy into Judgment. AS A RESULT OF THEIR SINS, ATIK YOMIN IS NOT REVEALED OVER ZEIR ANPIN AND CONSEQUENTLY ZEIR ANPIN THAT IS CALLED YUD HEI VAV HEI ACTIVATES JUDGMENTS. It is written: "AND HASHEM RAINED UPON SODOM...from Hashem out of heaven," which refers to Zeir Anpin. That is the meaning, since it says, "Out of heaven (Heb. *shamayim*)," WHICH IS ZEIR ANPIN REFERRED TO BY SHAMAYIM. SHAMAYIM CONTAINS THE LETTERS OF fire (Heb. *esh*) and water (Heb. *mayim*) THAT INDICATE Mercy and Judgment, to exclude whoever does not contain any kind of Judgment, THAT DOES NOT REVERT TO JUDGMENT.

230. תָּאנָא, הַאי חוֹטָמָא זְעֵיר. וְכַד שָׁארֵי תְּנָנָא לְאַפָּקָא, נָפִיק בִּבְהִילוּ, וְאִתְעֲבֵד דִּינָא. וּמַאן מְעַכֵּב לְהַאי חוֹטָמָא דְּלָא יָפִיק תְּנָנָא, חוֹטָמָא דְּעַתִּיקָא קַדִּישָׁא, דְּהוּא אִקְרֵי אֶרֶךְ אַפַּיִם מִכֹּלָּא.

230. We have learned that the nose OF ZEIR ANPIN is short. When the smoke starts to emerge, it leaves in a hurry and Judgment is executed. Who delays the nose so Judgment will not emerge? It is the nose of the holy Atik, who is referred to as longsuffering (lit. 'long-nosed') to everyone, BOTH TO THE RIGHTEOUS AND THE WICKED.

231. וְהַיְינוּ רָזָא דְּתָנֵינָן, יְיָ' יְיָ' פָּסִיק טַעֲמָא בְּגַוַוייְהוּ. בְּכֻלְּהוּ אֲתָר דְּשְׁמָא אַדְכַּר תְּרֵי זִמְנֵי, פָּסִיק טַעֲמָא בְּגַוַוייְהוּ, כְּגוֹן אַבְרָהָם אַבְרָהָם. יַעֲקֹב יַעֲקֹב. שְׁמוּאֵל שְׁמוּאֵל. כֻּלְּהוּ פָּסִיק טַעֲמָא בְּגַוַוייְהוּ. חוּץ מִמֹּשֶׁה מֹשֶׁה, דְּלָא פָּסִיק טַעֲמָא בְּגַוַוייְהוּ. מ"ט. אַבְרָהָם אַבְרָהָם, בַּתְרָאָה שְׁלִים, קַדְמָאָה לָא שְׁלִים, דְּהַשְׁתָּא שְׁלִים בְּעֶשֶׂר נִסְיוֹנֵי, וּבְגִין כָּךְ פָּסִיק טַעֲמָא בְּגַוַוייְהוּ, דְּהַשְׁתָּא לָא הֲוָה אִיהוּ כִּדְקַדְמֵיתָא.

231. That is the secret that we have learned. "Hashem, Hashem" (Shemot 34:6): There is a separating musical note between them. THAT IS, THERE IS A DIVIDING LINE SEPARATING BETWEEN THE FIRST HASHEM AND THE SECOND HASHEM. The same applies all over where you have a name mentioned twice. A note separates between them, as we find in: "Abraham, Abraham" (Beresheet 22:11); "Jacob, Jacob" (Ibid. 46:2) and "Samuel, Samuel" (I Shmuel 3:10). In all cases, there is a separating note BETWEEN THE FIRST AND SECOND NAME except by "Moses Moses" (Shemot 3:4). There is no separating note between THE FIRST MOSES AND SECOND MOSES. What is the reason? It is since "Abraham, Abraham" THAT IS MENTIONED TWICE INDICATES that the second ABRAHAM is complete AND ABRAHAM, the first, is not complete, since it is only now that he is completed with the ten trials. Therefore, the note separates between them TO INDICATE that now he is not as he was before.

232. יַעֲקֹב יַעֲקֹב, בַּתְרָאָה שְׁלִים, קַדְמָאָה לָא שְׁלִים, דְּהַשְׁתָּא אִתְבְּשַׂר בְּיוֹסֵף, וְשָׁרֵאת עֲלֵיהּ שְׁכִינְתָּא. וְעוֹד, דְּהַשְׁתָּא אִשְׁתְּלִים בְּאַרְעָא, אִילָנָא קַדִּישָׁא כְּגַוְונָא דִלְעֵילָּא, בִּתְרֵיסַר תְּחוּמִין, בְּשַׁבְעִין עַנְפִין, מַה דְּלָא הֲוָה בְּקַדְמֵיתָא. וּבְגִינֵי כַּךְ, בַּתְרָאָה שְׁלִים, קַדְמָאָה לָא שְׁלִים, וּפָסִיק טַעֲמָא בְּגַוַוייהוּ. שְׁמוּאֵל שְׁמוּאֵל, טַעֲמָא פָּסִיק בְּגַוֵיהּ. מ"ט. בַּתְרָאָה שְׁלִים, קַדְמָאָה לָא שְׁלִים, דְּהַשְׁתָּא הוּא נְבִיאָה, וְקוֹדֶם לָכֵן לָא הֲוָה נְבִיאָה. אֲבָל מֹשֶׁה מֹשֶׁה, לָא אַפְסִיק טַעֲמָא בְּגַוַוייהוּ, דְּמִיּוֹמָא דְּאִתְיְלִיד, שְׁלִים הֲוָה. דִּכְתִיב וַתֵּרֶא אוֹתוֹ כִּי טוֹב הוּא.

232. The same applies for "Jacob, Jacob." It indicates THAT the second JACOB is whole and the first is not whole. It is only now that he has been told the news that Joseph IS ALIVE and the Shechinah dwelt upon him, WHICH WAS NOT THE CASE WHEN HE WAS MOURNING FOR JOSEPH AND THE SHECHINAH WAS GONE FROM HIM. Moreover, the holy tree was now perfected in the land, WHICH IS JACOB, in the likeness of above, LIKE ZEIR ANPIN THAT CONTAINS twelve boundaries, THAT IS THE TWELVE PERMUTATIONS OF YUD HEI VAV HEI, and the seventy branches, SINCE TWELVE PERMUTATIONS SHINE IN ALL ITS SIX EXTRMITIES, AMOUNTING TO 72, THAT IS THE SECRET OF THE SEVENTY MEMBERS OF THE SANHEDRIN AND TWO WITNESSES. THE SEVENTY MEMBERS OF THE SANHEDRIN ARE REFERRED TO AS SEVENTY BRANCHES. THE HOLY TREE IN THE LAND, THE SECRET OF JACOB, ALREADY BEGOT TWELVE TRIBES THAT EXPANDED TO SEVENTY SOULS which he did not have before that. Therefore, the second JACOB is complete and the first JACOB is not complete and the note separates them. The same applies for "Samuel, Samuel" that the note separates them. What is the reason? It is because the second SAMUEL is complete. The first SAMUEL is not complete. Now he is a prophet, but before he was not a prophet. However by "Moses Moses," there is no separating note, since he was complete the day he was born, as it is written: "And when she saw that he was a goodly child" (Shemot 2:2). MEANING THAT IMMEDIATELY WHEN HE WAS BORN, THE SHECHINAH DWELT UPON HIM, ABOUT WHOM IT IS SAID, "THAT IT WAS GOOD" (BERESHEET 1:10).

233. אוֹף הָכָא יְיָ' יְיָ', פָּסִיק טַעֲמָא בְּגַוַוייהוּ, קַדְמָאָה שְׁלִים, בַּתְרָאָה

שְׁלִים בְּכֻלְּהוּ. וּמֹשֶׁה, בַּאֲתָר דִּינָא אָמַר, לְנַחְתָּא לוֹן מֵעַתִּיקָא קַדִּישָׁא, רַחֲמִין לִזְעֵיר אַנְפִּין. דְּהָכִי תָּנֵינָן, כַּמָּה חֵילָא דְמֹשֶׁה, דְּאָחִית מְכִילָן דְּרַחֲמֵי לְתַתָּא. וְכַד אִתְגְּלֵי עַתִּיקָא בִּזְעֵיר אַפִּין, כֹּלָּא בְּרַחֲמֵי אִתְחֲזוּן. וְחוֹטָמָא אִשְׁתְּכִיךְ, וְאֶשָּׁא וּתְנָנָא לָא נָפִיק, כד"א וּתְהִלָּתִי אֶחֱטָם לָךְ.

233. Here too, "Hashem, Hashem." There is a note separating between them, since the first YUD HEI VAV HEI is whole but the second YUD HEI VAV HEI is complete in its entirety. THE SECOND YUD HEI VAV HEI IS ZEIR ANPIN DURING THE PERIOD IT RECEIVES FROM THE THIRTEEN CORRECTIONS OF THE BEARD IN ARICH ANPIN, AND ALSO HAS THE THIRTEEN CORRECTIONS OF THE BEARD LIKE HIM. Moses, in place of Judgment, WHICH IS ZEIR ANPIN, wanted to bring down THE THIRTEEN MEASURES from the holy Atik, which is Mercy, to Zeir Anpin. Since this is what we have learned, how wonderful is the power of Moses that he brought down the THIRTEEN measures of Mercy FROM THE HOLY ATIK below. When the holy Atika was revealed in Zeir Anpin, all appear in compassionate. The nose (Heb. *chotem*) is calmed, and fire and smoke do not emerge, as it is written: "And for my praise I will refrain (Heb. *echetom*: Eng. 'nose') for you" (Yeshayah 48:9), WHICH INDICATES THE TIME WHEN THE NOSE OF ZEIR ANPIN IS IN STATE OF MERCY.

234. וְתָאנָא, בִּתְרֵין נוּקְבִין דְּחוֹטָמָא, בְּחַד נוּקְבָּא נָפִיק תְּנָנָא, לָהִיט, וּמִשְׁתַּקְּעָא בְּנוּקְבָּא דִּתְהוֹמָא רַבָּא. וּמֵחַד נוּקְבָּא, נָפִיק אֶשָּׁא דְּאוֹקִיד בְּשַׁלְהוֹבוֹי, וּמִתְלַהֲטָא בְּאֶלֶף וְאַרְבַּע מְאָה עָלְמִין דְּבִסְטַר שְׂמָאלָא. וּמַאן דְּגָרִים לְקָרְבָא בְּהַאי, אִקְרֵי אֶשׁ יְיָ'. אֶשָּׁא דְּאָכְלָא וְאוֹקִיד כָּל שְׁאַר אֶשִׁין. וְהַאי אֶשָּׁא לָא אִתְבְּסַם, אֶלָּא בְּאֶשָּׁא דְמַדְבְּחָא. וְהַאי תְּנָנָא דְּנָפִיק מִנּוּקְבָּא אַחֲרָא, לָא אִתְבְּסַם אֶלָּא בִּתְנָנָא דְּקָרְבְּנָא.

234. We have learned of the two openings of the nose. In one opening, the smoke emerges glowing hot and settles in the crevice of the great depths. From one opening emerges a consuming fire burning with flames and glowing in 1,400 worlds on the left side. Whoever manages to get near this is referred to as the fire of Hashem, who is a consuming fire burning all other fires. This fire is not firmly established except through the fire of the altar. The smoke that emerges from the other opening OF THE NOSE is firmly established only with the smoke of the offering.

235(1). וְכֹלָא תַּלְיָיא בְּחוֹטָמָא, בְּגִין כָּךְ כְּתִיב, וַיָּרַח יְיָ׳ אֶת רֵיחַ
הַנִּיחֹחַ. דְּכֹלָא בְּחוֹטָמָא תַּלְיָין, לְאָרְחָא הַאי חוֹטָמָא, בִּתְנָנָא, וְאֶשָׁא
סוּמָקָא. וּבְגִין כָּךְ אִתְקַבָּל בִּרְעֲוָא. וְהַאי דִּכְתִּיב, וַיִּחַר אַף יְיָ׳. וְחָרָה אַף
יְיָ׳. וְחָרָה אַפִּי. פֶּן יֶחֱרֶה אַף יְיָ׳. כֹּלָא בִּזְעֵיר אַפִּין אִתְּמַר, וְלָא
בְּעַתִּיקָא.

235a. All THE SWEETENING OF THE JUDGMENTS depend on the nose, and therefore it is written: "And Hashem smelled the sweet savor" (Beresheet 8:21). Everything is dependent on the nose, which should smell the smoke and the red fire THAT ASCENDS FROM THE OFFERING. Therefore, THE OFFERING is received favorably. This is what is written: "And the anger (lit. 'nose') of Hashem was inflamed" (Bemidbar 12:9), "and then Hashem's anger (nose) be inflamed" (Devarim 11:17), "and My anger (nose) shall be inflamed" (Shemot 22:23) and "lest the anger (nose) of Hashem your Elohim be inflamed" (Devarim 6:15). All this is said of Zeir Anpin and not of Atik THAT IS ARICH ANPIN.

31. The ears of Zeir Anpin

A Synopsis

We read a description of the ears of Zeir Anpin, that hear both good and bad and distinguish between them. The voice that enters the ears causes the brain to awaken and to bring mercy to the righteous and vengeance to the wicked. Rabbi Shimon says to hear means to understand. He explains the meaning of the full name Yud Hei Vav Hei Elohim, that is comprised of both mercy and judgment.

235(2). תָּאנָא, כְּתִיב הַטֵּה אֱלֹהַי אָזְנְךָ וּשֲׁמַע הַאי אִיהוּ אוּדְנָא דְּאִתְעָבֵיד תְּחוֹת שַׂעֲרֵי. וְשַׂעֲרֵי תַּלְיָין עֲלֵיה. וְאוּדְנָא אִתְעָבֵיד בִּרְשׁוּמֵי רְשִׁימִין לְגָאוּ. כְּמָה דְּעֲבֵיד דַּרְגָּא בְּעֲקִימָא, מ״ט בְּעֲקִימָא. בְּגִין לְמִשְׁמַע טַב וּבִישׁ וְתָאנָא, מֵהַאי עֲקִימָא דִּבְגוֹ אוּדְנִין, תַּלְיָין כָּל אִינּוּן מָארֵי דְּגַדְפִין, דִּכְתִיב בְּהוּ, כִּי עוֹף הַשָּׁמַיִם יוֹלִיךְ אֶת הַקּוֹל וּבַעַל כְּנָפַיִם יַגִּיד דָּבָר.

235b. We have learned that it is written: "O my Elohim, incline your ear, and hear" (Daniel 9:18). That is the ear that was made under the hair and the hairs hang over it. The ear was made with impressions of impressions in its innermost interior, as if someone had produced a slanted step. What is the reason that it is slanted? It is in order to hear good and bad. We have learned that from this slope within the ears, all the winged beings are suspended, about whom it is written: "For a bird of the sky shall carry the sound, and that which has wings shall tell the matter" (Kohelet 10:20).

236. בְּגוֹ אוּדְנָא, נָטִיף מִגּ׳ חַלְלֵי דְּמוֹחָא, לְהַאי נוּקְבָּא דְּאוּדְנִין. וּמֵהַהוּא נְטִיפָא, עָיֵיל קָלָא בְּהַהוּא עֲקִימָא, וְאִתְצְרִיף בְּהַהוּא נְטִיפָא, בֵּין טַב וּבֵין בִּישׁ. טָב, דִּכְתִיב כִּי שׁוֹמֵעַ אֶל אֶבְיוֹנִים יְיָ׳. בִּישׁ, דִּכְתִיב וַיִּשְׁמַע יְיָ׳ וַיִּחַר אַפּוֹ וַתִּבְעַר בָּם אֵשׁ יְיָ׳.

236. Within the ear, it flows from the three cavities of the brain OF ZEIR ANPIN, WHICH ARE CHOCHMAH, BINAH AND DA'AT, into this opening in the ears. From these drops, the voice enters into that slope and combines with those drops either for good or for bad. Good, as it is written: "For

Hashem hears the poor" (Tehilim 69:34) and bad, as it is written: "And Hashem heard it; and his anger was kindled; and the fire of Hashem burned among them" (Bemidbar 11:1).

237. וְהַאי אוּדְנָא סָתִים לְבַר. וַעֲקִימָא עָיֵיל לְגוֹ, לְהַהוּא נוּקְבָּא דִּנְטִיפָא מִן מוֹחָא, בְּגִין לְמִכְנַשׁ קָלָא לְגָאוּ, דְּלָא יִפּוּק לְבַר, וִיהֵא נָטִיר וְסָתִים מִכָּל סִטְרוֹי. בְּגִ"כ הוּא רָזָא. וַוי לְהַהוּא דִּמְגַלֵּי רָזִין, דְּמַאן דִּמְגַלֵּי רָזִין כְּאִילּוּ אַכְחִישׁ תִּקוּנָא דִּלְעֵילָא. דְּאִתְתְּקַן לְמִכְנַשׁ רָזִין, וְלָא יִפְּקוּן לְבַר.

237. This ear is sealed from the exterior and that slope enters inside to the opening in the ear, which contains the flow from the brain, in order to carry the voice inwards so it will not slip out, so it would be kept guarded and concealed from all sides. Therefore, it is a secret. Woe to the one who reveals the secrets, since it is as if he diminishes the uppermost structure that was prepared in order to gather the secrets WITHIN, so they do not escape to the outside.

238. תָּנֵינָא, בְּשַׁעֲתָא דְּצַוְוחִין יִשְׂרָאֵל בְּעָאקָא, וְשַׂעֲרֵי מִתְגַּלְיָין מֵעַל אוּדְנִין, כְּדֵין עָיֵיל קָלָא בְּאוּדְנִין, בְּהַהוּא נוּקְבָּא דִּנְטִיף מִמּוֹחָא, וְכָנֵשׁ בְּמוֹחָא. וְנָפִיק בְּנוּקְבֵּי דְּחוֹטָמָא. וְאִתְזְעַר חוֹטָמָא, וְאִתְחַמַּם, וְנָפִיק אֶשָּׁא וּתְנָנָא מֵאִינּוּן נוּקְבִין, וּמִתְעָרִין כָּל גְּבוּרָאן, וְעָבֵיד נוּקְמִין.

238. We have learned that when Yisrael scream from their woes, and the hairs are unveiled from over the ears, the voice enters in the ears in that opening which gets the flow from the brain. It gathers FROM the brain and emerges through the nostrils of the nose, and the nose becomes shorter and warmer. Fire and smoke exit from these nostrils, and all Gvurot are roused and execute vengeance.

239. וְעַד לָא נָפְקִין מֵאִינּוּן נוּקְבִין אֶשָּׁא וּתְנָנָא, סָלִיק הַהוּא קָלָא לְעֵילָא, וּבָטַשׁ בְּרֵיחָא דְּמוֹחָא, וְנַגְדִּין תְּרֵין תְּרֵין דִּמְעִין מֵעַיְינִין, וְנָפַק מִנְּחִירוֹי תְּנָנָא וְאֶשָּׁא, בְּהַהוּא קָלָא דְּנָגִיד לוֹן לְבַר.

239. Prior to the emergence of the fire and cloud from the nostrils, that voice ascends above and pounds the fragrance of the brain. Two tears flow down from the eyes and cause smoke and fire to escape from his nostrils through that noise that He carries out to the exterior.

240. בְּהַהוּא קָלָא דְּעָיֵיל בְּאוּדְנִין, אִתְמַשְׁכָאן וּמִתְעָרָן כּוּלֵּי הַאי, בְּגִין כָּךְ כְּתִיב, וַיִּשְׁמַע יְיָ' וַיִּחַר אַפּוֹ וַתִּבְעַר בָּם אֵשׁ יְיָ'. בְּהַהִיא שְׁמִיעָה דְּהַהוּא קָלָא, אִתְּעַר מוֹחָא. תָּנָא, כְּתִיב הַטֵּה אֱלֹהַי אָזְנְךָ, כְּלוֹמַר אַרְכִּין. שִׁית מְאָה אֶלֶף רִבּוֹא אִינּוּן מָארֵיהוֹן דְּגַדְפִין, דְּתַלְיָין בְּאִלֵּין אוּדְנִין. וְכֹלָּא אִתְקְרוּן אָזְנֵי יְיָ'. וּמַה דְּאִתְּמַר הַטֵּה יְיָ' אָזְנְךָ, אָזְנֶךָ בִּזְעֵיר אַפִּין אִתְּמַר.

240. In that voice that enters the ears, all those MENTIONED ABOVE are drawn and awakened. Therefore, it is written: "And Hashem heard it; and his anger was kindled; and the fire of Hashem burned among them." With that listening of the voice THAT ENTERED THE EARS, the brain is awakened, BECAUSE FROM THERE THE VOICE DRAWS MERCY TO THE RIGHTEOUS AND VENGEANCE TO THE WICKED. We have learned that it is written: "O my Elohim, incline your ear, AND HEAR," meaning to say down below. There are six hundred thousand ten thousand winged beings that hang on these ears and all are referred to as the ears of Hashem. In the words: "Hashem, incline your ear," the ear refers to Zeir Anpin, SINCE THE ACTIONS OF THE LOWER GRADES ARRIVE THUS TO ZEIR ANPIN.

241. מִסִּטְרָא דְּחַד חַלָּלָא דְּמוֹחָא תַּלְיָין אוּדְנִין. וּמֵחַמְשִׁין תַּרְעִין דְּנָפְקִין מֵהַהוּא חַלָּלָא, דָּא הוּא תַּרְעָא חַד, דְּנָגִיד וְנָפִיק וְאִתְפְּתַח בְּהַהוּא נוּקְבָּא דְּאוּדְנָא, דִּכְתִיב כִּי אֹזֶן מִלִּין תִּבְחָן. וּכְתִיב וּבוֹחֵן לִבּוֹת וּכְלָיוֹת. וּמִסִּטְרָא דְּאִתְפַּשְׁטוּתָא דְּהַהוּא חַלָּלָא, דְּחַמְשִׁין תַּרְעִין דְּאִתְפַּשְׁטוּתָא בְּגוּפָא, בַּאֲתָר דְּלִבָּא שָׁארֵי, מִתְפַּשֵּׁט הַהוּא חַלָּלָא דְּחַמְשִׁין תַּרְעִין, וְאוּדְנָא קָרֵי בֵּיהּ בְּחִינָה, וּבְלִבָּא קָרֵי בֵּיהּ בְּחִינָה, מִשּׁוּם דְּמֵאֲתָר חַד מִתְפַּשְּׁטִין.

241. From one side of the brain space IN ZEIR ANPIN – THAT IS, THE LEFT SIDE – the ears are suspended. From the fifty gates that emerge from that hollow, there is one gate that continues to emerge and open up within the ear opening, as is written: "For the ear tries words" (Iyov 34:3), and: "Tries the hearts and reins" (Tehilim 7:10). From the aspect of the expansion OF THE BRAIN in the cavern in the fifty gates that spread through the body, BEHOLD in the place where the heart resides, THE BRAIN STARTS to expand in that cavern of the fifty gates. THEREFORE, in relation to the ear, the word "tries" is used and "tries" is also used in relation to the heart, because they expand from the same place.

242. תָּאנָא בְּצִנְיעוּתָא דְּסִפְרָא, כְּמָה דְּאוּדְנָא דָא אַבְחָן בֵּין טַב וּבֵין בִּיש, כַּךְ כֹּלָּא. דְּבִזְעֵיר אַפִּין אִית סִטְרָא דְּטַב וּבִיש. יְמִינָא וּשְׂמָאלָא. רַחֲמֵי וְדִינָא. וְהַאי אוּדְנָא כְּלִיל בְּמוֹחָא וּמִשּׁוּם דְּאִתְכְּלִל בְּמוֹחָא וּבַחֲלָלָא חַד. אִתְכְּלִיל בְּקָלָא דְּעָיֵיל בֵּיהּ. וּבְאוּדְנָא קָרֵי בֵּיהּ שְׁמִיעָה. וּבִשְׁמִיעָה אִתְכְּלִיל בִּינָה. שְׁמַע: כְּלוֹמַר, הָבֵן אִשְׁתְּכַח דְּכֹלָּא בְּחַד מַתְקְלָא אִתְּקַל. וּמִלִּין אִלֵּין לְמָארֵיהוֹן דְּמָארִין אִתְיְהָבָן, לְמִשְׁמַע וּלְאִסְתַּכְּלָא וּלְמִנְדַּע.

242. We have learned in the hidden book that as this ear distinguishes between good and bad, so it is applicable to everything, MEANING TO ALL THE SFIROT OF ZEIR ANPIN. In Zeir Anpin, there is a good side and a bad side, WHICH ARE right and left, Mercy and Judgment. This ear is included in the brain. Because it is included in the brain and in one cavern, it is included in the voice that enters it, which is considered hearing once it is in the ear. Binah is included in the hearing. Hear means understand, WHICH IS BINAH, UNDERSTANDING. All this amounts to is that everything has equal import. Those matters were given to those who are seated on the benches of justice, to hear, observe and know.

243. ת"ח, כְּתִיב, יְיָ' שָׁמַעְתִּי שִׁמְעֲךָ יָרֵאתִי וְגוֹ', הַאי קְרָא אִשְׁתְּמוֹדַע, דְּכַד נְבִיאָה קַדִּישָׁא, שְׁמַע, וְאִסְתְּכַּל, וְיָדַע, וְקָאֵים עַל תִּקּוּנִין אִלֵּין, כְּתִיב יָרֵאתִי, תַּמָּן יָאוּת הוּא לְדַחֲלָא וּלְאִתְבַּר קַמֵּיהּ, הַאי בִּזְעֵיר אַפִּין אִתְמַר.

243. Come and see that it is written: "Hashem, I have heard the report of you, and I was afraid" (Chavakuk 3:2). This verse is well known. When the

holy prophet heard and observed and knew and understood about these structures IN THE EAR, WHICH IS: "I HAVE HEARD THE REPORT OF YOU," it is written: "I was afraid," since there it is proper to fear and break before him. That is said about THE EARS OF Zeir Anpin. AS RESULT OF THE REVELATION OF LEFT COLUMN WITHIN WHICH THAT CARRIES ON, AS MENTIONED ABOVE.

244. כַּד אִסְתָּכַּל וְיָדַע מַה כְּתִיב. יְיָ' פָּעֶלְךָ בְּקֶרֶב שָׁנִים חַיֵּיהוּ. הַאי לְעַתִּיק יוֹמִין אִתְּמַר. וּבְכָל אֲתָר דְּיִשְׁתְּכַח, יְיָ' יְיָ', בְּיוּ"ד הֵ"א תְּרֵי זִמְנֵי, אוֹ בְּאָלֶף דָּלֶ"ת, וְיוּ"ד הֵ"א, חַד לִזְעֵיר אַפִּין, וְחַד לְעַתִּיקָא דְּעַתִּיקִין. וְאַף עַל גַּב דְּכֻלְּהוּ חַד, וְחַד שְׁמָא אִקְרוּ.

244. After he saw and knew, it is written: "Hashem, revive your work in the midst of the years" (Ibid.). This is said of Atik Yomin, since wherever you find Yud Hei Vav Hei, Yud Hei Vav Hei, twice with Yud-Hei, or ONE with Aleph-Dalet and ONE with Yud-Hei, one NAME IS for Zeir Anpin and one NAME the most ancient among the ancient, even though ZEIR ANPIN AND ATIK are all the same and are called by the same name.

245. וְתָנֵינָן אֵימָתַי אִקְרֵי שֵׁם מָלֵא. בְּזִמְנָא דִּכְתִיב יְיָ' אֱלֹהִים. דְּהַאי הוּא שֵׁם מָלֵא דְּעַתִּיק דְּכֹלָּא, וְדִזְעֵיר אַנְפִּין. וְכֹלָּא הוּא שֵׁם מָלֵא אִקְרֵי. וּשְׁאַר לָא אִקְרֵי שֵׁם מָלֵא, כְּמָה דְּאוֹקִימְנָא, וַיִּטַּע יְיָ' אֱלֹהִים, שֵׁם מָלֵא בִּנְטִיעוֹת גִּנְתָּא. וּבְכָל אֲתָר, יְיָ' אֱלֹהִים, אִתְקְרֵיא שֵׁם מָלֵא. יְיָ' יְיָ', כֹּלָּא הוּא בִּכְלָלָא. וְהַהוּא זִמְנָא אִתְּעָרוּ רַחֲמִין בְּכֹלָּא.

245. We have learned the name is considered full when it is written Yud Hei Vav Hei Elohim, because this is the full name of the most Ancient of all and of Zeir Anpin, SINCE YUD HEI VAV HEI IS THE SECRET OF ATIK AND ELOHIM IS ZEIR ANPIN. All of it is referred to as the full name, but the other NAMES are not considered a full name, as we have explained: "And Hashem Elohim planted" (Beresheet 2:8). That is the full name THAT PLANTED among the plantings of the Garden. Yud Hei Vav Hei Elohim is always considered the full name. TWICE Yud Hei Vav Hei, Yud Hei Vav Hei is all inclusive, THAT IS ZEIR ANPIN AND ATIK, AS MENTIONED ABOVE, BUT IS NOT YET REFERRED TO AS A FULL NAME - SINCE mercy is

awakened is everything during that period, but IT IS NOT INCLUDED IN JUDGMENT. HOWEVER, YUD HEI VAV HEI ELOHIM IS COMPRISED FROM MERCY AND JUDGMENT, SINCE ELOHIM POINTS TO JUDGMENT. THEREFORE, IT IS A FULL NAME.

246. יְיָ' פָּעָלְךָ בְּקֶרֶב שָׁנִים חַיֵּיהוּ, לְעַתִּיק יוֹמִין אִתְּמַר. מַאן פָּעָלְךָ. זְעֵיר אַפִּין. בְּקֶרֶב שָׁנִים, אִינּוּן שָׁנִים קַדְמוֹנִיּוֹת, דְּאִקְרוּן יְמֵי קֶדֶם, וְלָא אִקְרוּן שְׁנוֹת עוֹלָם. שָׁנִים קַדְמוֹנִיּוֹת אִינּוּן יְמֵי קֶדֶם. שְׁנוֹת עוֹלָם אַלֵּין יְמֵי עוֹלָם. וְהָכָא בְּקֶרֶב שָׁנִים, מַאן שָׁנִים. שָׁנִים קַדְמוֹנִיּוֹת. חַיֵּיהוּ לְמַאן. חַיֵּיהוּ לִזְעֵיר אַפִּין. דְּכָל נְהִירוּ דִּילֵיהּ מֵאִינּוּן שָׁנִים קַדְמוֹנִיּוֹת אִתְקַיְּימוּ, וּבג"כ אָמַר חַיֵּיהוּ. בְּרוֹגֶז רַחֵם תִּזְכּוֹר, לְהַהוּא חֶסֶד עִלָּאָה דְּעַתִּיקָא דְּעַתִּיקִין, דְּבֵיהּ אִתְּעַר רַחֲמִין לְכֹלָּא, לְמַאן דְּבָעֵי לְרַחֲמָא, וּלְמַאן דְּיֵאוֹת לְרַחֲמָא.

246. THE VERSE: "Hashem, revive your work in the midst of the years" is said to Atik Yomin. HE ASKS: What is "your work"? HE REPLIES: It is Zeir Anpin THAT EMANATES FROM ATIK YOMIN. "In the midst of the years": These are the primordial years referred to as the days of old and not everlasting years, since the years of old are the days of old, THAT IS THE SFIROT OF ATIK YOMIN. Everlasting years (lit. 'the years of the world') are the days of the world WHICH ARE THE SFIROT OF ZEIR ANPIN. It is written: "In the midst of the years." Which years are they? The primordial years OF ATIK YOMIN. "Revive": revive whom? "Revive" Zeir Anpin, that all his light survives thanks to these primordial years OF ATIK YOMIN. Therefore, it says "revive." "In wrath remember mercy" (Chavakuk 3:2), MEANING REMEMBER the supernal Chesed of the most ancient among the ancient, in whom Mercy is awakened for whoever requires mercy and whoever deserves mercy.